A PLACE
IN THE NEWS

*From the Women's Pages
to the Front Page*

By
KAY MILLS

*With a New Preface
by the Author*

COLUMBIA UNIVERSITY PRESS
New York

*This book is dedicated to my mother, Mary S. Mills
and to the memory of my father, Morris H. Mills.*

---

*Acknowledgment is made to W. W. Norton for permission
to reprint the lines from* When We Dead Awaken *by
Adrienne Rich.*

Columbia University Press Morningside Edition
Columbia University Press
New York   Oxford

Library of Congress Cataloging-in-Publication Data

Mills, Kay,
A Place in the news : from the women's pages to
the front page / by Kay Mills.
p.   cm.
Reprint, with new pref. Originally published:
1st ed. New York: Dodd, Mead, 1988.
"A Morningside book."
Includes bibliographical references.
ISBN 0-231-07416-6.
ISBN 0-231-07417-4 (pbk.)
1. Women journalists—United States—History.
I. Title.
PN4784.W7M55   1990
071'.3'082—dc20
90-37380
CIP

Morningside Edition 1990

Casebound editions of Columbia University Press books are Smyth-sewn and
printed on permanent and durable acid free paper

Printed in the U.S.A.

c 10 9 8 7 6 5 4 3 2 1
p 10 9 8 7 6 5 4 3 2 1

CONTENTS

The fact of being separate
enters your livelihood like a piece of furniture
—a chest of seventeenth-century wood
from somewhere in the North.
It has a huge lock shaped like a woman's head
but the key has not been found.
In the compartments are other keys
to lost doors, an eye of glass.
Slowly you begin to add
things of your own.
You come and go reflected in its panels.
　　　—Adrienne Rich, 1971,
　　　from When We Dead Awaken

Preface to the Morningside Edition

Newspapers today are increasingly corporate. Their offices resemble banks or insurance agencies. They seem more interested in marketing the news than in covering it. But there is one area in which corporations know self-preservation when they see it and newspapers have not matched their pace: the care and feeding of female staff members, especially executive staff members. Newspapers are back in the inkstained wretch department on that score. Their (male) executives appear to have been reading Charles Dickens, not John Naisbitt and Patricia Aburdene.

Women make up two-thirds of journalism school graduates. They are one-third of the newsroom work force, and climbing. They are half of American newspaper readership. But in too many cases they are still hidden behind a newsroom pillar, unseen when promotions are passed out. Corporations know better. Time was when *Megatrends 2000* authors Naisbitt and Aburdene spoke before business groups, women were the exception in their audience; now they are the rule, maybe not a majority, but certainly a healthy presence. And corporations like AT&T even have created new jobs to manage work and family issues for employer and employees. As we go into the 1990s, too few newspapers are paying this kind of attention to hiring, promoting and retaining women on their staffs, not to mention listening to their ideas on news coverage. Then they wonder why readership is down.

And down it is, as the Newspaper Advertising Bureau tells us. In 1982, 61 percent of women surveyed read newspapers frequently; five years later, only 45 percent did—a cut of one-fourth in five years. That drop cannot be entirely explained by the fact that more women work outside the home. More women may have simply decided newspapers don't cover enough subjects of interest to merit making time to read them.

Women are interested in defense; it is their children who will go to war or serve now in the military. Women are interested in ferment in Eastern Europe; they know the appeal of an open society in which all may speak and strive for better lives. But women are also interested in what drugs do to the human body and how to prevent addiction; instead, they see coverage couched in war metaphors. Women are aware of the psychological cost of abortion, either performed or denied, but increasingly they see coverage centered on the political fallout of the issue. Women would have liked every step of the way to read the ins and outs of child care legislation, but they never got the same degree of detail that surrounded coverage of the bailout of the savings and loan industry.

Truly shrewd marketers would be seeking to recapture this female readership instead of courting men by piling on more professional sports coverage. Susan Miller, director of editorial development for the Scripps Howard Newspapers, suggests that newspapers ought to compare their readership surveys with the way they allocate their staffs and their hole for news. For example, women rank investigative reporting, business news, and local sports coverage low on their list, Miller says, yet most newspapers put more than one-fourth of their staffs on those topics. Women, she adds, are not inherently disinterested in sports or business. They just don't like the way newspapers present them. Women try to keep fit, so they participate in sports rather than watch pro football and read about it. They also want to know about their kids' teams. They are more interested in small businesses, which they now start in greater numbers than men do, than in giant corporations. Women also want stories about career management and family issues. Newspapers have people on transportation and oil industry beats; why not children's issues as well?

There is clearly a link between what is covered and who assigns the coverage, between what is covered and who does the coverage. The presence of more women at the page one conferences of America's newspapers will not revolutionize coverage, but it can't hurt. It might, for example, have kept The New York

Times from overplaying a shaky medical story linking women's job performance to their estrogen level, as it did on page one on November 18, 1988.

Again, having a female photo editor made a difference between the Detroit News' picture coverage of the skating competition during the 1988 Winter Olympics and that of the Detroit Free Press. American skater Debi Thomas fell while competing with Katerina Witt and lost any chance of a gold medal. The Free Press, with a male photo editor, ran a photo of Thomas falling with her legs wide open. The picture represented what News photo editor Joan Rosen said "is often referred to as a crotch shot." Rosen rejected the same Reuters photo and the News ran Thomas's fall in slight profile. As Rosen wrote later, "The story that night was Debi Thomas losing a gold medal, not her dignity."

In short, having more women in top jobs might allow newspapers to reflect better the concerns of all readers, not just white males between thirty-eight and sixty. It is entirely possible that if defense spending does decrease in the years to come and other issues surface, they may prove to be the issues that women have been associated with all along, from neighborhood concern about pesticide spraying to improving prenatal care for children. The newspapers that get out among 'em today could be ahead of the game tomorrow.

I would like to be able to report that since the initial publication of *A Place in the News: From the Women's Pages to the Front Page,* newspaper managements had experienced an epiphany and were not only righting all past wrongs in terms of personnel but were also doing so in terms of coverage. I can't do it. Yes, important, positive developments have occurred, which I will outline in a moment. Big personnel changes have been made, some advancing women, others overlooking them. Some papers are doing better in terms of content. A few—like USA Today—have already recognized that women are a major part of their audience. No matter what anyone thinks of its brief, breezy style, USA Today offers women more news about themselves in every one of its sections than any other major paper.

Yes, there is progress but it is spotty. It is not nearly what it should be, considering how many women work in newsrooms and read newspapers. Too many newspapers that could do a better job in covering the issues about which women would read are not doing it. Too many of the key jobs on major newspapers still go almost automatically to men. The glass is fuller than it once was but we should not sit back and drink too deeply; there simply is not as much to rejoice over as we would like or as there should be by now.

Consider, first, personnel: Here the evidence seems contradictory. There was a veritable flurry of changes at the top at American newspapers in 1989. The Los Angeles Times, the Christian Science Monitor, and the Chicago Sun Times got new editors. Men. The New York Daily News got a new managing editor. Male. The Orange County Register in California got a new managing editor. Female.

So Kay Fanning, a former president of the American Society of Newspaper Editors, is no longer editor of the Christian Science Monitor. Jean Sharley Taylor retired as the ranking woman at the Los Angeles Times in the spring of 1989 and for the remainder of that year there was no woman's name on the Times's masthead. Fewer women are Washington bureau chiefs now than when this book was written. Women of color still are more visible in editorial page meetings around the country than at page one planning sessions.

But women have also made great gains: Geneva Overholser has become editor of the Des Moines Register. Nancy Woodhull has become president of Gannett News Services. Early in 1990 Narda Zacchino was named to succeed Jean Taylor as associate editor at the Los Angeles Times and Carol Stogsdill followed Zacchino as Orange County editor. Linda Mathews is now editor of the Los Angeles Times Magazine. Jenny Buckner is a vice president of Knight-Ridder. Carolyn Lee is now assistant managing editor at the New York Times. Meg Greenfield remains editorial page editor, Mary Hadar is Style Section editor and Karen de Young is national editor at the Washington Post. Ellen Goodman is associate editor of the Boston Globe. Mary L. Dedinsky is managing editor at the Chicago Sun Times. Beverly Keys has become editor of the Fresno Bee. Indeed, as you read this book as it was originally published, you will find still other women who have since switched jobs, won promotions, quit journalism. It would only be news if that were not the case in our business.

What else is new, and what does it mean?

More women are covering more diverse subjects. Some women continue to demonstrate a commitment to covering neglected subjects or to keeping the people in mind when covering highly politicized subjects. And more women are thinking about change, writing about it, organizing to try to bring it about.

Women are now mainstays in political coverage at major newspapers. Women regularly write sports, although these women report that virtually each time a female reporter joins a newspaper that hasn't had any women on the sports staff or covers a team never covered before by a woman, she faces the same hassles and tests from colleagues and athletes. Women's bylines are common now from Bucharest to Beijing, although some newspapers still send women to some foreign beats and not others. The pool of women seeking the good beats and the promotions is larger today than at any time, but there are also more male editors willing to send anyone anywhere, regardless of gender.

By and large, it is columnists who have the most freedom to cover most consistently issues with special resonance for women— Ellen Goodman at the Boston Globe, Judy Mann and Dorothy Gilliam at the Washington Post, Anna Quindlen and Mary Cantwell at the New York Times, Glenda Holste at the St. Paul Pioneer Press Dispatch, Carol Ashkinaze at the Chicago Sun Times, Carol Kleiman at the Chicago Tribune.

But in a world in which abortion is being shoehorned into the standard form of political coverage—winners and losers— and the women forgotten, Karen Tumulty of the Los Angeles Times has continued to write notable stories about women's concerns and needs for late abortions or about the people in Operation Rescue who oppose all abortions. Margaret Wolf Freivogel of the St. Louis Post-Dispatch continues to cover abortion and other political issues as they affect women, and Melinda Voss of the Des Moines Register regularly writes on women's concerns. Molly Ivins of the Dallas Times Herald often turns her wit on women coping with the world of the Texas good old boys. Connie Koenenn of the Los Angeles Times created a beat on how people are preparing for the future and has focused among other things on changes in housing and transportation design and environmental awareness that have especially been fostered by women.

In the midst of a sensational murder case in Boston, Eileen McNamara could call upon years of experience in covering brutality toward women to remind readers that women are most often killed by someone they know.

"Eileen McNamara's work shows the merits of having someone with a memory of these cases and knowledge of how the judicial system responds. When you see coverage like this, you realize how you are cheated on so many other issues," says Bernice Buresh, director of the Women, Press and Politics Project sponsored by the Joan Shorenstein Barone Center on the Press, Politics and Public Policy at Harvard University.

The fact that Harvard University sponsored the work of Buresh, former Boston bureau chief for Newsweek, brings me to the next bright spot: More studies are being conducted by more groups and more women are organizing to see what is happening in the media and to try to redirect media focus.

With the help of the Gannett Foundation and the University of Southern California, Nancy Woodhull and feminist leader Betty Friedan have pulled together conferences on women, men and media which have kept the issue in the public eye and produced reports underscoring the need for change. The conventions of the American Society of Newspaper Editors and the Associated Press Managing Editors have addressed the questions of what holds women back and how to advance them in their careers.

At an APME convention, for example, women who have stayed in the newsroom and one who has left gave the executives tips for doing more than just talking about advancing women. Jeannie Falknor, former assistant managing editor of the Charlotte Observer, who had worked on that newspaper's Pulitzer Prize-winning investigation of televangelist Jim Bakker, told the group the male managers should be more flexible in dealing with employees with children. They should talk to their staffs, encourage discussion of any tensions between work life and home life, help a mother of a young child build support systems among her colleagues, conduct seminars to help employees survive life with teenagers or deal with the empty nest syndrome, and provide the same kind of day care, especially for sick children, that they write about in their newspapers. "I don't think top editors can afford to be passive about these issues any longer," Falknor told the APME audience. "You need to anticipate stress points and take aggressive roles in acknowledging the conflict for some employees between personal and private lives."

These discussions did not necessarily occur out of the goodness of men's hearts, although that helped. They occurred because there are more women in the hierarchies of newspapers and newspaper organizations so that there is a critical mass now forcing discussion of issues of concern to women. They also occurred because there are more young men taking an active interest in their wives' careers and their children's upbringing. Life, in short, is undeniably better for women in the newsroom because there are more of us and we have insisted that our ideas and our concerns be taken more seriously. But we are by no means where we should be.

After the lawsuits, after the women's caucuses, after the initial breakthroughs, women seemed to think we had done all we could do to open doors in our profession. We hit a plateau, and we coasted. We seemed to share the thinking of one editor quoted in *A Place in the News* who said that, with the number of women coming into the profession, he had believed change would take care of itself. But eventually we realized more could be done, more should be done, and we started getting organized again. Joining the older and larger Women in Communications, Inc. in airing women's professional concerns now are the Association of Women in Sports Media; the Association for Women in Journalism, a Texas-based group; The National Press Photographers Association's women's committee; and the Journalism and Women Symposium. Each seeks to give women a chance to come together for both relaxation and professional recharging, and several produce newsletters to maintain links forged at their meetings.

As this organizing has been occurring, our professional magazines—Columbia Journalism Review, Washington Journalism Review, Quill—have also shown more interest in issues of concern to women journalists. Another smaller magazine, the quarterly Media and Values in Los Angeles, produced a thoughtful two-part series in 1989 on gender and the media. There remains, of course, the Media Report to Women as a source of diverse information. Newspapers themselves, however, rarely run anything more on the question than reports on the women, men and media conferences or an occasional consultant's report that surfaces.

As a headline in Quill proclaimed, "We've come a long way, maybe." I repeat, as I did earlier in this volume, nobody wants to return to the way we were. How many women have come up to me with their own "everyday indignities" since this book came out? Too many. Nonetheless, women are in many respects at last fully acknowledged journalists, capable of controversy and compassion, just like the guys.

This book tracks where women are in the newspaper business, how they got there and where they still have to go. More important, it tells what difference it has made that more women are assigning, writing and editing the news. It may be up to the generation of journalism students who read this book to write the final chapters, to show the bosses once and for all that women add substance, not merely a little spice, to the mix of news that is covered. Their journalism professors (and too few of them are women) are going to have to help them understand that the world was not always the equal-opportunity employer it professes to be today. It can easily slip backwards if not pressed to go forward. Women who are already in the media must also work harder to build bridges to these students and help them both understand what is ahead and meet any challenges.

The female students who read this book may, in the words of Betsy Wade of the New York Times, have to muddy their skirts. Much as we might like, she says, we cannot carry them across to complete realization of their goals. But they may at last become the ones who are themselves the bosses, working in good harmony with their male colleagues who have seen that diversity pays. It will not be enough, however, for them to become the editors or the managing editors if they conduct business as usual. They will only make true change if they insist on opening new areas of coverage rather than covering the same stories the guys have always covered.

It may seem odd to quote the late Walter Reuther, president of the United Auto Workers, in this context, but Reuther, in talking about gains by blacks in labor unions, said something that applies equally to the attitude of women in the newspaper business today. "We have made progress," Reuther said, "but progress is a relative thing. We are in the middle of a social revolution and when you are dealing with the dynamics of a revolution, people will not judge where we are or where we have come from, they will judge us based on how far we still must go."

And we still have a distance to go.

Kay Mills
March 1990

CHAPTER

1

Out of the Picture

"We have a very small bureau, and I'm afraid I can't hire you," the *Newsweek* bureau chief in Chicago was telling the nervous young woman seated opposite him. The year was 1966, and the woman worked for United Press International. Ambitious, she was eager to cover the news as it was being made rather than sit behind a desk rewriting wire copy for broadcast news scripts. She was job-hunting.

"I need someone I can send anywhere, like to riots," he said. "And besides, what would you do if someone you were covering ducked into the men's room?"

Time dims memory. But not that kind. Somewhere in a corner of the brain, one little cell never forgets. It keeps the song that, heard again, recreates the room, the person, the moment. It preserves the phrase or the laugh or the gesture that resurrects a friend long gone. It knows precisely where you were and what you were doing when you heard about Pearl Harbor if you're old enough, or Kennedy's assassination, or Martin Luther King's, or the *Challenger* explosion. Every detail is frozen in memory, despite all the years. It keeps the innocuous question, too. The question that sometime later, when all the synapses are working, produces the epiphany, the moment when you're driving along and you realize that finally you understand. And why did it take you so long?

So much for why I remember, for, of course, I was the nervous young woman. The bureau chief could have asked me the logical, albeit painful question, "Why don't you come back when

1

you have more experience?" He didn't. The restroom question was hardly the worst ever asked a job applicant. But it did reflect its times. For many a female journalist over a certain age today, it carries a twinge of recognition: you've just been told there's no place for a woman. No place in the newsroom—and no place in the news.

That was then, and this is now. Then I had no answer for the bureau chief, no challenge to his assumptions. I did not suggest that it was equally dangerous for men *and* women to be sent to cover riots but that either should be given the chance. Nor was I glib enough to say that who goes into a men's room must come out. And why the *men's* room? I certainly wasn't bold enough to tell a prospective employer that his question was irrelevant and unfair. 1966 may have been two decades ago in time; it is further back in mindset.

I did try, feebly, silently, to think of a female newsmaker who, seeing an earnest young male reporter coming, might duck into the women's room. (We called them ladies' rooms in those days.) A distant Ceylonese ruler or a former cabinet secretary simply didn't fill the bill. They were the only ones I could think of. It never occurred to me to wonder why there were no women I might be covering. Or what difference it made to people reading newspapers that women were rarely the objects of serious coverage —or rarely the ones doing the covering. That's where the epiphany came in. That's what this book is about.

Four jobs later, I started to put it together. Women had not been in the news because they had not been performing tasks or living lives that men considered important. Women had comparatively little role in defining what was important and therefore what was news. Since then, the definition of news has changed because America has changed and journalism has changed (even if not all its leaders recognize that yet).

Several major factors have altered the press. Television tells people the news faster, with pictures. Television gives people the evening news; fewer afternoon newspapers do. Changing work patterns, as well as competition from television, have led to deaths in the afternoon press. Vietnam and Watergate left the nation, and especially the press, with far more skepticism toward the word of the government. And people have become more vocal in expressing day-to-day concerns, whether they are outraged about oil spills that tar beaches and birds or airliners that are slow to leave and quick to crash. New issues emerged, and new voices were heard: blacks, Asians, American Indians, the handicapped, the homosexual. All had stories to tell and wanted a hand in telling them.

And women. More powerful than any demonstration for the Equal Rights Amendment, more influential than any speech by a female politician, more far-reaching even than the development of the birth-control pill (although certainly related) was the simple fact that women went to work. Lots of women went to work, just as they had during World War II. But this time the men weren't off at war. When women went to work, they didn't like some of the conditions that they found—pay discrimination, limited chance for advancement, low expectations, a workplace geared toward the lives of the men who dominated it. One by one, they spoke up. Slowly, they started to change conditions they disliked because their work was needed—if not always valued.

One of the places they went to work was down at the newspaper, down the street or downtown or out of town. More women were going to college, more women branched out from traditional female jobs. More went into the news business lured by the chance to ask questions, to witness life's drama, to cover a murder trial, or to walk down a foreign boulevard and then to write stories that made readers feel they had been there.

Working for a newspaper is a ticket to history. Working with newspaper people keeps you from taking yourself too seriously. Journalists have eclectic and eccentric tastes, from climbing mountains to cooking huevos rancheros. They tell tales well; that's their job. Journalists grouch about every paper they've ever worked for because they know every paper can be better and that's what they want. The comments in this book about the *Los Angeles Times*, where I work and which I cite repeatedly because I know it best, have that end in mind: the fullest use of everyone's talent toward producing an even finer newspaper.

There is a clear and current interaction between the women's movement, the presence of women on American newspapers, and the coverage of women by American newspapers. No one planned such interaction. It was not a conscious act. It is one segment of a massive social evolution, and it is the focus of this book.

The relationship of women in the press to coverage of women

3

by the press, almost symbiotic, can be traced to the earliest days of American journalism. But successful or visible women in the press remained the exception until recent decades. Women moved in increasing numbers into the press corps in three distinct phases, all involving constant struggle against prejudice. First, Eleanor Roosevelt allowed only women to cover her White House press conferences. That meant Washington newspapers and news bureaus had to employ at least one woman to cover the news properly because Eleanor Roosevelt made news. Then during World War II, women flocked to newspaper jobs. In the 1950s and early 1960s, sturdy souls kept alive women's presence in the profession; their perseverence paid off when women's activities gained news coverage and women increasingly became news coverers in the 1970s and 1980s. It is a story I would never have imagined during that job interview in 1966.

That same summer of 1966 I was also turned down for a job at *The Chicago Daily News*. Reason: the paper already had three or four women. That was a great many for a newspaper then. It didn't seem fair, but it was the way things were. You might question the logic, but there didn't seem much you could do about it. It had been that way when I was a little girl, too, when the boys got to play softball without having first to prove they knew how.

Not until years later could I pin a name on the act of discrimination. If I were black, I would have recognized it immediately (and most assuredly would have experienced it much sooner). Discrimination against women was accepted practice in what was at least an era of candor—that is, you were told outright why you weren't suitable. It wasn't brainpower or table manners or even job experience. It was simply your sex, just as it had been, for blacks, simply one's race. The use and appreciation of everyone's talents, the diversity that should have added strength and depth to society, were ignored. But that was then. I didn't know what to call this attitude of employers. It disturbed and disappointed me, but only as an individual. I had not moved from the individual to the universal, from the personal to the political.

None of us has any way of knowing what our careers, our lives would have been like had men and women begun from the

4

same starting line. I have already done more than I ever dreamed possible in the world as it was constructed when I graduated from college. In a different world, could I have done more? Could Eileen Shanahan, once a star *New York Times* correspondent, have done more if the system had been more nearly fair when she started her career? Could Margaret Dempsey McManus, who trailed many a good story for *The Baltimore Evening Sun*, have done more? Could Beth Short, Associated Press correspondent in Washington during the Eleanor Roosevelt years, have done more? Would Marguerite Higgins, the inner-driven war correspondent, have done as much? We can only speculate. But we can wonder, too, about those who were discouraged, who turned to less challenging sections of the newspaper or less challenging fields. It is not enough to look at those who made it, who do not seem unduly scarred but who clearly could have gone further in their profession if they were just starting now. What talent was lost? How many men would have gotten to the posts they now hold had they had to compete with half the human race all their lives?

But back on that interview day in 1966, I held no such thoughts. As an only child of college-educated parents, as a good student, as a participant in school activities including the junior high, high school, and college newspapers, I had simply assumed that if you did a good job, you would get rewarded often enough to make it worthwhile. Other people might get a job you wanted, but only because they were more qualified. I had a lot to learn. I was not alone.

Only in recent years have I come to realize why, on that day in that small office overlooking Michigan Avenue, I couldn't think of an American woman newsmaker—no one but Oveta Culp Hobby, who was out of government office by then.

No women other than Hobby and Frances Perkins had ever served in the U.S. Cabinet. Neither John Kennedy nor Lyndon Johnson, the Presidents of whom a 25-year-old would have been most aware, had named any. Few women were in Congress. Few headed corporations. In short, few did anything that the news media considered news. Then as now, the media helped define our reality, and government was one of the prime anchors of that reality. My male rival for the *Newsweek* job didn't have to worry about female newsmakers heading for the restroom or the smoke-filled room or the boardroom. Women weren't in government and women weren't in business, so women weren't in the news.

And that says something about the definition of news. My Webster's Dictionary defines *news* as "(1) a report of a recent *event*; tidings. (2) *matter of interest to newspaper readers*."[1] News, therefore, at least to an extent is what newspapers say it is. By the 1920s and 1930s and 1940s the leading newspapers had evolved into journals that reported on wars and politics and treaties. They covered murders and trials and sensational escapades. In short, they covered events.

Until television entered the picture. Radio had reported the news first, to be sure, but television reported an assassination that occurred at midday only moments later—with pictures. It could take viewers to Kennedy's funeral or to the March on Washington live—and with pictures. So newspapers then had to start telling not just what but *why* or *how*.

The need for depth to hold readers—and advertising—began a transition that would later broaden the definition of news itself. But as that transition began in the 1960s and early 1970s, it was still easier for editors to assign in-depth stories about groups they felt they knew: politicians, diplomats, business executives, doctors, and lawyers. The politicians, diplomats, business executives, doctors, and lawyers were mainly men, white men. News was thus about white men. Women rarely were elected to office, and if they were, they were outspoken exceptions like Bella Abzug who clamored for attention and got it. Women were rarely ambassadors. Women apparently ran few small businesses; those who did were invisible in the press.

When women were news at all, it was because they were exceptional. When men were news, it was because they were merely doing what they always did: exercising power. And the men in power were being covered by men in journalism. It's no accident then that, in his 1969 book *The Kingdom and the Power*,[2] Gay Talese constantly referred to the *men* at the meetings, to the *men* in the newsroom, to the *men* who ran *The New York Times*. He never said *people*, he always said *men*. Even today, that exclusionary use of language is a quiet little tipoff to how people really think.

If women—with the exception of Charlotte Curtis, then editor of the *Times*'s women's page—were invisible to former reporter Talese, they were certainly invisible to his former employers as well. News was what men said it was.

If women wanted to read about themselves, they had to achieve success in male arenas: politics, business, medicine, law. As they moved into those arenas, a few brought their own issues and styles, trying—with mixed results—to achieve their goals collectively and with flexibility. But more often they found themselves alone in a crowd of men and adapted with equally mixed results to the styles around them. To workaholic lifestyles. To from-the-top-man-down work styles. To business-suit-and-tie dress styles. As their numbers increased, however, women started developing their own styles, proving that they do not necessarily act, think, vote—or dress—alike. They have also started to bring their own agendas to bear more forcefully in these previously all-male arenas.

In the news business, that does not mean women bias their coverage; it does mean they broaden it. Little statistical evidence exists to quantify the changes that women have brought to American newspapers, either through reporting or editing. Most of the academic studies that have been attempted are just as subjective as anecdotal evidence or are so dry and removed from the realities of newsrooms as to be meaningless. But anecdotal evidence is compelling that the presence of more women assigning, writing, and editing the news has altered the definition of news, although not firmly enough. As this book will show, women do indeed bring different voices to the news pages.

As women have moved into traditionally male professions, they have also moved into other jobs men had dominated: police officer, firefighter, telephone installer, truck driver. It was that surge, as well as the steady movement of women into the newsroom, that reshaped the news. Still downplayed in favor of congressional maneuvering or diplomatic imbroglios, the movement of women into the workforce and the way that movement has changed people's home lives remains *the* ongoing revolution. Long after men such as former presidential crony Bert Lance are forgotten, Geraldine Ferraro and Sally Ride will occupy the history books. They succeeded in a man's world but exemplified women's insistence on being as equals. Their arrival on the national stage was part of the evolution of news toward looking at all the people and at all their concerns—at developments that change lives, be they medical discoveries, new understandings of how children learn, evolving patterns of home ownership, or new jobs that technology creates.

The best newspaper people have always tried to convey the feel of events, "the smell of cabbage cooking in the halls," as sports editor Stanley Woodward once instructed Red Smith.[3] The best papers explored how these events affected people in Peoria or Portland, focusing on what people cared about rather than on what newspapers thought they should care about. News mainly covered events when I started in the business in 1964. But pushed into new depth by television's greater speed in covering events, newspapers began moving more into covering the stuff of daily life. Individually, the stories were small items. Collectively, they recorded the events that produced social change: reactions against the day-to-day bias that blacks encountered, the anger of consumers over cars unsafe at any speed, the determination of dedicated people to preserve the woods from clearcutters, the frustration of a woman in a dead-end job that shouldn't be dead-end.

Even so, news about average women—their daily lives, and their searches for identity on their own terms and equality in no uncertain terms—was still largely absent from the sections of newspapers that those in power considered important. My grandmother, who raised five children in a small Virginia mountain town as a storekeeper's wife, who chopped chickens' heads off with skill and plucked them pretty much clean, made the papers only when she died. Nobody thought to ask her about the changes she had seen in rural America, the way the automobile changed her small town when the main roads bypassed it.

My mother—who grew up crossing New River on a small ferry boat to go to school, who became the first in her family to finish college, and who was fired from her teaching job because she got married—carries in her mind a first-person view of Depression-era Washington. She worked for the Rural Electrification Administration filing papers that told the story of a changing America. Yet she too rarely made the papers. She made them for the PTA committees on which she served and for a fashion therapy project in which she worked to help mental patients just released from the hospital. (That story came during the evolution of the kind of coverage I'm discussing.) But mainly she made the papers as a survivor when my father, an Air Force officer, died.

8

Special to me, these women were not unique individuals by any means, and they were not much different from thousands of other people whose names appear only when they are born, marry, and die—if then—in our big-city papers. They didn't run for office, and they weren't stars. Along with me, the journalist, they represent women's transition from generation to generation in the twentieth century. Their stories are the stuff of social history books now. No reporter would have looked at them twice decades ago.

Today, to a limited extent, as an editorial writer for the *Los Angeles Times*, I help shape what one part of the media in one city says. That is new. And that agenda has changed to some extent. The press covers the illnesses and the interests of average people more intensively. It chronicles the many groups and individuals who are trying to get ahead, not just the elite.

But the press still relies obsessively on politics to fill its pages, although the wonders of science and medicine concern more people more intimately. And different papers are at different stages in this development. The *Los Angeles Times*, for example, was busy writing about the machinations involved in President Reagan's tax proposals in 1985—an important story but one covered in exhaustive detail—while it buried on page ten an eight-paragraph wire-service story about a key breakthrough in discovering the cause of toxic shock syndrome, a disease of concern to millions of American women. *The New York Times* carried a far longer, staff-written story on the front page, where it belonged. The news balance in American newspapers is still tilted toward government. But politics is "olds"; today, social movements and sciences are "news"[4]—tidings, if you will. Tidings of change.

No less a political authority than David Broder of *The Washington Post* has acknowledged this blind spot. The press missed the beginnings of the women's movement, Broder wrote in *Behind the Front Page*. Neither *The New York Times* nor *The Washington Post* nor *The Washington Star* considered that Betty Friedan's book *The Feminine Mystique* required reviewing in 1963. *The Washington Post* did not report the 1966 founding of the National Organization for Women, and *The New York Times* reported it in the women's section with a "cutesy" lead.

The press covers official, organized events diligently, Broder said, "but when an idea, a concept or a movement emerges outside those official beats, we do not usually respond unless or until there is an event that compels coverage. . . . Somehow, we in the press have to broaden our perspective and expand our range of vision. . . . We remain trapped in the assumptions and parochial limitations of our regular beats and the conventional thinking of the institutions and people we regularly cover."[5]

But women reporters did know about this movement. They were living it. This book examines their attempt to break out of the trap of which Broder spoke and to change coverage of women by American newspapers. It is about newspapers only. Not television; television news is having a midlife crisis—it doesn't know whether it is news or entertainment. Newspapers remain the medium with the resources to chart social change in depth—when they care to do so. This book is not about news magazines, either —even though I cheated in including my *Newsweek* story, but it is typical of stories I heard from countless other newspaper women.

If your favorite journalists or women at your favorite newspaper aren't featured, it is because this book is not a yearbook but a guidebook to the evolving role of women in the press. It is, in the pattern if not the style of poet Adrienne Rich, a modest attempt to open "a book of myths in which our names do not appear."

There has been no conspiracy to change newspaper coverage —no one could ever accuse anyone in the media, male or female, of anything that organized. Simply put, the presence of more women in the newsroom has changed some attitudes of their male editors. The presence of more women covering stories has led to more women being interviewed. Many men see only men as subjects for quotation while women, who are used to listening to both women and men, interview both women and men as a matter of course. The presence of more women (not many more but more) editing stories has given some reporters pause before they described a woman's physical attributes or marital status. How relevant were those, after all? The presence of some women on assignment desks has meant that stories about rape-law reform, abortion, and sexual harassment and about local women who are politicians might get straight news treatment.

Women in the newsroom didn't do it all, of course. Changes in hiring practices and news practices would not have occurred without the alliance of men who understood the changing society. They have helped women get where they wanted to go and have heard what women were saying. When a senior male editor backs a story or writes a column or editorial about discrimination against women, it often carries more weight than the same words from a woman. The man is somehow perceived as an objective observer. The support of a male colleague often helps win a small skirmish or a big war. The change in men's attitudes and in the definition of news also would not have occurred without the employment of more and more wives of more and more of those men—employment that changed attitudes and understanding about the need for stories on child care, equal pay, and child custody. When a male publisher has a working wife and a three-year-old, that makes a difference.

Ignoring the news judgments of women journalists sometimes still leads male editors to overlook or misplay stories. Women reporters spotted the Equal Rights Amendment as a developing story in the early 1970s, but as the ratification deadline drew near a decade later, the day-to-day campaign for the amendment and the social forces against it were abysmally covered. The death of a constitutional amendment affecting banking or football or almost anything else would have generated reams of copy for months before the deadline. The forces that beat the Equal Rights Amendment were the same ones that backed Ronald Reagan, so women journalists who had covered the ERA, unlike their male counterparts, were hardly astonished at the strength of the New Right. Had their editors paid more attention to what women were learning about this emerging political force, they might not have been taken by surprise when politicians from the New Right started winning elections.

Times have changed, you say? Not entirely. Female reporters kept watch over women in politics long after their male editors thought the story had come and gone. For men, the new woman was old copy as the 1970s turned into the 1980s. But women in the press saw the effort developing to get a woman on a national political ticket in 1984. Watching the methodical organizing, these reporters realized that there was indeed an outside shot for a woman to receive the vice-presidential nomination. Furthermore, they knew who it was likely to be. Their editors largely ignored

11

their female reporters' instincts until Geraldine Ferraro's selection was virtually assured. Newspapers and magazines were focused on Ferraro by June 1984; but female reporters had been aware of activities on her behalf months earlier. Perhaps if newspapers had taken Ferraro seriously sooner, they might also have looked at her husband's business practices sooner as well. That Ferraro's nomination was a political story makes it doubly puzzling that men failed to spot it—more puzzling than their ignoring stories about toxic shock syndrome or child-care shortcomings.

Given the need to cover a wide range of stories, and given the records of individual women who have covered wars, reported on European politics, and probed the treatment of the mentally ill, one can only wonder why the profession did not open its doors to women earlier. A few did crash the gates; they are the women on whose shoulders the rest of us stand.

It would be best if this book were history more than current affairs, but it will not be history until women cover more of the national and especially international beats that earn front-page bylines, until women help set policy for newspapers and help determine the range of news that shall be covered. With more women graduating from college and more women entering the professions, the newspaper business is out of step with the world it covers. Newspaper staffs and often their stories mirror only a fragment of that world. The world may long remember that which newspapers only cover marginally.

Life comes full circle. In the middle 1970s a Senate committee was grilling members of the U.S. Consumer Product Safety Commission about its budget request and its priorities for making rules about potential or real hazards. It was no big deal in the eyes of the media, unlike a Supreme Court confirmation hearing or an investigation into a weapons-cost overrun—just a little Capitol Hill story that might bear on whether people's toes got cut off by lawnmowers or children's heads got stuck in crib slats.

As the hearing wore on, one of the commission members, Barbara Franklin, who had been the Nixon Administration's recruiter of women for top government jobs, stepped across the hall into the restroom. One reporter followed. By then, I was covering for Newhouse News Service's Washington bureau, and I had known Franklin for more than a decade since we had been classmates in a Penn State economics course. I told her about the *Newsweek* bureau chief's question of so many years before, the one about following a newsmaker into the men's room. We could laugh that day. Events had finally started to overtake the question.

Everyday Indignities

Jane O'Reilly calls it "click! the housewife's moment of truth" —women's realization that no matter their role, they are the odd ones out.[1] I call them the Everyday Indignities after a line from Andree Brooks in *The New York Times* that "certain women insist that the small, everyday indignities can corrode their will more than the larger issues."[2] There's no point in trying to define the phenomenon—when your jaw drops open and you don't believe what just happened, you've got it.

The Washington bureau for *The Reporter* magazine was only a two-person operation. It was too small to have its own wire-service teletype printers, so Douglass Cater regularly went upstairs to the National Press Club in the same building to read the wires. Later when Meg Greenfield (now editorial page editor for *The Washington Post*) joined the same bureau, she couldn't do that. The National Press Club didn't admit women. Greenfield explained to the club that she did not want to eat lunch there or even peek into the dining room. She did not want to use the bar or the gym. She simply wanted to read the wires. No chance.

It was 1961.

CHAPTER

2

Publishers and Pundits

Debating women's place was a luxury few could afford in the American colonies and the young United States. Work was a family affair. Later, machinery took many jobs out of the home and into factories and offices. Labor was divided then—men outside the home, women inside. Wars, economics, education, and birth control eventually broke down some of that division.

In the eighteenth, nineteenth, and early twentieth centuries, women were always in the newspaper business, unlike some other fields. But they were so rare that the same names pop up over and over again in the histories. Elizabeth Timothy. Margaret Fuller. Jane Croly. Ida Wells Barnett. Nellie Bly. Dorothy Thompson. Cissy Patterson.

Contemporary scholars are restoring these and other women to the collective memory of the profession. This outline of their work illustrates that women entering the profession today are not standing on thin air. There is a foundation beneath them that has been laid by independent-minded women who felt the attraction of newspaper work, recognized how they could contribute to public information, and sometimes offered perceptive analyses of women's roles.

In journalism past as in journalism present, there were publishers and then the rest of us. Until recently, virtually no woman who was a publisher achieved that rank without being born into a publishing family or marrying into one. Men also inherited their publishing empires, like the Sulzbergers and Chandlers, Hearsts and McClatchys, or married into them, like Philip Graham and the first Chandler publisher. The critical difference is that men started those empires. Only when there were no male candidates did women become their leaders.

As America was being settled, as fields were cleared, communities built, businesses started, clothing stitched, and candles made, women worked alongside men. Work was split somewhat along gender lines, but it was done together, around the home. Newspapering could be family work, and in an era when disease and death struck early and often, it was sometimes women's work entirely.

More than a dozen women printed newspapers in colonial times, including Anna Maul Zenger, widow of John Peter Zenger, famous for his early defense of freedom of the press. The first American woman journalist was publisher Elizabeth Timothy. She and her husband Lewis, a French Huguenot, arrived in Philadelphia in 1731 from Rotterdam, and Lewis Timothy, who knew printing, went into business with Benjamin Franklin. In 1734, Franklin sent the Timothy family off to Charleston, South Carolina, to help with his developing journalistic empire there. Lewis Timothy was named editor of *The South Carolina Gazette*. His wife was busy with educating her growing family, which by 1738 included eight children.

Then smallpox struck. Lewis Timothy died in December 1738. The next month the newspaper carried a notice that, in their son Peter's name, Elizabeth Timothy was taking over the paper. She hoped to make the paper "as entertaining and correct as may reasonably be expected." The widow Timothy was not the compositor her husband had been, but Ben Franklin found her a far better business partner. Her accounts were clearer, she collected on more bills, and she cut off advertisements if payments were not current. The *Gazette*'s content was much like that of other papers of its day: speeches by the governor, sermons, ship arrivals, local events, foreign correspondence (literally—it came by mail), and advertisements.

In November 1740, a devastating fire ripped through Charleston. The *Gazette* covered the event and for days thereafter served as a community bulletin board, carrying announcements of relocated businesses and pleas for housing for the homeless. In May 1746, Elizabeth Timothy turned full-time operation of the paper over to Peter. After he died in 1781, his widow Ann continued the family tradition by running the paper.[1]

Historians have paid little attention to the family contexts of American newspaper dynasties—especially to women who have worked alongside their better-remembered husbands. Eliza Otis, wife of the founder of the *Los Angeles Times* chain of leadership that has continued for a hundred years, often stepped in for her husband, Harrison Gray Otis, as his newspaper career developed. Studying Eliza as a "journalistic comrade," historian Susan Henry of California State University, Northridge, found that Otis's wife in essence ran *The Santa Barbara Press* for her husband when he became a U.S. Treasury agent in the Seal Islands off Alaska in 1879.[2] Her writing had already been appearing in the paper for three years, although she had little practical newspaper experience.

Eliza Otis believed in hard work, both to ease her lonely heart while her husband was away and to keep from being "a mere domestic machine." In the late nineteenth century, it became increasingly acceptable for women to write; that acceptability, combined with the necessity for frontier publishing families to work together setting type, folding newspapers, and selling advertisements, helps explain Eliza Otis's emergence as a partner in her husband's newspaper enterprises.

The couple moved to Los Angeles, where Otis was hired as editor and then became owner of the *Times*, while Eliza Otis wrote poetry for the paper as well as doing local reporting, a regular travel column, editorials, and household advice. Their daughter married a *Times*man, Harry Chandler, and the Chandler name has been on the paper's masthead ever since.

A handful of modern publishers also started with family ties to publishing. Helen Rogers was social secretary to Elizabeth Reid, wife of the publisher of *The New York Tribune*. She wed the Reids' son Ogden. Ogden inherited the *Tribune*, and Helen busied herself with the New York women's suffrage campaign. Soon, however, she started selling ads for the *Tribune* and proved to have far better managerial skills than her husband, an alcoholic.

Helen Rogers Reid became vice president of the newspaper and helped bring Walter Lippmann to the *Tribune*. "It was not politics, though," writes *Tribune* chronicler Richard Kluger, "but Helen Reid's lifelong feminism that provided the main conduit

17

for her liberating and liberalizing influence on the Tribune."[3] She hired food writer Clementine Paddleford, whose descriptions made readers taste the food she was discussing and whose consumer suggestions helped them in practical matters. Helen Reid also made sure there were women in other departments, including Irita Van Doren as book editor. She brought Dorothy Thompson to the paper and later approved sending Marguerite Higgins to Europe during World War II. Reid's husband died in 1947. She was president of the company for six years until she turned the post over to her son.

Helen Reid had married into her newspaper dynasty; Eleanor (Cissy) Patterson was born into hers. Her grandfather, Joseph Medill, directed the *Chicago Tribune*; her father and brother were both editors of the *Tribune*. Brother Joe Patterson also founded the New York *Daily News* with her cousin, Col. Robert (Bertie) McCormick, who took over the *Tribune*. Cissy Patterson grew up to be a spoiled rich kid and fell in love with a handsome Polish nobleman. She married him despite his reputation as a philanderer but soon realized that she couldn't live with his indifference. Returning to America, she took up a dizzying party life in Washington but at 49 decided she wanted to do more with her life than exchange insults with Alice Roosevelt Longworth.

In 1930, she persuaded William Randolph Hearst to let her run *The Washington Herald*. Her only previous newspaper experience, other than listening to her beloved grandfather, her father, and her brother talk about their papers, had been in covering a murder trial for the New York *Daily News*.

In a front-page editorial, she wrote that having a woman as editor shouldn't be odd. "Men have always been bossed by women anyway, although most of them don't know it." In a radio talk she added, "Perhaps a woman editor is resented because an editor is supposed to possess wisdom, and something in the masculine mind objects to the suggestion that a woman can know anything except what she has already been told by a man. . . . There is . . . no part of a newspaper management that need necessarily be beyond her power to control."[4]

In an era when newspapers were becoming more and more alike, Patterson's *Herald* had a distinctive voice, wrote her biographer, Ralph Martin. She created a gossipy feature, "Page 3," to which Washingtonians turned to "find out who was doing what to whom." In less than two years after Patterson took over the *Herald*, she was able to tell Hearst that she had built the paper into the largest morning circulation in Washington, some ten thousand papers ahead of her nearest competition. Hearst made her publisher as well as editor.

In 1932, as the Depression got worse, Patterson herself went out to see how the poor lived. She put on her shabbiest clothes—hard to find in a fashion plate's wardrobe—and was dropped by her limousine near the Salvation Army at 11:45 at night. She worked ten days on the series and got so caught up in her alter ego that she cried during job interviews. That series led her to undertake other investigations such as checking on hungry children and on the problems of the Bonus Army of veterans camping in Anacostia Flats.

She continued to hire women and urged them to do more. "Women are the best reporters in the world," she once said. "In regards to feature writing—by which I mean emotional writing—women from the very start have headed for first flight. I think men have shoved them out of many a position in which, to my mind, they could prove themselves superior."[5] Always insecure, Patterson turned increasingly to drugs and alcohol, Martin writes, and slowly her interest in her paper diminished. She died on July 24, 1948, at 67.

Her niece Alicia Patterson's career began more conventionally. Unable to talk his daughter out of going into the newspaper business, Joe Patterson gave her a job on the New York *Daily News* as a cub reporter. She muffed a divorce story—she got the names wrong—and as a result the paper faced a libel suit. She dabbled in journalism through the 1930s but concentrated more on flying and writing about it. She married Harry Guggenheim, heir to a copper fortune. Together they bought *The Nassau Daily Journal* in Hempstead on Long Island, New York.

Alicia Patterson was in full charge of the editorial side of the paper, which was renamed *Newsday* in a contest. (She joked that she wanted to call it the *Courier-Irritant*.) Its first issue appeared in 1940; the paper was thus in position when the New York suburbs boomed after World War II. It covered local news intensely and irreverently and investigated everything. In 1954 the newspaper won a Pulitzer Prize for exposing a construction union shakedown at Long Island harness racing tracks.[6]

Originally aimed at 15,000 circulation, *Newsday* had 375,000 readers by mid-1963, when Alicia Patterson died of bleeding ulcers. Journalists remember Alicia Patterson today for creating a fund for fellowships to permit them to travel and study.

At the same time, in Manhattan, Dorothy Schiff's *New York Post* was advocating "honest unionism, social reform and humane government programs." Schiff was devoted to politics—she switched from the Republican to the Democratic Party after hearing Franklin D. Roosevelt's "Rendezvous with Destiny" speech in 1936. Her devotion was reflected not only in the editorials but also in the coverage of news. Schiff was a working publisher who for several years wrote her own column, one of many in the *Post*. She had bought the paper at the suggestion of her husband, George Backer, in 1939, and became the *Post*'s publisher in 1942; in 1976, she announced the sale of the paper to Rupert Murdoch.[7]

In California, two women whose papers held opposite political views were propelled into their jobs through family connections, Eleanor McClatchy and Helen Copley. McClatchy had trained to be a playwright but became president of the McClatchy Newspapers—*The Sacramento Bee, The Fresno Bee, The Modesto Bee,* and later *The Anchorage Daily News*—in 1936, after her father died. A reticent woman, she used her papers to champion liberal causes and candidates. She died in 1980.[8]

Helen Copley, a secretary, married her boss and succeeded him as publisher of the arch-Republican *San Diego Union* and other Copley papers upon his death in 1973. Feeling shy and ill-equipped for her new role, Copley hired a speech instructor to drill her for public appearances. She thereafter worked on shifting the flagship San Diego paper into a more moderate political stance.

At her first national publishers' convention, Helen Copley received a call in her hotel room from Katharine Graham of *The Washington Post*. "I know what you're doing because I used to do the same thing. You're staring at the wall and planning to have dinner in your room," Graham said. They ate together that evening and talked about shared experiences.[9]

Katharine Graham moved into the publishing ranks after the death of her husband, Philip Graham. Her father had picked

Philip Graham and not his daughter to succeed him at the helm of the *Post*. Phil Graham, a bright young man around Washington and adviser to Presidents, killed himself in 1963. Kay Graham, who had worked as a reporter in San Francisco after graduating from the University of Chicago, slowly emerged from her deferential shell and guided the paper through its severest test, Watergate. She has been president of the American Newspaper Publishers Association and was the first woman on the Associated Press Board of Directors. She remained chairman of the *Post*'s board after she turned the publishing job over to her son Donald in 1979.[10] If Americans know the name of one woman in journalism today, it is likely to be Kay Graham's.

These women did not get their jobs by reading the classified ads. They were clearly unlike the vast majority of working women. Until recently, many employed women worked only until they got married or because they were impoverished immigrant or minority women or genteel poor whose husbands had died. Or they were unmarried women whose families had no money to support them. They could aspire to becoming teachers, nurses, or secretaries; many were restricted to work as domestics or waitresses.

A few women, all of an especially independent strain, broke society's restraints, often with the inadvertent help of fathers who had educated them too well to be content with embroidering doilies. Some of these women were early feminist leaders like Elizabeth Cady Stanton. Others were journalists.

Margaret Fuller's dour father saw to it that she was widely read. Timothy Fuller had his daughter reading Latin when she was six and Shakespeare at eight. She learned Greek, French, Italian, and German. Her knowledge was not wasted. When her father died in 1835, Margaret Fuller went to work teaching at Bronson Alcott's progressive, experimental school in Boston.

Fuller was soon moving among the intellectual giants of the day—Ralph Waldo Emerson, William Ellery Channing, Theodore Parker, Henry David Thoreau. This group held endless discussions on moral and literary topics; the editor of its journal, *The Dial*, a woman treated with equality in a circle of intellectual men, was Margaret Fuller. Fuller also presided over philosophical conversations in women's homes. In her book *Woman in the Nineteenth Century*, Fuller wrote that women, like men, should be educated

21

and have the same opportunities. A mild plea today, it was radical in its age.

More than her feminism and social analysis, however, her colorful descriptions and her interview style caught the eye of pioneering *New York Tribune* editor Horace Greeley, who hired her as his paper's literary editor. Initially, Greeley criticized Fuller for writing in a ponderous Germanic style. Eventually, he called her "the most remarkable, and in some respects, the greatest, woman America has yet known."[11]

Central Park was a goat pasture when Margaret Fuller arrived in New York. She soon became a reporter as well as the *Tribune*'s literary editor. She wrote about conditions for prostitutes imprisoned at Sing Sing or the insane shunted away in corners at the asylum on Blackwell's Island. When Fuller's long-sought chance to travel abroad finally came, she was not as excited as she might have been earlier in her life, feeling that her mind and character were already formed. Nonetheless, she recognized the importance of a foreign tour. "I feel that, if I persevere, there is nothing to hinder my having an important career even now. But it must be in the capacity as a journalist, and for that I need this new field of observation."[12]

At 36, Margaret Fuller sailed for Europe. From England, she wrote home about the new parks and public libraries for the workers of Manchester. She observed that there was a woman "nominally, not really" in charge of a Liverpool education institute. In France she inspected the crèches of Paris—day-care centers where working mothers could leave their children. Her most sustained foreign coverage was of the Italian edition of the revolutions of 1848. Despite the political ferment and despite her personal ferment in a romance with an Italian marchese, Giovanni Angelo Ossoli, whom she may or may not have married (that tidbit of history has never been clear), Fuller did not neglect observations about women.

Anticipating feminists' frustrations a century later, Fuller said in a dispatch from Rome: "I am very tired of the battle with giant wrongs, and would like to have some one younger and stronger arise to say what ought to be said, still more to do what ought to be done. Enough! If I felt these things in privileged America, the cries of mothers and wives beaten at night by sons and husbands for their diversion after drinking, as I have repeatedly heard them these past months . . . have sharpened my perception as to the ills of woman's condition and the remedies that must be applied. Had I but genius, had I but energy, to tell what I know as it ought to be told! God grant them to me, or some other more worthy woman, I pray."[13]

Fuller covered politics and war in Italy, writing of class conflicts sure to come as Italy became a state and of the Pope's loss of political influence within Italy. Fuller survived the shelling of Rome by the French but drowned with Ossoli and their young son in a shipwreck within sight of Fire Island, New York, on a trip home.

Jane Cunningham Croly became a journalist and reformer under the pen name Jennie June. Like Fuller, she received her early education from her father, in his library in Wappinger's Falls, New York. Like Fuller, Cunningham had to go to work after her father died and left her virtually penniless at 25. And like Fuller, Cunningham wrote her first newspaper articles for *The New York Tribune*. She used the name Jennie June to hide her real identity—journalism was still no place for a lady.

Her husband was sickly and there was not enough money for their large family, so Jennie June wrote fashion, drama, straight news, and advice over the next forty years. She concentrated much of her editorial advice on sensible fashions and proper eating habits for women as well as on opening new careers for women in bookkeeping, teaching, nursing, and secretarial work. "It is somewhat ironic," writes historian Sharon M. Murphy, "that she used her influence to promote as careers for women the very types of work in which many modern-day women now find themselves trapped. But at the time she was writing, she was pressing for horizons then unfamiliar to many of her readers."[14]

When Charles Dickens visited New York City in 1868, the New York Press Club held a banquet at Delmonico's for the famous author. Jennie June, by then one of the country's best-known writers, was denied a ticket. In reaction, June and other literary women formed their own club, Sorosis. One hundred years later, Jennie June's feminist descendants were still fighting for admission to male-only groups like the National Press Club.

Jennie June insisted on being judged on the quality of her

work alone, saying, "There is no sex in labor, and I want my work taken as the achievement of an individual with no qualifications, no indulgence, no extenuations simply because I happen to be a woman, working along the same line with men."[15]

For years, if there was a woman on a newspaper who didn't write on fashion and food, she was the paper's "stunt girl." The most legendary stunt girl of them all was Elizabeth Cochrane Seaman—pen name, Nellie Bly.

Born in 1865, Elizabeth Cochrane lived with her mother in a series of boarding houses in Pittsburgh after her father died; there Cochrane learned life was hard for women alone. Reading a *Pittsburgh Dispatch* editorial arguing that girls should stay home and not seek careers or the vote, Cochrane wrote a rebuttal that women had a right to seek interesting lives. The editor printed her article. She then wrote another—on divorce, not a popular topic in those days—and the editor hired her at five dollars a week in 1885. She called herself Nellie Bly, after a Stephen Foster song. "She was a reformer who wanted to go out among the poor, into the tenements and factories, firsthand, talking with people, especially immigrants," writes historian Madelon Golden Schilpp.[16]

Later, for *The New York World*, Bly feigned insanity to expose conditions at the mental asylum on Blackwell's Island. She checked into a seedy hotel, pretended that she had just arrived from Cuba and spoke little English, and became so irrational that the matron called the police. Three medical experts found she was suffering from dementia, so off she went to Blackwell's Island. Other papers carried the story of her commitment, not knowing it was a gimmick by the *World*.

In the asylum, Bly was appalled at the way patients were treated. Buckets of ice water were thrown on patients for a bath, and the food was garbage. After a week, publisher Joseph Pulitzer's lawyer finally sprang her. Then she did a front-page finale to the story, calling the asylum a "human rat trap."[17] She also posed as a poor working girl to expose sweatshops. She stole fifty dollars from a woman's purse to see how women were treated in jail. She even played a chorus girl, complete with scanty outfit.

Bly's most famous stunt was her attempt to beat the fictional record "set" in *Around the World in 80 Days*. Her editors were reluctant to let a lone woman undertake such a journey. They relented but then worried that she would need too much baggage. Bly took one satchel and a pocket watch set to New York time. With headlines blaring about a "Feminine Phileas Fogg," Bly set off on November 14, 1889. She became America's sweetheart, a merchandiser's bonanza worthy of E. T. There were, historian Schlipp notes, Nellie Bly games, Nellie Bly clothes, Nellie Bly songs. After twenty-four days the *World* received her first cheerful dispatch about her seven-day sail across the Atlantic. From England, she detoured to Amiens in France to meet Fogg's creator, Jules Verne, at his elegant estate.

Off she hurried to the Mediterranean, Port Said, Ceylon, Singapore, and Hong Kong. Monsoon rains buffeted her ship en route. The *World*'s circulation rose as readers followed her bargaining in the markets, looking at Buddhist relics, witnessing a Chinese funeral. Then came the turbulent trip home, when some in the crew wanted to throw Bly's pet monkey overboard. They considered it a jinx. Finally the ship steamed into San Francisco Bay. Nellie Bly and the monkey headed for the welcoming reception, then boarded a special train that the *World* had hired to take her east. When Bly arrived in Jersey City, the timers called out, "Seventy-two days, six hours, ten minutes, and eleven seconds."

It was a hard act to follow. Bly kept reporting, doing stories on anarchist Emma Goldman and on the Pullman strike in Chicago. She left the newspaper business when she married Robert Seaman, a wealthy man more than twice her age. Less than ten years later, Seaman died. His widow took over his hardware business, only to lose it to dishonest employees. After World War I, the Nellie Bly byline reappeared because the widow Seaman badly needed money. Hired by her old friend Arthur Brisbane, Nellie Bly worked quietly in a corner, handling a column on abandoned children for *The New York Evening Journal*. She died three years later of pneumonia. In her obituary the *Evening Journal* said simply, "She was the best reporter in America."[18]

There were stunt girls and there were sob sisters. One of the first of the latter breed was Annie Laurie, whose real name was Winifred Black. Her first story for the *San Francisco Examiner* in 1889 was overwritten. Her editor told her, "We don't want fine writing in a newspaper. There's a gripman on the Powell Street line—he takes his car out at three o'clock in the morning, and

25

while he's waiting for the signals he opens the morning paper. It's still wet from the press, and by the light of his grip he reads it. Think of him when you're writing a story. Don't write a single word he can't understand and wouldn't read."[19]

Soon, like Nellie Bly, Winifred Black was dressing as a bag lady (before anyone coined the phrase) to check on conditions among women at a San Francisco hospital. In preparation, she asked a doctor she knew to drop belladonna into her eyes so that she would look desperate. (Belladonna, a drug made from the deadly nightshade plant, was used as a narcotic and dilated the pupils.) Black then wandered along Kearny Street and fell to the ground. She was tossed roughly into a prison horse cart, bounced at full speed over cobblestones, pulled from the wagon, and dragged into the hospital. After being treated with an emetic of mustard and hot water, she was pushed back on the street. Her story brought a furious reaction from the hospital, a governor's inspection, the firing of many on the hospital staff, and the beginning of ambulance service in San Francisco.[20] Black also did stories on a leper colony in Molokai and on conditions in cotton mills and fruit canneries—all in punchy sentences with emotional impact.

She was the first reporter from outside to reach Galveston after it was struck by a tidal wave that washed away much of the city. Disguising herself as a boy because she knew no woman could get through, she stepped over bodies and wrote about people so dazed they barely knew what had happened. She helped organize relief efforts. Later, she was in Denver when she saw headlines about the San Francisco earthquake. A succinct telegram from her boss, William Randolph Hearst, read: "Go."[21]

Trials brought out women reporters in force. Winifred Black missed few in forty years. One of the most famous was the trial of Harry Thaw, who was accused of killing famed architect Stanford White for his attentions to his wife, Evelyn Nesbit Thaw. Dorothy Dix, Ada Patterson, and Nixola Greeley-Smith covered that trial with Black. At this trial, according to Ishbel Ross, a famous phrase was born: "A cynical colleague, looking a little wearily at the four fine-looking girls who spread their sympathy like jam, injected a scornful line into his copy about the 'sob sisters.'" The sob sisters' function, as Ross defined it in *Ladies of the Press*, "was to watch for the tear-filled eye, the widow's veil, the quivering lip, the lump in the throat, the trembling hand. They did it very well."[22]

Dorothy Dix not only covered trials, she was an early "Dear Abby," writing one of the first personal advice columns. Her real name was Elizabeth Meriwether Gilmer, and she was another who as a girl was encouraged to use her family's fine library, making her a confirmed bookworm. Her husband developed an incurable mental illness, so she went to work freelancing and was hired by *The New Orleans Picayune*. William Randolph Hearst, who in his neverending battles to boost circulation advanced women's careers as much as anyone in the early days of the twentieth century, hired her away from the *Picayune*. She covered Carrie Nation's saloon-smashing tour of Kansas as well as murder trials. In her columns, Dix counseled people to take charge of their own lives, supported women's right to vote, and campaigned for women's education and employment.[23]

However one defined it, news received a different slant from some women from their earliest professional days. In part, that was because women could get into places where men would have been suspect. They could get victims to talk more readily. So they had different information and wrote different stories. Those who succeeded also dared to be different because they had little to lose, and they weren't going to get the job or be able to do it if they didn't have a gimmick such as going around the world or exploring the seamy side of life.

The press was blatantly biased; objectivity was rarely prized. If people didn't like what they read in one paper, they could buy another. Big cities had four, five, sometimes even ten competing papers. Reporters—male and female—readily adopted causes, and for some those became more important than their careers.

Ida Wells-Barnett was the daughter of an emancipated slave and grew up in Holly Springs, Mississippi. She challenged seg-regation early, at 22: a train conductor tried to make her go into a smoking car with the rest of the black passengers. She refused and bit the conductor's hand. She sued over her treatment and won in circuit court, but the state supreme court reversed the decision.

Like many women of the era, Wells-Barnett got into jour-nalism by freelancing. She wrote an article for a black church weekly about her fight with the railroad. The editor of the Negro Press Association hired her to write for his paper, and she went to Washington. Then she was offered a share in the ownership as well as the editorship of a small paper in Memphis, *The Free Speech and Headlight*. She wrote about poor conditions in black schools and was fired from a teaching job, so she went into journalism full time. In 1892, three black Memphis grocery store operators were lynched—mutilated and shot to death—possibly because their store was draining off business from white store owners. Wells-Barnett wrote outraged articles. While she was out of town, local racists ransacked and destroyed her newspaper office.

Friends warned her that her life would be in danger if she went back to Memphis. So she started working for *The New York Age* but vowed to fight against lynching all her life. She did. She was a founder of the National Association for the Advancement of Colored People and a suffragist.[24]

Josephine Herbst's life paralleled the intellectual currents of the twentieth century. She was a bohemian in the 1920s, knee-deep in Communist Popular Front activity in the 1930s, withdrawn from public life in the 1940s and 1950s, and ultimately revived by the social turmoil of the 1960s. In radical literary circles in New York in the 1920s, Herbst wrote mainly fiction at first, producing a trilogy of novels that only thinly disguised her own family history. In the 1930s she gave more time to journalism, writing about the midwestern farmers' strikes, an uprising in Cuba, German resistance to Hitler, and the Spanish Civil War for publications as varied as the *New York Post* and *New Masses*.[25]

Call it social notes or call it gossip, but intrigues and innuendoes have always been rich newspaper content. Washington and Hollywood are the richest mines, places that thrive on personalities as well as politics. Gossip has a long lineage in Washington, going back to the days of Anne Royall, considered by many historians one of the first women to establish her own reportorial reputation.

After finding a niche as a travel writer to "new" places like Alabama, Royall settled in Washington in 1830 to publish a four-page newspaper. She was already notorious from being tried the year before on charges of being a common scold—she had sworn at a group of evangelists harassing her. Now Royall turned her paper's attention to exposing Washington nepotism and scandal.

The stories bore Royall's unmistakable gossipy style. Few people were neutral about her reporting.[26]

Nor were residents of the other intrigue center—Hollywood —neutral about the reporting of Louella Parsons and Hedda Hopper decades later. Parsons started in Chicago, then went to New York and in 1923 became movie editor for *The New York American*, owned by William Randolph Hearst. Two years later he made her movie editor for his Universal News Service, and she moved to Hollywood in 1926.

Parsons became powerful because she had Hearst's influence behind her. She could make or break stars; her columns talked about their private lives as well as their public careers. She considered her two greatest scoops to be the breakup of the marriage of Douglas Fairbanks and Mary Pickford in 1935 and Ingrid Bergman's pregnancy in 1949 as a result of her affair with Italian director Roberto Rossellini. Parsons's power faded in the late 1950s, when she lost touch with the younger film stars and the rock music world that was changing the tone of the times.[27]

Hedda Hopper, Parsons's chief rival, started as an actress; she ran away from home to join a theatrical troupe after the eighth grade. She appeared in many of the hastily made films of the 1920s for M-G-M and then took up writing because the studio executives wanted to create competition for Louella Parsons. They thought Hopper could be controlled.

Benign at first, Hopper's column took off when it started reporting scandals and divorces. Hopper scooped Parsons on the divorce announcement of James Roosevelt, the President's oldest son. She called her house in Beverly Hills "the house that fear built." Known for her flamboyant hats, Hopper got her tips where she could. She learned, for example, that Clark Gable was entering the Air Force from the dentist who was fixing his teeth so he could pass the physical. After the war, Hopper became increasingly conservative and urged a boycott of films by writers, actors, and directors with Communist connections. She helped persuade Richard Nixon to run against Helen Gahagan Douglas for Congress in the race that launched his national political career. She praised J. Edgar Hoover and Ronald Reagan so often that some newspapers refused to run her column, saying that it was supposed to be about movies and not politics.[28]

Gossip and gore weren't women's only realm. Although there

were still many stubborn holdouts that refused to hire women, some papers had at least one woman reporter, a few of whom covered politics, social issues, and foreign affairs. Among them were Sigrid Arne, Genevieve Herrick, and Dorothy Thompson.

Sigrid Arne grew up in Cleveland and knew at age 6 that she wanted to be a writer. By high school she had focused her attention on newspaper writing. In the 1920s Arne worked for papers in Muskogee, Oklahoma, Oklahoma City, Detroit, and Cleveland, then joined the Associated Press in Washington in 1933.

While she was working in Oklahoma City, Arne set out to expose that babies were being peddled like groceries. Using a marked fifty-dollar bill, she "bought" a twenty-four-hour-old baby boy and then wrote a series of articles exposing the racket. She hoped the Oklahoma legislature would appropriate money for child care to allow women to keep their children. Instead, she wrote, "They voted $100,000 for tick eradication." Long before John Steinbeck's *The Grapes of Wrath* took the Joads from Oklahoma to California, Arne wrote a fourteen-part series in 1929 showing the plight of real people in real places.

At the start of the New Deal, Arne went to Washington. She wrote about National Recovery Administration codes governing various industries and about the Social Security Act. Studying the NRA code for the textile industry, she realized that textile prices would increase dramatically, so she went out and bought a huge supply of linens, curtains, and other household products—a supply she was still using years later. For her Social Security Act stories, she pasted up sheets and sheets of paper to chart how much money workers might expect to receive. She had hundreds of questions for government officials, who had to study Arne's chart themselves before they could give her answers.

She covered the Bretton Woods international monetary conference in July 1944 and the United Nations conference in 1945 for the AP. She wrote everything from a comprehensive study of postwar planning to the annual Christmas fiction story. As it customarily did with women, the Associated Press retired Sigrid Arne at 55. Beth Campbell Short, who worked with Arne, called her the model of a conscientious, smart reporter.[29]

Genevieve Forbes Herrick covered police and politics and showed that the woman's angle could be front-page news. Herrick consistently paid attention to women in politics, and according to historians Linda Steiner and Susanne Gray of Governors State University in Chicago, "her work was instructive to newly enfranchised women readers trying to define their political goals and responsibilities."

Herrick became a reporter for the *Chicago Tribune* in 1921. To investigate conditions on Ellis Island, Herrick disguised herself as an immigrant and traveled from Ireland to America. The *Tribune* published a splashy thirteen-part series on her trip that led to a House investigation of corruption and cruelty within the U.S. Immigration Service.

Best known for her crime reporting, Herrick covered such headline events as the 1924 Leopold-Loeb trial. But she also did a series of articles on Rep. Ruth Hanna McCormick, who ran for the Senate in 1930, and about women delegates to national political conventions. In 1928 she wrote a twelve-part series on the intersection of society and politics in the nation's capital, calling it "Washington—Democracy's Drawing Room." Ultimately, her friendship with Eleanor Roosevelt got her in trouble with *Tribune* publisher Robert McCormick. He accused her of being "socially subsidized" by Mrs. Roosevelt, whose politics he abhorred. Herrick quit and turned to magazine writing.

Herrick's contribution was to explain to readers the ambitions of activist women, according to Steiner and Gray. "Presumably these articles promoted understanding on the part of male readers unused to seeing women active in political life apart from specific reform movements."[30]

Dorothy Thompson's name appears on any list of the most famous women in American journalism. She was sufficiently famous and forthright to be the subject of *New Yorker* cartoons, to be the first reporter thrown out of Hitler's Germany, and to help make the political candidacy of Wendell Willkie in 1940.

Dorothy Thompson's professional skills and force of personality created that fame. Yet sometimes she could not reconcile her public role with the role of happy wife that she thought she wanted. Throughout three marriages—including one to author Sinclair Lewis—she wrestled with conflicting desires to throw her things in a suitcase and undertake new adventures or to foster an environment in which creative men could work. The former won out more often.

After graduation in 1914 from Syracuse University—where

31

she was notorious for what became a lifelong habit of monopolizing conversations—Thompson worked for the suffrage movement. In 1920 she and a friend sailed for Europe, where Thompson worked for the Red Cross and freelanced for the *New York Post* and *The Christian Science Monitor*. She wrote articles without pay from Vienna for *The Philadelphia Public Ledger* until she had done so many pieces that the paper hired her as a full-time correspondent.

She covered nine European countries and always seemed to be at the right place at the right time. Or so she told people, promoting her own legend. She disguised herself as a Red Cross nurse to interview the grandnephew of Franz Joseph, who wanted to reestablish the Hapsburg throne. By 1924 she was the *Ledger*'s Berlin bureau chief, covering the swirling economic and political controversies of the Weimar Republic. She was the first woman to head a major American news bureau overseas.

After a brief retirement during her marriage to Lewis, Thompson returned to Europe and interviewed Adolf Hitler, who was not yet chancellor but already the Nazi Party leader. She wrote a book about the experience, beginning it by saying, "When I walked into Hitler's salon, I was convinced that I was meeting the future dictator of Germany. In less than 50 seconds I was sure I was not. It took me just that time to measure the startling insignificance of this man who had set the world agog." She said Hitler was "inconsequent and voluble, ill-poised, insecure."[31] But Thompson soon changed her judgment of Hitler and started warning Americans of fascism and decrying American isolationism.

William Shirer, reporting from Berlin at the time, recalled Thompson's expulsion from Germany by Hitler in 1934. Thompson was taken to the train station under police escort and sent out of the country because Hitler was enraged about what she had written in her book.[32] Thompson returned to the United States and wrote on fascism for *Foreign Affairs*. In 1936 she began writing a column for *The New York Herald-Tribune* at Helen Reid's insistence. A cover story in *Time* magazine proclaimed Thompson and Eleanor Roosevelt "undoubtedly the most influential women in the U.S."

At odds with President Roosevelt's liberal New Deal social policies, Thompson boosted Wendell Willkie's nomination for President in 1940; then she changed her mind because she decided that Roosevelt's world leadership was more important than his faulty domestic policies. The *Herald-Tribune*, which was pledged to Willkie's candidacy, cancelled her contract the next year.

Thompson's greatest contributions to journalism seemed to be behind her. Marion Sanders, her biographer, feels that Thompson lost her greatest cause once the United States entered the war. "Politically," a friend of Thompson's told Sanders, "she was like a great ship left stranded on the beach after the tide has gone out."[33]

Little ties together these women in the history of journalism except the fact of their being separate from the rest of women in their day, of their being different from other journalists. But their stories form an important backdrop against which to observe the emergence of women in journalism that accelerated in the 1930s through today.

Everyday Indignities

Flora Lewis, now a foreign affairs columnist for *The New York Times*, was covering the first meeting of the United Nations Security Council in London years ago. "A big issue was the U.S. effort to make the Soviet forces withdraw from Azerbaijan (northern Iran), and there was tension between the U.S. and the Soviets.

"Edward Stettinius, then secretary of state, suddenly got up from the table and strode out. Several of us in the press gallery went running downstairs to follow him, thinking there might be an important development. I chased down the hall with the others and saw them go through a door. It was only at the last moment that I noticed it had a sign, 'MEN.'

"My male colleagues roared with laughter when I complained that they had taken unfair advantage. A couple were good enough to brief me on the meaningless things Stettinius had said."

CHAPTER

3

The Roosevelt Rule

Beth Campbell's first day at the Associated Press bureau in Washington started briskly. A small, energetic woman not yet 30, she arrived in the nation's capital after working for newspapers in the Midwest, where she had covered bandits who ranged the Plains as well as soup-kitchen survival in the Depression. She had gone to college and had been trained by a tough editor. She was ready for anything. Almost.

No sooner did she get off the train from Oklahoma City at Washington's Union Station on the wintry morning of December 21, 1936, than she was greeted by directions to report right away to the bureau. She had a story to write, and then, she was told, she was "going to sing 'Silent Night' at the White House tonight."

She walked into the AP office at Eleventh and Pennsylvania Avenue, was introduced around, and was told to produce a night lead on the Gridiron Widows by 2 P.M.

It was all quite confusing. "I didn't know anything to say to an editor but 'yes, sir.' But I didn't know what the Gridiron Widows were. I hadn't been to the White House. And I wasn't sure what was going on." She had worked for afternoon papers and didn't know what a night lead was—she didn't even know how long it should be. She did know she'd better find out. She discovered that she, a rookie just off an overnight train, had to write her first story out of Washington, a piece of about 350 to 400 words, by early that afternoon. It would be transmitted to morning newspapers for their use in editions they were putting together that evening. Night leads were for morning papers; day leads were for afternoon papers.

Campbell also learned that the Gridiron Widows were the wives of fifty reporters attending the exclusively male Gridiron Club dinner. Eleanor Roosevelt had invited these women and the wives of their husbands' prestigious guests to the White House; she also invited the Women's National Press Club to perform. It was Beth Campbell's introduction to the woman who had indirectly helped her get her break in Washington.

The 1930s marked the first major turn in the fortunes of women reporters like Beth Campbell—and the force behind that turn was Eleanor Roosevelt. She brought women into government and brought their ideas to bear on government. She had been influenced by the social workers with whom she dealt in New York and still kept their concerns before her husband. At the suggestion of her friend Lorena Hickock of the Associated Press, Eleanor Roosevelt insisted that only women cover her news conferences. Since she made news herself, newspapers and wire services were forced to hire at least one woman to cover her activities or to keep on female staffers, whose jobs were otherwise at risk in the Depression. At newspapers all over the country there was a woman here, a woman there—women covering trials, investigating mental hospitals, advising the lovelorn, and preparing social notes—isolated individuals. They had experience but little opportunity. Washington, then as now, was the journalistic mecca, but women rarely could make the pilgrimage.

Eleanor Roosevelt helped change that. She took the press out to the people. Miners, poor farmers, people who had never seen a President's wife before saw this one. And the press corps that went with her was female. Its members protected her too much on occasion, telling her at times that surely she didn't mean to say what she had just said. But its members were also staking out their share, albeit a small one at first, of national coverage, casting issues in human terms. Women were getting a chance on the national stage, covering a national player.

The AP's Lorena Hickok had been one of the first to report on Eleanor Roosevelt, although in initial encounters while covering the Democratic National Committee in 1928, she had found her poor copy. Hickok had reported for *The Milwaukee Sentinel*, *The Minneapolis Tribune*, and *The New York Daily Mirror* before landing at the AP. In correspondence with Bess Furman in the

Washington bureau, Hickok complained that "the AP wouldn't let me handle a big story, not if there was a male cub, not yet dry behind the ears, within 50 miles of the place."

She persevered, covering the Lindbergh baby's kidnapping, and became the only woman assigned to cover Franklin D. Roosevelt's campaign in 1932. The night FDR was nominated, Hickok asked his wife whether she was excited about going to the White House, and Mrs. Roosevelt only glared back. That led Hickok to suggest that someone be assigned to cover the candidate's wife because she saw Mrs. Roosevelt as not the usual potential First Lady. She didn't want the job herself but inherited it when the other reporter, Katherine Beebe, left for the West Coast. Hickok eventually became a close confidante of Mrs. Roosevelt. Too close, she eventually realized, because she learned things she felt she could not report and passed up scoops that had never even occurred to her at the time. After the inauguration, she did not report on Eleanor Roosevelt again.[1]

Mrs. Roosevelt soon demonstrated her news-making ability. Franklin D. Roosevelt took office on March 4, 1933; Prohibition was repealed with the ratification of the Twenty-First Amendment on December 5, 1933. The amendment had gone through the ratification process with the speed of white lightning after passing Congress earlier in the year, but it was still a touchy topic. Would Eleanor Roosevelt, a teetotaller, allow liquor to be served in the White House? President Roosevelt, using his wife to deflect controversy from himself, told reporters they'd have to get their answers from her. Mrs. Roosevelt called a news conference that male reporters clamored to cover but could not.

On the morning of January 29, 1934, the White House's chief usher handed each of the women reporters a paper saying that although no liquor would be served at the White House, wines would be and, when served, "will of course be simple ones, preference being given to American products."

"We were told to hold this statement for release until the end of the conference, but one lady who apparently did not hear this injunction dashed out to telephone the story to her paper," recalled reporter Marie Manning. Since Mrs. Roosevelt "had been at great pains to persuade the President to let the women, rather than the men reporters, have this sensationally important scoop—

repeal at last!—she declined to allow the non-cooperation of one reporter to defeat her plan. She quickly sent Ruby Black of the United Press, Bess Furman, then covering for the Associated Press, and me, of International News Service, to three telephones in nearby White House bedrooms so that we might phone the story to our own editors."[2]

Eleanor Roosevelt was not talking to female reporters plucked unprepared out of a secretarial pool. Like Beth Campbell and others, these reporters had been at work building the credentials that would get them to the White House.

Growing up in Oklahoma, Beth Campbell had originally wanted to teach home economics in Latin America. But after being co-editor of her high school newspaper in Bartlesville, she was hooked. While at the University of Oklahoma, Campbell met Sigrid Arne, then of *The Oklahoma City Times* and later an Associated Press reporter. She asked Arne to recommend the best editor for whom a young reporter could work. That was George Olds, Arne replied. So Campbell went to work for Olds at *The Springfield Leader*, an afternoon paper in Springfield, Missouri, in 1929, despite an offer from the larger *Austin Statesman*. She wanted to learn.

There must be an Editors' School somewhere that turns out people like George Olds. All beginners should have one to make them do it right in spite of themselves. Nearly six decades later, Campbell vividly recalled the time Olds sent her to cover a pet parade soon after she started work at the *Leader*. She rushed back to the office and told Olds about it in lavish detail. Then she wrote her story. After she handed the copy in, he called her over and tore up her lifeless story. "Now go back and write that story you told me," he said.

Olds also specialized in memory training. He sent Campbell out to cover meetings and told her she could only write—and he would only print—what she could commit to memory. First it was only a paragraph or two at a time; eventually, it was whole stories.

"After a year, he said I could be trusted with death notices. He said getting a name wrong on death notices was the worst thing you can do" because it was the only time some people got their names in the paper. He also made sure she got the closing stock figures correct. "People have jumped out of windows since the crash so you see how important it is to have the number correct," he told her.

Years later, the training paid off. Campbell got an interview she had been seeking for months with Washington socialite Evalyn Walsh McLean, who didn't like talking to the press. McLean was news because during that Depression era it was rumored that she had spent $100,000 on a debutante party for her daughter. She called one afternoon and said she'd do an interview if Campbell would get right out to her home. When she arrived after a hurried cab ride, Campbell found that the prime ground rule was that she could take no notes. The interview lasted four hours. But Evalyn McLean didn't know about George Olds. Campbell remembered what she needed to remember, especially when she asked McLean about the $100,000 party. "That's a lie," she told Campbell. "I never spent more than $50,000 for a party."

Campbell remembers no discrimination between men and women in the 1930s. "I got to cover every kind of story. I subbed for the sports editor. I had to cover a wrestling match. I sat in his seats right under the apron and blood spurted on me. I thought, 'Well, I have to learn everything.' " And she covered almost everything. Bandits roamed the Southwest; massive posses tracked them down. Competing with reporters from all over the country, Campbell covered the search for the Young brothers, who had killed five peace officers. On a tip from attorney Thomas Benton, later a U.S. senator, she was the only reporter covering the brothers' funeral in Joplin, Missouri, after they killed each other.

Campbell wrote stories to demonstrate the meager Depression diet on which many Americans lived by allowing herself twenty-five cents a day for meals for ten days. She had no trouble finding her first meals—the five-cent sandwich and the seven-cent oatmeal (with butter). But she couldn't keep writing the same story every day so she had to keep looking. She emerged from her story successful but hungry. She continued her interest in the lives of average people with a series called "Real Folks at Home." She'd drop in on a different family each night to see if she could get a story. She picked the rich, the poor, the educated, the ignorant. At only one place did she encounter any problem. It was an omen of the future. "The man said, 'You can come in but I wish you wouldn't.' He had been labeled a communist and lost his job in higher education. Now he finally had a job. Any publicity would blow his family out of the water," she said. She left.

She also covered religion. As church editor, she wrote a column, "The Very Idea," on local ministers' sermons. After listening to a particularly dismal message from the pulpit, she wrote in her column, "Even I could preach a better one." G. Bryant Drake of the Congregational church took her up on it. She was to speak at an evening service. The cab broke down en route, but her date fixed the car. They wheeled up to the church as the bells were ringing. Campbell preached on "Rejoice in Thy Youth," certain she'd get the paper in trouble with her temerity. The editor loved it and carried a big story on her sermon.

Leaving the *Leader* to be closer to home, Campbell went to work at *The Daily Oklahoman*. Associated Press editors saw her work and she was asked if she'd go to Washington for them. The wire service had to get the permission of its member papers to raid their staffs, and her editor, Walter Harrison, wouldn't let her go. She kept on reporting for the *Oklahoman* and covered the Oklahoma delegation at the 1936 conventions. "Nowadays, everybody kisses everybody," she recalls, "but that wasn't the case then and I slapped a senator who kissed me at one of the meetings."

The next time the AP called, Harrison did let her go. Bess Furman, who had been covering Mrs. Roosevelt for the AP, was pregnant, and the Washington bureau needed a replacement. But Harrison insisted that Campbell stay around to write a story on the birth of the city's Christmas baby, the holiday newborn on which the paper lavished great attention. Once that assignment was finished, she headed off to Washington. She took with her seven years of varied experience under rigorous editors. She might not know what the Gridiron Widows were, but she knew how to find out.

Beth Campbell Short, as she soon became after marrying AP reporter Joe Short, was not without misgivings about her new assignment. She had read that Mrs. Roosevelt nurtured newspaperwomen and that they nurtured her. "I said I couldn't do that. If she thinks giving me scrambled eggs out of a chafing dish in the White House is going to make me treat her any different than if I didn't have those eggs, she's wrong. I don't ever want to make close friends with a news source."

So the new Mrs. Short kept her distance. But she came to admire Mrs. Roosevelt, partly because she didn't undercut journalists. She recalls one summer when Joe went to Hyde Park to cover the President. The women of the press had an agreement that they didn't cover Mrs. Roosevelt on a daily basis in the summer, so they did not go to Hyde Park. But Beth Short got lonesome. To get to Hyde Park to see Joe, she decided to do a feature on what Mrs. Roosevelt did in the summer. She arranged to have lunch with her at the New York estate.

At lunch, Mrs. Roosevelt told her that they would be entertaining the King and Queen of England. Mrs. Roosevelt had decided that although they had to be formal in Washington, it would be more in keeping with summer in Hyde Park to serve hot dogs to their guests. But Sara Roosevelt, the President's indomitable mother, thought this choice was too informal. "That was the whole point. Hot dogs were America." They'd had one of their recurring disagreements, and the President's wife decided to have hot dogs anyway. She discussed it casually with Short, who wrote a news story.

The next day, just as those reporters who were at Hyde Park were about to go to Mrs. Roosevelt's cottage, Val Kill, for a swim, one of them, a woman, was paged. Returning, the woman peevishly asked Mrs. Roosevelt, "Did you see what Beth did to you?" Her office had called her to match the story on the hot-dog debate.

Mrs. Roosevelt was unfazed. "No," she said, "I didn't read the story, but I'm sure Beth wrote what I told her yesterday."

Beth Short left the AP in 1940 because she and Joe were expecting their first child. Women voluntarily left the newsroom when they were pregnant—but often they were fired. Time was, says Elsie Carper of *The Washington Post*, that the day a woman even said she was getting married, much less having a child, was the day she was in effect resigning from newspaper work.

But one woman's pregnancy could be another's career break. Because Mrs. Roosevelt insisted on being covered by women, the AP went to Chicago for a replacement for Short. Like Short, Ruth Cowan had handled various assignments for many years before coming to Washington. Cowan, however, had had a taste of discrimination. She had worked briefly for *The San Antonio Evening News* in 1928, then started covering the legislature in

Austin for United Press under the byline R. Baldwin Cowan. One day the Kansas City regional manager called. He wanted to talk about possible promotion, and he asked for Baldwin Cowan.

"Speaking," Cowan said.

"No, I wanted to talk to Baldwin Cowan. You are a woman. The United Press doesn't hire women."

"You've got one," Cowan replied in her best blunt manner. But not for long. Cowan was fired after three productive months on the job. She sent a telegram to Kent Cooper, the Associated Press bureau manager in Chicago. In staccato telegraph language, she informed him that she'd just gotten fired but that she'd lasted a while and did he have anything for a woman? She joined the AP's Chicago bureau in 1930. "I had a good time. They didn't know what to do with me. I sort of decided what I wanted to do. They thought I wanted society. I didn't."

Chicago was gangland in the 1930s. The police were still investigating the St. Valentine's Day Massacre; she covered that probe. For another assignment, Cowan hitched a ride to a gang-ster's funeral in a milk wagon. When the back door opened for the milkman, she walked in, too, although there weren't supposed to be any reporters inside. "It was the first time I had seen the floral wreaths the gangsters sent around among themselves. Some reached right to the ceiling," she says, her voice filled with awe even years later. "I decided I'd better go look at the corpse. This big guy came over and asked, 'How does he look?' When it became evident I didn't know how he looked because I had never laid eyes on him before, the big guy asked me who I was and threw me out. But I had enough for a good story. The editors decided I'd get along all right after that."

Cowan covered the 1932 Democratic Convention in Chicago and wrote extensively about the World's Fair in 1937 before going to Washington as Short's replacement.

One of the most experienced pioneers of this era was Bess Furman. Furman worked on newspapers in Nebraska for a decade before moving to Washington and the Associated Press in 1929. She wrote her way to Washington with her coverage of the 1928 presidential campaign. And she wrote her way into journalism history not only through her sustained coverage of the women's side of the White House but later when she spotted early on the chance to develop an important beat covering the Social Security, health, and education stories that originate in Washington.

Even a reporter as good as Furman faced obstacles because of her sex. In her autobiography, *Washington Byline,* she described the first birthday she had ever spent away from Nebraska, covering the opening of Congress "from the woman angle." She recalled: "It was a cold and stormy day, and a tense and strenuous one for me. In the months I had spent in Washington, with a special session on, I could easily have made the acquaintance of the eight women in Congress. But the AP men on Capitol Hill kept it as holy ground, on which I was not supposed to set foot without explicit orders. And so I had to meet and interview all eight Congresswomen in one day, in addition to picking out the women notables in the galleries."[3]

On more than one occasion, however, Bess Furman turned being a woman to an advantage. She had arrived in Washington in an era when Presidents shunned publicity. President and Mrs. Hoover kept their private life private. Furman got wind of a Christmas Eve party at which a Girl Scout troop would be caroling. Deciding it would be good for the Girl Scouts (and for her), Furman arranged to infiltrate the troop. Tucking her hair tightly into her hat, scrubbing off her powder and lipstick, she was soon "one in spirit and presence, if not in age, with the gray-green girls who went in a herd of forty through the southwest gate of the White House." Security then wasn't what it is today.

"Among the tallest of the forty little girls, I was on the back row," Furman wrote in her autobiography. "Holding our lanterns high, we stood facing the white columns and poinsettia-filled boxes that blocked off the central corridor." Furman knew none of the words to "Good King Wenceslaus," which seemed interminable, so she gave up singing, moved her jaws in rhythm, and concentrated on memorizing what she was seeing. Her story drew raves, even from Mrs. Hoover, who never asked how she got it.[4]

For about three years, Furman wrote about Mrs. Roosevelt for both the AP and *The Washington Star.* Finally, she told the *Star* she couldn't continue doing double duty. The *Star* editors looked to the women on their society desk for help, but they were not interested. So the editor turned to a young woman who had come in to town from South Carolina, Frances Lide.

43

Lide had decided after a year at Converse College that she wanted to work for newspapers. She was hired by *The Greenville Piedmont*, where she covered schools and churches from 1928 to 1931. The town was encircled by cotton mills, and she remembers that she was constantly waking up people who worked on the night shift to get information. Later she worked a seven-day week at *The Greenwood Index-Journal*, where there were only a telegraph editor, a city editor, and herself, the society editor. The paper had so little money that the telegraph editor left. Lide began doing that job as well as the society editor job at half the pay at which she'd started.

"Everybody else was going to football games while I was working two shifts on Saturday." Lide was young and wanted more out of life, but there seemed to be no place to go. She saved up two hundred dollars, quit her South Carolina job, and went to Washington to try her luck. Her suitcase was stolen the first night she was in town. She got a job as a government clerk-typist and wrote a column in her spare time for some South Carolina papers.

Lide made the rounds of the five papers that then published in Washington. No one had any jobs. She went back to the *Star* on a Saturday night after learning the paper needed someone to cover Mrs. Roosevelt's press conferences because of Furman's ultimatum. Frances Lide got the job—and worked for *The Washington Star* from 1935 until her retirement in 1970.

"It shows what a dramatic impact it was to have a First Lady making news," says Lide. At her news conferences, Eleanor Roosevelt brought in distinguished women from science, aviation, health, and education, and through her they got press attention. Her role in bringing women into the press corps in Washington and increasing their visibility once there is in many respects a footnote in a major era of American history. But it was key to bringing women and their bylines up from the outlying cities and small towns and onto the front pages of major papers.

"I would not have admitted Mrs. Roosevelt's importance at the time," Beth Campbell Short said some fifty years later. "I had never felt discrimination at my early jobs and never felt it at the Associated Press. It didn't matter if there was a story on the Hill or Mrs. Roosevelt doing something; if I was the one who was free, they sent me. But I've thought about it lately. If the women hadn't insisted on press conferences and if she hadn't had the policy of only women covering them . . . well, that's what really gave people like me and Ruth Cowan our break."

Bess Furman, Beth Campbell Short, Ruth Cowan, and Frances Lide were, of course, not the only women whose careers reporting the news started or advanced in the 1930s. Edith Evans Asbury, Katherine Beebe (later Pinkham, then Harris), Jane Conant, and Mary Ellen Leary were virtually the only women in their newsrooms. Although many of the pioneering women of their era are gone now, these four had firm memories of their work.

"I was very good at covering trials," says Edith Evans Asbury, who retired from *The New York Times* in 1981 after twenty-nine years on its cityside staff. Her career began in Ohio in 1929. "Most people don't want to cover trials. You're tied up for days and days. It can get boring. When there was a sensational trial that was on page one all over the country, a man took over. He'd get all kinds of help. When I covered equally difficult trials, I did it without a transcript or any other help. That's part of the story: women have to be twice as good as men to hold their own. We took it for granted."

Asbury, a short woman with white hair piled up like a Norman Rockwell grandma's, had a reputation that belied her kindly look. She would step on your grave to get a story, it was said; she had first demonstrated her doggedness while looking for a job in New York over eighteen long, lean months during the Depression. Even though there were nine or ten papers in Manhattan and several in Brooklyn and Newark, many qualified people were still on the street. "I was extremely persistent in job hunting. I felt I was demonstrating the persistence that I must show as a reporter."

She finally landed with the *New York Post*. "I did brilliantly there because I was interested in nothing else but working, throwing myself into the job." Once she spent an entire day watching a man threaten suicide. When she called the office, they said to come back in. "I'd been let out"—laid off, fired. Eventually she landed with the Associated Press after the war started. The AP man said it was hard to find women with news experience. "I told him it was his own damned fault. 'You wouldn't let them get any.'"

Katherine Beebe Pinkham Harris had better luck with the Associated Press but not without pursuing, pursuing, pursuing.

Her aunt had told her California was the place to live, so, armed with ambition to work on a newspaper, she took a secretarial job in the publications office at Stanford University in 1923 and wrote a letter every day to one of the editors on her list. The few encouraging replies were in their own way discouraging: "We have a man in Marin who is so bad," one editor replied, "that even a woman wouldn't be worse."

Finally she got a job with *The Oakland Tribune*, whose editor, a Stanford man, asked her what was going on at Stanford. She wrote a story on the possible abolition of sororities on the Palo Alto campus, a story that ran on the front page. The *San Francisco Chronicle* called Harris's former boss at Stanford and wanted to know why it didn't get stories like that from Stanford. He said, "My secretary came to you for a job and you didn't hire her. She wrote that story."

After working in a variety of other cities, often starting on women's pages and moving off when cityside was shorthanded, Harris landed a job in the AP bureau in New York. She wanted to get back to California but had to quit to do so. She applied at the bureau in San Francisco, which had about thirty people but no women. The bureau chief was reluctant to hire her because the place was such a dump. "You'll have to get used to seeing me without my coat on," he added.

She was made the "outside man" because the men were uncomfortable with her in the office. So she covered the San Francisco general strike when there were no phones or streetcars ("you walked everywhere"), the birth of the United Nations, the trial of dockworkers' leader Harry Bridges, and the Tokyo Rose treason trial. The men who had been uncomfortable with her presence in the newsroom lost good assignments because of that discomfort, while Harris was doing what makes the news business fun: seeing history, being there. When she left the job, there was no shortage of male applicants to replace her.

The Associated Press retired women at 55—not men, just women—and by midcentury Harris knew that if she ever wanted to work in Europe, she had better get there soon. Her husband had died in 1948, and she was restless. And she was already getting pension material from the home office, material she was resolutely ignoring. "I spoke to Wes Gallagher," then the head of the AP, "and he said, 'When I was in Germany, I wouldn't have wanted a woman foisted off on me, and I won't do that to somebody else.'" He wouldn't send her to Europe, but he did tell her that when she got there on vacation to stop by the office in Paris. She thought they wanted to use her to cover Elizabeth II's coronation in 1953, which they did, without paying her way over. She retired from the AP in 1957 after twenty-five years of service.

Men and women alike found the Depression the worst of times for starting careers. Jane Conant graduated from the University of California at Berkeley in 1933, when there were no jobs for anyone. She considered herself rich on the twenty dollars a week she got from *The Oakland Post-Inquirer* as women's club editor. "I paid off my twelve dollars in debts and was never so far ahead again." But teas bored her, and she agitated to get onto cityside.

She did, eventually starring on rewrite for *The San Francisco Call-Bulletin* and retiring in 1976 from what was by then the *San Francisco Examiner*. "Jane did a man's job today" was a compliment in those days, one Conant remembers receiving after she did rewrite duty when a ship blew up in the munitions depot at Port Chicago, killing about three hundred people. "It meant you were cool, competent, professional."

Described years later by more than one colleague as the best in the business on rewrite bank, Conant says that that was the limit of her ambition. "I never wanted to be city editor. I don't know what would have happened if I had. I probably would have had to fight for it. I liked what I was doing. I made a lot of people look good. Rewrite was where I really seemed to do best and enjoyed thoroughly. I was not personally a fighter for myself—but I would fight with reporters to get the information to do the job right."

It was still very much the Depression when Mary Ellen Leary got her master's degree in English from Stanford University in 1937. Learning she'd have to master shorthand to be a secretary but not to be a reporter made her decide she'd be a reporter. Nonetheless, she worked three years as a secretary to the city editor of *The San Francisco News*, writing stories on the side, before she got her break. The *News* had two women reporters already, and it was "not about to have three." Finally one left.

In the fine old tradition of Nellie Bly, female journalists in

47

the 1930s and 1940s—and indeed until fairly recently—posed as mental patients or maids or substitute teachers to get the "inside story." Leary posed as a single woman on welfare. "I went out to get an abortion, which was of course illegal then. I wanted to expose the police corruption that allowed abortion rings to flourish. I made seven abortion appointments in five days." Not pregnant, she could go only so far with the ruse, but she wanted to see how each place operated. Once she faced a physical examination but avoided it by bursting into tears.

When war came, she got the assignment to cover politics because the regular reporters had gone off to war. She never left, becoming one of the foremost political observers in California. She knew when she started that her competition had been writing for twenty-one, sixteen, and six years respectively and that she couldn't compete doing it their way. She wrote in a totally different style, reporting what she saw and explaining it to readers who knew no more about Sacramento than she had when she first arrived. She described how the politicians stood on the Assembly floor trading votes in stories that took readers to the scene and instructed them on how legislation really got passed.

Like Winifred Black, Leary had one reader in mind: the streetcar motorman. "He worked for the city so he was interested in government. He was in touch with people and he knew what concerned them. But he was tired as the devil when he got home so I had to catch his attention."

Good reporters, male and female, have long written for the motorman or the Kansas City milkman. But good female reporters, like Mary Ellen Leary, may have had an advantage. Outsiders, they could view a story from a new perspective. They knew what it was that readers didn't know because they often hadn't known it themselves at first. Without an image to maintain, they could ask the basic question that yields the basic answer. The fact of being separate, as Adrienne Rich put it, "enters your livelihood like a piece of furniture." It can enrich as well as deny.

Everyday Indignities

A few of the good ol' boys were sittin' around the desk in the city room down at *The Charlotte Observer* back in the middle 1970s. Elizabeth Rhodes, now with *The Seattle Times*, was an earnest young feature writer who came up with ideas for serious stories that she thought belonged in the news section. As she recalls, she had one of her ideas—maybe one about the ratification of the Equal Rights Amendment, then before the North Carolina legislature. She thought there should be some investigation into the motivations of businesses providing financial backing for the ERA's opponents. One of her editors said no, he didn't like that approach. But he might consider it, he said, if you "take off all your clothes and then give me the story idea."

CHAPTER

4

Rosie the Reporter

Blaring Movietone newsreels filled the theaters with images of women trading their sewing machines for machine tools and their cookware for rivet guns as the nation mobilized for World War II. Legions of women went off to work in shipyards and airplane factories. Men left the newsroom as well as the assembly line, and women took their places behind typewriters and at copy desk rims. While a handful of women landed assignments in war zones, the real breakthrough was occurring on the home front. Rosie the Reporter was born.

Eleanor Roosevelt had cracked the door for a few news-women to work in Washington. World War II left that door ajar for a few years, long enough for some women to see what they could do and to realize that they did not have to be men to do what had hitherto been almost exclusively men's jobs. Any man entering the military was supposed to get his job back; men and women alike who replaced GIs often had to sign forms that waived any permanent right to the job, and most felt that that was as it should be. The doors of employment for women slammed shut on all but the most persistent at war's end. Women would not return to the nation's newsrooms in any numbers again until the 1960s.

It was a distinguished group of women whose bylines began appearing—or, in the case of Bess Furman, reappearing—during the war. Furman left the Associated Press in 1936 to give birth to twins and in 1943 started to work at the *New York Times* Washington bureau, becoming the first woman in that office to make a lasting name for herself. She held that job until 1961. She covered education, science, and medicine as well as Eleanor Roosevelt.

Elsie Carper started at *The Washington Post* during the war; she is now its assistant managing editor. Eileen Shanahan, Helen Thomas, and Charlotte Moulton were at the United Press in Washington, and they held on at war's end. As Shanahan describes it, "Charlotte was kept on for the right reasons: she was covering the Supreme Court, as she did for many more years, and reporting rings around a whole series of Associated Press reporters and other competitors, getting complicated court decisions exactly right when nobody else quite did. They were afraid to fire her. As for Helen and me, one might think, given our successful subsequent careers, that we, too, were kept on because of our perceived excellence. Not so. Nobody else wanted those lousy jobs rewriting the news from the local papers for the radio wire with a choice of working either 5:30 A.M. to 2:30 P.M. or 3 P.M. to midnight."

News was more in demand than ever during the war, and women had never had so much responsibility in the newsroom. Marj Paxson, now a retired Gannett publisher, covered everything from the legislature to the courts for the Lincoln, Nebraska, bureau of the United Press. At war's end, the man Paxson had replaced didn't return. She was replaced by a man anyway. Grace Darin became the first woman on the copy desk at *The Baltimore Evening Sun* in 1943 and remained until her retirement in 1978. Darin used the Columbia School of Journalism as her avenue into the newspaper business and out of the small town of Virginia, Minnesota. Woman after woman used such extra credentials to legitimize their presence in the newsroom.

Women were in reporting jobs all over the country. Ann Sullivan started in 1942 at *The Portland Oregonian*, where she covered medicine and science for twenty years. During her long career, she often covered trials and even got to know some of the convicts. Once, in the late 1960s, one of them tipped her on tensions at the state prison at Salem that were about to blow up. She interviewed the new corrections chief and prison guards for one story, then was called to the prison because rioting had indeed broken out and prisoners had seized hostages. Although some of the prisoners wanted to kill everybody, others said they would negotiate with the corrections chief—"and Miss Sullivan." Years later, she said she wished she could remember what she had told the men as she talked through a bullhorn, but could not; whatever it was, it worked. The hostages were released.

Mildred Hamilton, a graduate of the University of Oklahoma, worked on a virtually all-female news staff for the Baton Rouge newspapers, *The Morning Advocate* and *The States-Times*, starting in January 1944. Ultimately, in 1958 she joined the *San Francisco Examiner*, where she maintained a long interest in international organization and in the women's movement. She combined those interests as the one of the few correspondents sent to the women's conference in Copenhagen in 1980.

And Ann Holmes, who had really wanted to write plays, became the military editor at *The Houston Chronicle*, and then had to write the story of her own brother's death in the war. Then she became the paper's arts critic with what even she considered no real background at the time. For many years the *Chronicle's* arts editor, Holmes has won major travel grants to expand her expertise. "I wouldn't have made it for a minute," she says, "if the men trained for the job and who had held down the job for years were around. Women were everywhere then."

Years later, as a few wartime legacies held on, newsrooms would have a woman here who had been covering courts for decades, a woman there who wrote features. Younger colleagues, unaware what prejudices these women had struggled against, often ignored them or dismissed them as out of touch. Some were; others were not helpful to young reporters, feeling that they'd made it on their own and others could, too. But still others remembered their own struggles and tried to help younger women.

One of the women who began her career during World War II—Eileen Shanahan—has played a central role in the evolution of women's status in American journalism. Her career has spanned the most far-reaching changes for women in the profession and in American society. A reporter who specialized in economics and taxes, she was nonetheless one of the first journalists to spot the political and social implications of the new women's movement. She along with other women at *The New York Times* put their considerable careers on the line by suing their own newspaper for discrimination. In addition to her groundbreaking work at *The New York Times*, Shanahan has been an assistant secretary at the Department of Health, Education, and Welfare, assistant managing editor of *The Washington Star*, assistant managing editor of *The Pittsburgh Post-Gazette*, and executive editor of *Governing*, a magazine on state and local governments.

A thorough, tough, demanding professional, she has shunned the Queen Bee syndrome. Instead, she has taught in the University of California's minority journalism program and has served as a one-woman network to help blacks, Asians, Latinos, and women find jobs around the country.

One is not born knowing that life is unfair. But as a sixth grader in the 1930s, Shanahan saw that girls couldn't become school-crossing guards. As a teenager, she discovered that girls didn't qualify for a prestigious scholarship that one of her sister's male high school classmates had won. "Right from the git-go, I had a sense of [discrimination] being systemic," Shanahan says, "I certainly knew it was a pattern."

Growing up in Washington, D.C., Shanahan decided without any doubt that she was going into the foreign service. "I was going to be the first woman ambassador." But what you start out to be, you often don't become. "I will never underestimate the role of luck and happenstance in life. I never do. . . . I was not thinking of journalism as a career. The girl who became my instant best friend the first week of college had been editor of her high school paper and wanted to go around to apply for the college paper. But she was diffident about going by herself and asked me to go with her. So I did. And here I am."

In the summer of her sophomore year at George Washington University, Shanahan got a job as a copy boy—that was the title for boy or girl, man or woman—at *The Washington Post*. The young men who had held the job before were being drafted. "They yelled, 'Boy!' and I jumped. I've always said that if I ever wrote an autobiography, I'd call one chapter 'When I Was a Boy.' "

Shanahan soon discovered the pull of the newsroom. How do you describe that pull to someone who has only seen the decorator version in the movies? In the days when newsrooms were newsrooms and not insurance offices, reporters slouched in rows, one draped over a typewriter seeking inspiration, another hunched over a telephone. Someone always had a desk that looked like your kid brother's room, but he could put his hands instantly on the notes from last week's interview under coffee cups and month-old newspapers. A drunk would lurch back from lunch. Teletypes chattered in the background.

Quick, quirky people shared their perfect quotes; they were waiting for the adrenalin rush that would come when the fire alarm bell rang or when an editor assigned a story that was "going out front" on page one. A rewrite man barked into his telephone headset and pounded his typewriter, his fists moving so fast they looked like hams. The noise intensified as deadline approached. An editor would rip the copy out of your typewriter, paragraph by paragraph, if you were on a big story. And you never knew when you walked in what the day—or night—might bring. Something new was always just about to occur. When it did, the room crackled.

"I think I had been there less than a week when I wrote my father that I had changed ambitions," Shanahan recalls. "He was good about it. It took him just a little while to adjust and adopt my dream as his dream. And he did. I regret that he didn't live to see me on *The New York Times*."

The swirl of working at *The Washington Post*—even if the job did involve cleaning paste pots and making grub runs—tempted Shanahan to quit school before her senior year. But a far-sighted *Post* editor said he would never promote her to reporter if she didn't finish school, and so she stayed on until she graduated. She got a job as a dictation girl at the United Press. Like every ambitious copy kid and dictationist who ever lived, she haunted the veteran journalists with requests for something to do. She rewrote press releases and watched and listened. Soon she was promoted over two people into an opening on the radio desk "basically rewriting the local news out of the papers without even checking it." It was February 1945, just before her 21st birthday.

"I worked there until 1947 doing that and shaking free to try to do a few bigger features one day a week or one day every other week until I left for my first baby in 1947—with at that time no sense that I would ever come back to work until the kids were all in high school. That's how I was raised. . . .

"But after 18 months at home, I really went through a deterioration that it took most women 10 years to go through. I think medically and clinically you might even call it depression today. I never neglected Mary Beth, but I didn't do anything else. I took care of her. I would go for days without washing any dishes. I couldn't do anything. . . .

"It wasn't post partum. I was a happy young mother at home with my baby for a time. And then quick-zap. It was actually my husband who finally said, 'Go get a job.' Wise man. How did he get so smart at 23 or 24? I don't know. He said, 'You don't hate that kid yet, but you will. You've got to get out of here. You've got to get back to work.'

"Well, it was pariah city out there." A mother leaving her baby at home when she had a husband and he had a job? She heard the same lines that women heard into the 1960s. The man at CBS radio said, "What on earth makes you think I'd hire a woman?" At ABC someone told her he already had one woman on the staff and that was all he could afford to have because it was a small staff and had to be flexible. "You couldn't ask a woman to work nights," Shanahan recalled that he said. "He was deaf to my argument that I'd been working 3 P.M. to midnight for UP for two years."

Shanahan worked her way down the floors of the thirteen-story National Press Building, where almost the whole news business was concentrated. Twelve, eleven, ten, nine. On the eighth floor she walked into the office of Walter L. Cronkite, Jr., who had covered the war for the United Press and was then a Washington correspondent for a string of midwestern radio stations.

"I walked through that door as it turned out the very day that he had decided he couldn't do it by himself. He was going to have to hire, he thought, an absolutely raw rookie with no experience, full-time. I walked in there with three years' experience. We talked, and I went home, and as I reached the apartment, the phone was already ringing, and it was Cronkite offering me the job. He had checked around . . . He hired me as part-time. I went to work for him on my 25th birthday, less than two full years before he went off to CBS and history."

Cronkite proved a generous teacher. "I look back on certain periods of my life as enormous growth periods, and that period of less than two full years was one of them. I was 25, he was 32, and there was that seven years and what he had done with it. He knew so much that I didn't know. It was partly that he was a willing, overt teacher and partly that I just watched him. . . . He let me do whatever I was capable of doing, and further he tried to get me on the air. One station in Cedar Rapids, Iowa, had a wonderful news editor, one of the best editors I ever worked for. There came time for the Republican fund-raising dinner in Washington, and Cronkite said, 'Let's see if they'll let you do it.' And WMT let me go on the air with an account of this dinner because it was obviously sort of semisocial and semipolitical."

Shanahan planned her second pregnancy so it would occur during a congressional recess—recesses were more predictable in those days—but she hadn't planned on Cronkite moving on. She tried to hold his string of stations together herself but couldn't do it. So it was back to job-hunting.

Soon it was wartime again. Shanahan did her first stint of economic reporting for the Research Institute of America, a newsletter publisher. "People don't remember what a big war in terms of the economy the Korean War was. In terms of its drain on the economy, it was much larger than the Vietnam War, which was much longer with many more casualties ultimately. . . . We had full-scale price and wage controls during the Korean War . . . and some industrial materials rationing. Steel, iron, copper, zinc, molybdenum—which I can still both spell and pronounce—and many other products were under industrial rationing.

"Covering price control is a great way to come to understand the anatomy and physiology of the economy and how different industries work." When the war was over, Shanahan stayed on and broadened her coverage to include legislation and Supreme Court decisions of interest to business. "That was the first time I really covered all three branches of government."

Restless, Shanahan wanted to work for a more prestigious newsletter. She got an appointment with Willard Kiplinger, even though her friends told her it was hopeless. " 'You wanted to see me,' he says, by way of opening the interview—and then says not another word. I talk of my qualifications and interests. He says nothing. I talk some more. He says nothing. I talk some more. Still nothing. Finally, desperately, I ask, 'Do you have some questions that I'm not answering?'

"He replied that he had wanted to see what kind of woman would apply for a job doing the kind of reporting *The Kiplinger*

Letter required—inside information. 'A respectable woman, the only kind of woman we would want here, just couldn't do it,' he said. I didn't ask him what kind of favors his male reporters gave in return for the inside information *they* got."

Shanahan bears a passing resemblance to the ebullient—but never flighty—side of TV character Edith Bunker. An emphatic talker, Shanahan tell her Kiplinger story and others like it with lingering outrage and incredulous amusement that such incidents ever occurred. One thing about Shanahan, you always know where she stands. Friends have been known to tell her of outrages or indignities just to hear her reaction. "You're just telling me that to get my blood pressure up!" she'll yell into the phone. It works every time.

While she was job-hunting, Shanahan went to *The Washington Post*, "where Al Friendly, newly anointed assistant managing editor, had covered the economic policy beat. He assured me that he did, indeed, know my work and thought it good but added that he couldn't possibly hire me because 'an economic story under a woman's byline just wouldn't have any credibility.' "

Shanahan went to work for the *Journal of Commerce* in 1956. The bureau chief of *The Wall Street Journal* used to greet her at work-related cocktail parties with a booming "I'd hire you in a minute if you were a man," although she'd never gone to him seeking a job. She left the *Journal of Commerce* in 1961 to work for the Department of the Treasury public affairs office.

"1962. *The New York Times* hires me. Hooray? Yes, indeed. But even in that success there was a reminder of the ever-present doubts of men about the capabilities of women. When I went to New York for my final interviews (Scotty Reston, in Washington, having finally decided that I was the one he wanted, since so many of his bureau staff said I was 'the best'), Clifton Daniel, then managing editor, inquired what my ultimate ambition was. Though even then I had some thoughts about wanting to be an editor, I gushed, 'Oh, all I ever want is to be a reporter on the best paper in the world, *The New York Times*.' Daniel replied, 'That's good, because I can assure you, no woman will ever be an editor at *The New York Times*.' "

Shanahan covered economics right away at the *Times*, although it was clear she did not have the top job. She was able to

grab tax policy; she covered the Securities and Exchange Commission and the Federal Trade Commission and she filled in on
other top economic stories for Ed Dale, who did have the top job.
"I had taken the job with that understanding so I didn't have any
legitimate beef in the sense of having been misled, although I got
a little more annoyed with it as the years went by." Nonetheless,
she takes great pleasure "each time I see a woman's byline on a
story about the economy or the budget or tax legislation. Those
frightened men who run so many of our newspapers, magazines,
and TV news operations probably don't do it consciously, but
perhaps some of them have buried somewhere deep in their sub-
conscious a sense that women can, in fact, cover such beats successfully because Eileen Shanahan did it. I like to think so."

When Shanahan started at *The New York Times*, there was only
one other woman, Marjorie Hunter, in the Washington bureau.
Hunter had replaced Bess Furman as the woman covering the
White House ladies. She also covered education when she could.

Hunter's preference to cover an education bill indirectly
launched Shanahan into the coverage she did in her spare time
of the women's movement. A lawyer in New York called Shanahan
and said, "Did you know that a constitutional amendment is coming up on the floor of the House of Representatives next Tuesday
and *The New York Times* has carried only one five-paragraph wire-
service story?"

"And I said to her, 'Oh, surely you must be mistaken.'

"She said, 'No, look it up. Somebody ought to cover it.'

"Okay. I went and looked it up. She was exactly right. The
Equal Rights Amendment is what I'm talking about. I then go to
the news editor, not expecting to cover it myself. It wasn't my
beat. I covered national economic policy and budget and taxes
and all that. And I said to the news editor, 'Did you know that a
constitutional amendment is coming up on the floor of the House
next Tuesday and we've carried one five-paragraph UPI story?'

"And he said, as I had, 'Well, you must be wrong.'

" 'No, I'm not.'

"Anyway, I just told him so he could put it on the schedule.
Marjorie Hunter was assigned to do it. She covered the House.
And the night before it was to come up, Maggie just happened
to stop by my desk to chat." In the chat Hunter said she would

prefer to continue covering an education bill in which she was interested. Shanahan said she'd like to cover the ERA debate and suggested that they talk to the news editor.

"Sure. She'd love that. He was astonished that I wanted to cover it, and I remember distinctly his saying to me, 'Oh, well, you don't cover women.' He didn't say, 'You cover important things like the federal budget,' but obviously that's what he meant. And I said, 'Well, I'm interested in this, and I'd like to cover it, and Maggie doesn't want to cover it.' And I didn't have anything on my beat I had to do that day. Well, no editor is sorry when anybody volunteers for work, and so I was allowed to do it, though I was considered very strange for wanting to."

The amendment didn't pass Congress until the next year. "It's always hard to remember what you thought at a time past, but I must have known even then that this was a matter of some importance. And so I covered it. I didn't have any concept of how important and how broad [it would be], nor did I know what was going to flow from it."

One story does flow from another. Shanahan did a comprehensive piece on cases being brought at the Equal Employment Opportunities Commission under legislation outlawing discrimination that had passed in the 1960s. At the same time, there were two vacancies on the Supreme Court. Sentiment developed to appoint a woman, so Shanahan did a piece on women in the legal profession and in law schools. "There were some law firms where I could get hold of managing partners or people who were hiring associates who were discovering that women lawyers really could work all night in a hotel room when they were trying to put a merger together and 'guess what, we talked with the wives and they said they didn't mind, they knew it was work.' "

By 1971 or 1972, "I knew this was something large. The founding meeting of the National Women's Political Caucus was right in that same time. I really can't reconstruct how I knew that the Equal Rights Amendment was more than just a story, but I knew it the minute that woman called me. . . . I obviously knew that it wasn't just a story, that it was a movement."

Shanahan's credibility as an economics reporter enabled her to tell an editor that a women's movement story was a news story. "I'm not sure I was ever assigned to any of these stories. I began

59

simply to keep track. I knew when the NOW conventions or the founding meeting of the Coalition of Labor Union Women were and asked to cover them ... Happily, they almost all ran from Friday evening through 2 or 3 P.M. Sunday because the women then and I fear now didn't have the kind of jobs where they could just take off the way men did. They had to have them on the weekends and they ended promptly at 2 or 3 P.M. Sunday so everybody could get on their airplanes and get home and wash their hair and get ready to go to work Monday morning. So a lot of it was no conflict. I covered my 'important' beat, my economics beat, through the week and then toddled off to women's meetings on the weekend. . . .

"I knew enough not to try to cover anything borderline," Shanahan says. "As a beat reporter who had been a beat reporter much of my life, they were used to hearing suggestions from me. They were used to my saying, 'Listen, I want to drop the tax bill today and cover the Joint Economic Committee and here's why,' and I would say that over the years at the *Times*, probably 95 to 98 percent of all those suggestions were accepted. I was somebody who knew my beat, and it was accepted that I understood this beat, too."

Shanahan not only had a track record but was also still covering economics, an area considered increasingly vital in 1970s Washington bureaus. "There was a time when I quite seriously considered going to the powers that be at the *Times* and saying, 'Look, this women's movement has gotten to be such a vast and diffuse story, it really is becoming a full-time job. It would make sense to headquarter it in Washington, where I live and want to live, and give it to me. Make it sort of a national women's movement beat, headquartered in Washington but involving traveling around the country.'

"I never made that proposal, and I never made it out of sheer fear. I reckoned—I think correctly, though occasionally I berate myself for cowardice on the point—I reckoned that as long as I could cover a tax bill, I would be listened to when I said a women's story was worth page one. If I stopped doing that and went to doing women full-time, within six months I'd be 'crazy Shanahan who's always screaming and shouting and wanting to cover some silly-assed women's story.' I strongly suspect I was right.

"I was in the process of proving every day that I was sane. Sane and competent. A real professional. I was covering tax legislation. I was covering the budget. I was covering the Federal Reserve. I was covering all that stuff that the male power structure respects.

"I think you have to prove it in an ongoing way. Don't put that in the past tense. I think you simply have to submit ongoing evidence that you are rational and professional. Never mind if you've got a twenty-, thirty-, or forty-year history. Are you sane today, or have you gone into a feminist tizzy? I really think that evidence has to be there. I don't see any signs that the need for that has abated."

Shanahan and other women have learned from experience that they often are called before a different judge than men for assessment of their professional demeanor as well as their talents. No discussion of women at work, especially women in as pushy a field as journalism, can ignore this pressure on women to fit precut patterns. Men sometimes don't fit them either, but allowances are made for them more often. They are viewed as individuals, not as types.

A former government lawyer who discussed Shanahan with me hissed that she was shrill, that she pushed too hard for a story. Some journalists feel she overreacted to sharp (or dumb) questions when she dealt with the press for Joseph Califano when he was Secretary of Health, Education, and Welfare. Such behavior by a man in a similar post would have drawn little or no comment. If men are applauded for doing aggressive reporting and maintaining high standards for preparation and accuracy, shouldn't women be, too?

It is commonplace to say that women face a double standard, commonplace because it remains true. As Karen Elliott House, foreign editor for *The Wall Street Journal*, says, "If men take their children to the office, they are seen as warm and caring; if women do, they're guilty of mismanagement. If men have a fit, they are seen as brilliant but difficult. If a woman does, she's too emotional." If a woman in the newsroom or the editorial page conference reacts to an absurdly sexist statement, she's viewed as having no sense of humor. She mustn't lose her temper, even when losing it is perfectly justified. Her views still need reinforcement by male colleagues to be taken seriously.

In any discussion on journalistic style or substance, I want Shanahan on my side. And Molly Ivins, who has also had questions thrown at her about her style. Ivins is big and she's brash, like

Texas, and if the state fits, wear it. Which she does; she returned to a political column on the *Dallas Times-Herald* after six years caught in the Cuisinart that is *The New York Times.*

As a writer, Molly Ivins can turn mush into a metaphor. *The New York Times* seemed to want it the other way around. Once the desk changed Ivins's description of a man with "a beer gut that belongs in the Smithsonian" to a man with "a protuberant abdomen" and edited "squawks like a $2 fiddle" into "like an inexpensive musical instrument." "Write that down: writers remember this stuff," she commanded me. "They put everything in this purée machine, and it comes out with no flavor."

Anyway, you get the picture. Molly Ivins enlivens. This is all by way of background for her tale about a job evaluation conducted during her six-year career at *The New York Times.* As Ivins recalled it, "An editor, for whom I had a good regard, told me they liked my writing and reporting. I should have said thank you and walked out. I didn't. I waited for the 'and.' And, he said, you laugh too loud. That is true. And, he said, you don't dress too well. That was true. He was forgetting that when I had worked at *The Texas Observer* before going to the *Times*, I was living below poverty. My wearing blue work shirts was considered a political statement, but it was all I had. Then he said I was known to walk around the office in bare feet. True. I take my shoes off wherever I work. But none of that is the goddamned business of *The New York Times.* I cannot imagine the personal style of a man getting that much attention."

Ivins put her finger on a problem that still bars advancement for many women in the newspaper business. Too many editors, blocked by notions about how women ought to behave but sometimes don't, cannot see what they have before them. These women on their staffs are bringing perspectives and specific stories that they might not otherwise have carried, that reach readers they might not otherwise have reached.

The stereotypes are breaking down, but not before they retarded the careers of the women who entered the newspaper business during World War II and proved themselves then, when their talents were needed. But those women persevered, so that when women moved into the profession in greater numbers in the late 1960s and 1970s, there were a few female mentors. In a fairer world, they would have been mentors who were also editors of newspapers.

Everyday Indignities

Women in Communication, an organization of women in news, public relations, and academic journalism, selected Eileen Shanahan to honor as one of its women of the year at a dinner in New York in 1975. Shanahan was told that she could invite her newspaper executives, just as the other honorees were doing.

Invitations went out to the top brass at *The New York Times*. Shanahan confesses to a rare instance of naïveté: she didn't check who had accepted. Came the night of the dinner, and Shanahan, her husband, her sister, and her brother-in-law were seated at their table. Other tables filled with guests of the honorees. Still only Shanahan, her husband, her sister, and her brother-in-law sat at their table.

The next day Shanahan arrived at the Washington bureau and ran into managing editor Seymour Topping. What, she asked, was he doing in Washington? Oh, he'd come down from New York to attend a dinner honoring George Tames, the *Times* photographer. He said he'd never heard about Shanahan's honor, apologized profusely, and vowed it would never happen again. But once was enough.

It was 1975.

CHAPTER

5

Bridging the Gap

Blurry memories from Fifties front pages: men, balding or gray-haired, gray-suited, untanned, undifferentiated, all white, all gray. Dwight Eisenhower, John Foster Dulles, Ezra Taft Benson, Charles Wilson, Sherman Adams. The Eisenhower era was, in the words of UPI's Helen Thomas, "eight years of feeling older than we should have."[1]

It was more than just feeling older, and it lasted longer than the eight years Dwight D. Eisenhower was President. From the end of World War II into the 1960s, the United States went through a cycle of conservatism that was both personal and political. Undercurrents of the protests that would erupt in the 1960s rippled beneath the surface, sometimes breaking through when blacks boycotted buses in Montgomery, academics resisted taking loyalty oaths, or women picketed for peace. But vast numbers of Americans, their families delayed or decimated by World War II, moved into the suburbs (or wanted to) and watched Sid Caesar and Imogene Coca on their new television sets. The wounds of upheaval inflicted by Depression and war needed time to heal.

It was a comfortable mold, and many women settled into it easily. It was what they wanted to do; it was what their men had fought for and what they had sacrificed for on the homefront; and it was what society was telling them to do. But what of those who didn't fit the pattern or, by force of circumstance, couldn't? What of the woman who wanted to be a writer but who, like *Los Angeles Times* associate editor Jean Sharley Taylor, knew she didn't want to wear a cameo and toil away in the attic?

Through the late 1940s, 1950s, and into the early 1960s, the same kind of women who had been welcomed at the city desk in wartime couldn't get past the front desk. Some of the men who blocked their way merely mirrored the views of the day. Woman's place was in the home; the newsroom was no place for a lady. Decent fellows when pressed, they sometimes changed their views, or they made an exception for what they considered the exceptional woman. Others held deeply rooted prejudices against anyone who was not like them—blacks, Jews, Puerto Ricans, Mexicans, Chinese, women, you name it.

Newspapers rarely hired women. When they did, it was to work on the women's section. The decade and a half immediately after the war was critical for today's generation because the men who were hired then now edit American newspapers. It is no accident that there are so few women in their ranks. It is no accident that many of them have had difficulty working with women as equals; they had so little practice for so long.

Women's absence from the city room was a double whammy: not only did few women get newspaper jobs in the 1950s, but when women did break through in the mid-1960s, they had few guiding lights ahead of them. I was among the first batch of women to supervise the national broadcast desk at UPI in Chicago; no older women worked in my section and few in the entire bureau. In 1967, I was only the second woman in *The Baltimore Evening Sun* newsroom since World War II; the few other women on the paper were on the women's pages, on the copy desk, or in the suburbs. No older women (and only one other woman) were working at the Newhouse bureau when I arrived there in 1972, and only one other woman had ever been on the editorial page at the *Los Angeles Times* before 1978. My situation was hardly unique. Finding someone to confide in about successes and slights, real or imagined, someone who understood because she had been there, was tough.

So what? Men didn't need anybody to confide in. Maybe they really did, or should have. But men, white men, were not alone in the newsroom. Picture yourself as an outsider, the only one of your kind in whatever situation, expected to adapt to another culture, subtly questioned about your judgment, not given the jobs you know you can do but passed over solely because you are

65

different, even left out at lunchtime. If you're a man, imagine that every person in authority at your paper and virtually everyone you interview is a woman or, if you're white, that all these jobs are filled by blacks, and you'll have some sense of the isolation.

Who did break the mold? No commonality can be seen in the careers of these women except quiet determination. Some of the women who succeeded during this era had been in the newsroom before and during the war. Building on the base of reporting experience she got during the 1930s and World War II, Agness Underwood ultimately became a city editor of legend at the old *Los Angeles Herald-Express*. Others held on to the toehold they had gained during the war. Laurie Johnston, who had worked in Oregon, Utah, and Hawaii, became a general assignment reporter for *The New York Times* in 1949.

Talented newcomers worked their way up in the newsroom: Nan Robertson and Betsy Wade at *The New York Times*; Mary McGrory, now at *The Washington Post*; and Jean Sharley Taylor. Charlotte Saikowski, Washington bureau chief and former Moscow correspondent for *The Christian Science Monitor*, went to work for the *Monitor* in 1962 after earning a degree at Columbia University's Russian Institute immediately after World War II, teaching English in Poland, and working on the *Current Digest of the Soviet Press* for ten years.

Precious few black women moved into white newspapers until the late 1960s or even the early 1970s. Riots and civil rights protests compelled newspapers to do then what they had not had the foresight or awareness to do before—hire blacks.

One who made an early breakthrough was Marvel Cooke, who joined *The Compass*, a successor to the experimental *P.M.* in New York, in the late 1940s after a career on *The Amsterdam News* and *The People's Voice*. "My mother sent me a little clipping from a paper, a black paper, that said I was the first black woman in the country to work as a journeyman for a white daily. I don't know whether that was true or not. There had been columnists, but to get a job as a journeyman on a white daily, I had my difficulties, I must say."

If a woman was good, she stood out because she was alone in a crowd. But she might also be kept doing dog stories— literally—as Mary McGrory was, or overlooked for plum assignments. She might be ignored at promotion time because there were only certain things women did—or because, well, women really didn't need the money. Their husbands could support them, or if they didn't have husbands, they didn't need much money.

Each woman played it her own way. "I was a reluctant feminist," Meg Greenfield of *The Washington Post* acknowledges. "It has been a slow dawning. When things happened like not being able to use the Press Club ticker while I was at *The Reporter*, I'd just say, 'That's dumb.' It didn't occur to me to do anything. I just kept going. I got accustomed to just working through it. I just lowered my head."

Outrage—good old bristling, teeth-grinding anger—could have consumed other women if they'd let it. "You submitted because you knew if you didn't, you wouldn't last," Jean Sharley Taylor says. "You submitted in order to prevail."

But the anger, the discrimination, assuredly changed some women's view of the world. It made them think and see the links. In the fall of 1953, Betsy Wade was fired from the *Herald-Tribune* when she told them she was pregnant. "That radicalizes you forever," she says. Wade started putting the pieces together in her mind; in the 1970s she put her name on the sex-discrimination suit against *The New York Times*.

Career patterns were as varied as the women who cut them. No one cut a more distinctive swath than Aggie Underwood. By the time she was named the first woman city editor of a major American newspaper in 1947, Underwood was a supremely confident journalist. It hadn't always been that way.

Arriving in Los Angeles from San Francisco as a homeless teenager, Agness Sullivan, whose mother had died when she was little and who had been raised in a series of foster homes, went to work as a waitress. She married Harry Underwood at 18 and quit her job when the first of their two children was born. At one point she wanted a new pair of hose; her husband, who was making only $22.50 a week, wouldn't let her have the money. Just then, a friend called to ask her if she could go to work as a relief telephone operator at *The Los Angeles Record*. She did. She stayed in newsrooms for the next forty-two years.[2]

Aggie—that's what everybody called her—had little confidence in those early days. "It was particularly bad when there

67

were more newspapers, because you had an editor sitting and reading those newspapers, checking every story, and wanting to know if you had gotten them all. If you missed one or two, they'd start chewing you out. The first three months, I went home every night and cried myself to sleep."[3]

From Aggie's typewriter in the 1930s and 1940s came stories that produced a long, lurid chain of headlines: "SLAYER SEES VISIONS OF NOOSE IN HER CELL," "2 BOYS DIE; MOTHER DEATH TRY FOILED," "GIRL IN DANCE MURDER PROBE TELLS OF DOWNWARD PATH," "GIRL HUNGRY GI TELLS OWN STORY OF TRAGEDY." The headline on a 1937 story about three children from Inglewood who had been strangled was "SENSATIONAL NEW CLUES IN HUNT FOR FIEND." Aggie's lead: "What little Jeanette Marjorie Stephens loved in life—a ruffled blue organdie dress—will be her shroud in death."

It was the era of a deadline almost every minute, a new edition almost every hour, a new lead on stories for every edition. Aggie was not above manipulating the news to get her story, to get her new lead. When Police Capt. Earle Kynette was on trial for allegedly planting a bomb that injured Detective Harry Raymond, Aggie knew that if she were to make her deadline, Raymond would have to testify by 10 A.M. The competing morning papers wanted him to testify in the afternoon so that they could banner his testimony. Aggie got one of the attorneys to drag out the cross-examination of a previous witness so it would be too late to call Raymond to the stand in the afternoon. She went to the hospital where Raymond was recuperating, found out what he would wear the next day, had her photographer take his picture in that outfit in his wheelchair, and had an engraving made so the picture was ready for the paper the next morning.[4]

For all her image as a tough reporter and editor, Aggie loved her children and was outraged once when her boss fouled up her carefully arranged plans to have dinner with them. She changed her plans so she could work, and then the city editor told her another reporter would work instead because he needed the over-time money. The story has come down in several different versions, but basically Aggie went back to the darkroom and was lamenting her fate when somebody—there was a little drinking going on—asked her what she was going to do. She grabbed a dead fish that had either been given her by a sea captain, in one account, or that a printer had given her, in another, but that in any event was being stored in the cool water in the darkroom. She marched into the city room and shouted at the editor. "Then I smacked him across the face with the fish. He ran around the desk and I chased him and kept hitting him with the fish.

"Out of the corner of my eye I saw Mr. Campbell [the pro-verbial hard-boiled managing editor]. Oh, oh, I said to myself, I'm going to be canned for this. But Mr. Campbell, laughing, yelled, 'Hit him again, Aggie. Hit him again!' "

It was the wacky *Front Page* era when Aggie Underwood presided over the city room. *Los Angeles Times* columnist Jack Smith worked for Underwood and remembered her newsroom being far different from today's quiet preserves in which security guards keep the parade of "anarchists, paranoids, evangelists, antivivi-sectionists, inventors, elephant boys, and self-promoting strippers from intruding on the ascetic lucubrations of reporters," sadly dispelling "the wonderful illusion that a city room is the circus with typewriters."[5] Aggie also would never have tolerated today's endless story conferences. "How the hell are you going to get anything in the paper by sitting around talking about it?" Aggie asked an interviewer.

Aggie kept a baseball bat on top of her desk to use against obstreperous press agents and a gun loaded with blanks inside her desk that she is alleged to have fired off at the ceiling if the place got too quiet.

None of Underwood's predecessors had lasted more than four years as city editor. When she took the job, bets were placed that she'd last three months, but she stayed seventeen and a half years, until 1964, when she was named assistant managing editor. She hated leaving the trenches, though, and retired three years later. "I had to be tough and hard, or those men would have taken advantage of me and I would never have gotten any work out of them," Underwood told an interviewer years after her retirement.

"I told [the reporters] never to lie to me. Give me a chance to protect myself. Like with Pat Folley. He called in one day with a story, and I said to him, 'Pat, you're drunk. Get the hell off the beat. Don't let people see you like this.' And he says to me, 'Madame, how dare you tell me I'm drunk?' And I told him, 'Because, you son of a bitch, you've phoned in the same story three times already.' "[6]

Covering police, one comes in contact with, shall we say, some less-than-desirable acquaintances, and Aggie was no exception. She became a friend of gangster Mickey Cohen and sometimes that helped; sometimes it hurt. Once when a bookie's collector was slain at the same table at which Cohen was sitting in a restaurant in the San Fernando Valley area, he called Aggie first. She had a reporter and photographer there twenty minutes before the police were notified.

When Johnny Stompanato, Lana Turner's boyfriend, was stabbed by Turner's daughter, it was a front-page story all over the country but especially in Los Angeles. Aggie called Cohen and asked him if he knew whether Stompanato had ever written any letters to Turner. She had the letters within an hour. A bit later he called back and said, "Hey, Aggie, could I have just one or two of those letters back? The *Examiner* is giving me hell."[7]

In her last years, Underwood was involved in a complicated lawsuit because of her friendship with Cohen. Ovid Demaris repeated in his book *The Last Mafioso* the charge that Underwood ran a hoax story about the sinking of an Israeli arms shipment as a cover-up to allow Cohen to pocket $1 million in donations that he had raised to buy the arms. Underwood said that no such article was ever published and sued. The suit was still pending when she died in 1984; it had been dismissed by lower courts and her lawyer was pursuing appeals.

As a reporter, Aggie Underwood succeeded because she got people to talk to her. A young bride confessed to Aggie that she fed her husband ant poison "because I wanted to prove I loved him by nursing him back to health."[8] Aggie attributed her empathy for life's losers to her miserable childhood. "I had been in almost every circumstance the person I interviewed had been in. Maybe it was because I could sympathize with them."[9]

She knew her city. In an era when events, not trends, were news, Aggie had a knack for maneuvering her reporters and photographers so that they got to the news while it was still happening. She was at her desk at 3:45 in the morning and she stayed for twelve or fourteen hours, never leaving even for meals. Without looking, she knew where a street would be in the fat map book others needed to consult. She knew what bar a reporter was calling in from—even knew the bartender's name.

It reflects the unquestioned sexism of her times that when

she was named the first woman city editor of a major American daily, *Newsweek*'s description of her said that she wore baggy black dresses, that her hair looked as if it was vacuum cleaned, that she had a voice like a foghorn and legs like Marlene Dietrich. Not a word about talent.

Tongue firmly in cheek, one of her former reporters said she always looked ladylike, "even when she was trimming her nails with the huge black copy shears that were chained to her desk. And no vacuum cleaner could make her hair look like that, it was just electric energy generated from within." Her voice, he said, was "more like a ripsaw going through a two-inch board."[10]

Like Underwood, Margaret Dempsey stayed on the newspaper scene after World War II because she got stories that other people didn't. She had showed her ingenuity in getting her job in the first place. Growing up, Dempsey had always wanted to be a reporter, and after graduating from the College of Notre Dame in Baltimore, she presented herself for an interview in 1942 at the office of Sunpapers' executive editor Neil Swanson, "an editor right out of the movies." Swanson wouldn't see her.

"But in calling and calling, I made such good friends with his secretary that finally once when I called she said, 'This looks like a good day. Just come down and sit.' I did. Finally, he opened the door and I walked in. He was most forbidding-looking. He asked what I wanted. I told him I wanted a job." She got it. Dempsey was not deterred when the *Evening Sun* city editor cursed about having "another one of these goddamned women."

Exhibit A in the list of stories Dempsey got by using her wits: Dorothy Henn, an English war bride, had returned with her husband Charles to the Baltimore area and was about to have quadruplets in December 1946. Everybody knew; everybody was eager to get the story. Those were the days before fertility drugs made multiple births far less extraordinary than they were then. "We got word that she'd gone to the hospital, and I knew everybody would try to see her husband at the hospital and that wasn't possible. No way the hospital would let us go near him," Dempsey recalls.

Dempsey hailed a cab and drove to the house in Catonsville, telling the cab driver not to leave, no matter what. "I hadn't paid him for the long ride out, and there was no way to leave without him, which he knew. He just kept the meter running." Henn's mother "was an old lady and all by herself. She said she didn't know if she should let me in. I said, 'Look, you're going to be besieged. Let me sit with you and help you.' So I came in and locked the door and pulled down the shades. I'd answer the phone when other papers and the wires called and say nobody was there but me. I waited and waited. Around midnight [Henn] came in. I was there when he told his mother it was quadruplets," three boys and a girl.

It was 2 A.M., and her taxi was still waiting. She sped back to the office, paid the cabbie about $200—she'd drawn a cash advance before she left—and stayed up all night doing the story. "Then I went home and slept three hours and went back. I wasn't going to let anyone else in on my story."

Exhibit B: "A mother had left her baby in a carriage outside her home. When she came back, the baby was gone. We got the word, and I dashed over. I was followed in another cab by my competition, Eleanor Healy of the *News-Post*. But I had the house number firmly in mind. It was a row house, and remember, they all look alike. I could see Eleanor wasn't clear on the number, so I dashed up to the door and almost had to push my way in. The family was in near hysterics."

This was a time where being a woman was an advantage. "We look less forbidding," Dempsey says. "A guy reporter showing up at a time when people are in great distress can look pretty scary. We look sympathetic." Dempsey sat in the kitchen with the family drinking coffee, and finally a cop came to the door and said, 'Do you want to see your baby?' They had found the child. I looked out the door and Eleanor had left, perhaps to pursue another angle. I would never have left. I would have just sat outside until someone came out."

Dempsey married fellow reporter Jim McManus, who, as Jim McKay, became a premier televison sportscaster. She left the *Evening Sun,* and they moved to New York for his television job. Looking back on her newspaper career, she says that she and the other women who succeeded may have done so because they approached stories differently from the way the male reporters did. "Although I covered the same things, I covered them from a different angle, the human angle. So perhaps the men didn't feel I was competing with them. . . . On a brilliant staff that included William Manchester and others, women held their own. They were not considered garbage to be gotten rid of. They carved out a niche and held on to it."

Theo Wilson's niche was trials. Wilson dates the events in her life by what trial she was covering; she retired from the New York *Daily News* before the John DeLorean conspiracy trial and after the Claus von Bülow murder trial. Her career in the courtroom began at *The Richmond News Leader*, where she got a first-hand legal education while dictating her stories from a judge's chamber. If she used a legal term incorrectly, the judge would set her straight while she was still dictating.

Not long after Wilson got to New York, the Sam Sheppard murder case "broke in all its glory." Sheppard, a Cleveland doctor, was charged with killing his wife. Wilson had never been out of town on an assignment for the *Daily News*, and she ended up in Cleveland with Dorothy Kilgallen, H. D. "Doc" Quigg, and Bob Considine, reporters who were celebrities in their own right. "I had no idea that what I was sending them was selling papers." It was. Wilson, it turned out, had an ear for the question-and-answer that makes courtroom reporting dramatic. The paper gave over four or five total pages for trials, and for readers, "it was like following a soap opera."

Dr. Sam Sheppard. Then another Sheppard trial. Then Bernie Finch. Carol Tregoff. Candy Mossler. Carl Coppolino. Trial buffs from the 1950s and 1960s will recognize the names. Then Jack Ruby. Sirhan Sirhan. Charles Manson. Patty Hearst. Jean Harris.

"I don't know any trial I have covered without women. You go out of town and you don't know the women, but where they come from, they're famous. There are of course some wonderful men who can do it. I was asked once if I was a sob sister. I said, 'No, *he's* sitting over there.' I don't want to stereotype people, but I think women have an eye for detail . . . a more intuitive sense. A woman hears some things better than men do because she listens. She's had to because of the way she was raised.

"Women have more patience. Some men cannot sit that long without moving. Some women can't either, of course. I always tell young people, 'Don't leave a trial during the courtroom action ever.' The guys who went out for a smoke during the Manson trial missed the moment that made page one, when Manson raised a pencil like a dagger at the judge and yelled, 'You deserve to die.' They hustled him out and we ran for the phones and the guys were yelling, 'What happened?' "

Women had an ear for trials and an eye for the good feature. Ellen Goodman, who worked for two years in Detroit before returning to her native Boston, recalls that her *Free Press* colleague Jean Sharley Taylor could make even the annual zoo story zingy. But Taylor kept her personal ideas about the role of women in check, unlike Dorothy Jurney, her editor at the *Free Press*. "Jurney didn't apologize for being a woman. She would be a good editor on any paper today. She had self-esteem as a woman. I was inclined to think you'd better keep your interest in these things under wraps. I never rebelled about writing women's page stories," Taylor says.

Not that Taylor didn't seethe at times over her treatment. In the mid-1960s she was sent to do front-page color for a series of crucial games between the Detroit Tigers and the New York Yankees. "I couldn't use the press box at Yankee Stadium. So I turned over a garbage can, put my Olivetti on it, and phoned in the story from a pay phone while my colleagues sat in the press box lowering cups of coffee."

Nan Robertson of *The New York Times* needed a long time to become confident in her intellectual powers. "I would demean myself," says Robertson, a small woman with a pixie's cap of white hair. "I can understand almost everything except for nuclear physics. I am smart. But I called myself Pinhead. I was being made a feminist. I was always loved by men, patted on the head. I guess you could say I was affectionately patronized. Like many women of my generation, I was not taken seriously."

Some of Robertson's best work, melding personal and professional interests, has centered on creative people. She credits her grandfather with instilling in her a love for the life of the mind. "I've always liked classical music, opera, drama, literature. I like best of all to talk to creative figures because I think what they do is the only thing that lasts. Sports figures don't last. Economists don't last. But the fact that Mozart put some black notes on a page that still stirs feelings among the people that play them, the audiences that hear them—that's something."

Growing up in Chicago, Robertson decided at 11 that she wanted to be a journalist and so went to Northwestern, one of the country's best journalism schools. She sailed for Europe a few weeks after graduation in 1948 and went to work for *Stars and Stripes* in a little village thirty kilometers from Frankfurt.

Over the next seven years, Robertson worked for the Paris edition of *The New York Herald-Tribune* and was a stringer for *The Milwaukee Journal* and *The Gary* [Indiana] *Post-Tribune*. As a stringer, she did features more than straight news and found it a critical time to be in Europe for the first years of the Marshall Plan, the Berlin blockade, and the beginning of the Cold War. It was "a Europe that was reeling from the war, devastated, rationed—a Europe in want."

Back in New York at 28, Robertson landed on *The New York Times* as a fashion writer. "The only reason for that was that I had once done public relations for Christian Dior."

The *Times* "automatically put me on the woman's pages as if those seven years in Europe hadn't mattered at all." As Gloria Emerson did before she became a *Times* correspondent in Vietnam, Robertson slogged away at shoe styles and hemlines for four and a half years. She also wrote about how unions established the prices for each element of a dress—the buttonholes, the sleeves; she wrote about fashion piracy; she wrote about male models; and she wrote about the atmosphere in the garment district.

One day, her boss, Elizabeth Penrose Howkins, told Robertson that Frank Adams, the city editor, kept asking that Robertson be loaned to him to do some stories. Howkins had turned him down. "I said, 'Mrs. Howkins, the city room is where young reporters aspire to be, where they go to learn the tools of the craft. The next time he asks, say yes." One month later, Adams asked again, and Howkins said yes. Robertson joined a small group of female reporters—"we even sat together"—that included star reporter Edith Evans Asbury. Robertson covered crime, courts, and fires before settling into feature writing.

Which she resisted initially. "But ultimately I realized that I was by instinct a feature writer. I was 'Queen of the Second Front,' the page where features played at the time. For a while I minded, but that's where the writing shows. That's where you reveal your-self. Feature writing is the only semiliterary form in the news-paper." In 1963 she transferred to the Washington bureau for a ten-year stint as a general assignment and feature writer.

"Apparently there's something about me that makes people talk. If there's a sensitive subject—somebody's child has just been killed—or somebody's difficult to get at, they say, 'Send Nan— she'll get through to them.' "

It worked. "I got one of the first stories from Jackie Kennedy after her husband was nominated for President by the Democratic Party. She said bitchy things about Pat Nixon and that just wasn't done. She said, 'You know that stuff about Pat wearing her old Republican cloth coat. Well, she buys her things at Elizabeth Arden and nothing there costs less than $250.' Remember, this was 1960. I asked her if it was true that she and her mother-in-law Rose Kennedy spent $30,000 on Paris fashions. She said they couldn't spend that much on Paris clothes unless they wore sable underwear."

Robertson spent three years in Paris for the *Times*, then returned to New York to translate her interest in creative people into news stories. She got a rare interview with E. B. White in which he talked about his wife Katherine, who had been an editor with him on *The New Yorker*. On that one, Robertson imagined White the stylist looking over her shoulder as she wrote.

The bare bones of her resumé make Robertson's success sound almost easy. But it wasn't, not for a moment. In November 1981, while visiting her sister and brother-in-law in Rockford, Illinois, she abruptly became violently ill. In a stroke of fortune, Robertson was taken to a hospital whose consultant on infectious diseases knew about toxic shock syndrome and accurately diagnosed her case. "Most doctors have never seen or have failed to recognize a single case of this rare malady," Robertson wrote later. "Yet the St. Anthony doctors had treated two before me."[11]

Robertson's fingertips had to be amputated because of gangrene caused by circulatory damage. Told what was going to happen, she was "filled with horror. I was certain I would never be able to write again. I was still on the respirator and speechless." Abe Rosenthal, the *Times*'s executive editor, telephoned a friend who was at the hospital with her and said "something that carried me through many of the hardest days," Robertson recalled. " 'For Chrissake, tell Nan we don't love her for her typewriter, tell her we love her for her mind.' "

Returning home after ten and a half weeks in the hospital, Robertson found that "I could not turn a single knob on any door, or any faucet, or the stereo or the television set. I could not wash myself, dress or undress myself, pull a zipper, button a button, tie shoelaces. Punching the telephone numbers with one thumb, I called Nancy Sureck, perhaps the most maternal of all my friends, awakening her and her husband, David. 'Help,' I said. Nancy was at my side within the hour, taking charge."

It was months before she could open a taxi door on her way to and from her rehabilitation appointments. "The cab drivers of New York, with one exception, invariably sprang to my rescue with a gallantry that amazed, amused, and touched me. I had decided to try a frontal, self-confident approach to all strangers in this tough city. I would hail a cab, hold up my hands, and say with a smile, 'I have a bum hand—could you open the door for me?' Without an instant's hesitation, the drivers would leap around to the back door and open it with a flourish. As we approached our destination, I would hand them my wallet, tote bag, or purse, and they would hold up each bill and coin like a rosary or miraculous medal or baby to be blessed. 'This is a dollar bill,' they would say, 'this is a quarter,' and then return the rest of the money to its place. One driver said, 'Even my wife won't trust me with her wallet,' and another muttered, 'Anyone takes advantage of you should be shot.' "

She came back to tell her compelling story in a cover article in *The New York Times Magazine* of September 19, 1982. In anguished detail, she described not only her own illness but the story of the disease itself and the efforts to track down its cause and its cure. She concluded, "My story is almost over except for one crucial detail: My deepest fear did not materialize. I have typed the thousands of words of this article, slowly and with difficulty, once again able to practice my craft as a reporter. I have written it—at last—with my own hands."

The next spring she was awarded a Pulitzer Prize.

Back at the paper and elated with the world the day the prize was announced, Robertson ran into one of her senior editors, a man of considerable polish and charm whom she was kind enough not to name in this story. They embraced, and then he held her at arm's length and said, "What's a little bitty thing like you doing winning the Pulitzer Prize?"

"I pulled myself up to my full height and said I had more moxie than any man in the room. I told that story to a group in New Jersey later. The women gasped; the men didn't understand."

Nan Robertson describes herself as someone who for many years did not get angry at the way she was treated. Many of the men in the newsroom—big-name men—went out of their way to help her. But Robertson realized by the 1970s that in many ways she could have gone farther faster if she had not been a woman.

"In my generation of women, we really didn't think about this. I didn't. It would have made me so goddamned angry. It probably would have soured the joy I felt as a reporter. I didn't allow myself to feel that anger until I became active in the *Times*'s women's caucus in the 1970s. It was retroactive rage when I realized that, yes, I had been respected and loved, but patronized as well."

Today Nan Robertson's picture hangs in the eleventh-floor hallway of the *Times*, which is filled with pictures of its Pulitzer winners. Anne O'Hare McCormick is there for foreign commentary in 1937. Ada Louise Huxtable won for architecture criticism in 1970. "I used to go look at those pictures and in the 1950s I'd say to myself, 'I'll never be up here.' Not because of the Pulitzers but because in those days women didn't get the good assignments that would be eligible for the prizes. But it was my dream. In those days it was an impossible dream."

Everyday Indignities

Fran Dauth, now city editor for *The Philadelphia Inquirer*, started out with *The Alameda Times-Star* in the Bay Area in California. With a circulation of 10,000, the paper had two reporters with roughly the same limited experience. They did the same thing and everything. He was paid $125 a week; she was paid about $65. "I asked why and was told he was a man and 'you can't pay a man that little.' "

CHAPTER

6

Through the Door

The Sixties. Beatles. Bob Dylan. Beads. Braided hair. Bearded hair. Shows about hair. Songs about protest. Civil rights. Women's rights. Hey, hey, LBJ. Boycott grapes. Rebellion on the campus. Reform at the political edges. Cesar Chavez. The Berrigan brothers. Fannie Lou Hamer. Rachel Carson. Ken Kesey. Tom Wolfe. Hippies, yippies. New gurus. New freedom. New Journalism. New questions.

New questions. New generation. Not just twenty years younger, as all generations are, but different as well. Told by John Kennedy that the torch was being passed to them. Told that what they did mattered—and believing it. Women in the generation still got mixed messages—that they could do whatever they wanted but on the other hand there still were some things women didn't do. That journalism was no place for a lady—but that there had always been some women who were journalists. Women seeking jobs were getting some of the same questions their predecessors had gotten, but some of them had new answers.

"What if you get married?" a male editor asked Jane Brody as he considered her job application at *The Minneapolis Tribune.* "Aren't you married?" she shot back. She got the job. Today Brody writes the "Personal Health" feature for *The New York Times.*

Some had the nerve to ask new questions, even if they didn't like the answers they got. Peg Simpson's AP bureau chief in Texas just hauled back and laughed when she asked him, "If I don't want to be a reporter all my life, what should I be thinking about?"

" 'It's a good thing you like being a reporter,' he told me, 'because you can't be a bureau chief. To be a bureau chief, you have to sell editors on the service. To do that, you have to drink them under the table, and if you did, their wives wouldn't like it. And you can't be a foreign correspondent because you wouldn't fit in to some foreign culture.' " Today Simpson covers Washington for the Hearst newspapers.

When Sara Fritz asked *The Pittsburgh Press* in 1966 why she had to go on the copy desk rather than be a reporter, she was told that reporters had to work at night and women couldn't do that. This double standard applied to even the smallest things: Fritz realized that men could smoke at their desks but women couldn't; "ladies" had to go to the restroom to smoke.

After six months, "one of the editors told me I ought to find another occupation. I was not a very good headline writer, I must confess. But within a year, I had my revenge. I landed with UPI in Pittsburgh, and I had done an investigative piece on teenagers using phony prescriptions to get drugs. The *Press* carried it with no UPI logo but with my byline on the front page. The guy at the *Press* called me and apologized that day." Fritz now covers Washington for the *Los Angeles Times*.

Joann Byrd was told at the morning paper in Spokane, Washington, that the only opening was to cover police and that she "couldn't be a cop reporter because you never know what you might see." It was not her first encounter with sexism. Her journalism adviser at the University of Oregon in 1961 had told her that women had no place in journalism. "He suggested I go to Lane Community College because it had a good secretarial course." Byrd later became executive editor of *The Everett* [Washington] *Herald*.

Sue Hobart of *The Portland Oregonian*, Elizabeth Rhodes of *The Seattle Times*, and Margie Freivogel of *The St. Louis Post-Dispatch* all tell similar tales of responses to their efforts to get jobs even in the 1970s: "You can't work at night" (all three of them have); "You'll just have babies" (all three of them have); "You won't stay in the business" (all three of them have).

It wasn't just male editors who asked questions of women that they never asked men. Women asked themselves a question that men never had to ask: "Will I work on the society page?"

"Yes, it's a foot in the door, a place to show you can write, a supportive environment," said the side that did work on women's pages. "No, it's not taken seriously, it's a female ghetto, it's a dead end, I'll never cover politics or the arts if I start there," said the side that didn't. Both sides were right.

"I had gone to a women's college and it was rather natural to go to the women's section," says Judith Martin. She started as a reporter at *The Washington Post* in 1960. "I looked at what happened on cityside. Women either couldn't get jobs or couldn't get assignments because they were told women couldn't be out on the streets at night. In the women's section we were out at night all the time covering parties."

Eleanor Randolph, who later covered politics and government for *The St. Petersburg Times*, the *Chicago Tribune*, and the *Los Angeles Times* before moving to *The Washington Post*, started on the society section at the Pensacola paper. "I covered weddings, clubs, all that, but I always let my editor know I wanted to be a reporter. It was good training. If you get something wrong in somebody's wedding, they call you."

"I started at *The Memphis Commercial-Appeal* in 1962, and there was no question but that I would work on the society page," recalls Connie Koenenn, a University of Missouri Journalism School graduate who now edits the daily arts coverage for the *Los Angeles Times*. "That was the South and the only place a woman could work." It was considered revolutionary enough that she was going to write features for the society section; God forbid she would want to work on news.

One more: Phyllis Austin, now with *The Maine Times* after ten years with the Associated Press, explains that she had studied religion at Meredith College in South Carolina and discovered that she had naïvely prepared for something she couldn't use unless she kept studying it in graduate school. Family friends owned a little weekly, *The Johnstonian Sun* in Selma, North Carolina, so she started there. "I could do everything—write headlines, write editorials, do the stories, and still sweep up." But her first break at daily journalism came with *The Raleigh News and Observer*—on the women's pages. "I had to sit through those club meetings and write them up seriously."

Flip side: Susan Jetton hated home ec; she had always sworn that she would never do food, fashion, or furnishings. She turned down a summer internship with *The Tennesseean* in Nashville because the internship was with the women's section. Instead, she became the sole reporter covering courts, education—everything —and writing editorials for *The Logan County News-Democrat*, a weekly in Russellville, Kentucky. After graduating from the University of Missouri in 1966, she didn't bother with job interviews because she thought she was in line to run the *News-Democrat* if its editor went off for a Nieman Fellowship at Harvard. But the owner, a woman, said she didn't think advertisers wanted to see the paper in the hands of a 21-year-old girl. And she did use the word *girl*.

Jetton scrambled around and went to see the personnel director of *The Charlotte Observer* in Charlotte, North Carolina, who said, "We'd love to hire you for the women's department." There were no reporting openings but there was one on the copy desk, "but we've never had a woman on the copy desk." "I said, 'Maybe it's time to start,' and I did." Jetton worked at the *Observer* ten years before becoming a political writer for *The San Diego Union* and then press secretary for California Assembly Speaker Willie Brown.

Jane Brody, who had a master's degree in science writing from the University of Wisconsin, a fistful of clips from covering the medical school for the university news service, and two years' experience with *The Minneapolis Tribune*, was told in a *New York Times* interview that they were looking for a technology writer, for which she hadn't been trained. But would she take a job if the only position available was on the women's pages? "I said I would not take it. I had a perfectly good job. The reason I wanted to leave was because I wanted to be a science writer."

And Molly Ivins: "I was determined not to go to any women's sections. That was all huff and puff." Ivins, now a political columnist for the *Dallas Times-Herald*, did not go on any women's sections, but she did recognize that they were covering the women's movement and other important issues.

Whichever way women came down on the question, the point is that they were starting to have a choice. And more of them were making choices. Why? Why the 1960s? Because more women were graduating from college. Women were marrying later. Increased awareness of birth control—and the development of the

Pill—allowed some control over starting a family or having one at all. The Victorian-era father who wanted his little girl to stay at home, even if she was well educated, was gone; other fathers, like mine, gave no sign that their daughters shouldn't go to work. As better jobs opened, women found it harder to resist the lure of better pay, and new families often needed two incomes to survive or prosper. More women's parents had attended college, and more women's mothers had worked, at least for a few years before marrying or having children. Did they pass on to their daughters the dreams they still carried?

Still, women entered some fields and not others. Why newspapers? Shakespeare says that "the readiness is all," and schoolgirls had long been encouraged to write. Writing was an outlet for creativity that was considered appropriate for young ladies. Susan Jetton knew when she was eight that she wanted to write. Gayle Pollard, an editorial writer for the *Los Angeles Times*, had a first-grade teacher who encouraged her writing. I wrote a short story —my only one ever—in the fifth grade, and the teacher encouraged me to do more writing. When Carmen Fields was nine years old, she started her own newspaper with typewriter and carbon paper in her neighborhood in Tulsa, Oklahoma; she went on to *The Boston Globe* and a Nieman Fellowship.

The Columbia Journalism School played a role as well, as did master's degree programs at other leading schools, such as Northwestern and the University of Missouri. While law schools, medical schools, and other professional schools were slow to admit women, Columbia did, albeit on a quota system for a time. For decades, women have used that credential and the contacts made at Columbia to move into a world in which they felt they needed a little extra help. Grace Darin found that *The Baltimore Evening Sun* regularly took women from Columbia Journalism School during World War II. Among others using Columbia as an extra plus were Betsy Wade of *The New York Times*; Molly Ivins; Dorothy Gilliam of *The Washington Post*; Gayle Pollard, Kathleen Hendrix, Terry Pristin, Itabari Njeri, Laurie Becklund, and Kathryn Harris of the *Los Angeles Times*; Betty Bayé of *The* [Louisville] *Courier-Journal*; and Caryl Rivers of Boston University, who turned to teaching and writing novels after reporting in New York, Connecticut, and Washington.

Women's sense of needing an extra boost has changed, says Ivins, adding, "Women today have an even shot at getting hired. That's improved dramatically." But for Bayé, Columbia was invaluable training. She'd been a civil rights activist and didn't start college until she was 27. She had had no involvement with journalism at all when she started at Columbia in September 1977. "All the basics that I learned, I learned at J-School."

Women of drive have long used Columbia as a stepping-stone, but none has done so more flamboyantly than war correspondent and columnist Marguerite Higgins. Doors of the city rooms of New York had slammed on her after she graduated from the University of California. Higgins applied to the Columbia Journalism School right before classes were to start in the fall of 1941. She was informed that the eleven spaces in the class alloted to women were already filled, but that didn't matter to her. She was determined to show she deserved to be there, to break the quota, so she corralled the necessary recommendations almost overnight. Her impressive hustling got her in, and she became the first to achieve success in her class, which included Elie Abel and Flora Lewis.

"Even in a class full of stars, she stood out," recalled Professor John Tebbel. She became known "as a reporter who could get absolutely any story no matter how difficult," Tebbel told Higgins's biographer, Antoinette May. "Naturally that was a challenge to us, and we tried to think of assignments that would really challenge her." She did them. She went to the *Herald-Tribune* and got a job.[1]

English and journalism, then, were acceptable majors in college. If a young woman like Fran Dauth didn't want to teach after graduating in English from the University of Colorado, it was not such a long leap to newspaper writing. Dauth, now city editor at *The Philadelphia Inquirer*, had had a friend in high school whose father was an AP sportswriter, and newspapering seemed like an exciting life. "I hadn't really thought I'd have a career—I wanted to see Afghanistan. Then I figured I'd marry and have three kids and live in the suburbs."

Like Dauth, Anne Cabot Wyman, an editor at *The Boston Globe*, was an English literature major and had had no career in mind when she graduated from Radcliffe. She worked for a publishing house and then took a job in the promotion department at the *Globe* before moving into reporting. Judith Martin, an English major at Wellesley, got into the newspaper business even more by accident. Her parents wanted her to get a summer job, and she didn't want a summer job. She applied to the *Post*, figuring she wouldn't get hired but she could tell her parents she tried. It didn't work—the *Post* hired her on the spot as a copy girl.

Another journalist majored in English, taught it, and then turned to newspaper work. "I went into teaching because I was told women had no future in the newspaper business," says Solveig Torvik of *The Seattle Post-Intelligencer*. "One day I walked into the teachers' room with a huge stack of themes to grade. The gym teacher was sitting there taking it easy and so were some of the others, and I said, 'I can't take it anymore,' and I threw the stack of papers up in the air and walked to the phone to call the University of Utah to see if I could get a master's degree in journalism." She taught during the day and worked at UPI at night until she got her degree.

War played a role once again in women's careers in the 1960s. "I am one of many women my age who got our break because our male friends in college would be asked first off about their draft status" as Vietnam escalated, Susan Jetton says. Draft calls rose from 112,000 to 231,000 between 1964 and 1965 and stayed that high until 1970. "If they were 2-S, it was, 'Come back when you've done your two years.' "

It is easy to forget the climate of the times in trying to recreate the motivations that set more women to working and more to working in the newspaper business. The civil rights movement triggered a reevaluation of treatment of Chicanos, Indians, the handicapped, and women. The long hard look at America that occurred in the 1960s and early 1970s resulted in civil rights laws that tried to put black Americans on a firmer footing. Often those laws covered conditions faced by women as well. The Equal Pay Act became law; the Equal Employment Opportunity Commission was established. Title VII of the 1964 Civil Rights Act specifically forbade employment discrimination against women. The Education Amendments of 1972 said that no institution that received federal aid could discriminate against women in any of its programs. Its Title IX directly benefited college athletic programs for women. In 1972 the Equal Rights Amendment passed Congress.

Newspapers were hardly immune from the reexamination of the times. Reporters and editors started to see the hypocrisy of covering civil rights developments without themselves acting on the issues they raised. Newspapers started hiring more women because everybody was hiring more women.

More women started to show up in newsrooms because, over time, a few women had made a name for themselves in journalism. The term *role model* is overworked but cannot be overemphasized. Beth Campbell had met Sigrid Arne in college and decided she wanted to be a good reporter like Arne. Mary McGrory speaks of how very kind Doris Fleeson was to her.

For me, it was May Craig, who wrote for newspapers in Maine. I never met her, and today she might not be my ideal choice. I have no idea how well she wrote. I have learned that she marched in a suffragist parade in Woodrow Wilson's day, broke Navy tradition by being the first woman on a battleship at sea when she covered air-sea maneuvers on the carrier *Midway* in 1949, and was the first woman to fly over the North Pole, in 1952.[2] I also know she was viewed as a joke by many men in the press corps, but I only suspected that at the time. What stuck in my brain was that May Craig and her funny little hats was on "Meet the Press" Sunday after Sunday with all those men. The men being interviewed had to answer her questions. For me, that meant that being a newspaper reporter was feasible.

For Ellen Hume of *The Wall Street Journal*, Brenda Starr in the comics was her "only red-headed role model." Later, for Eileen McNamara at *The Boston Globe*, Eileen Shanahan's byline in *The New York Times* was an inspiration. "She was writing economics. She was writing what the men wrote and for an Eileen McNamara to see an Eileen Shanahan . . ."

Established women in journalism subliminally showed younger women that it was okay to try to be a journalist, and sometimes the few that were there kept the beginners from dropping out. Tad Bartimus, an AP regional correspondent based in Colorado, still talks about how "Helen Thomas kept me in the business." Bartimus had gone to work in the AP's Miami bureau and remembers that Thomas would "come to Florida with Nixon and take me out to dinner. She'd feed me because I had no money, and when we were through, she'd go around the table and gather up the leftovers, which would feed me for three more days. Not

87

only did she feed me, but she gave me pep talks, telling me how important and exciting it was to be doing what we were doing."

Women were moving off the women's pages and sometimes onto the front pages. Hilda Bryant covered Seattle's racial climate for the *Post-Intelligencer* in the late 1960s. Peg Simpson was in on the AP coverage of the Kennedy assassination. Susan Jetton became the first woman to cover city hall and later the first in the statehouse bureau at Raleigh for *The Charlotte Observer*. She'd paid her dues writing every cute story that came along, whether it was riding the elephant in the circus parade or playing the water ballet mermaid. "You couldn't say no, and I never would have thought of turning anything down. I worked twice as hard as the men. All the time I was still trying to be a serious reporter. Nobody ever said they wouldn't let me cover stories because I was a woman, but still I didn't get many crime stories late at night."

Every woman was a first in something in those days. Molly Ivins was the first woman *The Minneapolis Tribune* had sent on the police beat in 1967. "They had other good women, but they sent me because I looked the part. I'm six feet tall. Nobody ever looked at me and said, 'Oh, you poor sweet dainty little thing. We can't send you out to cover a riot.' It was more, 'Ivins, get your ass out there.'" Cops give any green reporter, male or female, a hard time, "but to be a woman covering an almost all-male organization was as bad as I thought it could be, although when I got to the Texas legislature, I found a whole new dimension of sexism."

Timing, in addition to size, helps. Soon after Linda Deutsch started with the Associated Press in Los Angeles in 1967, Robert Kennedy was killed. She worked second string, covering the Sirhan Sirhan trial. Then Sharon Tate was killed. The reporter from New York took one look at how long Charles Manson's trial was expected to last and left. It lasted ten and a half months, and Deutsch was on her way to one of her specialties, courtroom coverage. She has since reported on the trials of Angela Davis, Claudine Longet, Daniel Ellsberg, John DeLorean, and the Hillside Strangler.

Deutsch swears by her beat because it contains movie stars, hippies, drugs—you name it. "You can trace social history through trials. Trials are the only story you see from beginning to end. I've been asked how I can go from covering movies to trials. But how can anyone forget the drama of the judge announcing from the bench that Hunt and Liddy had broken into Ellsberg's office or Manson threatening the judge?"

Before there are trials, there are crimes. And where there are crimes, there are reporters. More and more women were getting assignments to cover crime stories in the 1960s. Fran Dauth was about 25, brand new at *The Oakland Tribune*. A woman had been found at her elegant home with a battered skull. Dauth's city editor called her, demanding to know what she was doing on the story. It happened that Dauth had no idea what to do, but she looked in the phone book and called up the woman's husband, a psychiatrist. He said to come on over to the couple's home. As she arrived, a police detective was also arriving to question the man. She fully expected to be thrown out but instead was ushered in and sat there taking notes while the detective took notes. When he left, the doctor suggested to Dauth that she stay for a drink and look around.

"He seemed to like the attention. So I was able to draw diagrams and get a good story." When the first edition of the paper came up with her big front-page story, it had the byline Frank Dauth. The printers had decided that no woman would have been sent on a murder.

One of the premier police reporters in the country is Edna Buchanan of *The Miami Herald*. She won a Pulitzer Prize in 1986. Few win Pulitzers; fewer still are profiled in *The New Yorker* magazine. Calvin Trillin started his piece with a discourse on "the classic Edna lead," one that is "simple, matter-of-fact . . . that registers with a jolt." He liked the one about a woman who was about to go on trial for murder conspiracy: "Bad things happen to the husbands of Widow Elkin." Trillin went on to tell how Buchanan knows not only most of the police officers in the Miami area but often what shifts they work.[3]

She got interested in criminals when she read the New York tabloids to her Polish grandmother, who didn't read English. She decided she could be a writer during a creative writing evening class at Montclair State Teachers College. The teacher, said Trillin, told Buchanan it was a rare pleasure to come across such writing, that "one section reminded him of early Tennessee Williams. It was the one radiant New Jersey moment."

Buchanan got a job at *The Miami Beach Daily Sun*. She wrote society news as well as politics, crime, and movie reviews, then started covering the cops for the *Herald* in 1973. "Most reporters would sooner cover thirty weeks of water-board hearings than call a murder victim's next of kin, but Edna tries to look on the positive side," Trillin wrote, adding that Buchanan has never forgotten that people like to talk about their loved ones, even if they've just been wiped out in a gang shooting.

"Perhaps because a female police reporter was something of a rarity when she began, some policemen took pleasure in showing her, say, the corpse of someone who had met a particularly nasty end," said Trillin. Buchanan survived and prospered. "It's better than working in a coat factory in Paterson, New Jersey," she told one questioner.

By the late 1960s and early 1970s, then, women not only were getting first jobs and covering front-page stories, they were also starting to work their way through the system from the state capital bureaus and the medium-size papers into the top spots: Washington bureaus, *The New York Times, The Washington Post*, the *Los Angeles Times, The Wall Street Journal*, and others, slowly but steadily.

Peg Simpson was one. Simpson, who "never met a reporter until I became one," worked summers for *The Hondo Anvil Herald* and Edna, Texas, weeklies during the summers when she was at North Texas State College. As a child, she had traveled a lot because her father was a hurricane specialist, so places in the news became real to her. When it came time to declare a major in college, "I didn't want to be undecided, so I said I was a journalism major."

She worked eighteen months as editor of the Hondo paper after graduation, even though advertisers started pulling ads because of her city council coverage. "I was just quoting the guys directly, but they weren't used to that." A celebrated murder case was about to go to trial in Hondo, and the Hearst paper in San Antonio was too cheap to send someone to a month-long trial. It asked the AP to cover the trial, and the AP asked her. Someone suggested it was okay for her to call UPI as well, and she did. "By the end of the month, it was the lead story across Texas because somebody had been feeding UPI and AP—and it was me."

Simpson moved to Dallas as a vacation relief person and helped cover the Texas legislature in Austin for the AP. She was in the city hall basement when Jack Ruby shot Lee Harvey Oswald. She transferred to Washington in January 1968 and stayed there with the AP for ten years before shifting to the Hearst Washington bureau. Simpson helped develop the coverage of women in Washington and reported on the International Women's Year meetings in Mexico City in 1975 and Nairobi in 1985 as well as every political convention since 1972. She had a Nieman Fellowship in 1979.

Scores of other women moved into the newspaper business and upward once in it. Women's bylines started appearing over front-page stories about the powers-that-be in Washington in the papers that are the powers-that-be in the press.

What hooks women on the business is the same thing that hooks men—the kaleidoscope of events and people and power. You interview a wife-killer one day; the next day you profile a handicapped man. Follow the school board's talk and tedium, and one day it ends up on the front page, banner headline, when the board decides to fire a controversial staff member. Ride the circus elephant, go to the zoo, work twice as hard and don't complain, and one day you go to the city hall and then the state house. Nag, cajole, pester, work hard, and finally you get sent to to Vietnam, to cover the story of the era. Albany. Sacramento. Washington. Moscow. Beijing. Stories, headlines, bylines. Women were starting to be there in some numbers, telling the stories in their own words.

Everyday Indignities

Carol Richards was working for the Albany bureau of the Gannett newspapers, reporting regularly on the New York state legislature. One day, her bureau chief sent her out to buy a tie for the elevator operator at Christmas.

Richards was so flabbergasted at his directive that she went to the best store in town and spent twenty dollars. (Ties then cost about four or five dollars.) Her boss asked her for his change. She said there wasn't any. "I didn't do it out of malice, but I wanted him to know that if he was going to send me out on errands, I knew good stores and he'd have to pay for it."

CHAPTER

7

The Girls in the Balcony

The Associated Press and United Press International are like dueling banjos: faster is better. Especially in the days before television brought events instantly into American living rooms, minutes were as golden for wire-service reporters as for trauma surgeons. Wire-service reporters have been heard saying to one another, as they rush out of an event, that just once they'd like to write about something *after* it happens.

Readiness isn't all in this case. If you're a wire-service reporter, you also need to have your tools to be ready: a nearby phone, accessibility to the person being covered, a speech text if one exists. For more than a decade Helen Thomas of United Press International faced a constant professional problem when she had to cover speakers at the National Press Club (NPC) in Washington. She had to sit in the balcony because the Club didn't admit women. Not as members, not as luncheon guests, and not as direct questioners. Thomas, who covered the Justice Department in the middle 1950s, did not sit alone in the balcony, but she worked for a wire service, which made her distress greater: it was directly proportional to her distance from a telephone. And there was no telephone near the balcony.

Thomas also headed the Women's National Press Club, which gave her a vehicle to try to correct the situation. Joined by her opposite number at the Associated Press, Frances Lewine, Elsie Carper of *The Washington Post*, Bonnie Angelo of *Newsday*, and others, Thomas set about doing just that.

The National Press Club, founded in 1908, is located only

blocks from the White House, a convenient location, in which many newspapers house their Washington bureaus. The Club has not only meeting rooms but a restaurant, a library, a gym, and a bar. Women could not use the wire machines in the Club, nor could they eat there, and they certainly could not visit either the gym or the bar. Press agents who were not active reporters could; women who were active reporters could not.

Personally galling, the exclusionary policies became professionally offensive when more women began reporting affairs of state and as the National Press Club became the most consistent site of major speeches by government officials and visiting foreign dignitaries. Women's fight to end the men-only policy of the National Press Club and the equally offensive (but less professionally harmful) men-only policy of the Gridiron Club marked their coming of age. They transformed what some thought a trivial issue in the late 1950s into major victories in the early 1970s, victories that occurred not only because women mobilized for the effort but also because a majority of the men affected also agreed with them by that time.

Women journalists had meanwhile founded the Women's National Press Club in 1919 as their own forum for professional discussions and socializing. Columnists May Craig and Doris Fleeson worked for years individually to try to break down discrimination against women. The unified effort got underway in 1953 when ever-pesky Texas journalist Sarah McClendon suggested to the women's club that it form a committee to monitor admission to press conferences and other matters bearing on the fair treatment of women news correspondents with men. Said McClendon, "We might make our position clearer and present it with more weight and greater dignity if we acted as a club rather than as individuals."[1]

Don Larrabee, bureau chief for a string of New England newspapers and president of the National Press Club when it finally went co-ed, commented that "the struggle for admission to the National Press Club by Washington women journalists did not surface publicly until after the club admitted its first black male in 1954. To be sure," Larrabee added, "there was closet sympathy for admission of women among some of the men" who aspired for club office, "but no real crusaders, to my knowledge.

94

It was regarded as the kiss of death for a candidate to run on a platform favoring women members."[2]

In February 1954 the battle became official. The Women's National Press Club "unanimously adopted a resolution urging the National Press Club to permit accredited newspaper women to cover its news events and simultaneously voted to send letters to cabinet members and other high officials advising them that women reporters were barred from the National Press Club," recalled Fran Lewine. "The NPC did not respond to this gentle pressure." The women also went to the State Department and to foreign embassies in Washington to urge them not to send overseas dignitaries to speak to the National Press Club.[3]

The Club inched slightly away from intransigence in February 1955, when its board admitted women to the club balcony to cover luncheon speeches. "It wasn't that we weren't grateful," Helen Thomas said. "But it was humiliating. It was going into purdah to go into the balcony. But we did feel it was a step forward, and Liz Carpenter did make that possible in her era [as Women's National Press Club president]. But all the PR people, all the lobbyists were on the floor, and there you were. I cannot believe that we had to go through all that."

This denial of equal access to the news hurt women's ability to do their job. Sometimes it even meant that they lost assignments. Susanna McBee, then with *The Washington Post*, was assigned to cover the civil rights march on Washington in 1963. She interviewed march leader A. Philip Randolph and others in New York. But when the civil rights leaders came to Washington for the march itself, they decided to have their only press appearance at the National Press Club. McBee would have had to sit in the balcony and wouldn't have been able to ask questions, so the *Post* pulled her off that day's developments in the story. The man who covered the news conference then wrote the *Post*'s main story on the march; McBee ended up doing a sidebar on Martin Luther King Jr.'s speech.

Why do clubs restrict membership? What justification does a professional organization have for keeping out fellow professionals? Why do little boys pull up the ladder and keep girls out of the treehouse? Protecting the bar, not the luncheons, may have been the main concern, judging from the clamor that followed the brief appearance of Mollie Thayer of *The Washington Post* in the bar in the 1950s. "I just heard fun noises and wandered in," Thayer said in a letter of apology to the Club president. "If it's any consolation to you, I didn't see a thing in the Men's Bar except a score or so of well-tailored backs. So its secrets are still inviolate."

The "newswoman question," as it was called in the Press Club newsletter, escalated in the late 1950s and early 1960s, when the club pulled out of the Joint Committee of Press, Radio and Television, which had been formed in 1951 to entertain visiting foreign dignitaries. The Club didn't want to compete for lunch guests because it could probably get most of them anyway. Helen Thomas objected because women would lack equal access to the speakers. Press Club president William Lawrence of *The New York Times* characterized Thomas's views in a memo as "the usual yak yak by Miss Thomas about how her members were 'Jim-crowed' into the balcony and thereby denied opportunities to cover the news. She said her members didn't wish to join the NPC, and I assured her membership would not be forced upon the women. There was a lot more ad nauseum."[4]

The women were by no means unanimous that protesting the Press Club policy was a proper course. Many women worked in women's sections and didn't see the need to attend Press Club functions. Others found vehement protest unladylike. Even some who covered government, rather than society, felt that they had made it on their own and didn't need to gang up on the Press Club, Helen Thomas recalls. "I certainly didn't agree with them."

"Once we were going to picket in the lobby of the National Press Building against some speaker who was coming that day, and I particularly remember Esther Tufty [who ran her own news service] being horrified at the idea of picketing in the lobby of the National Press Building," says Isabelle Shelton, who worked for *The Washington Star* at the time.

The women found an ally when Soviet Premier Nikita Khrushchev refused to speak at the Press Club in 1959 unless women were permitted to cover the event. Columnist Doris Fleeson remarked that "the Ambassador of the Soviet Union, Mr. Menshikov, personally intervened to insure our presence at the Khrushchev luncheon. . . . I did not share the Ambassador's amusement over this, and I cannot imagine that the State Department did."[5]

Thomas and her colleagues kept trying to enlist State Department help. The Department regularly replied that embassies made their own arrangements and that it advised only if asked. The women felt the State Department should play a more activist role to counter the fact that many embassy press attachés were members of the National Press Club, giving the Club easy access to ambassadors. Baffled at "why the State Department persists in discrimination against the newspaperwomen of Washington," Fleeson wrote a letter of complaint to Secretary of State Christian A. Herter in March 1960. "It is a professional question in which the government has intervened to our disadvantage, not just an internal division in the press itself." To Thomas, she commented, "How tiresome all these people are."[6]

In Helen Thomas the women had as a leader someone who had finally won assignment to White House coverage after seventeen years at UPI. At the White House, she first covered the Kennedy family, then presidential news as the third person on a team headed by Merriman Smith. Ultimately, she would cover Presidents Kennedy, Johnson, Nixon, Ford, Carter, and Reagan and become dean of the White House correspondents, the senior wire-service reporter who says "Thank you, Mr. President" to close news conferences.

"Thank you" was not all she said to Presidents and Prime Ministers; Thomas never feared standing eye-to-eye with leaders as formidable as Britain's Margaret Thatcher or as elusive as Ronald Reagan. Best known for asking questions and unloading volumes of information onto the rewrite desk, Thomas was also the chief listener to take seriously the nocturnal telephone calls of Martha Mitchell, wife of Attorney General John Mitchell, in the midst of Watergate.

A relentless worker, Thomas remembered how long it had taken her to get the job she had, and she was determined to wring every bit of information from the beat. Getting her to take time off was like trying to pry a toy out of an infant's grip. "I have been a women's libber all my life," Thomas wrote in her 1975 book *Dateline: White House*, "and discrimination against women at all work levels has always been distressing to me. Throughout my career, I've tried to move forward in this male-oriented profession. My biggest ambition was to be a good reporter, knowing full well that in my career you are only as good as your last story."[7]

During her term as president of the Women's National Press Club, which began in 1960, Thomas launched a letter-writing campaign to win support from heads of major bureaus and newspapers in Washington for opening foreign dignitaries' meetings with the press to all correspondents. The group best able to handle such functions would be the capitol's standing committee of correspondents, she argued, because that committee was elected by correspondents and governed arrangements for covering Congress. It did not exclude legitimate reporters. Response was decidedly mixed.[8]

Walter T. Ridder of Ridder Publications said the arrangement would be "perfectly okay with me. I am not so sanguine as to believe that this will avoid uproar and tumult and bitter feelings, but it sounds like the best arrangement. For what it is worth, you have my vote of 'Yes.' " John L. Steele of *Time* agreed with Thomas that women should be admitted to cover heads of state, but he thought the Press Club remained the best hope. He proposed to support Club officials who would agree to abolish "the archaic ground rules now in force."

From Walter Trohan of the *Chicago Tribune*: "I have no objection to your proposal to handle distinguished visitors. As a matter of fact, I think it is an excellent one, and should have been done long ago." Columnist Drew Pearson: "I think you're quite right, and you can quote me accordingly."

But Kenneth Crawford of *Newsweek* disagreed, saying the Press Club should simply move some functions to a bigger auditorium. And James Reston of *The New York Times* was evasive: "It is my understanding that the Standing Committee of Correspondents was not intended and is not constituted to arrange such functions as you describe, and that they do not want to. In view of this, I would not be able to give you the opinion you request."

The women kept after the White House as well. Asked about the issue at a news conference on November 29, 1961, President Kennedy replied that when an official visitor speaks at the Press Club, "all working reporters should be permitted in on a basis of equality. That is not a social occasion but a working occasion. That happens to be my personal view and the members of the Press Club . . . are entitled to have any arrangement they want on social occasions."

The Press Club balcony had become to Washington women "what the wall is to West Berliners," wrote Merriman Smith. He couldn't resist having fun with the issue, pointing out that Arthur Krock "has been writing about it in *The New York Times*, credential enough for any crisis because Mr. Krock does not vend our national troubles lightly." Still, wrote Smith, "it would seem to be a problem that most any Rotary Club could handle back home. But not in Washington, the current seat of most western wisdom."[9]

Art Buchwald joined in after women had had to sit in the balcony to cover A. Philip Randolph. He went to the Press Club bar, he wrote, where "one correspondent spoke for several members at the bar when he said, 'Our women were very happy to sit in the balcony until outside agitators from the North came down here and started causing trouble. Women prefer to be together. That's why they have women's colleges and women's magazines. We've always treated our women good, but they wouldn't know what to do with equal rights if we gave it to them.'

"Another newspaperman agreed. 'You said it. You start mixing the sexes and you know what you'll wind up with? Babies! I've seen it happen during the war.'

" 'We don't ask to go to their beauty parlors,' a columnist said. 'Why should they ask to come to our club?' "[10]

Ridicule helped. So did White House interest. President Kennedy refused to attend a White House Correspondents Association dinner unless women could attend. Since his presence was one of the main reasons for the dinner, he won. He went, and they went. Public attention and the women's constant efforts bugged—and budged—the boys. But only a bit. In 1963 the National Press Club allowed "ladies" to have lunch in the East Lounge. They could not, however, go into the members' bar.

The women kept the pressure on. Bryson Rash, a local television newsman and Club official, complained in 1963 that "some non-members of the NPC"—read women—"have sought intervention by officials of the Federal Government in the affairs of our organization. It seems to us that people who deal in news and its dissemination are best served by keeping the federal government or any other government as far away from our affairs as we possibly can. It is not in our interest to encourage news management in any shape or form."[11]

News management was not, of course, what the women wanted. They simply wanted equal access to the news.

But Rash kept up his resistance. In a December letter to a *Washington Star* editor, he complained about a column by Isabelle Shelton. "It seems to me to be rather a pity," Rash wrote, "that the columns of such a great newspaper as yours can be used by individuals with an axe to grind. Especially when the issue is a private one and really has little or no interest to the great public which you serve."[12]

The women renewed their campaign to keep foreign dignitaries from accepting speaking invitations at the National Press Club. Elsie Carper and Fran Lewine fired off telegrams by the dozens. The Women's National Press Club protested West German Chancellor Konrad Adenauer's speech in November 1962; the Germans had asked the Press Club to change its rules, and it had refused. Adenauer was obviously aware of the controversy because he corrected himself several times when he said "ladies and gentlemen." Finally, he said, "I am sorry there are no ladies here. There must be some ladies up there in the gallery."[13]

Carper and Lewine, co-chairs of the Women's National Press Club's professional committee, tried strenuously during the spring of 1963 to keep British Labor Party leader Harold Wilson from speaking at the National Press Club. They showered telegrams onto the British press and urged women members of the British Parliament to ask Wilson not to appear. He appeared, but "the next time British officials came to town they held press conferences at their embassy or at places open to all—men and women correspondents," Lewine said.

In January 1963, Nelson Rockefeller snubbed the women by having his first appearance in Washington as a declared presidential candidate at the National Press Club. Columnist Vera Glaser wrote, "The decision is viewed by the women's press corps as a studied slight." Contrasting Rockefeller's disdain with Nikita Khrushchev's insistence that all correspondents be permitted to cover his appearance on an equal basis, Glaser pointedly told readers that "female writers in Washington had a communist dictator to thank for temporarily lifting them from their second-class status."[14]

To get more attention for their case against the National Press

Club, the women appeared before the Presidential Commission on the Status of Women in April 1963. The Press Club's intransigence was working a concrete hardship on female journalists who needed equal opportunity to do their job, they told Commission members. "It has been pointed out that reporters are used to working under difficult conditions—including covering events from balconies," the women reported. "But normally there is no competitive disadvantage among reporters in such circumstances. They are all in the same boat (or balcony).

"On one occasion at the NPC, a woman reporter on the balcony lost out on a bulletin story when her male competitor on the floor had fast access to telephones. In addition, she lost the chance to share in use of the speakers' text, which the male reporter was able to get because of his closeness to the head table." Without access to speakers and telephones, women would not get assignments to cover newsmaking events at the press club, the women said, adding, "The government, by failing to take action, is condoning this situation."[18]

That August came the March on Washington. The day A. Philip Randolph and other march leaders held their conference at the National Press Club, women reporters issued a press release reminding them that "the balcony as well as the back of the bus should have special meaning to civil rights leaders."[15]

Joining the women reporters in protest was black feminist Pauli Murray, an Episcopal minister and attorney. "You who have struggled against the rigid views of your own brethren in the AFL-CIO need no reminder that human rights and human dignity are indivisible and that in 1963 discrimination solely because of sex is just as morally indefensible as discrimination because of race," Murray wrote Randolph. Tokenism, she added, "is as offensive when applied to women as when applied to Negroes."[16]

Columnist Betty Beale added this footnote: "Perhaps the most ironic note of all was that a Negro member of the WNPC, Alice Dunnigan, also was relegated to the balcony."[17]

That fall, Lewine could report that "the slow drip, drip method seems to be working finally in our crusade. . . . Although they still have not made any public statement of policy, the State Department now is quietly advising presidential visitors that one fair solution to the problem of press appearances is a press conference in the State Department auditorium, open to all accredited reporters."[19]

"We have not had to send as many irate telegrams," Lewine also said. The following June, Lewine could report that no visiting head of state had gone to the National Press Club. The campaign was being felt. In 1964, the National Press club made tables available on the ballroom floor for "working, non-member press" at its luncheons, with Bill Gold, a *Washington Post* columnist, offering the successful resolution.

By this time Lyndon Johnson was in the White House and was being goaded on the issue by his wife's press secretary, Liz Carpenter, a past president of the Women's National Press Club. Elsie Carper recalled that Johnson told the State Department not to let foreign visitors go to the National Press Club unless women reporters were admitted on an equal basis.

In 1966 the State Department's protocol office said women should be allowed to cover luncheon speeches by foreign dignitaries on an equal basis with men. NPC president Windsor Booth wrote James Symington, chief of protocol, to complain that few women covered recent discussions of television programming or Senator J. William Fulbright's talk on Vietnam or Agriculture Secretary Orville Freeman's speech or one by the Treasury Secretary. "There are fewer than twenty-four newswomen in Washington who regularly cover national and international news. The National Press Club has made a minimum of twenty-four of the best seats in the house available. They simply are not interested."

Not content to blame the victims—who might not be covering Vietnam or agriculture or the Treasury because of the discriminatory policies of the very newspapers whose editors belonged to the National Press Club—Booth went on: "It seems to me that our women reporters, a number of whom are very able indeed, made it perfectly plain yesterday in your office that they are not interested in covering the news. All they are interested in—and they were perfectly frank to say it—is the glamour and drama of sitting in with news people when heads of state, and only heads of state, are visiting in Washington."[20]

But Booth's was a waning opinion. By December 1968 William Hickman of McGraw-Hill proposed, albeit unsuccessfully, that women be admitted to full Press Club membership.

Another idea that twenty-five-dollar-a-year guest memberships be created was shelved because it would treat women as "second class citizens."

On November 24, 1969, according to Don Larrabee's chronology of the process, the National Press Club board "adopted a new policy under which women members of the working press with official credentials could attend luncheons on the ballroom floor but could not use the middle bar. . . . Bartenders were instructed not to serve women. Any woman remaining in the main lounge one-half hour after a luncheon was to be asked to leave the club."[21]

Finally, on June 4, 1970, Larrabee, by then NPC president, read a letter to a club meeting from Hickman proposing that women be admitted. The "time is overdue for addressing the issue of women's membership," said Hickman, adding, "No longer, I submit, can the National Press Club rest on its professional laurels so long as female professionals are barred from our society. . . . I think we can all agree that men no longer hold a lock on journalistic talent. To me, such a change is necessary for our club to maintain its credentials as a professional organization." Even Hickman said that "the sanctity of the men's only bar should not be violated, but ladies should have similar facilities if they so desire."[22]

The first vote, conducted by mail, failed because the proposal to admit women did not receive the required two-thirds of the majority of the total membership, although those who voted favored it two to one. Larrabee told a television interviewer that the issue "goes to the heart of the club's professional status. We have to do this; otherwise, we are nothing but a social club. . . . I'm going to fight for this."[23]

The issue came to the floor at the Club's annual meeting the next January; women needed two-thirds of those present and voting to win admission. First the men would have their say.

Vernon Louviere, a leading opponent, argued that admitting women would alter the character of the Press Club. He did not say how. He claimed that the NPC board had received no formal overtures from any women journalists wanting admission and had done no studies to determine the economic impact of admitting women or the "likelihood of unpleasant incidents." And he wrote in a letter circulated to fellow members, "The argument that admission of women would add to our economic base is specious. The spending habits of women argue against that."[24]

Ralph de Toledano, a columnist, was more to the point. The National Press Club was a men's club and had always been a men's club, although certainly it practiced no discrimination, he said. "If the good Lord had thought there would have been discrimination by having men and women, he would have given us unisex." De Toledano predicted there would be only two or three or four women at most applying, and for that the men would have to curtailing their privileges as members. "We are not discriminating against them. We want our club as it is."

The man who ran the golf tournament said the tournament would be irrevocably harmed. Members would have to watch their language in the bar, said another.

In a letter to members favoring admission, Robert Ames Alden said that "as long as the National Press Club refuses to recognize women as part of the national press corps, its credibility as the National *Press Club* is chipped away." If it refuses to admit women, Alden said, "we should consider changing our name to the men's Press Club of Washington, D.C. or the 14th and F Street Men's Club."[25] Others noted that the reason women hadn't applied was because they didn't feel welcome.

Larrabee called for the vote. Only those attending were counted this time. The vote was 227 to 56 in favor of admitting women. The Press Club record reported, "Some victors celebrated by inviting women reporters to have a drink at the Men's Bar." The Washington Press Club, successor to the Women's National Press Club, and the National Press Club merged in June 1985.

Press clubs were not the only facilities that had to be liberated as women moved into journalistic ranks. Restrooms have evidently been a problem ever since indoor plumbing. There was no restroom for women in the Capitol Hill press galleries until May Craig protested. Women's restrooms remained inadequate for years until Joan McKinney of *The Baton Rouge Advocate* threatened to turn one of the men's bathrooms into a unisex facility.

The same situation prevailed in other state capitals as recently as the early 1970s. There was only one bathroom for the press at the capitol in Harrisburg, Pennsylvania, and it was for men. "Women had to go downstairs," says Sara Fritz, who served for two years as UPI's Harrisburg bureau chief. "Now, I get too involved in a story to go downstairs. So I just went in and locked the door." Christy Bulkeley of Gannett remembers going to American Press Institute seminars in the middle 1970s and finding no women's rooms on the floor where the sessions were conducted.

But there were also good guys in opening access to the news to women. Patricia Wiggins of UPI was covering President Eisenhower, who played golf at the Burning Tree Country Club. Even thirty years later, Burning Tree allowed women on the grounds only to pick up their husbands or to shop at Christmastime in the pro shop. Back in the 1950s, male pool reporters were allowed to watch Eisenhower tee off, but Club officials wouldn't allow Wiggins to do so. But in her defense, Press Secretary James Hagerty protested that she was part of the official pool and that she would go in or the pool would not go there and furthermore Eisenhower himself would not go there. On this one occasion, Burning Tree let Wiggins in.

When Susan Jetton was covering city hall for *The Charlotte Observer*, Mayor John Belk, head of a big department store, once played host to North Carolina mayors for golf, lunch, and a business session at the local country club. Jetton was the only woman there. The luncheon for some inexplicable reason was set up in the men's locker room—which Jetton says may have been because it looked more like a sun porch than a locker room. The club said that Jetton could not attend. "Belk said, 'You mean she can't be in the locker room, not in the club. So put the tables where she can be.'"

As women were winning their fight with the National Press Club, they turned their sights on still another target, the Gridiron Club. Composed of fifty male Washington bureau chiefs and editors, the Gridiron Club offered only an annual affront: the Gridiron Dinner. In his book *Without Fear or Favor* Harrison Salisbury of *The New York Times* described the Gridiron Club as "an assembly of troglodytes, the wise and stuffy Old Men of Washington journalism." Outside Washington the members' names were unknown, but within the Beltway "their names were golden. Young correspondents were expected to genuflect at the mention of the institution," in which membership "seemed to confer an extraordinary life-span."[26]

The Gridiron Dinner, seemingly the only reason for the club's existence, included a show that lampooned the news of the year and the people who made it. Often the script reflected wit otherwise unknown to the journalists' regular readers. But the show was not the thing as much as simply being there. The brass came from back home, press organizations threw lavish parties before and after the dinner, and bureau chiefs' stock rose or fell according to what cabinet secretary, senator, or Supreme Court justice sat at whose table. Based on the theory that journalists who have eaten and drunk and laughed with the big shots may get their phone calls returned and news tips confirmed, the Gridiron Dinner was a Washington social gathering that competitive journalists wanted to attend.

Harrison Salisbury recorded that some Washington hands felt that "the institution was a total anachronism" and that the women who picketed the dinner in 1971 "should have been celebrating not protesting their absence."[27]

The women picketed in evening dress, surmising that the police would be hesitant to rough up "ladies" nicely dressed. Each year the number of picketers grew, with men joining the women. In 1972 the Club decided to open its doors to a few "prominent women"—as guests only, not as members. Eight women attended the dinner in 1972, and seventeen the next year.

At this, the women of Journalists for Professional Equality, as the protesters by then called themselves, were "almost more insulted than before the tokenism," Bella Stumbo reported in the *Los Angeles Times* on April 8, 1974.[28] The group pressured the women who had been invited to the dinner to stay away. "It was full membership or nothing. And such women as Anne Armstrong [a prominent Republican], Pat Nixon and Shirley Chisholm did stay away." In 1973 Chisholm sent the Gridiron Club a telegram saying, "Guess who's not coming to dinner?"

Years later, Katharine Graham of *The Washington Post* told an audience at the National Press Club about the ambivalence she felt in deciding whether to accept the invitation. The daughter of one publisher and the widow of another, she'd heard for years about the Gridiron Dinner. She really wanted to go. But "the women at the *Post* wrote me a letter urging that I stay away. If women couldn't be members, they said, we shouldn't go at all. Some of our reporters were planning to picket outside the dinner. They were right. I decided not to go. I couldn't bring myself to picket, however. The most I could do—and I've never said this in public before—was get into the car and drive by." Later that evening, she joined the picketers at a buffet dinner at Eileen Shanahan's home, and stayed late.[29]

In 1973 the club voted on admitting women. Twenty-six members voted to admit, but the move failed because it needed a two-thirds majority to carry. Marty Nolan, then bureau chief for *The Boston Globe*, resigned in disgust.

The following spring, a small knot of protesters met to plot their strategy. Toni House, who was then with *The Washington Star*, recalls that her colleague Isabelle Shelton brought Elsie Carper, Fran Lewine, and Eileen Shanahan to join the younger women because they were "veterans of the battle of the balcony." Picketing was fine, Carper told the group, but better to wreck the dinner. And how better to wreck the dinner than by getting big-name people not to go?

The women rented the gym at Mount Vernon College and held a Counter-Gridiron party, a grown-up carnival with booths and celebrity auctioneers. Former Attorney General Elliot L. Richardson autographed copies of his doodles. Dr. Janet Travell, who had been John Kennedy's physician, demonstrated the healthful effects of rocking chairs. Senator Charles Percy spent the evening working as a roving photographer. Two colleagues from Capitol Hill, Edmund Muskie and Walter Mondale, turned up as well. The hit of the evening was Martha Mitchell. For five dollars and the price of the phone call, Mitchell agreed to call whoever you asked her to call for a brief chat as a benefit for the Reporters Committee for Freedom of the Press. After her publicized middle-of-the-night phone calls to Helen Thomas, people wouldn't believe it really was Martha Mitchell on the line; they were sure some friend was playing a joke.

In 1975 the Gridiron Club voted to admit women. Helen Thomas was the first. Fran Lewine followed a year later. Said Thomas, "Once the doors had been opened, I have made it a policy to walk right in. When the National Press Club . . . opened

107

its membership to women, I joined. I also joined Sigma Delta Chi, the formerly all-male journalist society, and when the Gridiron Club . . . invited me in 1975 to become the first woman in its ninety-year history, I did not hesitate."[30]

But the Club had not acted quickly enough to head off a second Counter-Gridiron event, which turned into a celebration instead of a protest. Martha Mitchell made sixty-three phone calls that night, Baltimore City Councilwoman Barbara Mikulski and Sen. Ed Muskie called bingo games, and Gloria Steinem signed pardons for past male chauvinist sins. There was cause to celebrate.

Everyday Indignities

A young woman reporter went off to the Washington bureau of her newspaper early in the 1980s. She was married, and because of his job her husband couldn't accompany her. She agreed to commute on weekends and paid for her weekend trips herself, on the understanding that it was one of the prices of a modern lifestyle. Later she learned that her paper was paying for similar trips for a male reporter who had been sent to the bureau in the middle of the school year before his family could join him. He was commuting home on weekends to see his six-year-old.

That's not all. She had arrived in the bureau to find she had no office, only a desk in the hall. A nonstaff writer based in the bureau, a man, did have an office. When she protested, they didn't move her into an office. They built a wall around her desk.

CHAPTER

8

Stylizing the News

Hard news? Soft news? Where did these terms come from? Their sexual implications fairly leap from the page. Hard news is news about foreign policy, the federal deficit, bank robberies. Historically, men's stuff. The right stuff. Soft news is news about the Four F's—family, food, fashion, and furnishings. Women's stuff. Back of the book. Plays, movies, books. Lifestyle. The things I like to read. And ain't I a woman?

But what could be "harder" than the labyrinthine legal corridors being opened by surrogate parenthood? Isn't covering that covering a family issue? Aren't homeless people on every front page every winter? Don't men eat? Aren't women the ones overwhelmingly impoverished in a country that spends more on guns than on butter or babies? The hard news–soft news distinction is becoming increasingly absurd. Yet it still governs the way some newspaper people distinguish what is important, who should cover it, and who should supervise that coverage.

The evolution of the women's pages into today's feature sections marked a belated recognition that all parts of a newspaper should be prepared for all people, not just for female people or male people. This evolution occurred partly because of social pressures and partly because of economics; newspapers always need to sell ads, and appealing to readers, not offending them, sells ads. To appreciate the transition away from women's pages, one has to understand the origin of that species.

Women were virtually invisible in early newspapers, which carried perhaps a column of women's news. Women had their place, and that place was not in reporting on government, foreign affairs, business, or sports. Their place was in the women's sections that began in the late nineteenth century as newspapers competed vigorously for readers and realized that some of those readers were women.

The initial treatment of news for women was "florid and romantic." Food and fashions were "the chief drawing cards of the woman's page." By the 1890s, "the woman's page was a definite feature in the larger papers," Ishbel Ross said in her encyclopedic *Ladies of the Press*. "It took in clubs, which were just beginning to impinge on the social consciousness; society, which was riding high; and all subjects that were supposed to interest women."[1]

Club news was news. The formation of women's clubs was one of the first efforts women made at collective activity outside their homes. These clubs often aimed at self-improvement or community improvement; the women studied literature, or they became active in prison reform, physical culture, or gardening. The Women's Christian Temperance Union was founded in 1873, and the General Federation of Women's Clubs in 1890. Members worked in settlement houses, campaigned for women's right to vote, and sought improvements in the public schools. Later the clubs rarely produced news, but women had to cover the tedious sessions anyway.

Society news was taken so seriously that for many years virtually all the society editors and reporters for New York newspapers were men. James Gordon Bennett of *The New York Herald* initiated society coverage by sending William H. Attree to a costume ball given by Mr. and Mrs. Henry Brevoort in February 1840.[2] "As time went on and society news became part of any well-conducted newspaper, the job seemed to fall by divine right to the unwanted woman on the staff," Ishbel Ross reported. A woman could best tell not only who was at society parties but what they wore.

Nothing got—and still gets—publishers' attention faster than a mistake in society reporting. A man at the *Herald* made one of the bigger flubs.[3] "Mrs. Stuyvesant Fish gave one of her most gorgeous balls on the same night as a prize fight and the make-up man got the two lists of names confused," Ross wrote. Mrs. Fish "would not believe it was a mistake and raised bedlam about it."

Society editors and writers held great power around the country in their day; some were good journalists, but others simply knew the publisher. Ishbel Ross, herself a cityside reporter, described the society sections in their heyday, the 1930s: "The society page is nearly always an accurate reflection of the community it represents. It may drivel or be discriminating, according to the intelligence of the woman directing it, the local sense of social values, or the policy of a paper. But it is rarely inconsequential, since it is a sound newspaper principle that names make news."[4]

Indeed, years after Edith Thayer retired as the social editor of the little *Lewiston Daily Sun* in Maine, she told Nancy Grape, a political reporter, that she had in no way felt shortchanged by being on the women's pages. "Most people only get their names in the paper three times—when they're born, when they get married, and when they die. I wrote all three of those stories."

Wedding coverage, however, could get out of hand, which frustrated younger reporters. Connie Koenenn was reporting for *The Memphis Commercial-Appeal* in the early 1960s when "the rich planters from the Mississippi Delta would come up and talk to the society editor. They not only wanted their daughters' wedding pictures on the cover of the section, but somehow the notion had gotten around that the upper left-hand corner was most desirable, so they wanted the upper left-hand corner."

Then the wedding itself had to be covered. "You planted yourself behind a potted palm somewhere and wrote down names. Now, I was totally inept at this because I didn't know anybody," Koenenn recalls. "I didn't know why I was frustrated, but after six months I wrote my mother and told her I didn't go to journalism school to cover weddings."

For too long, society news was the main news of the women's sections. Its emphasis on debutante balls and society weddings meant that the life and concerns of the average reader were rarely reflected. Today, society news has a limited place in newspapers. A good society reporter chronicles the power structure. Although this coverage reflects only the tip of the social structure, it is the tip that often controls access to culture in a community, decides which charities advance, and determines which politicians will work successfully with the moneyed interests.

The women who wrote club news and society news, fashion and food, often worked in a section of the newsroom that was separated physically from the rest of the newsroom. Regular news reporters who were women were separated as well. Before World War I, Ishbel Ross and Emma Bugbee, the only female reporters on *The New York Herald-Tribune*, were not seated in the city room but had to work down the hall.

Marie Manning Gasch, who wrote the "Beatrice Fairfax" column for many years, remembered that "when a man was being eased out of his job, or subjected to discipline, the higher-ups had a way of sending him to expiate his crime—real or imaginary—in the Hen Coop. Forcing a man to work in the same room with us was the equivalent of sending a dog to the pound or standing a child in the corner."[5]

Judith Martin, who covered the embassy-party beat for the women's section at *The Washington Post* and later created "Miss Manners" and her arch etiquette tips for achieving "excruciatingly correct behavior," found that editors in the front sections of the paper didn't take seriously any news that wasn't issued formally. However, Martin often got better quotes and more candid explanations about international events informally from diplomats at parties than the same diplomats gave State Department or political reporters working their beats.

Newspapers did not value nontraditional sources; nor did they question government sources as closely as they would after Vietnam and Watergate. For example, in the fall of 1961 John and Jacqueline Kennedy's baby Patrick was born with hyaline membrane disease, which is often fatal. Martin told the desk that she knew the chief pediatric resident at the hospital where the child was being treated, so she was drafted to help on the desk. Her source was virtually next to the incubator.

As deadline approached, Kennedy's press secretary, Pierre Salinger, briefed reporters, telling them that the baby's condition was improving. Eddie Folliard, the *Post* White House reporter, wrote that story. Martin called her source, who said, "No, that's not what we told Salinger. We told him that the downward trend has momentarily stopped." That did not mean that the baby was better. "What time does your paper hit the streets?" the doctor asked. "The baby is going to be dead when the paper hits the street." When Martin told this to the *Post* editors, they ignored the advice, but the doctor was right.

Unspoken, Martin says, was the *Post* editors' idea that not only was the official word right, but that a woman contradicting that word couldn't be right. "It was a combination of sexism and the old way of looking at things."

City editors often ensured that little live news got reported into women's sections, and so they became static, Ishbel Ross wrote. "But where a woman of wide newspaper experience takes hold, wonders can be done with the stepchild of the profession."[6]

Dorothy Jurney, Vivian Castleberry at the *Dallas Times-Herald*, and Marj Paxson at *The Houston Post* and *Houston Chronicle* started remaking women's pages into a different image. Stretching them to better reflect women's lives. Giving them a political bite that men didn't notice because men didn't read them.

Pivotal in this transition, Jurney was born into journalism. Her father owned the newspaper in Michigan City, Indiana; her mother had been one of the first women in the Indiana legislature. After graduating in journalism from Northwestern University in 1930, Jurney confronted bleak employment prospects in the Depression. She went to work for her father's paper, which had a circulation of six thousand in a town some sixty miles from Chicago. Her job was to go up and down Franklin Street and find out who had gone to Chicago for the day, who had company, and what people were doing—to listen to everyday currents. "To do that, I had to get the confidence of people."

Jurney married an engineer and went to Panama, where she got a job in the canal's press office. Not until World War II did Jurney and other women get to show what they could do in big-city papers. Jurney went to work in Washington, D.C., for the copy desk of *The Washington News*, a paper that had virtually no males left "except the physically handicapped and the drunks." She became assistant city editor and then acting city editor. The editor said that he wanted to make her city editor for real, but he didn't think it would work out and so he never did it. Then "he told me he had a young man coming back who had been a writer but not an editor and would I teach him the job? I tried for a month; he wasn't smart, and I got tired of it and quit."

Moving to Florida, Jurney got a job on the copy desk of *The Miami Herald*, then switched to the women's section. Sometime later the city editor's job came open, and Jurney was asked what her ambitions were. Chastened by the experience she had had in

Washington, Jurney replied, "I just want to do the best I can do every day."

"You mean you don't want to be city editor?"

"Why should I even try for that? I'm a woman."

Jurney didn't get the job, but she learned later that she had been seriously considered. "They took my answer to mean I had no ambition. Lee Hills, then in charge in Miami, was open enough to consider me. If I had shown any ambition, who knows?"

Hills put no restraint on Jurney and her women's section. "He made it possible for me to see news out there that others weren't covering." Tackling the fossilized club news, Jurney told the club leaders what really made news. "If they were working on neighborhoods or education, this we could report. But we weren't just going to write that they met and the secretary read the minutes."

She cut down on the brides, too. Her reporters covered blacks to a modest extent, "though this remained largely interviews with black entertainers. I remember our pieces on Lena Horne and Nat King Cole especially. It was a time when they sang in the plush Miami hotels but they weren't allowed to eat or stay there overnight. It was a beginning."

From Miami, Jurney went to the *Detroit Free Press*, where she stayed from 1959 to 1973. She changed the look, philosophy, and level of professionalism of the women's pages. Her feature writers, who included Ellen Goodman and Jean Sharley Taylor, covered everything from the early days of the women's movement and the growth of activities for women in the United Auto Workers to behavior problems and the rising problem of unwed teenage mothers in the black community. During this time Lee Hills, who had meanwhile moved to Detroit, told a new *Free Press* editor that Dorothy Jurney "is our women's editor, and if she were a man, she'd be the executive editor."

Jurney retired in 1975 as assistant managing editor at *The Philadelphia Inquirer*. Well into her 70s, she surveyed the slow movement of women into the top editing jobs and reported her findings in the bulletin of the American Society of Newspaper Editors. She helped with studies analyzing coverage of concern to women and sought financing for a novel set of seminars to

115

bring the day-to-day newspaper gatekeepers into contact with the thinkers who will shape the news in the twenty-first century.

Just as Jurney was revising the approach to news for women in Miami, Marj Paxson was doing the same in Houston in the 1950s. "I tried to see what other women's sections were doing," says Paxson, now retired from publishing Gannett's *Muskogee Daily Phoenix* in Oklahoma, "and I came across *The Miami Herald*. Dorothy Jurney was its editor, and the *Herald* became the leading women's pages in the country."

Like Jurney, Paxson challenged the prominence given to brides in women's pages when she became society editor at *The Houston Post* in 1948. For decades brides were a staple item for society sections, with young—and inevitably white—faces and miles of laces filling the front pages of society sections. Today pictures of brides, if they are run in big-city newspapers at all, are tucked away on a back page. Their weddings are important, but only to families and friends and not to readers as a whole—unless the brides are Madonna or Lady Di.

Paxson took brides off the front page of the *Post* society section. Soon the paper's owner, former Governor William Hobby, called Paxson to ask that she make an exception for the daughter of a friend of his who was about to be married. She said she'd rather not, thank you, sir. He replied that he'd ask his wife, Oveta Culp Hobby, who actually ran the paper. Oveta told Paxson to stick to her new policy.

Elsewhere in Texas, Vivian Castleberry was running the women's section of the *Dallas Times-Herald*. She, too, covered the women's movement and women's issues in the women's page. Castleberry and her reporters "got away with murder because the dumb male editors never bothered to read it," remembers Molly Ivins. "They were writing about birth control. Abortion. But it wasn't considered 'real news.' Even today it isn't. You have to be a moron to miss the crying need for adequate child care, but papers do."

In the 1960s, these women's-page editors and women's-section writers like Elizabeth Shelton of *The Washington Post* and Isabelle Shelton of *The Washington Star* consistently covered questions that affected women's daily lives. (The two Sheltons were not related, but mail for one regularly went to the other.) Women could rarely

116

read about themselves in the front sections of newspapers; they had no identity there because they did not participate heavily in conventional politics. They voted and they licked envelopes, but they weren't running for office in great numbers. The definition of news had not altered sufficiently to include events in which they did participate in the front pages. As a result, coverage of serious women's issues—not just clubs, weddings, and parties—in the women's sections was especially important to giving women a sense of themselves. This wasn't the main purpose of the coverage; serious women's issues were news and belonged in the newspaper. But increased self-awareness was a side-effect.

Women's sections were often the only place where women could prove themselves journalistically. Janet Sanford, now the publisher of the *Visalia Times-Delta* in a flat, prosperous-looking farm community south of Fresno, California, worked as a journalist, married, had children, went to college (in that order), and returned to newspaper work as women's editor at *The Phoenix Gazette* in 1970. "That's when I became more of a career person. The women's movement was in its infancy."

Sanford's new section "had been weddings, bad social columns—good columns can add news—clubs, that is, event-oriented. I changed all that because I'm somebody who has never done what other people do." To learn more, Sanford attended sessions at the American Press Institute. "I can remember what a difference it made in my life. I was exposed to great minds and experienced for the first time a camaraderie with other women journalists. I heard Dorothy Jurney speak there. I met Jennie Buckner, who's now a managing editor at *The San Jose Mercury News*, Nancy Woodhull, who's at Gannett. They had a great group of women sitting on the women's pages because there were no other jobs."

Sanford renamed her section into "Today's Living." It covered social issues and even provided some competition for the newsside, she recalled with pride. "No one was delving into how foster kids were being treated. . . . In 1976 we did stories on breast reconstruction after cancer operations and hit insurance companies for not paying for it. They called it 'cosmetic surgery.' We were hitting trends before they became stories."

Feminist leaders in those days often didn't understand that

117

the only coverage they could count on consistently was in sections such as Sanford's. Sanford recalls the day Gloria Steinem came to town and Sanford assigned herself the interview. Steinem was running on her habitually tight schedule, but finally Sanford got her for a minute.

"Steinem peered over her granny glasses and asked who I was. She said, 'That shows what your paper thinks about women's issues.' That made me think. I mean, newsside hadn't sent a reporter, but at least I was there."

For a time as Steinem, Betty Friedan, and others organized demonstrations and raised issues, newssides did send reporters. The women's movement flared into the front section, even into the front pages. The former women's sections that had once consistently covered those developments were replaced by jazzy new "Style" sections that covered people in the arts and entertainment, trends and trendsetters, and social change as well as society outings.

The new format was an attempt to upgrade the content and increase the readership of what had at too many papers become dowdy—and let's face it, boring—women's sections. The *Los Angeles Times* and *The Washington Post* took the lead. Now "View" and "Style" and "Living" and "Accent" and "Lifestyle" sections form a paper trail across the country.

Many people give *The Washington Post* trailblazing credit, perhaps because it's a visible eastern paper. But the *Los Angeles Times* was developing a comparable section at the same time, according to David Laventhol, who was the assistant managing editor delegated to supervise the changeover at the *Post*. "I know that because as part of my development effort, I read the *Times*, visited Times Mirror Square, spent considerable time with [editor] Nick Williams and others, and stole a lot of ideas."[7]

In the late 1960s, *Post* editor Ben Bradlee became unhappy with the old "For and About Women" section and wanted broader-based coverage. Bradlee, who came from a news-magazine background, wanted a section that resembled the "back-of-the-book" coverage that *Newsweek* and *Time* gave the arts, changing living styles, and the private lives of the people whose public activities were reported in the front section. Bradlee wrote his ideas down on one page, gave it to Laventhol, and said, "Look into this."

So Laventhol, who later headed *Newsday* and then Times Mirror, visited Dorothy Jurney in Detroit, went to the *Chicago Tribune,* and talked to the editors at the *Los Angeles Times.* He realized that a separate section for women implied that other sections were for men and not women, and was an anachronism in the modern world. "Television forced newspapers to look more closely at what they were doing" and to focus on more than hard news, he added. "The only surprising thing is that it took so long after the start of television to do it." The "Style" section debuted on January 6, 1969.

"Style" 's purposes were twofold, says Ben Bradlee: "First, to treat women as people and not as appendages to men, and second, to make the paper better organized." Loosely defined, that meant that you put in one section "what people do in their nonprofessional lives"—tend to families, go to the movies, and read books. The *Post,* unlike the *Los Angeles Times,* prints its "Style" section at night with the run of the paper. "If there is any contribution of the *Post* to twentieth-century journalism," Bradlee says, "it's the 'Style' section and the fact of its printing as part of the paper. That makes it timely and not 'just' a feature section."

The New York Times started its transition in the late 1960s and completed it only in the mid-1970s, when it established five rotating sections, one for each day of the week. Two of those sections—"Living" and "Home"—were handled by the lifestyle writers and editors. A.M. Rosenthal, executive editor at the time, says the decision to have five special sections was made strictly for business reasons. "We weren't going after new readers; we were trying to get readers to read every day. A newspaper needs to make money, and we couldn't afford to stay the same."

Well before these sections debuted, the *Times* was featuring the work of two women with distinctly different styles, Charlotte Curtis and Judy Klemesrud. Curtis wrote biting descriptions of the lives of the rich and famous, who often seemed flattered instead of embarrassed by the wickedly meticulous details that laced the stories. And Klemesrud not only etched quick and finely delineated profiles of the creative, she also found news where it had not been discovered before.

Before Charlotte Curtis's arrival in New York, Eugenia Sheppard of the rival *New York Herald-Tribune* had dominated the wom-

119

en's daily press scene. She was "the Boswell of pop fashion society," Marylin Bender, now a *New York Times* editor, wrote in *The Beautiful People*. Sheppard and John Fairbanks of *Women's Wear Daily* "created a new kind of celebrity, the fashion socialite," Bender said. "They instigated a merger of fashion and social gossip that spread like an epidemic through the press, even to supposedly liberal or middle-highbrow publications."[8]

A graduate of Bryn Mawr College and former society editor of *The Columbus Dispatch*, Sheppard joined the *Herald-Tribune* in 1940. She became women's feature editor in 1949 and remade her section with elegant typography and spacious fashion layouts. "No New York paper ran more fashion copy," said *Herald-Tribune* biographer Richard Kluger. Hers was a slick, "unashamedly elitist" section, never more so than in her "Inside Fashion" column begun in 1956, which portrayed the narcissistic love of clothes and parties among the rich whom she made famous.[9]

"Most papers covered fashion by press release and slavish devotion to visiting designers," Bender said in an interview years after she had written her book. "*The New York Times* didn't do that. Its coverage was honorable but boring." This tedium departed upon the arrival of Elizabeth Penrose Howkins in 1955. "She had magazine savvy and a tremendous respect for good writing. . . . She raised the esteem of the department." Convinced that the issues her section handled deserved the same competence the *Times* accorded Broadway and the arts, Howkins hired Craig Claiborne as food editor and brought in Gloria Emerson, Nan Robertson, and Marylin Bender as writers.

It was onto this stage that Charlotte Curtis, a Vassar alumna and former *Columbus Citizen* society editor, stepped in 1961. Clifton Daniel, then an assistant managing editor at the *Times*, was enamored of society columns. He read *Women's Wear Daily* and Eugenia Sheppard. "I think rich people are fascinating," he told *Times* reporters, and in 1963 he sent Curtis off to cover society, a beat she approached as a social historian.[10]

Curtis piled "pertinent and impertinent data" into stories, Bender recalls. She covered a West Point wedding and detailed how many flowers there were and what happened to virtually every drop of champagne. Her beat took her from Palm Beach to Paris, Southampton to San Francisco. She covered the 1970 cocktail party that Leonard Bernstein had for the Black Panthers, infuriating partygoers by writing exactly what they said.

In 1965 Howkins retired and Curtis became women's news editor; her title was changed to family/style editor in 1971. "Her big interest was American politics," says Bender. "She faced the whole question of whether politics should be in a women's section. It never had been. She thought that was ridiculous." Just as society had become sociology in her hands, other territories were opened —feminism, civil rights, politics—to be covered as news of the day in her section. "As time went on, there were no holds barred," Bender says. "If abortion was brewing, abortion was what we did. It may have been the *Post* that did 'Style,' but the spadework of reporting and coverage was the *Times*. I want us to get credit for that."

Curtis became editor of the *Times* op-ed page in 1974. As associate editor, hers was the first woman's name on the *Times*'s masthead. She died of cancer at 58 in April 1987. "She was absolutely passionate about news. Even in her last letter, she was offering a story idea," Bender said a few weeks after Curtis died. "The sad thing is, the only person who could have written it was her."

Judy Klemesrud, a graduate of the University of Iowa and the Columbia School of Journalism, was a *New York Times* reporter for nineteen years after starting her career at *The Chicago Daily News*. She wrote about the self-help health movement, the increasing participation of women in the work force, adoptions by single women, and teenage pregnancy and drug addiction. Angela Dodson, also of the *Times*, says, "I recently did a piece on displaced homemakers"—women struggling to get back on their feet after their husbands die or divorce them, leaving them with little means of support and less hope. "They credit Judy Klemesrud with discovering that story. It is the kind of issue that is almost untouched by male hands."

Klemesrud also did celebrity profiles. They became so well known that she once figured in a *New Yorker* cartoon. A sloppy-looking couple is sitting on the front porch. The woman says to her husband, "Judy Klemesrud called. She had the wrong number."

"She is one of the people we can say thank you to," said Betty Friedan after Klemesrud died of breast cancer at 46 in October

121

1985.[11] One of the last stories she covered was the National Organization for Women convention in New Orleans.

Meanwhile, on the West Coast, the *Los Angeles Times* had started "View" in July 1970 to provide wider feature coverage of a city and a region that were emerging as trendsetters. James Bellows, then associate editor, was trying to revitalize feature writing throughout the paper. His wife, Maggie Savoy, edited the "View" section briefly before her death in late 1970. Jean Taylor succeeded her in 1971 after working in Phoenix at *The Arizona Republic* as women's editor and associate editor.

When Taylor arrived at the *Times*, the "View" section had only three full-time writers and one part-time writer. She hired Bella Stumbo, one of the most observant writers ever to work at the *Times*. Stumbo did the kind of articles that "View" staked out to illustrate life in Los Angeles, focusing, for example, on barrio women and on people whose lives rarely appeared in newspapers but who were the soul of the changing city.

"We took the name 'View' very literally," Taylor says. "We were using the section as a mirror for society."

"View" actively sought male readership. "Women had such low esteem of what women did, so we artificially had to put esteem into women's sections by bringing men in, by running stories all people would be interested in," by hiring male writers like Michael Seiler and Charles Powers. "We did it by shortening stories, taking out lesser stories. We eliminated automatic author interviews of books that aren't any good." It was a fine line to walk. "Every time I felt we were demeaning news of women, I would pull back," Taylor adds.

Taylor moved up the masthead to associate editor in charge not only of "View" but arts, real estate, food, travel, television, and book coverage in 1975. Like some other editors, Taylor worries that feature sections in general may be losing their way, "not attempting to understand society. They may have gone too far in losing the unique women's perspective. . . . We have to reevaluate whether in attempts to bring honor and equality to women's pages, we may have forgotten there are real, genuine different interests of women. We need to say more often that it is valid that something a large bloc of our readers are concerned about is important. We don't have to apologize anymore."

The Washington Post faced a similar situation. "In the rush not to be 'For and About Women,' " says Shelby Coffey, "Style" editor for six years, "we were afraid we were overlooking areas of family life of concern to both men and women." During his tenure at "Style," the *Post* added "Style Plus." Every day the fifth page of the "Style" section carries articles about careers, personal finance, family questions, or "how to find whatever, how to enjoy ———, how to deal with ———."

"After all that ferment in the late 1960s, I am coming to think that these sections are now so general that they don't quite know what they are," says Scott McGehee, formerly a women's-page editor and now a Knight-Ridder executive. "They've reached a plateau, and it's time for more evolution," she adds.

So convinced was McGehee of the need to make the sections more relevant, she brought together at corporate headquarters not only the feature editors at Knight-Ridder but the very top editors as well "to get them to think about keeping these sections moving." She reports that both groups liked the exchange—the top editors because they needed to focus on those sections and the feature editors because they got their bosses' attention more directly than ever.

Women's sections suffered in the past because although they were often headed by women, what they were to cover was often defined by men. At some of her former papers, Elizabeth Rhodes of *The Seattle Times* found that the editors "would allow the leash to be extended to cover social issues as long as we did the clubs and teas. The editors' wives wanted that. Now women editors of lifestyle sections are starting to write their own rules. We are defining ourselves."

The Seattle Times's "Scene" section has a one-page written statement about its philosophy. In part, it reads, "If we could freeze a moment in the life of our area, and then begin writing about what we see in that scene, we would write about people, what they're doing and why they're doing it. . . . We write about the basics of people's daily lives—as basic as food, clothing and shelter. But we also write about other things people care about: their relationships, their health, their community, their time at work or play, the people around them, what they read, the things that make them laugh and cry. We bring home the news—whether

123

the threat of nuclear destruction or the latest toy—by telling how it affects the people who live here."

News about women has not been the only casualty of stylizing the news. Women editors have been pushed out of the only positions of authority they had. For example, the creation of the "Style" section at the *Post* cost women four jobs in two years, according to a 1972 memo from a group that went on to file a sex-discrimination complaint. "There has been no compensating hiring of women on the national, metropolitan, foreign, sports and financial staffs."[12]

Individual women have paid a price. Marj Paxson was a victim twice, once at *The St. Petersburg Times* and once at *The Philadelphia Bulletin.* "I still have not quite forgiven women's movement activists for turning against women editors," Paxson said.[13] "In the early days of the movement in the 1960s, most substantive newspaper coverage of the movement was on the women's pages. I considered myself a part of the movement and so did many other women's editors I knew across the country.

"But the activists wanted the movement news off our pages, and in their eyes we women's editors were traitors. When editors responded by changing women's sections to general interest feature sections, women's editors paid the price. We were not considered capable of directing this new kind of feature section. That was man's work."

There was irony involved. At *The St. Petersburg Times*, Paxson ended up the number-three person in the new section. Four months after the changeover, the *Times* was notified that she had won a Penney-Missouri award for general excellence—in the defunct women's pages. Six weeks after she went to Columbia, Missouri, to accept that award, she was fired. Paxson later became women's editor of *The Philadelphia Bulletin.* There the paper abolished its women's section for a "Focus" section with a male editor. Paxson stayed on, working off her frustration by pulling weeds in her garden, until she left to become a Gannett news executive and ultimately a publisher.

Some of the stories historically covered by women's sections have become institutionalized as legitimate front-section news at some papers. Women getting into political office. Women going into space. Corporations using their child-care arrangements as a recruiting tool. Child abuse. Poverty among women. But at other papers, where the decision-making editors are mostly men, it is never a sure thing that such a story will make the front section.

Lifestyle editors are confronted with a dilemma. "I'm constantly getting messages from the women who are assistant city editors that they can't muster up any interest in their own section in covering some story or event, and will my section cover it?" one female editor says. "I know it's important and it should be covered. But it belongs in the front section or the city section, not my section. I have my own mission. Should I turn my section back into a ghetto of women's news?"

The answer will come only when newspapers make a clearer definition of what should be covered in their feature sections and a firm commitment to covering a broader range of news throughout the paper. That broader range, in turn, may only emerge with more women in positions of authority throughout the paper to ensure that these stories are not just reported but also printed.

Everyday Indignities

When Judith Martin was covering White House and diplomatic parties for *The Washington Post* in the 1960s, she was instructed always to fill in the national desk if anything of substance was said.

One night President Johnson was dancing with Martin and told her, "I may have started World War III last night."

" 'Oh? How?' I said in my best party-reporter voice," Martin recounts. Johnson replied that he had bombed North Vietnam the day before. Another time, after Johnson had announced he wasn't running again, he had an interview with several women reporters after a party and told them he'd never really wanted to be President or Vice President.

Martin thus had a source at the top. One night, as she dropped off another solid item at the desk, one of the men said to the other, "Hmm, if that's true, we ought to put a reporter on it."

CHAPTER

9

Political Crossroads

A t the 1972 Democratic Party convention in Miami, women tried at the last minute to win the Democratic vice-presidential nomination for Texas Lieutenant Governor Frances Farenthold. To escape the press, they plotted their strategy in a women's restroom. It was commentary on women's political and journalistic standing that there were so few of them that they all fit in the restroom and that there were so few women covering the convention who could have followed them.

In 1984 women constituted half the delegates to the Democratic Convention in San Francisco, and a woman was selected to run for Vice President by the Party's nominee. Scores of women reported the event for major newspapers, magazines, and television. Political coverage was no longer the exclusive property of the good ol' boys and the Irish boyos. Women still rarely wrote the biggest political stories—the main convention wrapup, telling who got the nomination, or the election-night story, headlining who won. But one of the last male bastions had clearly started falling.

Several roads led to San Francisco. In the beginning there were women who were politically active—holding meetings, trying to redefine issues, raising money for women candidates, running for office, moving themselves forward in both the Democratic and Republican parties. There were also women at home and women at work who were starting to ask their elected representatives to pay more attention to their concerns about nuclear war, educational opportunities, equal pay, day care, parental leave, pension reform, and wife beating. And finally there were women who had been moving into American newsrooms in rising numbers who insisted on covering political parties instead of debutante parties and who were learning the names of the female political players. After running parallel for a decade and more, these women's paths crossed at the San Francisco Convention and, to a far lesser extent, at the Republican Convention in Dallas a month later.

Women were not breaking completely new ground in the 1970s and 1980s. Exceptional women had been covering politics for decades. Dorothy Thompson's political influence played a role in the 1940 presidential campaign. Mary Ellen Leary started covering politics while the male reporters were away at war and stayed on the job after the war as one of the first women to cover politics in California. Doris Fleeson reported on politics for forty years. Mary McGrory broke into the political-reporting ranks in the mid-1950s and went on to win a Pulitzer Prize. Sarah McClendon has plagued presidents with her pointed questions for decades. But it was no accident that Timothy Crouse titled his book on campaign coverage *The Boys on the Bus*. For a time there seemed to be more women running for office and running campaigns than covering them.

Politics, as it has traditionally been covered, involves individual contests to win the power to govern and then the victor's attempts to master the art of governing itself. But politics also concerns the reordering of social forces—the swing of the pendulum between the ins and the outs, between liberals and conservatives, between blacks and whites, between men and women. Women approached political writing from both these directions. One group of reporters provided the earliest coverage of the political arm of the women's movement. Others followed the pioneering steps of Fleeson and McGrory and insisted to their editors that their reporting experience prepared them for covering politics.

The men on the desk who decided what stories appeared in American newspapers played the early protests of the women's movement strictly for laughs. When women marched for equal rights in New York City on August 26, 1970, the New York *Daily News* headlined, "GALS UNBUTTON THEIR LIB." In hostile hands, the catch phrase "women's liberation" became derogatory. Few

128

women thereafter wanted to be identified as "women's libbers" or even as "feminists." To some, the protesters were "girls"—that's what one AP story on the demonstration at the 1968 Miss America Pageant called the women who dumped bras, girdles, and other items into a trash can to show their objection to the cult of beauty. Some of the early protests were easy to poke fun at. They were flamboyant. It took adventurous, nervy, noisy women to take to the streets, wave placards, and sit in at their bosses' offices or demand admission to a men's bar.

If you relied on newspapers to shape your perceptions in those days, you would think that few women cared about politics; it was the unusual woman who ran for office or voted on grounds any different from her husband's. Few women, if newspaper accounts reflected society, were in business, and few cared about anything more than home and hearth. Women were segregated into the women's pages as employees, as news subjects, and as readers.

But in Washington and elsewhere, a few women who were straight-news reporters and women's-section reporters saw the genesis of a story. They had followed the reports of the presidential commission on the status of women. Even if they had not covered it, they were aware of the formation of the National Organization for Women, outgrowth of that presidential commission, in 1966.

A few of them had covered the founding meeting of the National Women's Political Caucus. And a dramatic meeting it was. The women wanted to help elect more women and win the appointments of more women to government jobs. The session threatened to degenerate into partisan squabbling until Fannie Lou Hamer, the Mississippi civil rights leader, spoke. In the same booming voice that had seared the conscience of the 1964 Democratic Convention, Hamer told the women that they should be ashamed of themselves. She insisted that they work together; black women had fought too hard and endured too much brutality to get the vote to see their efforts count for nothing.

Women reporters—some, not all—understood what the women's movement was saying. They had seen their own attempts to join the National Press Club thwarted just because they were women even though they had professional qualifications as good as—sometimes better than—men who could become members. They juggled family and work. They felt that sometimes they weren't taken seriously by the men they loved or by the men with whom they worked. They saw that sometimes they were paid less than the men around them who covered the same hearings, worked the same hours, came from the same backgrounds.

Initial coverage of the political arm of the women's movement coalesced behind the passage of the Equal Rights Amendment and the fight for its ratification. Sara Fritz of UPI kept tabs on the amendment, and bureaus had standing orders to feed her information as each legislature took it up. Connie Koenenn, then with *The Arizona Republic*, covered the first legislative rejection of ERA. That debate made her aware early on of resistance to the women's movement, which would emerge full blown less than a decade later when conservatives swept Ronald Reagan to the Republican nomination and to the presidency.

As women belatedly mobilized to try to win ERA ratification, they also started to run for office in greater numbers than ever. New to political candidacy, they faced problems in raising money, gaining credibility, and learning political skills. They held conferences, exchanged ideas, trained themselves—and talked to women reporters, who went to their meetings and built their own networks of sources. Covering the National Women's Political Caucus, the National Organization for Women, and women's campaigns was the only way I could get into political coverage. Male reporters wrote all the key campaign stories on male candidates at the Newhouse Washington bureau, and politics was the only language my bureau chief understood.

Women reporters around the country (and David Behrens at *Newsday*) covered the movement in addition to education or religion or whatever else they did. But the reporters in Washington were pivotal because they were at the seat of political power and because they worked for news organizations with power. They included Eileen Shanahan, then with *The New York Times*; Isabelle Shelton of *The Washington Star*; Frances Lewine and Peg Simpson, both then with the Associated Press; Sara Fritz, then with UPI; Marlene Cimons of the *Los Angeles Times*; and Barbara Katz, then with *The National Journal*.

Women in Washington asked questions that Presidents weren't

expecting. In 1969 at his second news conference, President Nixon was asked by columnist Vera Glaser of the North American Newspaper Alliance "whether we can expect a more equitable recognition of women's abilities or are we going to remain a lost sex?" Out of two hundred top-level federal appointments, only three had been women, she said. A startled Nixon pledged to name more. Glaser's question and the reaction to it caused her editor in New York to ask her to write a five-part series about court decisions affecting women, their lack of economic and political power, and the groups emerging to seek improvement in women's status.[1]

At a televised news conference a few years later, AP's Fran Lewine asked President Ford if he agreed with his administration's guidelines urging federal officials not to patronize segregated facilities. He said he did. Then Lewine asked why he played golf every week at the Burning Tree Country Club, which still refused to admit women. Some of Lewine's editors were upset that the question was asked, and Ford's press secretary Ronald Nessen later wrote that her question was "the worst misuse of a question at a presidential news conference to advocate a personal point of view." It was a valid question; it was simply Nessen's problem that he could not distinguish between a reporter's personal point of view and her professional responsibility to raise questions.

Covering the women's movement required converting the vague unease among women and their sense of coming social change into the kind of hard realities that could be reported. Women were holding consciousness-raising sessions around the country—a fancy term for baring their souls, fumbling for answers or even the right questions, and learning that they were not alone in their quest. Women who were reporters knew what was going on, knew what the women were saying, and said some of it themselves.

But there was no conventional peg for a news story. In journalism there has to be an occurrence; something has to have happened. Consciousness-raising belonged in magazine articles. It was like something out of Marilyn French's fiction. You have not sold your story if all you can tell an editor is that you have a feature on women complaining about their husbands not taking out the garbage or how they feel like incomplete people because their

131

work is not valued. This inability to visualize the story, to cover an event, David Broder said, made much of the press corps miss the beginning of this social revolution.

Yet a handful of female reporters did see the story—and covering the political aspect of the movement gave them candidates to interview, fund-raising reports to review, campaign efforts to assess. Politics involves power; it is a framework male editors understand. "I think that's the reason I got the time I got to write a piece on the women in the legal profession pegged on . . . two Supreme Court appointments" that were pending, Eileen Shanahan says. "Power is recognized. Who's coming into positions of power through the elective process or through appointments" is a story, no matter who the people are.

Women in politics were not only talking about credit discrimination, child care, rape reform, and affirmative action; they were also talking about traditional political issues in terms people could understand. Barbara Mikulski, campaigning for the Baltimore city council and then the U.S. Congress, talked about the cost of feeding a family, the difficulty of finding a steady job, the scarcity of housing, the need for blacks and white ethnics to stop fighting for pieces of the pie and start demanding an interest in the bakery. Mikulski, Pat Schroeder of Colorado, and Bella Abzug were good copy. It was Schroeder, after all, who first called Ronald Reagan the Teflon President. These women raised issues that were getting in the papers.

To cover the rest of the movement beyond politics and legislation, reporters had to stretch, to talk to people who weren't usually interviewed. They had to delve into shifting roles in the workplace, at school, and in the home—the ultimate coverage of shifts in power that is the soul and substance of politics. These were the hardest stories to do, but they were often the best because they touched people's daily lives. Women who were reporters could find these stories because they were also living them. For example, her ability to translate statistics into real people and national events into real concerns with which people can identify has made Ellen Goodman's success as a columnist.

As Peg Simpson recalled, there was constant tension between editors and reporters over what should be covered and how. Even though the women's movement story "became progressively better and led in directions unforeseen a decade before," many editors "still did not recognize its significance, and as a result, many of the benchmarks of change in the 1960s and 1970s were ignored —even by the self-assigned specialists," Simpson said.[2] Among the missed milestones were Supreme Court rulings that struck down protective legislation that had kept women out of better-paying jobs. Few reporters or editors took seriously the addition of sex discrimination to the 1964 Civil Rights Act—a move that opponents of the bill had made to try to kill the measure.

Building their contacts and seeking new material for stories, women kept reporting on political conferences held by the National Women's Political Caucus, by NOW, and by the LBJ School at the University of Texas. With these meetings and these stories as a backdrop, women then started reporting the preparations for the 1977 National Women's Conference in Houston, a government-backed meeting that could never have happened a decade later. The media stars of the women's movement—Bella Abzug, Gloria Steinem, and Betty Friedan—worked alongside women from Arkansas and California, from Indian reservations and black communities, and from college campuses and hospital nursing stations, hammering out resolutions to try to set women's agenda. Across town, Phyllis Schlafly and Nellie Gray and other stars of right-wing, antiabortion groups held their own sessions.

Grace Lichtenstein, a fiery, no-nonsense reporter at *The New York Times*, knew the Houston meeting would be hot stuff, and she wanted to cover it. She had covered the movement from its earliest days until "more and more stories about women were in the news." Her request was turned down. "I was too involved, they said. I went from a period when I asked for and got assignments because nobody else thought it was news in 1970 to 1977 when it clearly was national news and I was refused. It was Catch-22." Instead, the *Times* sent Judy Klemesrud and Anna Quindlen.

Some feminists remained prickly about women reporters who wrote stories critical of other women. When Midge Costanza was eased out of her job as a White House liaison official in the Carter Administration, recalled Peg Simpson, "I wrote that she was fired not because she opposed Carter's politics limiting federal funds for abortions for poor women nor because she criticized Carter's friend Bert Lance, but because she was not competent to do her job." Simpson was told bluntly by leading feminists that she shouldn't have written that story even if it was true. Likewise, Marlene Cimons of the *Los Angeles Times* drew feminist criticism when she wrote about the clumsy tactics of some West Coast women lobbying Congress for an extension of the ERA deadline.[3]

Newspapers started to pay more attention to women in the work force when it became clear that their move from the carpool to the labor pool was not going to go into reverse. Government forecasters predicted that two out of three new jobs in the decade to come would be filled by women. Stories written by men and women alike on changing family styles, on the impact of women's move into the workplace on the fast-food and grocery businesses, and on the problems of single parents started to appear more regularly in the front sections of newspapers previously dominated by Presidents and international affairs. Because shifts in the work force obviously affect business and what affects business affects *The Wall Street Journal*, that newspaper has given front-page coverage to these trends. At virtually all newspapers, congressional coverage started to include abortion debates, bills on insurance discrimination, and maneuvering around attempts to pass the Equal Rights Amendment.

After the 1982 election, women's rights advocates such as Eleanor Smeal pointed to women's votes as the deciding factor in gubernatorial elections in Texas, New York, and Michigan. The "gender gap" that women activists had seen developing while lobbying state legislatures to ratify the ERA was now documentable in hard political numbers and made the front pages. Not only was Ellen Goodman writing about it now; so were David Broder at *The Washington Post*, who had been among the very first male political writers to see women as a force to cover, and Adam Clymer of *The New York Times*. The women's movement was now truly news—in editors' eyes as well as in the eyes of the women involved—because it could give people votes or take them away.

The parallel paths of women moving into politics and women moving into the press started to turn and merge. In 1983 some women formed to press for the selection of a woman vice-presidential nominee at the 1984 Democratic Convention. In November 1983 the *Los Angeles Times* "View" section carried a story and picture spread on possible women vice-presidential candidates; it was reported by two women and edited by a third. The next spring, the story moved to the front pages. The top editors "thought it was a nice story in a political year," said Jane O'Reilly of *Time*, who with Judy Mann of *The Washington Post* had been among the earliest writers to suggest the possibility of a woman on the ticket. "They loved the idea of a woman candidate but were totally baffled when the concept turned out to be a real woman."[4]

Editors remained skeptical when NOW president Judy Goldsmith had lunch at the *Los Angeles Times* in May 1984 and predicted that there was an 80–20 chance a woman would be on the ticket. At the same time, there was an imperceptible shift among the press that said that a woman on the ticket was a reasonable, serious political possibility. Ann Lewis, then the Democratic Party's shrewd political director, called that shift alone a victory. "Politicians are no longer debating whether to nominate a woman but when," Lewis told me for a *Los Angeles Times* article.[5] Asked whether having a woman on the ticket could be construed as mere tokenism, Lewis shot back: "Your token is my pioneer."

Throughout the 1970s, women in the press had been meeting women in political campaigns. In the 1980s the women in politics were running for office themselves, or they were working for governors, rising in political-party hierarchies, lobbying for major labor unions, and running voter registration drives. A small group of them convinced Geraldine Ferraro to let herself be mentioned as a potential vice-presidential candidate. They helped transform that speculation into a nomination. This group—known as Team A—met with Ferraro one night over Chinese take-out food in Joan McLean's Washington apartment, and they rigged the fortune cookies so that Ferraro couldn't miss their point. "You will win big in '84," read the one Ferraro got. "You will meet a man in San Francisco and travel with him," read another.[6]

Once Walter Mondale was clearly the Democratic frontrunner, newspapers and politicians alike turned their focus on the second spot, and women appeared on the front pages. San Francisco Mayor Dianne Feinstein went to Minnesota, where Mondale was interviewing potential running mates. Martha Layne Collins of Kentucky, then the nation's only woman governor, went to Minnesota. Ferraro went to Minnesota. They were on the front page. Mondale went to Miami to address the NOW convention.

That was on the front page; so was the story that NOW insisted Mondale name a woman and threatened that if he didn't, women delegates would lead a floor fight in San Francisco. Criticism of NOW's stand was on the front page. Women leaders such as New York City Council President Carol Bellamy and Rep. Barbara Mikulski went to Minnesota and told Mondale of the role women had played in their campaigns. Their visit made the front page.

Then Mondale picked Ferraro. Magazine covers hailed a "historic choice." Newspaper headlines blared it. And women reporters went off to the Convention with sources that were now valuable because they had made political news that the male editors understood. The years of going to conferences, of doing the how-politics-is-different-for-women stories paid off. For example, I had not been scheduled to help cover the convention. After Mondale picked Ferraro, that changed. My boss said to me, "You're the only one on the staff who knows those people." (Not quite accurate—Sara Fritz, who was also on the Convention team, did, and Marlene Cimons, who wasn't, knew them, too.) I wrote a long background piece on the political chain that had led from 1972 to 1984 and two op-ed page pieces, one on why the nomination meant what it did to women no matter what else happened. The other was on growing discontent among black women that they were continually left out of consideration for anything resembling power.

Among the men, Bruce Morton of CBS saw what was happening. One evening before the Convention began in San Francisco, he told his television audience that he had seen a small group of women, a mix of seasoned politicians and veteran reporters, joyously greeting one another in their excitement over the Ferraro nomination. He didn't know what it meant, Morton said, but it was clear that it meant something and that it might be what San Francisco was all about.

It was as if there were two Democratic conventions. Male reporters hopped around tracking the proposal that Bert Lance (and everybody remembers Bert Lance) would be chosen national chairman, to court the South. They chased that story long after it died. Editors sought copy on demonstrations that drew less attention in blasé San Francisco than had the arrival of the Olympic torch. They focused on potential platform fights. One male

136

reporter talking to Jane O'Reilly of *Time* said he'd just written a column about how bored everyone was.

"Bored? Who have you talked to?" O'Reilly roared back. "Have you talked to any women?"

Reporters assigned to the Ferraro plane in the early winging-it days tended to be women. Some had covered her before. Some protested that they didn't want to cover a candidate just because they were women. Women's objectivity was tested by the Ferraro candidacy, just as black reporters faced objectivity tests in covering the Rev. Jesse Jackson. It is legitimate to ask any journalist how he or she separates his or her own identity from the subject being covered. But that question was now being posed about whole categories of reporters, categories that were not in power in the newsroom. Black reporters, after all, were hardly uniformly enamored of Jesse Jackson, just as many women viewed their coverage of Ferraro as strictly that: coverage, not part of a personal crusade. As Peg Simpson of Hearst newspapers told Eleanor Randolph of *The Washington Post*, "Can a woman cover Geraldine Ferraro fairly? We can cover her as fairly as all those white male reporters have covered their white male candidates all these years."[7]

"We've all covered stories where our hearts were involved—stories about refugees, hostages, plane crashes—the key is not to let that stand in the way of what's really going on," added Ellen Hume of *The Wall Street Journal*.

Initial coverage of the Ferraro candidacy had all the nervousness of a couple on its first date: nobody knew quite how to handle this new person on their front pages. Ferraro campaigned in Mississippi where agriculture commissioner Jim Buck Ross talked to her about the state's new crop, blueberries. Ferraro said they grew wild on her Fire Island property. "You grow blueberries?" Ross asked. "Can you bake a blueberry muffin?"

"Sure can," Ferraro replied. "Can you?"

"Down here in Mississippi, the men don't cook."

Had Ferraro offended the southern vote? Should Mondale go through a door first? Should the candidates kiss or shake hands when they met? Was Ferraro a livelier candidate than Mondale? Ferraro flipped off a kidding comment about Italian husbands, and that buzzed through the papers. Questions about her congressional campaign reports, her family finances, and her husband

137

John Zaccaro's business dealings soon wiped sexism off the front pages and reminded the press that this was a real candidate with a real background to report. For better or worse for the Mondale-Ferraro ticket, press coverage of the rest of the campaign centered on their credibility and their ability and on issues like disarmament and the deficit.

Ferraro finally became "just a candidate" by the end of the summer, Peter Boyer wrote in *The Washington Journalism Review*. "But to get there, she had to live through a sort of instant processing by the press—first, the lionization, then its reverse, scandal. Both phases, it could be argued, were excessive, and both, probably inevitable."[8]

Because of the questions about the Ferraro-Zaccaro finances, about subsequent investigations concerning John Zaccaro, and about Mafia ties that the press unfailingly asks anyone of Italian heritage, there is no way of knowing based on the Ferraro affair how the press would have treated a woman candidate for a top office strictly as a woman running for that office. Questions of ethics and ethnicity will eternally cloud assessments of 1984. The fact that the media did ultimately treat Ferraro more as a candidate than as a woman may mean the transition is under way.

In her book Ferraro offered her own view. "The real test of my candidacy will come when the next woman runs for national office. Only then will we know if she, too, is going to be judged by a standard different from that used for her male opponents; if she, too, is going to have to be better in order to be judged equal. It will be interesting to see what the press will do to her on foreign policy. Was my siege peculiar to me because I was a three-term member of Congress—or because I was a woman? It will also be interesting to see how the spouse of the next female candidate will be treated."[9]

Ferraro's candidacy raised a question of newspaper style that women reporters had been fighting for years. Ferraro was married to John Zaccaro. She used the name Ferraro. Calling her Miss Ferraro did not accurately reflect her marital status. Calling her Mrs. Zaccaro did not reflect her professional preference.

For years, Eileen Shanahan, Peg Simpson, and Sara Fritz, among others, had lobbied diligently for stylebook changes to avoid such problems and to reduce belittling coverage of women.

They wanted newspapers and wire services to tell their reporters not to describe clothing, hairstyles, or family status in situations where the same information would not be included if the subject were a man. This group, all members of the Washington Press Club, failed initially to convince the AP and UPI to drop titles such as Mrs., Miss, and Ms., and in the case of *The New York Times*, even Mr. The negotiations on this point were strained; AP management was especially reluctant to be "forcing down the throats of editors something they don't want," although Knight-Ridder, Gannett, and even the conservative Copley News Service dropped the titles, Fritz recalled.[10]

Newspapers' insistence on using anachronistic titles often meant that reporters had to scramble to find out a woman's marital status even when it had no bearing on the story. Today it seems a petty annoyance, but sometimes asking a woman her marital status to meet the requirement meant that reporters asked one less question of substance; sometimes the question so annoyed the woman being asked that she wouldn't answer the question—or any others. And as Fritz pointed out, the policy led to such designations as "Miss Pat Carbine, editor of *Ms.* magazine."

Under rules existing then, Ferraro would have been identified as either Miss Ferraro or Mrs. Zaccaro. Neither was right in the context. So, quietly during the week before Labor Day, UPI advised editors that with the Ferraro nomination, "serious questions again have arisen over use of courtesy titles for women in news stories." Editors whose papers had largely stopped using the titles had been asking UPI to drop them, too. It was a burden to comb through all the wire stories to eliminate the designations, especially in an era when stories could otherwise go directly into print through computers. As a result, UPI agreed to drop the titles, too.

Once Ferraro was on the Democratic ticket, women working on other stories on women found far more receptivity, albeit fleeting, from their editors than they had found only months before. Stories about congressional passage of pension reform and child-support legislation made the front pages. The *Los Angeles Times* gave ten days of front-page play to a long-planned series on women in the workplace, edited by the only woman in a managerial position on the national desk. *The New York Times* ran a front-page series on day care. These stories had greater impact because readers saw elsewhere on those front pages articles about a woman running for office who was raising these issues. Women reporters also had their judgment validated that a woman would play a key role at the Democratic Convention and a woman might be nominated.

The parallel lines had met. Although the Mondale-Ferraro ticket lost, many politicians felt that despite the financial problems that dogged Ferraro during the campaign, she had not wilted under pressure and that she had made political candidacies for women more credible. Some of the women who had covered her campaign now joined the political rotation on their papers, trailing other candidates as well. Some moved into White House reporting afterward; others to covering Congress. When major tax legislation moved through Congress over the next two years, more women were there covering it every step of the way.

Newspaper editors and TV news producers became aware, Ferraro herself wrote, that "the majority of their women reporters were still automatically hired in 'light' news areas and allowed to have no political experience. . . . Covering gardening and cooking, and documenting new forms of 'relationships,' may be interesting for both male and female reporters. But a national political campaign is vital to all of us—men and women, reporters, viewers, and readers."[11]

Some of the "girls on the plane" got there because of their coverage of the women's movement. Some were comparative newcomers to reporting and had signed on because they were young, mobile, competitive, and ambitious—the same reasons young men cover national campaigns. A few others were veterans of other planes, other years. No longer were there no women or only one or two, as in the days when Doris Fleeson and Mary McGrory started out.

For many years Fleeson had been virtually alone in a man's world. She broke into the newspaper business after attending the University of Kansas. In 1927 she went to work at the New York *Daily News*, which belonged to what she described as the "who-the-hell-reads-the-second-paragraph school." Fleeson was soon assigned to the paper's Albany bureau, and then in 1933 she and her husband, political reporter John O'Donnell, were sent to

Washington, where they wrote a column together. Fleeson was the only woman reporter permanently assigned to travel with President Roosevelt on his campaign trips. Divorced in 1942, Fleeson reported on wartime conditions in Germany and then returned to the Albany bureau.

After the war, Fleeson started her own political column and became known for her sources within the government that yielded stories ranging from a feud between Supreme Court Justices Robert H. Jackson and Hugo Black to Gen. Dwight Eisenhower's plan to resign from the Army. A 1951 *Time* article on the Washington press corps called Fleeson one of "the best Washington newspaper reporters," the only woman it named in the company of Walter Lippmann, Arthur Krock, James Reston, and others. By the early 1960s nearly a hundred newspapers were carrying her columns.[12]

Like Dorothy Thompson before her and Mary McGrory after, Fleeson was able to demonstrate her ability to analyze politics and cultivate sources because she had started a column. It was she who was on the hook, not the newspaper. She was not writing as the voice of a newspaper, the way a political reporter may; she was representing not the newspaper but herself.

Mary McGrory, who covered some political events alongside Fleeson, remembers Fleeson as an "able, tough reporter, an ardent feminist who was very kind to me." Once, McGrory said with a soft smile of recollection, Fleeson was told that she thought like a man. "*What* man?" she shot back.

McGrory herself worked in obscurity for years, starting as a secretary for Houghton-Mifflin book publishers and then for the book review editor at *The Boston Herald*, where she also wrote a few dog stories (yes, stories about dogs). She went to Washington at 29 as a book reviewer for *The Washington Star*, writing reviews to which no one paid attention and an occasional profile for seven more years. Then Newbold Noyes, national editor of the *Star*, sent her to Capitol Hill to cover the Army-McCarthy hearings, advising her to observe and write it "like a letter to your favorite aunt." Since she had a favorite aunt, it was not a difficult assignment. "It was very liberating. All I did was an unprententious, simple account of how people were acting."

McGrory grew up Catholic in Boston after World War I,

141

always wanting to write. Asked about her schooling, she replied that she went to Emmanuel College but that she was *educated* at Girls Latin School, where she studied Latin every day for six years and learned the rules of French grammar in French. "It was an unrelenting classical education." It was an education that produced McGrory's precision with language.

Her columns, first syndicated in 1960 by the *Star*, won the Pulitzer Prize for commentary in 1975. When the *Star* folded in 1981, McGrory moved to *The Washington Post*. Her columns rely on an outsider's approach. "It has to be. George Will or Joe Kraft would have lunch at the White House. Or in Will's case, the President comes to his house. I've been to the White House exactly once in all my time. They don't return my phone calls. I don't blame them. So I have to get the information the long way around. I have to go to the hearings. That's when I see White House people. I read what they say. I go to their press conferences. It's not a very chic thing to do."

McGrory's has long been a liberal voice, unchanging even when liberalism became last season's fashion. She has an unabashedly romantic streak in her writing that often showed in her reporting on John Kennedy or on Vietnam veterans. Her prose can also be cutting. In 1972 she wrote of Nixon, "Will the President attend the Inauguration? Ask yourself, why should he? He didn't attend the election, and it went extremely well."[13] In 1986, writing of Seattle Archbishop Raymond G. Hunthausen's trouble with the Vatican, McGrory said that his backers consider him "guilty of nothing more than compassion, tolerance and openness." Sharp in her judgments of the intransigent or immoral, she was proud that her name showed up on the White House enemies list of the Nixon days. She even sent presidential aide Chuck Colson a thank-you note.

Often alone in a sea of male political reporters and commentators, McGrory has never been especially viewed as a feminist. "My dear," she once said to *The Wall Street Journal's* Jane Mayer, "I remember when it was ninety-three to one. I was the one. It was terrific. I never opened a door, carried a coat, bag, or typewriter for years."[14] In one of her columns, she said that a liberated young cousin had told her she was guilty of "veteranism," which was "to be expected of someone brought up in the school that a woman has to be twice as good to go half as far."

Much of her thinking was formed by her Aunt Kate. Kate, according to McGrory, was a feminist who believed that women could do anything but who still deferred to men, even when she could fix a toaster at which McGrory's father and brother could only stare helplessly. Kate, a bookkeeper through her working life, thought of men as sort of befuddled creatures who needed to be corralled this way and that, McGrory remembers fondly.

So McGrory was surprised when Aunt Kate approved of the Ferraro nomination. She often used Kate as a barometer for the nation's political highs and lows, and Kate had not failed her when Nixon was struggling to remain in the White House. Kate knew when he should stay, and she knew when he should go.

Kate, whose male chauvinism was "a scandalous joke in the family," was cool toward a woman on the ticket as the summer began, McGrory wrote in a column on "Ferraro's Magic" right after the 1984 Convention. "On the last day of the Convention, I called her up again and talked to a different person. She had watched—and loved—every minute of the proceedings. . . . When we got to the subject of Geraldine Ferraro, it was as if Bella Abzug, a woman Kate deplores, had seized the phone.

" 'She's very intelligent,' she enthused. 'Very capable. I think she could run the country.' "

It was then that McGrory realized the depth of the Ferraro phenomenon, and that it had stirred her as well. "When I heard it was Ferraro, I was joyful as those ecstatic old feminists in the Moscone Center who wept throughout her acceptance speech. Like them, I thought it was time and that she was right. For me, one of her prime qualifications is that she is the mother of a 20-year-old son. If we had someone like her sitting in the National Security Council during Vietnam, I always thought, we might have gotten smart much sooner."[15]

In the generation after Fleeson and McGrory, Judith Michaelson was among the first women to get the nod to cover politics. Michaelson, an honors graduate of Brooklyn College, had spent two weeks as a copy boy—and as in Eileen Shanahan's day, the word was still "boy"—for the *New York Post* before becoming the backup secretary for editor James Wechsler. She held that job for two years. Finally, in 1959 she got a tryout as a reporter and managed to be the first at a crime scene right after two teenage boys had been killed in Hell's Kitchen in Manhattan. "I walked

143

up, and there were all these women sitting on the stoop, including the mothers of the dead boys. It was a classic situation of coming upon people who were still in shock and talked and talked and talked." Michaelson clinched her reporting job that day.

Over the next few years, she reported politics "here and there," but it wasn't until the fall of 1964 that she was assigned full-time to a campaign, that of Robert Kennedy for the U.S. Senate from New York. "My city editor, John Bott, called me over and said, 'I'm not in favor of this, but the boss thinks we need a girl—and he said 'girl'—covering the glamour candidate. You've got him for a week.' That week became a month."

Post publisher Dorothy Schiff liked what Michaelson was reporting, and she stayed on the beat. Michaelson, who is hardly shy, remembers some tentativeness from her early days as a political reporter. When Kennedy appeared at the Overseas Press Club, reporters gathered in a semicircle around him. Michaelson stood behind that semicircle as if she didn't belong. Kennedy caught her eye. He shook hands, and she introduced herself. "I'm Judy Michaelson of the *New York Post*. This is my first campaign."

"Mine, too," Kennedy said boyishly. "I guess we'd better stick together."

Eleanor Randolph, who is now a colleague of Mary McGrory's at the *Post*, had to protest her way into political coverage. She was working at *The St. Petersburg Times* in 1972 when that paper outlined its coverage for the wide-open Florida primary. All eleven reporters assigned to the eleven candidates were male. Randolph and another reporter, Virginia Ellis, complained to the state editor that they, too, wanted to cover candidates.

"He just put his head back and laughed," Randolph says. "Then he asked, 'How can you share a room with another reporter [meaning that only men would be covering politics]? How can you cover politics when the guys are sitting in their shorts playing poker in the back room?' We said, 'That's ridiculous. That's not the only way to cover politics.' But there was no chance. So we went to the editor. He said no. He must have had a change of heart because he came out later and said, 'Who, other than Muskie, would you want to cover?' So I covered Wallace, and Ellis said [Sen. Henry M.] Jackson, and that was the beginning of my career covering politics. Even though I was through by the Convention,

I knew it meant that in 1976 I'd be on some campaign bus." She was, by then for *The Chicago Tribune.*

The Chicago Daily News followed suit in 1972, sending what Lois Wille describes as "its usual all white male contingent" of reporters to cover the Democratic Convention. Every woman on the staff signed a protest petition, so the paper responded by sending Wille to the Republican Convention.

The Associated Press did not initially assign Peg Simpson to the 1972 Democratic Convention, either, although for months she had been covering women's efforts to use new party rules to get more women delegates to the convention. "Dozens of my stories had dealt with the battle by women and minorities for more delegate seats. I was astounded. I was puzzled that a reporter who had become a specialist in an important area was not assigned to follow the story wherever it led—in this case, to the national political conventions," she wrote later. "Clearly, my editors and other media executives did not consider the women's political movement to be a bona fide story meriting continuing and expert coverage."[16]

Even when more women started covering candidates, they still needed extra fortitude. Cheryl Arvidson, *Dallas Times-Herald* Washington bureau chief, for example, has never been easily deterred from a story. Arvidson built up her sources over years of covering midwestern legislators on Capitol Hill for UPI. She parlayed that experience into trailing Walter Mondale during his 1976 vice-presidential campaign with Jimmy Carter. In 1980 Carter and Mondale were running again, and more women were covering their campaign and the Reagan-Bush ticket. Arvidson—for whom "ebullient" may be too tame a word—and her women friends on the campaign were "feeling pretty full of themselves."

They were traveling on the Reagan campaign and had "had sort of a religious experience when we realized that there was more than one of us. We were so pleased that finally there were enough of us to go out to dinner and fill a whole table. There was me and Sara Fritz and Ann Devroy and Rachelle Patterson, I think." When the women got to the restaurant, they saw that at a line of tables along the wall were most of the male correspondents, talking with campaign aide Lyn Nofziger. "Nobody in our group had even been asked," Arvidson remembers. "It was just devastating. It took the air out of us terribly."

The women sat at their own table and discussed when women reporters might be treated as equals. "Three more elections," the women concluded. "It will change. It will be easily three more elections. We do not practice what we preach. When you get to politics," Arvidson says, "you're talking about an old boys' game covered by old boys. It's the last hold of masculinity. When you look forward, you get depressed because you see how far we still have to go and how slowly we are getting there. But when you look back and see where we've come from, you can be pleased."

Of the country's best newspapers, only a handful have women regularly writing national politics. Even fewer have a woman writing the lead political story or directing political coverage. Among them, Ann Devroy is political editor at *The Washington Post*; Ellen Hume and Jane Mayer formed half the 1984 political team at *The Wall Street Journal*; Maureen Dowd and Robin Toner write national political stories for *The New York Times*; Sara Fritz and Karen Tumulty have covered politics and Congress for the *Los Angeles Times*; Maura Dolan and the late Nancy Skelton worked on the 1984 campaign for the *Los Angeles Times*. But the person who writes the convention wrapup, the election-day lead, is a man at *The New York Times*, *The Washington Post*, the *Los Angeles Times*, *The Boston Globe*, the *Philadelphia Inquirer*, the New York *Daily News*, *The Baltimore Sun*, and so on across the country.

Why cover politics anyway? It's only a game. Its metaphors are sports metaphors ("running a race," "striking out," "scoring"). Only the names change. The country lumbers along without the bulk of its citizens knowing—or caring—who headed George Bush's campaign or whether George Will saw a Carter briefing book in Reagan's offices. But politics is about power, the opportunity to make change or preserve values, a reflection of where people are willing to be lead. If you cover politics, yours is the lens through which people see who has power. That is a power itself.

Within American newspapers, the political reporter is the one whose stories make the front pages, whose travels are chronicled in books, whose political assignment may be parlayed into White House or state house coverage. The political reporter may someday become an editor or editorial writer. Nancy Grape, now an editorial writer at *The Portland Press-Herald*, got there by reporting politics for a smaller paper in Lewiston, Maine. She points out that if women lack access to political reporting, they may eventually also have less access to shaping the newspaper's policy on who should govern the community.

Women did not change the forms of political news coverage; Teddy White and television did that. What women have done— some of them, anyway—is to ask different questions on different subjects and to expand the focus of political coverage. More light falls now on women as candidates, on women as campaign work- ers, on women as voters, and on issues of interest to women as well as men. It is an accomplishment not solely of media women but also of the women who ran the races, raised the money, and tackled the issues. As a result, American politics and American newspapers now reflect more diverse elements in American life. That is one of the most far-reaching social changes of this century. It is an evolutionary process on both sides of the notebook. It is by no means complete.

Everyday Indignities

Patt Morrison of the *Los Angeles Times* is a versatile spot-news reporter who can turn out a quick feature with the best of them. She's the kind who has a ready response for the inevitable question of why she became a journalist. "I got into this job to see men type—something women traditionally did. Look around you in a newsroom," she says. "It's a leveler." Morrison also has arguably the largest collection of hats of any journalist extant. About three hundred hats. Pink hats. Hats with veils. Hats bought at a little shop in the French quarter while she was covering the Ginny Foat trial. She wears them in the newsroom as well as out, partly to have fun, partly to challenge people to think of her as an individual. "It disarms them, and they have to realize that this is not a news-sucking machine sitting across from them."

Folks in the *Times*'s newsroom are used to Patt's hats now. But early in her career, she wore a hat to a *Washington Post* job interview—an act, she will remind you, once considered a sign of good breeding. As she went from one office to another, the editor escorting her finally said, "Are you sure you want to wear that hat? They might think you want to be a society writer."

CHAPTER

10

If the Suit Fits . . .

Enlightenment alone did not unlock newsroom doors. Legal action helped.

It came from women who did not share similar histories, similar politics, even similar career patterns. Shirley Christian was born in a farmhouse near Windsor, Missouri, and grew up in the Kansas City area. Ginny Pitt's parents had both been journalists; she grew up in Huntington, West Virginia. Eileen Shanahan was born in Washington, D.C.; her father was a government accountant, and her mother died when she was 17. Betsy Wade was born in New York City and raised in Westchester; her father sold welding torches. These women did have one bond, however: together with a handful of colleagues they sued the Associated Press and *The New York Times* for sex discrimination.

There were other suits and discrimination complaints filed in the 1970s and into the 1980s—at *Newsday*, at *The Detroit News*, at *The Washington Post*, and at *The Baltimore Evening Sun*, among others. But the suits against AP and *The New York Times*—the former the national news-gathering organization subscribed to by more than 80 percent of America's daily newspapers, the latter the number-one paper in the country, the paper read by the movers and shakers—made the entire industry take notice.

Both sides, the women and their bosses, claimed victory. The women were clearly successful, not so much for themselves as for the women who came after them. The bosses were never judged guilty of discrimination by any court; the cases never got that far. Both sides gave up something—absolute proof versus absolute vindication—to avoid what A.M. Rosenthal of the *Times* called the "itchy part"—having to compare people in court, justifying, or not, why people were passed over for promotions, putting judgment calls on the record.

Most important to the public, the women's suits brought more women into all levels of both organizations, which changed the product. As a result, readers of the AP wire—that is, newspaper readers across the country—and of the *Times* won as well.

The women's suit against the Associated Press began with a discrimination complaint initiated by a group of black employees and Shirley Christian. That complaint languished for several years but was revived when a group of AP women, still including Christian, asked for help from their union, the Wire Service Guild.

Christian had started work for the AP in the mid-1960s and served three years as a United Nations correspondent and five years on the foreign and world desks in New York before winning a long-sought assignment as bureau chief for Chile and Bolivia. She had a master's degree in journalism and Latin American studies from Ohio State University. She had researched agrarian reform in Chile on a grant from the Inter American Press Association and had studied at Harvard on a Nieman Fellowship in 1973–74. Leaving the AP, she became *The Miami Herald*'s chief Central American correspondent in 1979 and two years later won the Pulitzer Prize and the George Polk Award for international reporting. She has since written *Nicaragua: Revolution in the Family*. She joined *The New York Times* in Washington in March 1985, transferring later to Buenos Aires.

"Shirley Christian had two major roles in this case," says Ginny Pitt, who was working on the desk in New York when the AP case was developing. "Because she had been part of the original group and was still with AP, we could keep that complaint alive. Had Shirley not remained enthusiastic and involved, we would have lost about three years of bureaucratic maze-running.

"Second, Shirley was an ideal point person. Her talent and skills were beyond reproach. She was very determined but not obnoxious and abrasive. . . . She won her Pulitzer Prize in precisely the area the AP would not send her"—Central America—"solely because she was a woman."

The women filed their complaint with the Equal Employment

150

Opportunity Commission in 1973. Five years later, the EEOC ruled that it had "reasonable cause to believe" that the AP was violating the 1964 Civil Rights Act. The women filed suit in September 1978, charging that the AP did not apply uniform criteria to hiring and promoting men and women, filled jobs through word-of-mouth recruitment that restricted women's opportunities, and relegated women to jobs with less prestige. Of forty-one domestic bureaus headed by a person with the title bureau chief, for example, none was headed by a woman in 1973. In 1977 there was still only one female bureau chief. The women also charged that they got fewer merit raises and unequal retirement benefits. Men earned average salaries of $20,359.56, the suit charged, while women earned $16,580.20.

The AP, adamantly opposed to paying one penny, ultimately had to provide more than $800,000 in back pay to women who had been working there between November 1972 and June 1983, when the suit was settled. The seven women named in the suit shared $83,120.

Ginny Pitt, who had worked for Cincinnati newspapers before joining the AP in Boston in 1972, initially insisted that she was not in the suit for the money. "I said I wanted to make AP better and wanted to help women. But I realized the bottom line is money. When you suffer the discrimination, you suffer it in the paycheck. And that's wrong." Pitt did not think she personally had been discriminated against when she heard of the original complaint. She kept track of the case as she moved up in the AP and became a supervisor on the New York general desk. "It was a pretty high position. I didn't have anything to kick about.

"Then I started checking around about salaries and found that I was making less than the men sitting next to me. It really came home when I started asking about being a bureau chief. I kept being given reasons why I couldn't. I had to prove myself. The general desk was a spawning ground for bureau chiefs," and the men didn't have to keep proving themselves.

"Then I was told I didn't look like a bureau chief. That I could be attractive, but I had to fix myself up and lose weight." It was a no-win situation, Pitt says. "Part of a bureau chief's job was to take publishers to lunch and dinner, and if you were terribly attractive, it would create problems for editors and publishers who were married. But if you were too unattractive, you'd be an embarrassment to the AP. . . . Women were getting hurt. But the AP was also getting hurt."

Many women in the AP feared getting involved in the case. With reason. When Pitt got involved, "I was immediately made invisible by being put on the overnight," midnight to 8 A.M. She had been working 3 to 11 P.M. To daylight folks, those may not seem glamorous hours, but they are prime time for editing stories to appear in the morning newspapers, which dominate the business. Being in charge during those hours means you are in effect in charge of the bulk of the AP's national report. Working the overnight meant "you don't have to see the brass—and they don't have to see you. You are also making no key decisions."

Ken Freed, who was active in the Wire Service Guild and had repeatedly championed the women's cause, is convinced that he paid a price, too. Freed had been the AP's State Department correspondent and was an AP delegate to the Guild's negotiating committee. He, too, got a Nieman Fellowship. At just that point, AP decided it would no longer make up the difference between a reporter's salary and the lower Nieman stipend. Then when Freed returned to Washington, the State Department job was no longer his. The *Los Angeles Times* offered Freed a job, and he took it.

Freed blames his problems at the AP on his activism. "I remember being at a grievance meeting in 1977 when Tom Pendergast [the AP's former vice president for personnel] said to me that I had done the worst thing ever done to AP with that women's suit."

Ken Freed, Pat Sherlock, and Dick Oliver were among the Guild men who supported the suit. "We wouldn't have had the money to go ahead without the Guild support," says Ginny Pitt.

All the women named in the suit have since left the Associated Press. Fran Lewine, for example, has worked since the suit for both the U.S. Department of Transportation and Cable News Network. She had started to work for the AP in Newark in 1944 and was passed up for moves into New York headquarters, even though men with comparable experience were moving to other bureaus or overseas. Finally, Lewine got to Washington in the middle 1950s, when Ruth Cowan was forced to retire at 55.

Lewine recalls that no matter what women did, it was never enough to earn good beats on a full-time basis. She had been covering the social side of the White House. "Say it's a Saturday, and President Nixon has an Oval Office press conference, and you're there. You'd get kudos for what you did, but they'd never consider that you could do it again."

Like Ginny Pitt, Maureen Connolly was the daughter of a former journalist. She had started on a small daily paper in Massachusetts, *The Newburyport Daily News*, covering the suburbs and writing engagements and family-type feature stories. In 1970 she had gone to *The Boston Record*, and when she asked during her interview how many women worked there, she was told, " 'You're it. We always have one.' I was 'the girl.' " In addition to covering federal courts and the school committee, Connolly was the one who would sit on Santa Claus's lap or write the front-page special with a headline like "KID COMES OUT OF A COMA AFTER A YEAR; MOM SAYS IT'S BEST CHRISTMAS PRESENT EVER." In 1972 she moved to Maine with *The Portland Press-Herald*, and the following fall she began as a state house reporter for the Associated Press in Augusta. She stayed until 1978 and is now a college teacher in Maine.

Connolly's frustration with the AP stemmed from its lack of direction. "I regularly told the bureau chief that I wanted to stay with the AP. I wanted to make it my career, but . . . no one ever told me of any options. They sent two new correspondents, one from New York with comparable experience, one from Albany with less. I was the one who trained the new people. . . .

"I was aware [of discrimination], and I certainly felt it was there. I felt I was an important part of the suit because I was part of a line bureau; the rest were from a hub. I felt I represented a lot of women who never saw Rockefeller Center," where AP headquarters are located. "AP is so spread out. It has so many little pockets, it's so decentralized. People didn't know what was going on," Connolly says. "They didn't look at patterns. The executives might look through the newsroom at Rockefeller Center, and they'd see different faces—and they'd think everything was okay where out in the bureaus it wasn't."

Virginia Tyson, who views herself as representing black women in the suit, started work at the AP's Dallas bureau after she received her B.A. from Yale and a master's degree in journalism

153

from Northwestern University. She did day rewrite for a year as part of a minority-training program and quickly got frustrated. "They were waiting for me to ignite. And I was waiting for them to tell me what to do." Finally she agitated for a full-time regular job and went to the AP's bureau in Omaha.

On her first day, the others in the bureau tested her by leaving early. Later they sent her to cover a story while she was also doing the radio shift, which meant that she was writing a story while writing scripts for local broadcasters. It was like being a one-armed paper-hanger, since each job requires concentration. Omaha was clearly going to be a test. "Within three days, I asked, 'How do I get out of here?'" Tyson stayed in Omaha two years, went to the Los Angeles bureau in 1977, stayed three years, and then joined the *Los Angeles Times*.

"When I had gotten stuck in Omaha, I thought who could I sue? When I saw news about the AP suit, including Shirley Christian, I realized these were names I had seen on the A-wire. I thought, if they were willing, so was I. I was really mad at AP for being treated like dreck. . . . The men would get a little talk about management; women had to ask when we could go on the desk. Men got the breaks, and women were the interchangeable parts who filled in the gaps. There was a great network of people who were disenchanted. I felt I was representing blacks' lack of opportunity."

What did she hope to get out of the suit? "Basically, I wanted them to be punished, which they never were. It was the idealistic sixties thing, wanting things to be better for people who'd come after me, so they wouldn't have to put up with this crap." Tyson thinks the suit accomplished little. "There are more women. And that's a good sign. It's a little more human. But like everything else, it never lives up to what you expected."

The settlement, negotiated between the AP, the Guild, and the EEOC, included not only back pay but a training program to prepare women for promotional opportunities and an affirmative action plan for women, blacks, and Latinos. The consent decree set a goal of thirty-seven percent women filling entry-level reporting and editing jobs as well as goals for promoting women.

Once the AP decided to settle, says Jan Goodman, the women's attorney, there was an almost complete about-face in its attitude. Where previously it had argued that its employment records were protected by the First Amendment, it then vigorously applied itself to affirmative action. "One thing about people in a hierarchical organization," says Goodman. "When they get the orders, they appear to march to them."

When the suit was settled in 1983, women made up twenty-two percent of AP employees; when the suit was filed, AP's news staff had been about seven percent female. Today it is twenty-five percent. Women have made up forty-four percent of new hires at the Associated Press since the suit was settled. In mid-1987 women were bureau chiefs in three of the forty domestic bureaus —San Francisco, Hartford, and Newark—and in three of the thirty-six foreign bureaus—Madrid, New Delhi, and Vienna. The AP's American-trained foreign staff is twenty-five percent female.

To understand what those numbers mean, bear in mind that the Associated Press blankets the nation in a way no other news organization does. United Press International is not a membership organization, as the AP is, and has always lacked resources to keep up; it often follows the AP's lead in personnel matters. AP reporters write about a chemical spill in the Southeast, a mine disaster in the West, and legislatures and school reform efforts in every state. Those stories go by wire to over three-fourths of the nation's daily newspapers. What the AP outlines as the nation's news is the nation's news to readers of those papers, most of which have no national or foreign correspondents of their own. Those readers do not also read *The New York Times* or the *Los Angeles Times*. Papers that run AP reporters' bylines over stories are now dotted with women's bylines as never before.

Ninety-nine stories out of a hundred that a wire-service reporter writes will be dictated by events—the train wreck, the legislative debate, the courtroom decision. But that hundredth story may be a feature, a story that the reporter uses enterprise to find. That story may now be about premenstrual syndrome or the link between women and the land in the open spaces of the West. Women don't always do stories on women, of course, but men did so with far less frequency.

"Today there are many more women at the grass-roots levels," says Tad Bartimus, AP regional correspondent based in Colorado. "Almost every bureau I ever worked in, I was the only woman. That's not true now. And where the news is concerned, there are lots of women doing stories about women. . . . The suit did that. Remember, this is a company that takes the path of least resistance. If you want to do a story, the bureau chief will say, 'Go do that and leave me alone.' Women have more initiative than men in this regard because they are still proving themselves. In the process they've changed the way the wires read across the board at that level.

"In this company the power of the news is made in Yakima, Washington, and Columbia, South Carolina, and that has changed because there are more women there. But AP has two levels. The top leadership is male—it answers to a virtually all-male board of directors coming from male newspaper leadership. Women may be powerful in the content of the news, but they are not powerful in determining the course of their lives."

Kelly Smith Tunney, director of corporate communications and assistant general manager, is the highest-ranking woman at the Associated Press. She was one of three AP management people who helped negotiate the settlement of the women's suit. When the decision was made to settle, Tunney says, the negotiators felt they would do it only "if it could be good for the AP. Time has proven that right," she says, adding that AP officials took to the affirmative action plan "like a duck to water."

The settlement "gave us an excuse to do something we needed to do anyway. The beneficiaries have been women, minorities, and all people. It has improved our whole community," Tunney says.

It is not so much any internal personnel changes that have affected the news report, Tunney says, but rather that the wire service is reflecting what newspapers want in the way of coverage. "Society has changed. Everybody's view of what's going on has changed. The Associated Press looks different. Television looks different. I think that has much more to do with it than any male-female thing" in reporting.

The AP suit had a reach beyond Rockefeller Center and even beyond AP offices worldwide. "The agencies produce a lot of the talent that then goes on to the *L.A. Times, The Washington Post, The Portland Press-Herald,* or wherever," says Ginny Pitt. "Most people stay at AP about six years. It's the best training ground in the world. The very worst AP reporter in many cases is better than the very best reporter at a local newspaper who hasn't had that experience. The other suits are very important, but AP and UPI—and UPI paid a lot of attention to the AP case—are the springboard. If women can't get that kind of training, they are going to be hampered throughout the industry." If women are getting that training now, Pitt goes on, "then clearly we won. The AP also won. Those women make other papers better, too, because they have the AP background."

The *New York Times* suit had a salutary effect on the newspaper industry. If that elite paper—the editorial supporter of civil rights, the paper of record for the nation—could be sued for discrimination, then anyone could be.

If the women were right, they had not only been underpaid and discriminated against at the entry level, they had also been unduly blocked from playing key roles as foreign correspondents, Washington reporters, and desk editors. These were roles that, filled by women, could help change the face of American journalism because they would carry the cachet of *The New York Times*. Success for women at the *Times* is so important because it says that now the most prestigious paper in the country thinks it is important that women do the same jobs as men professionally, that women be reporters in Bangkok as well as Brooklyn and write national security editorials as well as home furnishing news. It is arguable whether the still virtually all-male leadership at *The New York Times* thinks that women in general have the potential for success that it has long felt men in general have; it may still be looking for the exceptional woman more than the exceptional man. But at least now it is looking *at* her, not *past* her.

The genesis of the women's suit may be found in a letter that art writer Grace Glueck wrote to publisher Arthur O. Sulzberger —"Punch," for short—in 1970. "Abe Rosenthal, Arthur Gelb and others in an all-male cast had been promoted into the paper's top editorial jobs," and Glueck congratulated Sulzberger on his choices but asked why no women had been included. "My male colleagues . . . beamed benignly, as well they might. Back came a note from the publisher saying that the point was well taken, that he would consult with 'key management executives' when they came back from vacation. But apparently they never did. And some years later, well after we had started our group action, one of the men in the *Times he*-erarchy told me, 'Grace, you scared us with that note. We thought you had troops, and we were waiting for the other shoe to drop.' "[1]

The women looked at the payrolls and were stunned. "When we saw the inequities in pay, that's when we really hit the roof," says Grace Lichtenstein, who was then a *Times* reporter. "When Jane Brody, clearly a star, saw the list, she marched in, demanded, and got a raise," Lichtenstein recalls. Betsy Wade, a key organizer in the suit, found that men made an average of $59 a week more than women. Eileen Shanahan, star economics reporter and another named plaintiff, became the smoking gun in the suit when she found that while she was twelfth in seniority in the Washington bureau, she was nineteenth on the salary scale, making about $3,000 a year less on the average than men in the bureau. All the women in the Washington bureau were clustered toward the bottom of the payroll, with the lone black woman at the very bottom.

"This had an absolutely galvanizing effect on one of our reporters in the Washington bureau, who has since retired, who up until that time had had absolutely no interest in anything to do with the so-called women's movement," says Joan Cook. "She had been led to believe that she was extremely well paid and really a top professional, and here she found herself way down at the bottom of the list. She turned into a real tiger."[2]

Pay wasn't the only problem. Lichtenstein kvetched about the paper's rigid unwillingness to call women "Ms." instead of "Miss" or "Mrs." That unwillingness bespoke other, more complex rigidities. The men at the top at the *Times* simply could not envision women in many of the key jobs and, worse, didn't recognize their own blindness.

On Memorial Day 1972, the women's caucus presented its grievances to Sulzberger. The letter pointed out what Joan Cook calls "really serious lacks on the paper—that there were no women in photography, there were no women on the editorial board, there were no women on the masthead, there were no women in outside classified advertising sales, and so on the litany went."[3] The publisher promised to form a committee to deal with the complaints. (Only men served on it.) But a further sign of trouble was the arrival of two stars from the Washington bureau. "Nan Robertson and I went up from Washington for the meeting, and we were late," Eileen Shanahan says, remembering the look on Sulzberger's face. "When we walked in, Punch knew this was for real."

By 1972 the other shoe was indeed starting to drop. The women went to attorney Harriet Rabb of Columbia University's Employment Rights Project, who along with her colleague Howard Rubin was among the nation's best sex-discrimination attorneys. That fall, Ada Louise Huxtable was named to the *Times* editorial board, and Charlotte Curtis was named editor of the op-ed page. Neither had taken any part in the case. "This should surprise no one," Wade says. In 1974 the women took their case to court. In 1977 U.S. District Court Judge Henry F. Werker granted them the right to represent all other women similarly situated at the *Times*.

Although Curtis was not part of the women's suit, she later told *New Times* writer Judith Coburn—before the suit was settled —that "the women's charges against the paper are generally true."[4]

As with the AP case, it was critically important in the beginning that the women had the support of their union, Betsy Wade says. This logistical support was vital, as was the element of protection that the Newspaper Guild provided its members involved in a suit. "The law would have looked with great unhappiness" on any direct retribution, Wade recalls.

Still, the women did not want the Guild to press the case because they wanted it to apply to women outside Guild jurisdiction—that is, to women with pink-collar jobs and to some women who were classified as management with job titles like "confidential waitress." Wade noted an air of elitism in some discussions among the newswomen about the breadth of the suit. "The tenor of the discussion was, 'How could these people—women in classified, for example, whose idea of life [they thought] was to shop on lunch hour—how could they appreciate what this means?' This affects us all, and if they come for you tonight, they come for me tomorrow," Wade says. Ultimately, the suit covered a range of women at the *Times*.

Who are the women whose names finally appeared on the

suit? Louise Carini, an accountant who joined the *Times* in 1951, has since retired. Nancy Davis, a telephone solicitor for the advertising department, had applied for nine openings for a better job at the *Times*; later, she headed the advertising department for several publications. Andrea Skinner represented 130 "not white" women, as the formal description went. She had joined the paper as a clerk and moved to the children's fashion sections, lining up a greater variety of models so that "now the magazine does not speak with an exclusively white male voice," Wade says.

Of the four newswomen involved, Joan Cook had been a reporter with the *Times* since 1959. The files of the women's caucus showed that she had been repeatedly cited for bright writing in the in-house newsletter, "Winners and Sinners," yet she couldn't get a raise. Of her early days at the *Times*, Cook recalls that basically women were grateful for the few reporting jobs they had. If they wanted to advance, they had to do it one at a time; if someone were courting a particular editor for a promotion, "the rest of us would have a ladylike agreement not to queer the act and wait our turn, so it was very difficult to move on."[5]

Grace Glueck joined the *Times* in the 1950s and now covers art news. Betsy Wade describes Glueck as combining aesthetic judgment, writing skills, a sense of humor, and the reporter's flexibility not to mind being told "that she's going to look at the exhuming of some Maya ruins in about six hours and does she have some clothes for the jungle?"

The best-known plaintiff, Eileen Shanahan, had to be particularly staunch, Wade says, because she was the only plaintiff from the Washington bureau. She was isolated, without the support the women had in New York.

And Betsy Wade Boylan. As in *Boylan* v. *The New York Times*. Not only did her name come first alphabetically, she was also senior woman on the suit in terms of rank. Copyeditors tend to be anonymous, but Betsy Wade, as she is known professionally, was about as prominent within the *Times* as a woman could be in the early 1970s. She was head of the foreign copy desk at the time the suit was filed; she helped with the copyediting, for example, for the *Times*'s publication of the Pentagon Papers.

Wade came by her professional command of words through the half-hour she spent every night, at her father's insistence, on vocabulary building when she was growing up. In ninth grade she sold *The New York Times* at her school and discovered that all the history teachers subscribed. Wade earned a B.A. from Barnard College in 1951 and a master's degree from the Columbia School of Journalism in 1952. She went to work for Eugenia Sheppard on the women's pages of the *Herald-Tribune*, replacing Joan Cook, who was pregnant. She married James Boylan, a historian and founder of *The Columbia Journalism Review*, and was fired from her job when she became pregnant in 1953.

In 1956 Wade became the first woman hired for the copy desk at *The New York Times*. Even then, she said later, "you could see there was something wrong. There were no women ahead of me. There were no women doing what I was doing. There were no women alongside me. There were no women, except for the publisher's daughters, in any position of authority at the paper that you could see, get hold of, or understand."[6] For fourteen years, Wade worked on various desks at the *Times* and was named assistant head of the foreign copy desk in 1970 and head in 1972.

"I had a good job. I was not a disaffected person. But I felt it was important for me to be on that suit because other women could see that if there was anything going to happen to us as a result of the case, it was going to happen to me first." Like Ginny Pitt, Wade says she was well paid and had not entered the suit seeking financial compensation. "I had been seduced by money," she says. In the long run, money was what mattered because it was what mattered to management and it was the firmest measure of the discrimination women faced.

In reports prepared for the case, Dr. Orley Ashenfelter, a Princeton University professor of economics, concluded that there was "a sizeable difference between the salaries of male and female employees that cannot be explained" by any difference in productivity. The difference "almost certainly could not have arisen by chance alone," he added.[7] Barnard College economics professor Mark Killingsworth found a difference in pay of $5,160 a year between men and women and that only $1,425 of that amount could be attributed to the fact that men had more experience.

Yet in her *New Times* article, Judith Coburn quoted one of the *New York Times* attorneys as saying that "this is a case where . . . highly paid women, who have been well treated by the *Times*,

161

now assert for some reason undeterminable from their papers herein that they have suffered discrimination because of their sex. But their claims . . . are totally devoid of substance and rationality." To which Harriet Rabb replied, "It's like they believe that once you make over $17,000 a year you give up your constitutional rights."[8]

The judge in a pretrial hearing raised his eyebrows at Wade's salary and said the plaintiffs should find a "victim." Wade replied that the *Times* had promoted fourteen men to assistant editor jobs in twenty years who were no better qualified than she. "I make the amount of money I make . . . because I am one of the best editors the *Times* has and because after all, if I couldn't have the job, they thought that maybe if they gave me the money I would shut up."[9]

To this day, the *Times* management insists that it did not discriminate against women. "We thought it was unfair to single out *The New York Times*—that it was one more case of whacking *The New York Times* because it's so visible," associate editor A.M. Rosenthal said in an interview in 1986. "We didn't really feel we were treating women unfairly."

When Rosenthal became a top editor at the *Times*, according to Harrison Salisbury, there were complaints that his policies were not free of male chauvinism. ". . . When cases flared up about treatment of women on the paper, Abe found them hard to accept. He thought of himself as secure and at home in a woman's world and could not understand when the women in the city room reacted so differently."[10] When the *Times* settled the suit, "Rosenthal irritated several friends by insisting that the settlement represented 'a great victory' for the *Times*," Salisbury wrote. "When his friends pointed out that the settlement was an admission of fault, Rosenthal did not agree. Later he insisted to a friend that 'I have done more about women and blacks than anyone on the paper.' "

Years later, Rosenthal insisted that he helped put women in jobs that they had not held before. "People have asked me what would *The New York Times* be like without women. Today that's an unimaginable question, but twenty or thirty years ago, when I came back from being a foreign correspondent, that wasn't unimaginable. It was reality. There were no women on the metro desk when I became metropolitan editor. It was a like a monastery."

Rosenthal professed that he couldn't even remember the names of the women on the suit—only Betsy Wade Boylan's, because it gave the case its name. "It hit nerves, but not as many as people think. There was disappointment—but no sense of rage."

Perhaps not. But Grace Lichtenstein recalls being in the newsroom sometime just before the suit was filed while a local television station was doing a program on the *Times*. "They interviewed me on camera as sort of the token woman on general assignment. I made a mistake. I said, 'This is a great place, but there aren't enough women, there aren't enough blacks, there aren't enough Chicanos. There aren't enough American Indians.' I was just reflecting my times. But Rosenthal called me into his office, and I got the dressing down of my life. He was crazed. He told me what I had done was akin to McCarthyism. That being the 1970s, I had to think of which McCarthy. . . . In retrospect, it was dumb. In retrospect, I would have been more circumspect," Lichtenstein concludes. But it did reveal a certain oversensitivity among the *Times* management.

All during this time, Betsy Wade said years later, the women were redefining their relationship with *The New York Times*. "It required us to look at what it was that we had hoped for and what it was that we had wanted when we went to work there. It required us to look at what we wanted for the paper. I think this was finally what had the greatest impact on us: we all wanted the paper to be better than it was in certain particular ways that we felt were important. . . . It is the problem of a paper that speaks with a white male voice at all times. It does not speak with a voice that is many-colored and both-sexed."

Despite their ambivalence about the *Times*, Joan Cook adds, "our love affair was stronger than our anger."[11]

Many journalists aspire to work for *The New York Times*. Many come, and many leave in frustration because the paper is so big, so slow to change, so homogenized. Many stay because it is, after all, *The New York Times*, no matter its deficiencies. But to dream of working at the *Times*, to get the job, to move up in the ranks, and then to find yourself suing the paper for which you always wanted to work—what does that do to someone?

For Betsy Wade, her relationship with the *Times* has undergone "a flowing redefinition. It had been my ambition always to

163

work for the *Times*. . . . I never say 'we' anymore when I speak of the *Times*, and that was a terrible loss. It was like giving up a family member. I found I worked for them, and they endured me. It was shattering."

The *Times* was never found guilty of sex discrimination. It agreed to a stepped-up affirmative-action program, one that for the first time applied to top jobs. The *Times* committed itself to placing women in one out of every eight of the top corporate positions during the four-year life of the settlement. It agreed to place women in one in four of the top jobs in the news and editorial departments by the end of 1982, and to provide $233,500 in back pay for 550 women. The agreement euphemistically called that payment "annuities."

Ten years after the settlement, assessments of its impact are more mixed than those of the AP suit. Some call it a failure, saying the settlement was not sufficiently monitored and that thus the *Times* slid out from honoring its commitment to put women in a certain number of top jobs. Others say the women underestimated the ferocity of the reaction from the male management. Betsy Wade says that one reason the women settled rather than pursue the case into court was because they knew that they were like scorpions in a bottle. "You've got them and they've got you, and everybody has a lot to lose." Joan Cook adds, "Harriet told us that if we did come to trial, it was highly likely that we would, singly or in groups, be accused of everything from alcoholism to mopery."

For his part, Max Frankel, who succeeded Rosenthal as executive editor, says he thought the suit "didn't have much merit. The fact that it was settled for so little and quickly seems to have backed that up." Nonetheless, Frankel does say the suit may have increased management's sensitivity to the need to promote more women and to make sure pay scales are equitable.

Did the women win? "Certainly we didn't in money," Wade answers. "But when I see young women remaking a page in the composing room, I feel good. I think we may have advanced the process by five years."

If the *Times* had really been beaten, says another, there would have been women in the initial round of promotions in the fall of 1986, when Frankel replaced Rosenthal as executive editor.

164

The fact that in 1986 there were still no women's names among the likely successors to Rosenthal at a company that had been sued for sex discrimination shows that thinking at the very top had changed precious little. (There were also no names of women involved in the speculation over who would succeed Benjamin Bradlee at *The Washington Post* or Bill Thomas at the *Los Angeles Times*.) There still were none until Frankel completed his roster of editing changes. The first round of promotions involved only men: Frankel for Rosenthal; Jack Rosenthal for Frankel as editorial page editor; Leslie H. Gelb to succeed Jack Rosenthal as deputy editorial page editor; and Arthur Gelb to succeed Seymour Topping as managing editor.

The second round included only one woman, Judith Miller, who was named news editor for the Washington bureau, while men were named to the jobs of Washington editor, assistant managing editor for personnel, foreign editor, London bureau chief, metropolitan editor, senior editor for staff recruitment and training, and business manager. Finally, the third round contained three more women—Soma Golden, national editor; Karen Arenson, editor of the Sunday business section; and Donna S. K. Laurie, deputy editor of national editions. In that round, six men received new jobs.

Some women who join the *Times* today are convinced they have done it on merit. And that is possible now, just as it has always been possible for men. These young women are, however, as one *Times* staff member says, basically "apolitical yuppies" who lack a sense of history. Some have never heard of Eileen Shanahan, who is no longer at the *Times*, or of that relatively anonymous— to them—former copyeditor named Betsy Wade.

But Barbara Crossette is convinced that she moved up because of women like Betsy Wade. Crosette joined the *Times* in 1973 as a copyeditor on the foreign desk after attending graduate school in England and working for *The Birmingham Post* in England. "From the time I arrived here, I wanted to go back as a foreign correspondent. It took ten years." Wade was head of the copy desk, and whenever someone came looking for help on a project, she would prod Crossette to do the job. "She pushed women at her own expense. And she gave me a zillion pep talks. . . . I came at just the right time. The *Times* was just beginning to move women." After a 1980 Fulbright in India, Crossette worked in Washington for a year, served as deputy foreign editor, and then was assigned to Bangkok as the *Times* correspondent.

The New York Times. The Associated Press. *The Washington Post. The Detroit News. Newsday.* The targets were hanging there in the 1970s. "It was the temper of the times," says Gerry Shanahan, a copyeditor at *Newsday* when women there filed suit in 1975. New York was alive with protest. Women had paraded down Fifth Avenue in August 1970 in the first major march for equality. Women at *Newsweek* sued. Women at *Reader's Digest* sued. Women at *Ladies Home Journal* staged a sit-in. Women at NBC sued.

"We wanted the very things that every other women's suit called for," Shanahan, now a suburban editor at *The New York Times*, says. She and a group of friends on the *Newsday* copy desk "started talking about it because of when it was." They broadened their group when they realized that "three copyeditors aren't going to represent the collected stories of people, the experiences of a whole class of people. . . . We looked around and saw only a hand-ful of women in entry-level jobs and couldn't see any women beyond that. We saw that men got the plum assignments."

Memos were sent to editor David Laventhol about discrim-ination against women in salary, promotions, and assignments. Once a women's caucus was formed, the women identified four-teen grievance areas. The women circulated petitions among the women at the newspaper, saying that they all agreed about the charges. "We wanted to take away from management the notion the ability to say that this is a notion of three crazy women in the newsroom. At that point we had the whole newsroom."

The women met with management, which put off any res-olution of their complaints until after a union-organizing drive. The union won and in turn backed the women's demands. The company voluntarily issued an affirmative-action plan in April 1974, but in January 1975 the women sued anyway. It was a class-action suit with four named plaintiffs; two more were added later. Among the charges was one that "*Newsday* creates special jobs and job titles for men, but not for women, who are not considered competent or who are being phased out of their present positions" —a complaint that still sounds familiar today.

166

A consent decree settling the suit was signed in February 1982.[12] "Both sides claimed they won," Shanahan says, "but *Newsday* had to pay money. That's what hurts a company most." In addition to agreeing to certain hiring and promotion goals, *Newsday* agreed to pay $100,000 to eligible female employees and to a scholarship fund at Columbia University, $15,000 to the plaintiffs, and the plaintiffs' legal fees.

Encouraged by the receptive climate of the decade, more women filed cases against their newspapers. In Detroit, Mary Lou Butcher saw that her career was stalled and sued *The Detroit News* in 1976. Hired after graduation from the University of Michigan, Butcher started out writing wedding announcements, then pushed and prodded her way in to a suburban bureau and three years later into the city room. After six more years, she was given a weekend shift, the kind normally given only to new reporters. Men with less experience had weekends off. When she asked for better hours, she was told that she was being transferred back to the suburbs instead. Between 1972 and 1976, all eight women reporters who had been in the city room had been moved out—to the suburbs, to the lifestyle section, or to reader services—or they had left. She and three other women sued the paper, which agreed in November 1983 to pay $330,000 to about ninety employees.

Butcher left the newspaper business for public relations in March 1977 after filing her complaint with the EEOC. She knew that her own advancement at the *News* had been effectively blocked. The *News* has since been sold to Gannett, but well before that sale, Butcher says that there had been definite advancements for women. "The suit was instrumental in moving women into every area where they typically had not been—sports, photo, state and national bureaus—every area that women hadn't been allowed to venture," Butcher says, adding that it also led to clearing out some executives who had been discriminating.

"It was rewarding to me to see other women just treated as equals. The whole community benefits when you have a variety of people helping make the decisions on how a story is played, how it is edited, and what treatment it gets."

In the middle 1970s Sharon Dickman, who had worked her way up from editorial clerk to reporter for *The Baltimore Evening Sun*, saw continuing discrimination against women and minorities at that paper. A soft-spoken person, Dickman nonetheless pointed out various problems to management to try to get them solved, from an editorial that made light of women reporters trying to cover baseball locker rooms, to a photograph demeaning to women, to management's failure to open up jobs for women and minorities.

In 1974, acting for the fair employment practices committee of the Baltimore-Washington Newspaper Guild, Dickman filed a complaint with the Maryland Commission on Human Relations stating that the company "has discriminated in the areas of race and sex involving hiring, promotion, transfer, on-the-job segregation," despite statements in its affirmative action program.[13]

The complaint languished for several years and then was settled between the Sunpapers and the Commission without union participation. The agreement called for more detailed record-keeping on the hiring and promotion of women and minorities for a limited period of time. As for Dickman, she was named assistant metropolitan editor in 1979, the first woman on the desk.

In Washington, women and blacks took aim at the *Post*. Their case never went as far as a lawsuit, but after ten years a settlement was negotiated through the EEOC.

The *Post* case started slowly, once again the product of women looking at their own shop as consciousness of sex discrimination grew. "I think I can honestly say to you that I never personalized this," says Claudia Levy, who has worked in the *Post*'s metropolitan, business, real estate, and Maryland sections. "I felt the *Post* had a very un-up-to-date notion of what women could do. I did not think I was a high-powered reporter. I didn't think I personally had suffered enormously. It was more a case that women all over the country were organizing, and I was covering it, and here it was in my own backyard.

"I could see that untalented men were coming into this organization and women weren't getting in the door and weren't getting hired who had far more talent, and it made me furious. I think it was a case of seeing that women on the inside had an obligation—and that is an awful word, but an obligation—to point out what was happening and try to do something about it. I wasn't an aggressive person, and I believed them when they said I wasn't very good. It wasn't until later, when I became an editor, that I saw that I did have judgment and that I might have been able to handle some of the things that they said I couldn't do."

As early as 1970, women at *The Washington Post* (as well as at *The Washington Star*) sent their editors a memo that concentrated not on personnel practices but on purging stereotypes. The women asked in the memo that stories that by definition deserved front-page play receive it, that insulting or nongermane references to women be dropped, and that stories not stigmatize women simply because they were achievers by conveying the tone, "She's done pretty well—for a woman." The women also asked for newspaper backing in fighting discrimination when women were barred from covering assigned events, such as luncheons at the National Press Club or sports events.[14]

In response, executive editor Ben Bradlee posted a one-page memo reiterating the *Post*'s policy of equality in hiring, its assignment and promotion practices, and its policy of following through to elimate "unconscious but none the less offensive" discrimination in news columns.

Two years later, black reporters at the *Post* filed a complaint with the EEOC. Less than a month afterward, the women again petitioned the publisher and senior editors. They recalled that in June 1970, when Bradlee had first responded to them, "there were 287 news and editorial employees—244 men and 43 women. Women made up 15 percent of the staff. In March 1972 there were 294 news and editorial employees—254 men and 40 women. Women made up 13.6 percent of the staff." There were no women assistant managing editors, news desk editors, editors in financial, sports, or the TV magazine, or in the Sunday "Outlook" section, no women in foreign bureaus, and no women sports reporters.[15]

"Women are losing ground at *The Washington Post* at a time when more women are graduating from journalism schools and more are applying for jobs here. *Time* magazine recently reported that women now make up 44 percent of journalism graduates. We are told that about 40 percent of applicants at the *Post* are women," the women added.

"Many stories considered expendable deal with social issues of interest to the general reader but are given short-shrift in this

169

male-oriented, politically attuned newspaper. The issues of women's rights, health, consumer news, day-care, abortion, and welfare are examples of stories not being adequately covered and displayed. *The Washington Post* would be a better newspaper if it used the talents and perspective of more women in assigning and evaluating stories on such issues."

The women called upon the *Post* to recognize both its intentional and its unintentional discrimination against women in hiring and promotion practices and to institute an affirmative-action program to correct that discrimination. Failing to receive a response that they considered adequate, the women filed their own complaint at the EEOC on May 29, 1972. Two years later, the EEOC ruled that women as a class at the *Post* were denied equal access to higher-paying jobs and to assignments that could lead to promotion. The EEOC also found that the *Post* preferred single women for higher-level jobs in the news department, a preference it didn't show for single men.

Why did they complain? Notes from the files of the *Post* women's group show that one woman was assigned to the suburban weekly section over her protest, after she had had a baby. Another was denied a job in Latin America, told she couldn't have a traveling job, because she was an unmarried mother. One was paid a reporter's wage despite her assignment as a night editor for the "Style" section. One was criticized for supposedly marrying "beneath her" on the staff, although at least one man married a news aide and did not receive similar criticism.

B. J. Phillips represents the case of a gifted writer who got away. She had reported for *The Atlanta Constitution* but was assigned to do light features when she joined *The Washington Post*. In 1970 she was sent to Houston to write about the astronauts' wives. She was there when Apollo 13 blew up, killing the crew. Phillips wrote three front-page stories, only to return to Washington to find that her next assignment was to cover the opening of the cherry-blossom festival. She complained, asked again to go on the national desk, and finally quit when the national editor asked her how she would handle being the only woman with the "boys on the bus." She later went to work for *Time* magazine.[16]

Judith Martin started out working with men who, twenty years later, were editors while she wasn't. She was passed over for assignment to the New York bureau because she was married. When she took her first maternity leave, she inadvertently discovered that her papers were being processed as though she was quitting. She said she wasn't. Someone in the personnel office said that many women go on maternity leave and never come back. To which she replied, "I know a lot of people who go out to lunch and never come back, but you're not going to abolish lunch hour."

The case was settled in 1980 with an agreement that called for a five-year hiring and promotion plan. The *Post*, while not admitting to any discrimination, also gave cash settlements amounting to $104,000 to 567 women, established a $100,000 scholarship and sabbatical program for women employees, and paid $42,500 in legal fees. In a report to the EEOC summarizing its hires from June 1981 to June 1986, the *Post* said it had filled 40 percent of applicable news and editorial management positions with women. The goal in the settlement had been to fill one-third of the jobs with women. The *Post* also reported that it had filled 40 percent of its reporting, assignment-editor, and critic jobs with women.

Nonetheless, the Newspaper Guild remained unhappy about disparities between men's and women's pay at the *Post*. Martha Hamilton, a *Post* reporter and member of the Guild bargaining committee, found that "in the best paying jobs and in many of the largest job categories, *The Washington Post* pays white men significantly higher salaries on average than white women or blacks doing the same jobs. This is pay discrimination." Some of the disparities might have been due to the fact that men had been able to get good jobs at the *Post* longer than women had. But the Guild contended that pay discrimination still occurred among relatively new hires.

While white women reporters were paid 13.1 percent less than their white male colleagues in 1986, black women were paid 20 percent less, Hamilton reported. Learning that they were clustered near the bottom of the pay scale, seventeen black women at the *Post* began individual meetings with managing editor Len Downie and other top executives to discuss their careers. "It's interesting to me, who's been here a long time, that at last we finally have enough black women to talk about this," says veteran Dorothy Gilliam.

171

The problems attacked by women's lawsuits are by no means solved. The results have been uneven. Some male managers insist to this day that the best people at the newspapers were not involved in the lawsuits and other legal actions, but the collective achievements of the women who brought those suits give the lie to that claim. Benjamin Bradlee of the *Post* said, for example, that the equal-employment case "didn't facilitate anything—it made life more difficult" because it "created a hopelessly us vs. them" situation. People at the newspaper were not "working as a team." Having said that, however, Bradlee paused and added, "That's not fair. It probably made us conscious of numbers which we hadn't been before."

That younger women, who may understand only intellectually what discrimination is, lack a deep, visceral awareness of the problem is the truest sign that the suits have succeeded. Discrimination against women has diminished, at least at entry levels. Movement of more women into the workforce would, to be sure, have brought some changes. But women had been slowly moving into jobs outside the home for decades without much appreciable change in the newsroom. Without these legal actions, the laissez-faire attitude of management would have allowed male editors to go on denying women key assignments and promotions.

Women like Betsy Wade put their roles in perspective today. When she was a young reporter for the *Herald-Tribune*, she was assigned to cover a news conference that Eleanor Roosevelt was having. She told the press aide that she was there from the *Herald-Tribune*, and the woman replied that Emma Bugbee, a *Herald-Tribune* mainstay for over forty years even then, was already there.

"I thought, 'Who is this woman? Why does she block my way?' It was only years later that it dawned on me what she must have endured and how much of a pioneer she was and how much I owed her. I realized that young women at the *Times* might be looking at me the way I was looking at Emma Bugbee. Now I understand their attitude. I can only hope that someday when they've run up against that brick wall, they'll think, 'Oh, *Boylan* v. *The New York Times*. That was Betsy Wade Boylan. Now I know what she meant.' "

Everyday Indignities

The man who regularly covered the New York Yankees for *Newsday* was stuck out of town and couldn't get to the game. The editor asked everyone but Helene Elliott to fill in—including a guy who hadn't covered baseball since the Mets played at the Polo Grounds. (That was a long time ago.) Elliott said nothing at the time, although she points out, telling the story, that she had not been sitting behind a post when the man was looking for a substitute. When she left that night she asked the editor why she hadn't been asked. He got flustered and said he hadn't seen her. The next week she covered the Yankees.

CHAPTER

11

Women of Color

It is no accident that most minority women in the newspaper business—blacks, Latinas, Asian-Americans—are either under 40 or just hovering around that age. No accident—unless you consider discrimination accidental. The same newspapers that covered first the civil rights movement in the South, then the protests in the North, then the coming of age of other minority groups covered most of the milestones of those movements with white male reporters and occasionally with white female reporters.

In 1968 the Kerner Commission scored the journalistic profession for being "shockingly backward in seeking out, hiring, training and promoting Negroes." That panel headed by Illinois Gov. Otto Kerner and formally known as the National Advisory Commission on Civil Disorders, reported that "fewer than 5 per cent of the people employed by the news business in editorial jobs in the United States today are Negro. Fewer than 1 per cent of editors and supervisors are Negroes, and most of them work for Negro-owned organizations."

It would not be enough simply to seek out black journalists as a solution, the Kerner Commission said. The news business had to recognize that it was not an attractive field for young blacks because they had not been made to feel comfortable in the profession, which was also low-paying. The report urged early recruitment and training in high school and college as well as extensive internship programs. Not only should more blacks be helping report and edit the news, the report said, but stories about blacks' daily lives should be integrated throughout the paper—from the front page to the women's page, "if the media are to report with understanding, wisdom and sympathy the problems of the city."[1]

What that Commission said about blacks in 1968 was even truer about other minorities. The absence of Latinos and Asian-Americans from the group defining the news agenda was not yet as critical as was the absence of black reporters; the Latino and Asian-American populations had not grown then as they have in the two decades since the report was issued. But today representation of Latinos among American newspaper employees is worse than that of blacks—they constitute only 1.68 percent of all employees, as opposed to 3.62 percent for blacks. Asian-American journalists are not quite 1 percent of the total.[2]

A 1987 survey by the American Society of Newspaper Editors (ASNE) found that, taken together, minorities still constitute only 6.56 percent of the total newsroom work force. Yet minorities make up about 20 percent of the total population and may make up as much as 25 percent by the turn of the century. In California, minorities will be the majority by early in the twenty-first century. Progress has been made—minorities were 3.95 percent of a total journalistic work force of 43,000 people in 1978; that work force has grown by 11,700 people, while the number of minorities has more than doubled, from 1,700 to 3,600. Of journalists just starting out, 17 percent are minorities; 26 percent of interns hired in 1986 were minorities.

However, many of the young people who enter the profession with the best backgrounds don't stay. Lisa Chung of the *San Francisco Chronicle* told editors at their 1987 convention that a dozen of the nineteen people who had graduated with her from the 1980 Summer Program for Minority Journalists at the University of California at Berkeley were no longer in the news business. A stunning 56 percent of American newsrooms have no minorities. None. Only 3.9 percent of newspaper executives are minorities. With few women among newspaper executives, the dearth of minorities represents a double-whammy for women who are black, Latina, or Asian-American.

Newspaper editors have committed themselves to achieving minority representation in the nation's newsrooms equal to that in the general population by the year 2000. They probably won't make it. ASNE has particularly tried to help smaller newspapers,

175

which traditionally have provided entry-level jobs, by holding collective job fairs and by providing consultants to help editors who want help. However, Judith Clabes, editor of *The Kentucky Post* in Covington, and head of ASNE's minorities committee, reported in 1987 that there still seemed to be "too many who need convincing" that hiring and promoting minorities not only is the morally right thing to do but is also good for business. A better-integrated staff helps papers reach more potential readers, she said.

American newsrooms were double-barred against minority women's entry until the women who entered in college during (or as a result of) the civil rights movement graduated and were encouraged to seek newspaper jobs. There were only a few exceptions in the 1950s and 1960s. Women today know of Dorothy Gilliam, now a columnist at *The Washington Post*; Nancy Hicks Maynard, formerly of *The New York Times* and later director of the minority journalism program at the University of California; and Charlayne Hunter-Gault, who reported for *The New York Times* before joining "The McNeil-Lehrer Report" on public television.

Fewer have heard of Marvel Cooke. Cooke spent most of her career in the black press. (The experiences of women in that segment of the press should be the subject of another book.) An English major at the University of Minnesota, Cooke got her first job because her mother knew black intellectual leader W. E. B. DuBois. Leaving Minnesota, a state with few blacks where she had gotten more than a whiff of discrimination, Cooke knew she wanted to live in a black community. She headed for Harlem. She started work as a secretary for *Crisis*, the NAACP magazine that DuBois edited. When he got into political disagreements with the NAACP leaders in 1934, he left, and she had to find another job.

It was very difficult. "I applied to *The Amsterdam News*, which was the largest black paper in the East at that time. I got a job as the secretary to the women's editor. No women had jobs on the news side." Frustrated, she stayed a while, then got married and went to teach at a black college in North Carolina. She lost that job during the Depression. Back in New York for a visit, she bumped into the *Amsterdam News* editor, who was looking for someone to run a features syndicate. " 'The job is really for a man'—this is what he said to me—'but we don't have enough money to hire a man and a secretary. You could do the work, and

I wouldn't have to hire a secretary because you can type.' So that's how I got back into the newspaper field."

Cooke joined the fledgling American Newspaper Guild and went on strike for eleven weeks in 1935 as the union sought recognition as the bargaining unit. "We walked the streets in a very cold November. The strike was settled on Christmas Eve. We won, and we went back in. I got my first really authentic job then as a reporter at the *News* covering everything. Of course, there was a lot of prejudice against me [as a woman]."

"I remember the very first assignment I was sent on. The editor sent me out to cover a murder, and it was a grim, grisly murder. I had never seen anyone murdered before in my life. He thought I would cave in, which I did not."

She worked for *The Amsterdam News* for several years and then went to *The People's Voice*, run by Adam Clayton Powell, later congressman from New York. The editor was a drunk, Cooke recalls; he would go out on sprees and leave her to run the paper. Finally he decided he could no longer work. Powell asked him who was going to run the paper. "He said, 'Marvel. She's been doing it for the last year.' I was assistant managing editor, but they would not offer me the job of managing editor."

The paper folded in 1947. Cooke then got a job on *The Compass*, a successor of sorts to the liberal, experimental paper *P.M.* in New York. A friend who worked there had been urging the hiring of blacks. "*P.M.* and *The Compass* had concentrated on the black area, but there were no black workers there and no women."

Cooke soon proved her value to the paper. "A young black prisoner—he was in one of the prisons around here for the criminally insane—had been discharged back home in Brownsville, which is a section of Brooklyn. He hadn't been home more than two or three days before he shot up the place and killed a few people. . . . One of my fellow reporters, Daniel Gilmore, had been sent to cover the story. That community, which is mainly black even yet, had just closed around that family. A white reporter couldn't get through.

"So Dan called the office and said, 'Marvel's the only person I think could get through here. They're just not letting anyone through.' There were real barricades. It turns out the family was well liked. This was just a sick boy in the family. They weren't letting any of these white people through to write awful stories. So I got a taxi and went on over and met Dan. Dan and I were able to walk through. . . .

"When we said who we were, the woman said, 'I'm not letting anybody in.' I said—we were Negro then, not black—I said, 'I am Negro and I work for *The Compass*, and I do understand the problem as possibly a white reporter would not understand. I think somebody is going to write this story. It's going to be written. I think it would be better if I do it than somebody else.' Well, she did let us in, and we got a terrific story. After that, I sold the paper on doing a series on Brownsville."

Even after these successes, Cooke recalls that as the only black and the only woman at *The Compass*, she had "a very difficult time with the managing editor." He found fault with everything she wrote. Finally, he "had to admit that he did not want a woman on the staff because he couldn't use his four-letter words. I answered that and said, 'Well, I'm accustomed to them. I don't use them myself, but I've been out in the streets of Harlem.' " She also got him to admit eventually that some racism was involved. "And he and I got along after that."

Cooke was covering the Rosenberg trial when the paper closed in 1952. The millionaire who owned the newspaper ran for the state senate and used the paper for publicity; after he lost, he had no more use for the paper. That was Cooke's last newspaper job. In the years since, Cooke says, "I think that black men and women, but particularly women, have become trained. . . . It used to be for a black woman, you had to be a social worker or teacher, nothing else. Look what's happening to the women on TV. I wouldn't want that if I were young; I would rather sit down and work with words and ideas. But I look at the black women on TV—we have some beautiful black women on TV—and I say, 'Well, I was a forerunner.' There were not many opportunities when I came along, almost none."

Cooke has no regrets, though, about the era and the area in which she lived. The Harlem apartment building in which she has lived for decades was a home for the black artistic renaissance of the 1930s. "I knew and had a wonderful relationship with Langston Hughes," she says, holding out a book of poetry that Hughes had autographed for her. "Paul Robeson was around

Right, Bess Furman, who worked for the Associated Press and later *The New York Times,* greets the Truman family at a Women's National Press Club dinner in 1945.

Left, Ruth Cowan, Associated Press correspondent in England, interviews two U.S. Navy nurses newly arrived to serve in Britain in 1944.

Sigrid Arne of the Associated Press, with U.S. Army Engineers clearing the way for road crews on the Alaska Highway in 1942.

The Woman's Angle...

Know what we found out? More women read an afternoon newspaper than men.

And something else . . . Women don't look just for news about fashion and food. They want news of people . . . items of human interest . . . children . . . schools . . . and today's social problems such as drug addiction.

We know that today's woman (our reader) wants to be more aware. She looks for "in depth" news coverage.

We give it to her . . . information on the rising school population problem . . . the needs of a retarded child . . . the needs of the public library . . . things affecting her children.

R e p o r t i n g with the woman's touch here is Maureen Connolly. She covers those stories where a woman's views are essential.

Maureen grew up and resides in nearby West Newbury and is a graduate of Pentucket Regional High School. She attended the University of Massachusetts at Boston.

On the weekly Woman's Outlook, which she edits, fashion, food and social news is given.

Weddings, engagements and anniversaries, all are important events in people's lives, and we give news of these in daily and weekly coverage, plus daily news on clubs and organizations.

The modern woman's angle for the modern woman.

Today's woman wants to know more than just that mini skirts are "in" this year.

There's more to women's news.

The Daily NEWS

IT'S BIG on the LOCAL ANGLE

House ad in the Newburyport, Massachusetts, *Daily News* in 1968, promoting "The Woman's Angle" and its reporter Maureen Connolly, who later was among the women suing the Associated Press for sex discrimination.

Second from left, Frances Lewine of the Associated Press, and reporters Hazel Markel, Isabelle Shelton, and Dorothy McCardle with President Lyndon Johnson in December 1963 after a party at the White House.

The photograph of reporter Marvel Cooke that ran with her story in the *Daily Compass* in 1950 about exploitation of domestic help.

(Douglas Chevalier, Washington Post)

Dr. Robert Martin and Judith Martin, then a *Washington Post* staff writer, now Miss Manners, with their daughter Jacobina, picketing in 1972 against the Gridiron Club's refusal to admit women.

Karen Carter and her unique equal pay protest at the *Houston Chronicle* in 1977.

(Barbara Sorensen)

Gayle Pollard, then with *The Boston Globe,* at a church women's meeting. Pollard, now an editorial writer for the *Los Angeles Times,* is the National Association of Black Journalists' vice president for print.

Even into the 1970s, women who were reporters often did stunts on behalf of their papers to call attention to local events. One brushed a rhino's teeth; here Susan Jetton, then with the *Charlotte Observer,* rides an elephant in a circus parade.

Associated Press correspondent Tad Bartimus in Vietnam in 1973.

Hilda Bryant, formerly of the *Seattle Post-Intelligencer,* slipped into Afghanistan and traveled with Afghan guerrillas operating against a Soviet encampment in July 1980.

More women than ever covered the 1984 presidential campaign, including (from *left*) Alison Mitchell of *Newsday*, Elaine Shannon of *Newsweek*, Patricia O'Brien of Knight-Ridder and Lyn Sherr of ABC, who traveled with Geraldine Ferraro.

Center, Mary McGrory of *The Washington Post*, on the scene as usual, sitting at the press table while Lt. Col. Oliver North is being sworn in at the Iran Contra hearings, 1987.

A salute to the men and women

LEE P. WEBBER
AGANA, GUAM

CATHERINE SHEN
HONOLULU, HAWAII

SUSAN CLARK-JACKSON
RENO, NEV.

ROBERT B. MILLER JR.
BATTLE CREEK, MICH.

DAN A. MARTIN
HUNTINGTON, W. VA.

NANCY L. GREEN
RICHMOND, IND.

J.C. HICKMAN
BELLINGHAM, WASH.

MARY PARKS STIER
IOWA CITY, IOWA

VINCENT E. SPEZZANO
ROCHESTER, N.Y.

DAVID J. MACK
BINGHAMTON, N.Y.

PAM JOHNSON
ITHACA, N.Y.

MICHAEL J. COLEMAN
ROCKFORD, ILL.

GORDON R. BLACK
BOISE, IDAHO

KENNETH ANDREWS
JACKSON, MISS.

BERNARD M. GRIFFIN
ST. CLOUD, MINN.

FRANK J. VEGA
BREVARD COUNTY, FLA.

MICHAEL CRAFT
JACKSON, TENN.

RONALD E. DILLMAN
ST. THOMAS, V.I.

FRED L. FOSTER
BRIDGEWATER, N.J.

RICHARD L. HOLTZ
LAFAYETTE, IND.

WILLIAM R. STONE
SALEM, ORE.

DONNA M. DONOVAN
BURLINGTON, VT.

RICKI W. SMITH-COYNE
LANSDALE, PA.

KAREN A. WITTMER
SALINAS, CALIF.

ROBERT T. COLLINS
CAMDEN, N.J.

MALCOLM W. APPLEGATE
LANSING, MICH.

GARY T. STOUT
DANVILLE, ILL.

PAT THOMPSON FRANTZ
CHAMBERSBURG, PA.

WILLIAM T. MALONE
LITTLE ROCK, ARK.

DIANE L. BORDEN
SANTA FE, N.M

PETER A. HORVITZ
CHILLICOTHE, OHIO

GEORGE N. GILL
LOUISVILLE, KY.

MONTE I. TRAMMER
SARATOGA SPRINGS, N.Y.

GEORGIA C. VOYSEY
MARIETTA, OHIO

JOHN P. ZANOTTI
CINCINNATI, OHIO

GERALD A. BEAN
SAN BERNARDINO, CALIF.

A Gannett house ad appearing in *Editor & Publisher* during the American
Newspaper Publishers Association convention in 1987.

who publish Gannett newspapers

THOMAS FENTON
EL PASO, TEXAS

SARA M. BENTLEY
FREMONT, NEB.

JAMES T. BARNES JR.
MARIN COUNTY, CALIF.

MICHAEL A. LIND
COFFEYVILLE, KAN.

CHARLES T. WANNINGER
MARION, IND.

LAWRENCE R. FULLER
SIOUX FALLS, S.D.

BRUCE Q. MACKEY
SPRINGFIELD, ILL.

CHARLES C. EDWARDS JR.
DES MOINES, IOWA

CHRISTOPHER S. DIX
STOCKTON, CALIF.

SONJA CRAIG
WAUSAU, WIS.

VERNON "BODIE" McCRORY
MONROE, LA.

JANET SANFORD
VISALIA, CALIF.

MAURICE L. HICKEY
DETROIT, MICH.

CHRIS E. JENSEN
MUSKOGEE, OKLA.

E. ROANNE FRY
STURGIS, MICH.

RICHARD B. TUTTLE
ELMIRA, N.Y.

JOHN SEIGENTHALER
NASHVILLE, TENN.

CARLOS D. RAMIREZ
NEW YORK, N.Y.

PAMELA F. MEALS
OLYMPIA, WASH.

BROOKS JOHNSON
FORT COLLINS, COLO.

THOMAS A. BOOKSTAVER
TARENTUM, PA.

TERRY G. HOPKINS
FORT MYERS, FLA.

W. HOWARD BRONSON JR.
SHREVEPORT, LA.

JANET KRAUSE
NIAGARA FALLS, N.Y.

RICHARD S. FEENEY
NORWICH, CONN.

JOHN H. McMILLAN
UTICA, N.Y.

RONALD A. ORTIZ
VINELAND AND
MILLVILLE, N.J.

DENISE BANNISTER
GAINESVILLE, GA.

MICHAEL B. GAGE
GREEN BAY, MICH.

JAMES F. DAUBEL
FREMONT AND
PORT CLINTON, OHIO

C. DONALD HATFIELD
TUCSON, ARIZ.

KAREN A. OPPENHEIM
PALM SPRINGS AND
INDIO, CALIF.

PAUL B. FLYNN
PENSACOLA, FLA.

DUANE K. McCALLISTER
PORT HURON, MICH.

JOSEPH M. UNGARO
WESTCHESTER-
ROCKLAND, N.Y.

ROBERT E. ROBBINS
HATTIESBURG, MISS.

RICHARD K. WAGER
POUGHKEEPSIE, N.Y.

SAL DEVIVO
WILMINGTON, DEL.

CATHLEEN BLACK
PUBLISHER
USA TODAY

THOMAS CURLEY
PRESIDENT
USA TODAY

GANNETT

(Christian Science Monitor *photo*)

Katherine Fanning, editor of *The Christian Science Monitor* and the first woman to serve as president of the American Society of Newspaper Editors.

Janet Chusmir became the highest-ranking woman on a major newspaper when she was named executive editor of the *Miami Herald* in 1987.

(Miami Herald *photo*)

Marita Hernandez of the *Los Angeles Times*, on assignment in Nochistlan, Mexico, in 1984.

Dorothy Gilliam, pioneering reporter and now columnist for *The Washington Post*.

Jennifer Werner of the *Seattle Post-Intelligencer*, typically alone in a sea of male faces, photographing a news conference.

Left, Lisa Chung of *The San Francisco Chronicle* and Catherine Shen, *Honolulu Star Bulletin* publisher, at the first national convention of the Asian-American Journalists Association in Los Angeles in 1987.

From *left*, Christy Bulkeley, first woman publisher of a Gannett daily; Marj Paxson, retired publisher of the Muskogee, Oklahoma, *Phoenix;* and Peg Simpson of Hearst newspapers confer at the third annual Journalism and Women Symposium in Estes Park, Colorado, 1987.

during the 1930s, and I knew all these people. I think I've been very lucky. Somebody said to me not long ago, 'Do you mind being your age?' I said, 'Not at all.' If I weren't my age, I wouldn't have known W. E. B. DuBois. I wouldn't have known Langston Hughes. I wouldn't have known Paul Robeson. I wouldn't have missed it."

The professional climate had changed little for blacks by the 1950s, when Dorothy Gilliam began her career. She had worked at *The Louisville Defender*, the black weekly in her hometown, while a student at Ursuline College. The society editor there became ill and Gilliam, hired as a typist, became the new society editor at 17. "I had never written a story except for the high school newspaper. So I practically went out the door within moments covering some Louisville version of a fancy middle-class black party." The experience confirmed Gilliam's desire to be a journalist.

Gilliam later transferred to Lincoln University in Jefferson City, Missouri, where she got her bachelor's degree. "I spent several weeks—months, really—trying to find a job. I finally ended up going back to work for a black weekly in 1958." She ran into what she was sure were twin biases because she was black and female. She worked the next few years in the black press, then realized she was going to have to have "some white credentials" if she were to have any hope of getting a better job. She applied to Columbia Journalism School and was interviewed by a man who, she later discovered, wrote that she was good but "you know, this is a really dark-skinned black person." In other words, Gilliam says, there was not going to be any doubt about who she was. She enrolled as one of two blacks in the Columbia class of 1961.

The Washington Post routinely interviewed Columbia graduates, and its city editor, Ben Gilbert, interviewed Gilliam. He encouraged her to get more experience but to keep in touch. While on a fellowship in Africa, she wrote some pieces for the *Post*. "I'm sure they didn't set the world on fire, but they struck a little spark. . . . The times were beginning to change slightly. So when I got back, they offered me a job. . . . At the time there were three blacks. Some people say I was the first woman.

"It was pretty rough in many, many ways. There were lots of restaurants around here that I couldn't eat at. This was 1961. Remember, the Civil Rights Act didn't pass until 1964." Ben

179

Gilbert tried to help her feel more comfortable and asked Elsie Carper, a reporter who is now assistant managing editor at the *Post,* to be sure to go out to lunch with her. The women had to eat at the YWCA, bypassing segregated restaurants on the way.

Gilliam was determined to cover stories not only about blacks and women, but she met frustration. "I went to cover somebody's 100th birthday on Massachusetts Avenue—a high-rent district. First, the doorman really could not believe that I was supposed to come in the front door. This was a black doorman, right? Then when I got upstairs . . . I got, 'You are from the *Post?* Are you sure?' . . .

"I think I did a lot of repression. There really weren't ways to express it. There was nobody to talk to." She could share her thoughts with one of the black men on the staff, but even he thought she was cool and collected about handling the stress, when actually she was torn up inside. "In terms of keeping the job, I couldn't walk around storming and screaming." Although she did make friends with other blacks around the city, few could understand because so few had been in newsrooms.

Gilliam started to recognize that despite her misgivings, some of the best stories were about welfare. "The war on poverty was starting. The paper was also very interested. . . . I thought, 'You're missing all the good stories by trying to be general assignment,' so I sought after these beats."

After one series on Junior Village for homeless children, Sen. Robert Byrd of West Virginia, then chairman of the District Appropriations Committee, decided to investigate. "By that time I had gotten married and I was pregnant. I remember one day we were walking around Junior Village, and he was going from place to place, and there were all these children. The pathos was obvious. It was a very draining situation. I was six months pregnant and very tired and at one point I was really dragging. Senator Byrd reaches over and helps me across a ditch, and I wanted to say, 'This is the first southern black woman you've ever helped across a ditch,' but I decided I wouldn't do it."

Looking back on that portion of her career, Gilliam says, "I am sure some of the stories I got, I was able to penetrate more deeply because I was a black woman. . . . I was able to emphathize. I had for a brief period in my life been on welfare when my daddy died and my mother was trying to get her life reorganized, so I could sympathize with being on welfare, and I certainly could sympathize with being poor. It wasn't that there weren't white people who had some of the experiences, but I know that some of the people were happier talking to me. They said they were."

Gilliam traveled to Oxford, Mississippi, to help cover James Meredith's entry into Ole Miss. "In those days, they had to send two reporters if they were going to get to the black community. They knew they couldn't send me to do the white story. I remember a guy named Bill Chapman was covering the campus, and I was covering some of the black community. He stayed at the Sand and Sea Motel and I stayed at the black funeral home because there were no places for black people to stay.

"It was a fantastic story. If you can imagine a classic small town but overflowing with federal troops, then you have the picture. Federal troops on one hand and an a roused redneck populace. They were trailing any car that had Memphis tags. I had flown to Memphis and rented a car because I wanted to use a photographer that I knew from Memphis . . . and so he went with me and we were trailed. It was scarey; I was glad he was with me.

"One night when I was at the funeral home, there was all this commotion, and I thought, 'What is going on?' Two blacks had been killed during the night, and we figured out that these were the warning to the local black community—that there may be all that going on over there, but this is to let you know who's still boss, who still runs things. In many ways as I look back, I think that was one of the shining hours of the press in terms of really covering an American story that made a difference."

Gilliam became a columnist in 1979 after serving for seven years as an assistant editor in the "Style" section. Her subjects cover a wide range but repeatedly focus on sociological change from individuals' perspectives, on families, minority affairs, and education.

"I think a young black woman coming out with my background today—certainly the opportunities would be much, much broader today," Gilliam says. Yet there remains little mobility among black reporters. They break in, but they plateau and grow dissatisfied, according to a report by the Institute for Journalism Education, which runs the Berkeley summer program and an editing project in Tucson for minorities. Minorities actually stay at papers longer than white reporters, the Institute found; but many of them are thinking of leaving the business because they see few opportunities for advancement.[3] "The newspaper business is a scandal" in terms of the scarcity of minority executives, Gilliam says.

"The only move you see is lateral. Nobody sees any prospects for change," Gilliam said during an interview at the *Post*. "This paper is going to lose a lot of people as well, a lot of journeymen. Maybe from a corporate standpoint, they don't care. They can lose someone who's been around for ten or twelve years. You're paying them a lot more than you pay a young person. But you lose the long view, and if you understand the credibility problem newspapers are now having, you realize you can't afford to do that."

Not long after Gilliam started her career at the Post, Bea Hines broke in at *The Miami Herald*. Encouraged by the 1964 Civil Rights Act to find a better job, Hines, a widow with two sons who was working as a maid, answered ad after ad. The *Herald* was "impressed by the fact that I knew what a résumé and a letter of application were" and hired Hines to work as a library file clerk. She attended Dade Community College, where she met the *Herald*'s book editor, Fred Shaw. He told her she had a future in writing, but she was skeptical because there were no black reporters on the *Herald*. Hines then got a three-month tryout with Shaw's help.

She showed up for her first day of work "dressed in high-heeled shoes and my Sunday-go-to-meeting clothes," only to be sent to cover riots that had just begun. She didn't know how to do anything, she said years later, but she did know how to watch. She got a staff reporting job as a result of her coverage.[4]

Nancy Hicks Maynard, who has since gone into law and whose husband owns *The Oakland Tribune*, attended Long Island University. Her strategy was to "go to a school that had *New York Times* editors as teachers." Given a choice between a news assistant's job at the *Times*—a fancy title for clerk—and a reporting tryout at the *New York Post*, Maynard chose the tryout, even though she knew she might get dumped. "You always have to practice the highest art form, and that was reporting."

She started as a general assignment reporter for the *Post* in 1967 and a year later during the school strike went to *The New*

York Times. She covered education, then did general assignments, then went on special assignment to the science section to help cover the moon landing. She wrote about the learning process, psychology, sociology. Moving later to Washington, she covered health, education, and social policy.

Being female helped. "One of my first reporting jobs was to go in and be a substitute teacher during the strike. It started when I went in to do a story on Head Start because I looked like a kindergarten teacher. . . . The union accused me of strikebreaking. I covered education—maybe that's easier for women. I got an interview with Rap Brown when he was released from federal prison on weapons charges. A friend of mine helped me get into the car in which Brown was leaving. They may have thought I was Rap's girlfriend, and I didn't disabuse them of that."

Like other black women interviewed, Maynard has found that "the editing class"—as she calls the predominantly white male group that edits American newspapers—has less tolerance for mistakes by minorities than it does for those of its own members. "There is this underlying assumption of incompetence. It's one of those things that almost any mistake is attributed to that. It's not that you're young. It's not that you're inexperienced. It's not for all those reasons. One incident cannot make and break a career, but it can make a difference for a person of color. You don't get to make an awful lot of mistakes. . . . Women don't, either. But they have to overcome different issues. Their basic intelligence is not in question. Their ability to cope, their temperament, their toughness—but not their basic intelligence. It's a big moat to get over."

Being black is almost universally more of an identifying factor for black women in the newspaper business than being female. Talking about being one of a kind on an editorial page, Pat Fisher of *The Seattle Times* remarks that she thinks of herself more as the only black person on that staff than as the only woman. Like white women who took some time to find their voice as women in a man's newspaper world, some black women said that it is only recently that they have been willing to focus more on issues that really gripped them as blacks and as women.

Fisher, for example. A communications major at the University of Washington, she had tried to get jobs on the local newspapers, but they weren't interested—"not in me, anyway." She taught at the university, and years later, as riots were occurring, the papers suddenly were looking for black reporters. "They wanted a black who was a journalism major. They didn't dare *not* hire me." She covered higher education, courts, and general assignment and in 1979 became an editorial writer.

A few years ago she realized that the issues "that brought out passion in my writing were things about blacks and women . . . that's what my voice was. I made a New Year's resolution in 1984 to change the direction and scope of my writing. I had avoided, let certain things pass. Now I would seek them out." One thing she did was persuade the *Times* to send her to the southern region of Africa in the fall of 1985.

At roughly the same time, the same thoughts were occurring to Jerelyn Eddings at *The Sun* in Baltimore. When she was working for United Press International in Atlanta, Eddings recalls, "I had always resented doing the women's issues. I tried not to do black stories. I tried not to be typecast."

Stymied in her attempts to get to Washington, Eddings won an American Political Science Association congressional fellowship, which brought her to the nation's capital to work for then Rep. Paul Simon of Illinois and Sen. Daniel Inouye of Hawaii. In 1979, she finally got to Washington with UPI, and as is traditional in the wire services, she got the least desirable assignment because she was the new person in the bureau. For years, covering the budget had been the bottom of the heap. "It was a decent story in the last year of the Carter Administration, but it was absolutely *the* story when Ronald Reagan came to town. There I was sitting on what was supposed to be this awful assignment, and it was the biggest story on the Hill."

She was hired as only the second woman ever on *The Sun*'s editorial page in 1982, brought to Baltimore to write about the subjects she had covered in Washington—Congress, the budget. "And from January 1982 until September 1984 I wrote editorials on basically those subjects. But then I got a Nieman. That started in September 1984. In writing that Nieman application, I worked through some things I had been fighting since college. I realized that I'd succeeded and was doing all those things and now the question was how was I going to make all these things I'd learned work for people who might not have these choices? How would I make them useful for blacks and women?"

After her Nieman Fellowship year at Harvard, her editor, Joseph Sterne, suggested that she write a column. *The Sun* hadn't had a Nieman Fellow for some years and wanted to spotlight its winner. Eddings thought about ways to direct her attention, "now that I wasn't afraid of being shoved into things." In November 1986, for example, she wrote a column called "More Voices for the Choir"[5] about the progress made by women and blacks in journalism and the dearth of them in top newspaper jobs. "A newspaper can hardly serve a diverse community unless its own staff reflects the richness of those different voices," Eddings wrote. "Women represent 53 percent of the potential readers. Minorities are 14 percent of the population nationally, and a much larger percentage of large metropolitan areas. Until these groups are well represented throughout news staffs, something important is being lost."

After Dorothy Gilliam and after Nancy Hicks Maynard, a spurt of black women entered the profession. There were Fisher and Eddings and Eddings's roommate at the University of South Carolina, Betty Anne Williams, now an assistant managing editor at the Rochester *Democrat and Chronicle*. Karen Howze worked the police beat at the *San Francisco Chronicle* and covered municipal courts during her tour there from 1972 and 1978 and went then to *Newsday*, the Rochester *Times-Union*, and *USA Today* as editor of its international edition.

And more: Gayle Pollard, a graduate of the University of Michigan and Columbia Journalism School, started at *The Miami Herald* in 1972 before going to *The Boston Globe* and *Los Angeles Times*. Jackie Thomas, with a master's degree from the Columbia University School of International Affairs, joined *The Chicago Sun-Times* in 1974, had a Nieman Fellowship in 1983, worked at *The Louisville Times*, and is now associate editor of the *Detroit Free Press*. Pamela Moreland, a 1976 Northwestern University master's graduate, worked at papers in Oceanside and Pasadena before going to *The Los Angeles Herald Examiner* and then the *Los Angeles Times*. Carmen Fields, who like Gilliam went to Lincoln University because "it was the only predominantly black school with a degree in journalism," started at *The Boston Globe* in 1972 after getting a master's degree. She had a Nieman Fellowship in 1986. Angela Dodson worked at Gannett papers and at Gannett's news service in Washington before ending up at *The New York Times*. Sandy Banks was a sportswriter on *The Cleveland Call and Post* before joining *The Cleveland Press* and later the *Los Angeles Times*.

And in November 1981, when Gannett officials named Pam M. Johnson to head their paper in Ithaca, New York, she became the first black woman to be publisher of a general-market daily newspaper in the United States. Johnson came into publishing through the academic as much as the newsroom route. A graduate of the University of Wisconsin, Johnson joined *The Chicago Tribune* one year after Chicago's urban riots but then returned to Wisconsin, where she completed a Ph.D. in journalism and educational psychology. She taught at Norfolk State University in Virginia, where she caught the eye of Gannett recruiters, who sent her first to *The Bridgewater* [New Jersey] *Courier-News* as general manager and then to *The Ithaca Journal*.

Like Madison, where she attended college, Ithaca is a university town. "And Gannett gave me its best paper of the year," Johnson told a magazine interviewer. "I just knew they were setting me up for success."

What happened that brought these women into the newsroom? It wasn't that black women suddenly started to work. Hardly. They had always of necessity been in the work force in greater proportion than white women, even when their husbands had jobs, because pay was so low for all black workers. Most were day workers or took in laundry; others held the most onerous jobs in tobacco factories or fish-processing plants. Some, however, moved into teaching, where they received less pay than whites. The picture started to change for all working women during World War II as more jobs opened for women. After the war, black women, last hired, were first fired.

The civil rights movement of the 1950s and 1960s started the change. Colleges were picketed and protested and prodded into enrolling more minorities; by the late 1960s and 1970s these students were graduating. The civil rights movement—and damning reports like the Kerner Commission's—embarrassed the white media into hiring more minorities. Women like Betty Anne Williams acknowledge their debt to the people who came before them.

At 22, after six months with the Associated Press in Columbia, South Carolina, and one year in Charlotte, North Carolina, Williams went to the AP's Washington bureau. "I was the beneficiary of the civil rights movement that made news executives look around and realize they had no black people in their newsrooms."

Many of the black people who were hired were women because, as Nancy Hicks Maynard comments, newspapers seem more willing to hire black women than black men. "There is a fear of black men in so much of our culture. People hire people like themselves. White women are more familiar to white men than black women, black women are more familiar than black men. You would think it would be the other way around, but it's the softness and the fear of challenge. Black women are more educated in general than black men. There's a terrific attrition rate in the lives of a lot of black men."

The women who were hired endured slights and ran afoul of ignorant people—not only on their beats but in their newsrooms. And they were repeatedly asked whether a black person covering the black community could be objective. Says Betty Bayé, now an assistant city editor at *The* [Louisville] *Courier-Journal*, "I resented the question. I finally got so, when I knew I couldn't get the job anyway, that I said, 'Everybody knows only white male reporters can be objective. You've sent Jewish reporters to Israel and you don't ask them that.'"

Black women jump through the same hoops everyone else jumps through; then, just when a woman thinks she's going to achieve a breakthrough, one more hoop is invented. Carmen Fields tells about all the opportunities she had at *The Boston Globe* until 1977. She covered Jimmy Carter's campaign for the presidency; following the tradition of reporters who have covered a winning presidential candidate, she hoped to go to Washington after he won. "A lot of blacks had been stuck on his campaign because editors initially thought this peanut farmer wouldn't go anywhere. So Carter won and I said, 'I think I want to go to Washington.' There was great hedging and a lot of saying, 'Well, be patient.' You see, there had never been a black in the Washington bureau."

In general, says Gayle Pollard of the *Los Angeles Times*, "if you're a black woman and want to be an editor beyond the level of copy

187

desk, you have to work for a Gannett paper. Otherwise, you have limited choices. *The Sun* in Baltimore, *The Philadelphia Inquirer*, and some papers' neighborhood bureaus are willing to give people a chance. But the chance to be a foreign editor or national editor—even to be a metro reporter working downtown at some of the major papers—well, those doors haven't opened up."

Pollard, who was elected vice president for print of the National Association of Black Journalists in August 1987, says she regrets the distrust among the minority groups and between minorities and women when they must battle for those jobs white males don't get—even though she understands the origins of the feelings. She adds: "Black women simply do not enjoy the natural progression of young white men in their late twenties and, occasionally, young white women. We're expected to wait our turn. That would be okay if there were some guarantee that by being a good girl, it would pay off before you were 40 and considered too old to have anything to do with managing the people who work the streets."

There are still few black women who are editorial-page staffers or newspaper columnists. One of the most sensitive was Leanita McClain of the *Chicago Tribune*. As a columnist she had the freedom to focus on the pull she felt between the black working-class, housing-project culture in which she had grown up and the white professional world in which she found herself rising. She was angry about the racism in Chicago's mayoral election, angry also that it taught her she could hate.

I never heard of Leanita McClain until she died. She committed suicide on Memorial Day 1984.[6] But a posthumous collection of her columns, *A Foot in Each World*, reveals a writer of understanding, one who spoke with equal poignancy about the messages sports heroes could carry and about the realities of inner-city schools.[7] She was proud that she had made it from tough beginnings, and she told inner-city students they could make it, too.

She did not turn her back on her past. She couldn't. She'd go to a business lunch and find an old classmate waiting on her table, or she'd hear of a boy from church in prison for murder. "Sometimes," she wrote, "I meet my aunt getting off the bus with other cleaning ladies on their way to do my neighbors' floors."[8]

Intellectually, she seemed to understand her position; emotionally, it tore her apart.

Newspapers, like society, have not always made it easy for black women and other women of color, just as they are not easy on sensitive people of any shade, any sex. Where newspaper executives' consciousness has been raised, their efforts have focused largely on increasing the number of black reporters in newsrooms and less on increasing their comfort. Realization about the lack of Hispanic and Asian-American journalists dawned even more slowly, indeed has yet to dawn at some newspapers. The level of awareness seems directly correlated to the influx of immigrants into a given community or, in some cases, to pockets of Hispanics or Asian-Americans who already lived in an area. Thus, the odds of finding Hispanic or Asian-American reporters in newsrooms are greater in Miami, in some Texas cities and the rest of the Southwest, and in some California cities.

Among the most prominent Asian-American journalists is Catherine Shen, publisher of the *Honolulu Star-Bulletin*. A native of Boston, she graduated from Wellesley and the Claremont Graduate School and first worked as an art editor for a textbook publisher in San Francisco. Moving to Maine for a simpler life, she worked as a reporter for *The Brunswick-Bath Times Record* but found life almost too simple there and moved back to San Francisco. She became a copyeditor with the *Chronicle* in 1974 and stayed eleven years, copyediting, revamping the Sunday news magazine, and editing the feature section. Then a Gannett executive she'd met recruited her for *USA Today*, and one year later, in September 1986, she started as publisher in Honolulu.

Although Hawaii's newspapers have long been a preserve of whites, the *Star-Bulletin* had links with the Asian-American community well before Shen arrived. Chinn Ho, a Chinese-American, owned the *Star-Bulletin*, then sold it to Gannett for three times what he had paid for it. Still, Shen says, it's viewed as unusual to have a Chinese-American woman as publisher—and one perceived as young (even though she's now 40). "If you're a woman, you're always perceived as young. You're fighting being a woman, you're fighting anything that makes you seem less qualified."

189

Lisa Chung, a *San Francisco Chronicle* reporter, echoes Shen's words. Chung, who's in her early thirties, recalls an interview early in her career with a man whose chemical company had begun manufacturing explosives, raising community concern. The man clearly was uncomfortable talking to her and was patronizing her. "The interview fizzled. I hadn't gotten what I needed because I wasn't being taken seriously.

"Here I was, looking even younger than I was, being Asian, being short, being female. It all added up that he thought he didn't have to deal with me seriously." At that moment, Chung saw only one possible solution. "I was kicking myself for wearing this blouse with a scalloped collar because it looked frivolous," she says with the hint of a smile. "I was thinking maybe I shouldn't have worn that. It was the only thing about myself I could have changed. I should have worn a 'serious' blouse that day. And I shouldn't have had to worry about that."

Discomfort about ethnicity and gender affects editors as swell. The rapport between editor and reporter grows partly from how the editor perceives the reporter's abilities, but "it's also your persona," Chung says. "Editors who come from an area where there aren't a lot of whatever you are are uncomfortable."

Chung, who grew up in the Silicon Valley before it was called the Silicon Valley, got her first job at *The Hartford Courant* after graduating from Mills College and the Berkeley summer program. She joined the *Chronicle* in 1983 and now does general assignments there as well as covering the Asian-American community. Her own heritage, she says, has affected her reporting style in that she knows to "pay proper respects first." That background helps her do her homework first—gathering the background from ancillary sources, going in the side door, as it were—before going to the main source.

So does ethnicity make a difference? Certainly. How much? Hard to tell. Evelyn Hsu of *The Washington Post* emigrated from Hong Kong to the United States with her family when she was a child. She grew up poor in Los Angeles in a family with little command of English. But her mother made a point of reading newspapers, so Evelyn assumed that newspapers were important. She went to the University of California at Berkeley, later enrolled in the summer program, and then worked at the *San Francisco Chronicle*.

Today, she says, it is hard to separate out what stories she's done because she's a woman, an Asian, or poor when she was growing up. "Asian is probably easiest," she says, because there had been so few Asian reporters and the Asian community had always had an adversarial relationship with the *Chronicle*. One of her first big stories was covering a protest against a new Charlie Chan film that the Asian community found offensive.

Asian-American communities are relatively uncovered—or when covered, they are considered distinct from the rest of a city rather than part of the dailyness of life in the city. Asians of Chinese heritage, Japanese, Korean, and Vietnamese are sometimes hostile groups yet are often lumped together into one category with no recognition of conflicting interests.

And Asian-Americans have a unique set of problems when job-hunting. First of all, "Asians aren't perceived of as a minority," said Lisa Chung during a round-table discussion on the issue for the Associated Press Managing Editors.[9] One midlevel manager involved in that same discussion pointed to another problem for Asian-American journalists: "We are seen as reserved and hard-working, and that may not fit the profile of what senior executives are seeking for the managing or executive editorships," that is, creative self-starters. Family attitudes among immigrants can also work against young people going into journalism. Many Asian newspapers are tools of the government, and newspaper work is not considered an honorable profession.

Like blacks, like Latinos, like women, Asian-American journalists wonder whether they should specialize in covering their own groups, whose story may not be being told or is told wrong —or move into other areas and develop the same expertise as white male reporters. For the moment Lisa Chung does not mind covering the Asian community because she knows the stories might not get done otherwise. However, she might mind if she were at a paper in a city where that community was not as important as it is in San Francisco. "I don't like being expected to be the expert on every single Asian population that lives in the Bay Area."

Like blacks, Asian-Americans can make subtle differences in the way stories are covered. For example, Mei Mei Chan of *USA*

Today mentioned the lack of coverage of the Asian perspective on a black boycott of a Chinese grocery in Washington. Perhaps if there had been Asian-American journalists helping in the coverage, she said, "people would have opened up a bit."

Like blacks, like Asian-Americans, Latinas fight stereotypes. Yet they are middle class, they are poor; they are from families with long educational lineages, they are first-generation college graduates; they are immigrants themselves, they are native born; they are from Mexican heritage, Cuban, Panamanian, and Puerto Rican. They write about their communities, or they cover real estate.

Lorenza Rodriguez's mother's family had lived for generations in the Rio Grande Valley of Texas, yet she was born in Michigan during apple-picking season. Indeed, all the Rodriguez children were born during a different harvest season in a different part of the country. Her father, Rodriguez recalls, "had grand plans about sending us off to college." He settled into a job at Carnegie Steel in Milwaukee and had worked his way up to foreman before he died in an auto accident when Lori was six. Her mother moved the family back to Mission, Texas.

The women of Mission do unskilled work, packing grapefruit and oranges. Rodriguez herself helped with all the crops—cotton, canteloupe, citrus, beets. "I guess I've done everything. Most of what's grown in the Valley, I've picked or packed or done something to it."

Hating poverty and loving school, Rodriguez had the incentive to do well. "My mother did what Hispanic families do. She bought the *World Book*. Because we didn't have money for entertainment, we would spend evenings reading from it. *'No hay como la education.'* My mother hammered that into us, even when she was making tortillas out in the field. She was telling us this wasn't going to last forever. That we were doing this so we could buy clothes to go to school."

Lori Rodriguez told her school counselor, who was Hispanic, that she wanted to be a journalist. "Oh, no, Lori, that's a tough business. And you're Mexican and a woman," he said. "Go into science. They'll judge you for your talent." Rodriguez edited her school paper at Our Lady of the Lake College in San Antonio, then moved on to the University of Texas at Austin, where she edited the college paper. She worked after graduation for *The Houston Chronicle*, went to Washington with her husband, divorced, and returned to Houston. One editor told her she couldn't cover police except in emergencies because women didn't cover cops. But the city editor liked her writing, so she got feature assignments. She has covered Hispanic politics, women's political issues, the school board, and other stories.

Being in Texas, being in the South, Rodriguez finds herself no different from other women in one respect. "You're 'honey' and 'darlin' ' all the time. You face that from people you work with and for and people you interview. But if you're patient, you can get them to say things they might not say to a man. I'm not above doing that. But it is hard to be taken seriously."

Rodriguez, like others before her, resisted taking the Hispanic beat but finally saw the good stories that were available. Leyla Cattan, by contrast, wanted that beat from the start. She writes about it in Spanish for *The Arizona Star* in Tucson. Brought up in Panama and educated in Italy, Cattan immigrated to Arizona and learned English even though she writes in Spanish. She had worked for *El Dia* in Panama in the mid-1960s but wanted to do more than cover parties, weddings, and baptisms. "I wanted to interview ministers and secretaries of state, and I was finally able to manage to be a reporter on the street."

When Cattan moved to Tucson, she suggested to the local paper that she write articles in Spanish, but she got nowhere because the *Star* had no one in management who read Spanish: "I could be insulting their newspaper for all they knew." Finally, the paper hired someone in management—an Anglo—who knew Spanish. Cattan credits retired editor Frank Johnson with finally letting her do the column. She found that it was a job she had to want to do because of the technical problems involved. In the first years that she wrote the column, the *Star* lacked the facilities to print the diacritical marks—the accents and other marks needed for Spanish. So after Bill Waters, the Spanish-speaking editor, read her column, she had to send it to Nogales by bus; from there it was sent to Hermosillo, three hours away, where it was set; then it was sent back to Nogales, where someone would call her and she'd pick up the copy. She went through all this because she felt that what she wrote was important for Spanish-speaking people to learn, and she could afford to do it. Thanks to computers, the *Star* can now set her columns. Today, one of the *Star*'s five (out of seven) female editorial writers—Elaine Ayala—reads Cattan's copy.

Being Hispanic, writing in Spanish, Cattan felt she was reaching people who'd not been reached before. In 1975, for example, she interviewed Mexican-American women who had never been interviewed in connection with the International Women's Year meetings in Mexico City. She has written about Mexican-American families' achievements and about educational issues such as dropouts and privately financed scholarships from within the Mexican-American community. Hers is not a column in the opinion sense, Cattan says, but "just a window for them to come to talk. I can't pretend my background is universal. I didn't grow up in a barrio, picking cotton or fruit.

"I'm not a columnist commenting. I wanted to give them information. For many, that's something they've never had. If I start imposing my point of view on them, then I am not serving them. If we are more, than I can have the luxury of writing my point of view."

Marita Hernandez, one of the Pulitzer Prize–winning team on a Latino life series for the *Los Angeles Times*, had "a real middle-class background and was not very aware of a Latino heritage although I had lived in Mexico City as a child." She started journalistic life as a copy girl on *The San Diego Union* while attending San Diego State. On graduating, she got three or four job offers, mainly in heavily Latino areas. A Los Angeles native, she chose to stay in California and signed up with *The San Luis Obispo Telegram*.

The only Latina at her small paper, she took a special interest in covering the growing union-organizing activity of Cesar Chavez. Being a Latina covering Latinos wasn't really an issue there, she said, because the staff was small and the reporters banded together. "It was us against the system." Few Latino organizations had ever gotten coverage when Hernandez began at the *Telegram*. She spent a week with a farm worker family and found that her story on them was the first time the newspaper had had her perspective. "I lived with them, worked with them. By the end I had blisters on my hands and my back was sore."

To get more experience, Hernandez moved to *The San Jose Mercury News*. She had a rude awakening. Assigned to do reaction stories by interviewing people at a shopping mall, Hernandez complained that that wasn't what she'd been hired for. An editor replied, "I didn't hire you. We know why you're here"—implying she was there only to meet some quota. "It was the first time I'd confronted such racism. . . . I hadn't encountered another Latina in the newsroom until I came to Los Angeles. It's good to know that there are people there, that you have somebody else who understands where you are coming from."

Hispanic journalists are in the main young people because many of them, like Maggie Rivas of *The Dallas Morning News*, are first-generation college graduates. Rivas grew up in Devine, Texas, near San Antonio, where her father was a barber and her mother a housewife. In her parents' generation, "for kids to get a high school diploma was a big deal. The possibility wasn't there for them. . . . The only woman I knew who had graduated from college was a cousin who was a nurse."

After graduating from the University of Texas, Rivas went to Columbia Journalism School and then worked for UPI in Dallas. She won an Inter American Press Association fellowship that took her to Lima, Peru, for nine months. After that, she worked for *The Boston Globe* for three years, for a Dallas television station, and then for the *Morning News*'s business section.

Asked whether she thinks being a Chicana gives her difficulty in getting jobs today, Rivas replies in her infectious and not at all belligerent manner: "Whoever hires me knows what they're getting." That is, she has been an activist, interested in Chicano issues since she was in college. She and others need not always tailor their attitudes to those of the majority. Take her or leave her, she's herself. Today she has a choice, unlike the generation that came before her. Then, the world of journalism said to young women seeking jobs and not liking what they saw, "Take it or leave it." There is a generation of change in Maggie Rivas's statement, not change completed but change under way.

195

Everyday Indignities

One Saturday, young reporter Carmen Fields was sitting virtually alone in the *Boston Globe* newsroom. She was not sitting behind a post. Suddenly the phone rang: there was a big fire. It was cold and damp outside and Fields wasn't especially anxious to go out, but she thought this might be her big chance. The man in charge got on the phone to talk to one of his bosses to see who to send to cover to the fire, and Fields heard him say, "There's nobody here."

CHAPTER

12

Trenchcoats Come in Women's Sizes, Too

The *New York Tribune*'s correspondent in Rome was outlining for readers the qualities needed for an ambassador to Italy: "One that has experience of foreign life, that he may act with good judgment, and, if possible, a man that has knowledge and views which extend beyond the cause of party politics in the United States,—a man of unity in principles, but capable of understanding variety in forms. And send a man capable of prizing the luxury of living in, or knowing Rome; the office of Ambassador is one that should not be thrown away on a person who cannot prize or use it. Another century, and I might ask to be made Ambassador myself . . . but woman's day has not come yet."[1]

Margaret Fuller, writing in 1848, was prescient; woman's day had not come yet for ambassadors. It had also not come for foreign correspondents. Indeed, when Clare Booth Luce was named ambassador to Italy by President Eisenhower, not many more women than Fuller had become foreign correspondents.

Fuller reported from England, France, and Italy, in peace and in war, as America's first female foreign correspondent. It would be another seventy years—when Dorothy Thompson went to Europe—before another woman of such distinction, or indeed many other women at all, would report from overseas. Anne O'Hare McCormick was still a rarity when she won a Pulitzer Prize in 1937 for foreign commentary.

It is a given that any list of the top news stories of the year contains international crises and triumphs—coups, oil embargoes, religious warfare, evolutions of Latin American dictatorships into

197

fledgling democracies. Women have not often covered—and still are not covering—these top stories, events that shape readers' views of the world and help shape reporters' careers. The fact that a candidate for an overseas job is a woman still makes her invisible to some editors making foreign assignments. Women have had to fight not only to get into the newsroom but also to get out of it to go abroad for their newspapers.

World War II opened the door for an intrepid few women to become war correspondents. Ruth Cowan, who had covered Chicago gangsters and gone to Washington to cover Eleanor Roosevelt, got her Associated Press credentials as a war correspondent during World War II, picked up her military uniform, and headed off to North Africa. The AP bureau chief there had asked for reinforcements, but it turned out he didn't want women. So Cowan went to London and later went to the front for the Battle of the Bulge, hitchhiking back from the front with a French unit.

Loved and hated, admired and despised, Marguerite Higgins pushed her bosses at *The New York Herald-Tribune* to let her go overseas. It was 1944, and Higgins wanted to get to Europe before the war was over. She spoke French fluently, had studied German, and was learning Spanish and Russian. Getting nowhere, she bypassed her city editor; the publisher's wife, Helen Reid, made sure Higgins was sent to Europe.

After the war, Higgins, at 26, was named the *Herald-Tribune*'s Berlin bureau chief during the Soviet blockade of the city. When the German story shifted from Berlin to Bonn, Higgins wanted to shift with it, but she, too, was blockaded—she was told by her desk at home to stay in Berlin, essentially because she was not considered diplomatic enough to handle the complexities of the story. Then she was transferred to Tokyo, where her predecessor had been fortunate to get one story a week in the paper.[2]

Tokyo was dull at first, but Higgins was soon in the right place at the right time again when war began in Korea. With Keyes Beech of *The Chicago Daily News*, she made it into Seoul ahead of the North Koreans and then barely escaped. She covered the first week of the war for the *Herald-Tribune* by herself, traveling with Beech and scoring an exclusive interview with Gen. Douglas MacArthur, the Pacific commander, with whom she had hitched a ride back to Tokyo.

Once back in Korea, she and Homer Bigart of the *Herald-*

Tribune began a long-running feud. Bigart was designated the prime correspondent there, but Higgins was allowed to stay on over his protests because of the dimensions of the story. Bigart, a tested veteran of World War II combat coverage, "kept ignoring and resenting [Higgins's] presence long after she had demonstrated her qualifications for being there," Richard Kluger wrote in his study of the *Herald-Tribune, The Paper.*

"He thought her stories dealt too much with her own exploits, that she hero-worshipped MacArthur and was too reverential of the military command in general. . . . His bitterness was almost certainly the result of the conviction . . . that Higgins nearly got him killed in Korea for making him take chances he would not otherwise have had to—surely more of a confession of his own character than hers. 'No way can I make my behavior toward her appear in a favorable light,' he conceded years later. His dispute with her, he said, was territorial, not personal. 'I wanted her out of there in the worst way but couldn't get her transferred. . . . The desk in New York loved it."[3]

Keyes Beech covered the Inchon landing in September 1951 with Higgins "while the usually resourceful Bigart was left back on a big transport ship to file an overview of the vastest amphibious action since the Normandy landings six years earlier." The first four landing waves encountered little trouble, but the fifth—which Beech and Higgins were accompanying—was pinned down by heavy fire for hours behind a seawall. Beech, who quarreled with Higgins on more than one occasion, nonetheless said, "She had more guts, more staying power, and more resourcefulness than ninety percent of her detractors. She was a good newspaperman."[4]

Higgins and Flora Lewis were classmates at Columbia. Like Higgins, Lewis had difficulty persuading her bosses at the Associated Press to let her go overseas. They held out "until the very end, by which time I had covered a lot of international conferences including Dumbarton Oaks, the formation of the UN at San Francisco, and the Roosevelt-Churchill summit at Quebec. It was obvious that there was going to be a lot of diplomatic activity in London and Paris right after the war, and I had qualified for that kind of coverage. I was accredited as a war correspondent and had a uniform, but the war in Europe had ended while I was in San Francisco."

Arriving in London the day before V-J Day, Lewis found

"the trees along King's Way were festooned with toilet paper, in short supply but there wasn't anything else. People were dancing in the streets." Lewis eventually did get into war zones for the AP in the 1940s and 1950s and for *The Washington Post*. Lewis went on to become Paris bureau chief and is now a foreign affairs columnist for *The New York Times*.

But woman's day as a foreign correspondent has not yet fully come even today. Old prejudices and new obstacles still stand in the way, although they are being steadily eroded every year. Young women like Diana Henry, to be sure, have left beats on *The Baltimore Evening Sun* metro staff to go to Paris for *The Sun* (the morning paper). That's a transfer a young woman simply never contemplated—nor would it have been granted—two decades ago. Countless women have distinguished themselves from Paris to Peshawar, from Saigon to San Salvador. Countless others did not have the chance. They were either flat-out denied the opportunity or were so conditioned that they never even thought of going after the big stories of the day. This is the place to tell the adventures and observations of those who got overseas, but not without remembering those who didn't.

There is no one-and-only route to a foreign assignment. Some ask to go and keep asking to go until they get there. For others, the assignment seeks them out. Some, like Peggy Hull in World War I, paid their own way; her paper, *The El Paso Times*, could not afford to send her. Others go and prove themselves, as Kate Webb did, starting as a freelancer in Vietnam and becoming UPI bureau chief in Phnom Penh. Webb survived three weeks as a North Vietnamese prisoner after she and several colleagues were captured while trying to check on a battle.

Today, some women go abroad with all the trappings provided by a *New York Times, Washington Post, Los Angeles Times*, or *Wall Street Journal*. These major papers carry weight around the world; their status makes it easier for women to function in otherwise alien worlds. That women are correspondents for influential papers encourages women in second- and third-rank papers to try for choice assignments, too. Seeing women's front-page bylines may plant new possibilities in the minds of young women still in school.

Women's drive to be where the action is, to write the leading stories of their day, and to advance their careers is no different from that of any man who has packed off to London or Lagos. Their experiences in getting there and working there, however, are often different, especially when they seek a combat assignment. A boss may tell a man he can't have a particular assignment. A government official may treat him with contempt. It does happen often—but not because the man is a man. Many—men and women—are not qualified. Many—men and women—are barred from a place or event by foreign government officials because they are Americans or because they are reporters. The added element for a woman is that she is a woman.

Persistence. Persistence. Persistence. Gloria Emerson spent four years pushing and prodding *The New York Times* to take her off covering Paris shoe shows and put her on the Vietnam story. Finally in 1970 her editors relented. "I was equal at last, and often it was too much to bear," she wrote of her experience. "But the truth is, there were times when I was turned back, sent away, by Americans who did not want me with them on the line. Perhaps they saw I was clumsy or untrained; perhaps they thought I might bring them bad luck. I met soldiers, so much younger than myself, who felt that one dead white woman was more bothersome than ten dead men—and who needed more trouble?"⁵

Maggie Kilgore of United Press International drew only disbelief when she first asked to go to Vietnam. She was at a party at which UPI boss H. L. Stevenson was talking with some of the single men about going overseas. "How about me? I'd like to be considered," Kilgore said.

"You don't want to go over there. What's a nice girl like you want to do in Saigon?" Stevenson replied. "If you're so serious, write me a letter."

Kilgore wrote the letter. Nothing happened. One day in 1969 she was covering the Department of Agriculture. This was not a favorite relief duty; hog bellies produced few big bylines. Bureau chief Grant Dillman asked her to come in to talk to him. "I was walking up Fourteenth Street thinking he was going to ask me to stay at Agriculture the rest of my life," Kilgore groans.

"You wanted to go to Vietnam. Are you still available?" Dillman asked. Kilgore was being asked to cover politics in Saigon.

"I was so relieved. It wasn't Agriculture. I would have taken

Karachi instead, which was the pits." She got her shots and was on her way in January 1970.

Edie Lederer's third-grade teacher predicted that she would be an ambassador. Instead, she went overseas with the AP after five years of working in New York, San Francisco, and Sacramento. She went first on her own, traveling around the world with a friend and stopping in Afghanistan, Nepal, India, Thailand, and Vietnam. Ambitious young wire-service reporters on vacation often visit local bureaus, hoping to turn their dreams into realities; Lederer was no exception. When she got back, Wes Gallagher, head of the AP, called her in San Francisco and asked her if she wanted to go to Vietnam; the Saigon bureau chief had asked expressly for her. "It was the greatest story of the era, and I wanted to be part of it."

For Georgie Anne Geyer, there seemed not the faintest indication that she could ever be a foreign correspondent, she wrote in her book, *Buying the Night Flight*.[6] "I was 27. And I was clearly a woman. All the correspondents were men in their 50s and 60s." Geyer took matters into her own hands, applied for a Seymour Berkson Foreign Assignment Grant, and went to Latin America for six months. She stayed on as a correspondent.

In contrast, Sharon Rosenhause became the *Los Angeles Times*'s first female foreign correspondent without even asking. "If India had been posted [as a job opening], I doubt that I ever would have applied." She had been an editorial writer for eighteen months after joining the *Times* from *The Bergen Record* in Hackensack, New Jersey, when the editors asked her if she would go to India. They were faced with an emergency because *Times* correspondent Jacques Leslie had been expelled.

"I was stunned. It was not something I had thought about. You either want the adventure or you don't. I liked the prospect of getting back to reporting, but I had a job I liked, and India was not a place I had thought about going."

What finally decided it? "I figured that if I didn't go, for the rest of my life I'd wonder what I'd missed."

Washington Post reporter Joanne Omang was a self-described "beneficiary of the Equal Employment Opportunity Commission's aid." The *Post* had already been hit with an EEOC complaint by women on its staff when in 1974 a woman in its foreign department was turned down for a South American assignment. The *Post*, Omang said, was afraid that the woman would sue. So Omang was asked to go. "There I was, happily covering Alexandria [Virginia]. I was single, apparently a cheap person to send. I didn't speak Spanish, had never been to South America, and didn't especially care to go." She had, however, worked in the Peace Corps in Turkey for two years and had traveled in the Middle East. In 1975, after two years at the *Post*, off she went to South America.

Latin America was considered a journalistic backwater, an entry-level job for a foreign correspondent. Women went as freelancers and in a few cases as correspondents. They were there when the shouting turned to shooting in the late 1970s. "Nobody cared about it," Omang said. "Nobody wanted to go there, so you might as well send women. So when the area got to be important, the people who knew the most about it were women. They had become the experts."

A. M. Rosenthal, then executive editor of *The New York Times*, went to Central America to check out the situation in the 1980s, and as usual in a foreign crisis, he found the hotel lobby in San Salvador full of correspondents exchanging information. "I've been in a lot of those situations—the Congo, Lebanon—and this was the first time there were a lot of women," Rosenthal said. "Four of the best were women, and I would have hired them all if I could. I did hire Shirley Christian."

Hilda Bryant of Seattle took the path abroad that is least likely to be duplicated. Bryant, at the time a reporter with *The Seattle Post-Intelligencer*, had written stories about a welfare official who found a unique way to reduce his enormous backlog of child-support cases: he simply shredded the records. Bill Bonanno, a convicted mobster sitting in McNeil Island Penitentiary in the Puget Sound, read her stories and wanted to talk with Bryant.

Was she interested? "Sure. . . . I mean, I'd read *The Godfather* and gone to movies." Gay Talese had chronicled the Bonanno family in *Honor Thy Father*. Bryant interviewed Bonanno for thirteen hours over two visits. Meanwhile, a mobster was wiped out in New York and gangs were headline news again. "It was almost as if I'd put out a contract on him to promote my story."

Bryant's managing editor was pleased—so pleased that he let her use a ticket he had for an initial flight from Seattle to

Pakistan as a bonus for her Bonanno coup. Bryant devoured material about the civil war raging in Afghanistan on Pakistan's borders because her itinerary took her to Peshawar, a frontier city swarming with refugees from Afghanistan.

There she met an American-educated spokesman for the guerrilla resistance who was fascinated by, you guessed it, the Mafia. He had read about the exploits of Mafia families while being educated in New York and Boston, and "being a bloodthirsty Pathan and a tribal Afghan, that kind of outlawry appealed to him." He became her passport into refugee camps near Tarblea Dam on the Indus River on the northwest frontier of Pakistan. Later she made two trips into Afghanistan itself—one the following year after Soviet troops went in, and one when she was working for a Seattle television station. She was detained briefly as a possible Soviet spy in Peshawar on one trip and came under a Soviet artillery attack on another.

While in Peshawar on her original visit, one rebel commander said to her, "It's bizarre to see a woman from Seattle, Washington, sitting at midnight in the guerrilla nest of one of the biggest rebel organizations of the Afghan revolution. Do you understand that this place, where you are sitting, is the target of all kinds of potential terrorism and enemy violence?"

That didn't keep Bryant from coming back, disguising herself as a Pathan boy, and riding a donkey into Afghan battle areas. "The disadvantages of being a woman in this strict Muslim culture were outweighed for me by unique privileges. The tribesmen allowed me to go into the women's working and living quarters whenever I chose, to hold their infants, gossip with their wives in stunted Pashto, and denied me only their consent to take photos of their women. However, the women and girls, shy but eager to win the friendship of the foreign woman, occasionally consented to lift their veils for my camera when their husbands were not around."[7]

Fear for women's safety, in addition to outright discrimination, has often kept women out of war zones and off foreign assignments completely. Men and women alike appreciate editors' concern for their safety, but women, like men, want to share in those decisions that affect their lives.

Tracy Wood calls this attitude "gentlemanly concern." She

encountered it as she was heading for Vietnam for UPI. Her New York editors considered that assignment too dangerous for a woman, although they never thought a thing about the regular hazards she faced when she walked through the Port Authority Bus Terminal and Times Square to get to work at midnight or leave work at midnight. "Probably day after day that was more dangerous."

When she got to Vietnam, her bureau chief said he was never going to let her cover combat: "He couldn't stand the idea of a woman getting killed." With no combat assignments, Wood wouldn't be doing what she was there for. Assigned to tour Hué, Wood sat down there with veteran deskman Barney Seibert. "We had a couple of bourbons, and we just arranged things." Seibert told her everything she needed to stay alive and helped her file her copy so that she wouldn't be found out. Her plan was to do so much so well that by the time the bureau chief caught on that she was in fact covering combat, she'd have made her case. Eventually, Wood covered fighting north of Hué for several months.

Once Wood visited a firebase south of Da Nang that was constantly under threat of Viet Cong infiltration. Its commander was under enormous pressure and wouldn't have liked any reporters. "But he took it as a personal offense that anyone would send a woman to cover that story. He didn't care who I was with. The idea that I was a woman sent him into a rage." A major who didn't care what she was saved the day and helped her get her story.

Out of concern for its women correspondents' safety, the Associated Press told Edie Lederer and later Tad Bartimus that they had to stay at headquarters in Vietnam. "We just never found the headquarters," Lederer says.

Years later, with Lebanon the war zone, there was a tragic reversal of roles. "Male journalists are the ones who get kidnapped" in the male-dominated Middle East, said Nora Boustany, a Lebanese working for *The Washington Post*, so women actually fare better in covering some developments. "We begin to see terrible risks as opportunities for career enhancement." Boustany said that the men with whom she worked mistakenly thought she liked covering the daily disasters. "I have seen many able men journalists break down and cry covering a story. When I cry, I go into the bathroom. I hope one day we can cry together."[8]

205

Single women, like single men, find it easier to get assigned overseas. Their insurance costs are lower, they are more mobile, and their work is not likely to be affected by a spouse who is miserable in Moscow. But men with families are still far more likely to draw foreign assignments than women with families. It is still unusual for a man to quit his job when his wife transfers. A woman may do one foreign tour, perhaps even two, but a career abroad—rare indeed.

Female reporters married to other journalists—an occupational hazard—still give newspapers fits. Who gets the job? What is the status of the one not on assignment, usually the woman? Some newspapers have slowly had their consciousnesses raised.

One of the earliest cases was that of Sydney Gruson of *The New York Times* and Flora Lewis. They married in London shortly after V-J Day. "They had a rule then about not allowing a spouse to be on the paper, considering it nepotism. Nor was I allowed to work for what the *Times* considered a competitor," Lewis says.

Lewis worked for the *Post* as a stringer in Warsaw in the mid-1950s and went on staff in Bonn in 1958. She left the *Post* in 1967 after *The New York Herald-Tribune* folded and *The Washington Post* came to be considered competitive by the *Times*. "There was one period of twenty years when we moved seventeen times. I always continued working, but it was impossible to keep a regular job, so I had to change all the time, do freelancing, whatever I could get."

When Lewis and her husband covered the same event, she says, there generally was no problem because two people who were friends could cover the same event and not see the story the same way. "You make different decisions on what to go with. We had a rule of thumb that anything we found out because one of us was taking the kids to school—and it wasn't always me that was taking them—and the other went to the news conference, that was shared. But if it was obviously an initiative—the one who did it, did the story. That might be a difficult thing to legislate or write into any agreement, but it worked."

Lewis found that in war situations, men "seemed to think women would faint or cause some problem or embarrassment. As a result, I often had to go out on my own."

The necessity for a woman to patch together jobs overseas

as stringers or part-time correspondents was at least understandable, albeit discriminatory, given the climate of the 1940s and 1950s when women had difficulty getting fulltime foreign correspondents' jobs. But little had changed by the time Anthony Astrachan and Susan Jacoby, two *Post* reporters who were married, went to Moscow in 1969. Astrachan had reported for the *Post* from Africa; Moscow was his assignment. Jacoby, a bright young woman who had been an energetic education reporter when education was the big story, had to fight to get a leave of absence.

"We thought [the leave] would be granted as a matter of course to ensure the return to the paper of one of its better talents," Astrachan wrote in his book, *How Men Feel*.[9] "But the *Post* tried to refuse. 'Why should we give you a leave to go to Moscow?' Ben Bradlee, the executive editor, [asked Jacoby]. 'You won't learn anything there you'll be able to use when you come back.' Properly decoded, that meant, 'No woman is going to cover foreign affairs for us.' Flora Lewis had already been a foreign correspondent for the *Post*, and since then it has had other women foreign correspondents and a woman foreign editor, but there was no mistaking Bradlee's real, if unconscious, meaning in 1969."

In Moscow Astrachan put a joint byline—"By Susan Jacoby and Anthony Astrachan"—on a story on which his wife had worked. The *Post* desk removed Jacoby's name. The paper refused to pay her for her work on that piece, arguing that wives of other reporters helped their husbands without pay. Astrachan countered that the other wives had not been *Post* reporters.

"We had to live with the situation, of course," Astrachan wrote. In Moscow Jacoby was often excluded from lunches given by diplomats and other correspondents. "This was doubly ironic, because she spoke Russian better than I did and knew more about Soviet life than half the men at the table."

Asked about Astrachan, Jacoby, and the *Post* years afterward, Bradlee says the paper simply had budgeted for only one correspondent in Moscow at that time. "We never thought of sharing it. Neither did they."

Next in the evolutionary process was the case of Linda and Jay Mathews. Linda Mathews had been a reporter for the *Times* in Los Angeles and then in Washington, where she covered the Supreme Court. She was married to *Washington Post* correspondent Jay Mathews, who had specialized in Chinese studies in graduate school. When Jay was sent to Hong Kong for the *Post*, she asked for an assignment there, too. The *Times* refused. She quit and was soon hired by the Asian *Wall Street Journal*. Before long many of her stories were appearing prominently in the domestic *Wall Street Journal*.

The *Times* post of Hong Kong correspondent became vacant when its correspondent—Jacques Leslie again—quit. Linda recalls a phone call early one morning in Hong Kong. She answered; an editor in Los Angeles was on the line wanting to know whether Jay would be interested in working for the *Times*. "Ask him yourself," Linda steamed as she handed Jay the phone and headed off to take a long shower.

Jay was quite happy where he was, thank you, but what about asking Linda? A few weeks later, the editor called Linda, said he was tired of reading her stories in *The Wall Street Journal*, and asked her to work for the *Times*. Later she became the *Times* correspondent in Beijing when China allowed U.S. papers to open bureaus.

By the 1970s, journalists married to journalists on competing papers were no longer rare in places where there are many news organizations, such as Washington or New York. Occasionally husbands and wives covered the same stories. But in this case Linda Mathews would be in constant head-to-head competition with Jay Mathews—her husband. And the China story is not just in Beijing; it demands constant travel to understand a country as large as China, as caught between two worlds, the technological and the traditional. As part of the agreement that each correspondent signs with the *Post*, Jay Mathews had to agree that his own enterprise stories—pieces he did on his own initiative rather than in reaction to an event—would appear in the *Post* first, even if Linda had come along on the reporting trip.

Linda recognized that there had been some fear among her editors that she would defer to her husband and not do anything that would harm his career; other editors worried that she wouldn't defer to him and that their marriage would break up. Curiously, editors rarely showed this concern about strains on marriages when they transferred male reporters to Washington or Warsaw. The question, Linda Mathews says, is whether "a marriage is qualitatively different than being the best of friends? I never thought our situation was that different from people who traveled with friends and shared information. On any foreign beat, there are little networks, regular traveling pairs in which no competitive lines are crossed." The *Los Angeles Times* may go out on a story with Agence France Press or UPI, *The New York Times* with *The Toronto Globe and Mail*. There's a saying that "loners are either geniuses or idiots, and there are few geniuses."

Only once did the Mathewses abandon their practice of not talking about the stories on which they were working. "We were in Shanghai after the fall of the Gang of Four. Jay was doing a political story, while I was talking to people for a feature on consumerism in China. I came across some people eating hairy crabs, which are a delicacy. They were buying three male crabs and one female and pretending they were the Gang of Four—Madame Mao and her three allies. I thought it was a great anecdote and I told Jay about it. The next thing I knew, he'd used it in his lead. I griped, and he just said, 'Next time, don't tell me.' "

Newspapers still have difficulty dealing with dual-journalistic-career marriages, which are increasing, not decreasing. Only the biggest newspapers have sizable foreign staffs. Many of them naturally draw their correspondents from reporters experienced in covering Washington. As more women reach Washington jobs, more women who work, say, for the *Post* will be married to men who work, say, for *The New York Times*. They are all potential candidates for foreign jobs. But the *Times*, for example, refused to allow Philip Taubman's wife Felicity Barringer to continue reporting for the *Post* once they both went to Moscow. She reported on a part-time basis for the *Times* from Moscow.

Likewise, when *The New York Times* sent Steven Weisman to India, it would allow his wife Elizabeth Bumiller, a *Post* reporter, to continue reporting for the *Post* "Style" section only on a contract —not staff—basis. Since its clumsy handling of Astrachan and Jacoby, however, the *Post* itself has proved far more sympathetic to the problem. It transferred Karen de Young, its foreign editor, to London when she married a network producer based there, and it has sent a married team, Fred Hiatt and Margaret Shapiro, to Japan.

When J. Michael Kennedy, the young *Los Angeles Times* Beirut correspondent, married fellow *Times* reporter Rebecca Trounson, Trounson moved to Beirut, where she reported for CBS and *The Boston Globe*. She started writing features for the *Globe* but eventually was doing the *Globe*'s main story, even though she was a freelancer. Kennedy later was based in Houston for the *Times*, and Trounson reported for *The Houston Chronicle*, returning to Beirut to cover the TWA hijacking and helping to cover the Mexican earthquake.

Despite some continuing resistance, the opportunities for younger women today as foreign correspondents clearly are greater than they were for Flora Lewis in postwar Europe. "I don't think it's possible for editors today to get away with what they did to me," she says.

One couple that has made dual newspaper careers succeed, Linda and Jay Mathews, may have arranged their professional lives to their own satisfaction and to that of their bosses; dealing with the Chinese was another matter. "The Chinese have a veneer of egalitarianism," says Linda Mathews. "After all, Mao says that women hold up half the sky. Jay and I had separate credentials, separate offices, and separate interpreters. But the Foreign Ministry could never quite get used to the fact that I didn't work for or with him. I wanted notice of trips or reaction to some development, for example, and I'd find out about something secondhand and call up the ministry. 'But we just talked to Mr. Mathews ten minutes ago.'"

Dealing with people with different customs, different values, even different tones of voice poses problems for any reporter. The good ones adjust, learning what differences are worth fighting over and when they should compromise or simply give up. Sometimes being a woman is an advantage, as Tracy Wood found in Vietnam. "People tend to underestimate you because you're a woman. That becomes clear on about the second day on the job, and if you're smart, you figure it out and use it."

Nonetheless, women who are foreign correspondents inevitably can still point to times when their sex made their job harder. While she was working for the Asian *Wall Street Journal*, Linda Mathews traveled frequently to Korea and Japan and found operating there much more difficult than it was in China. In the mid-1970s there were very few Japanese professional women and only two or three women journalists that Mathews knew of. "They were considered oddities, but they were often very good. It was difficult for me to get appointments in Japan.

"Korea was almost as bad. The Koreans had had long exposure to the United States, but they still conduct much of their business at night with entertainment. It's like the Japanese use of geishas, but it is called 'giseng' in Korea. These would be parties with Korean government officials where people let their hair down. You needed to see these officials in those circumstances to know what they really thought. But they were for men only. So here I was limited to trying to see government officials during the day. I was seven months pregnant with Peter at the time, and every government official would say to me 'What are you doing here? Why is your husband letting you do this?' "

Finally, Mathews complained about her lack of access to officials and to the parties. " 'Okay,' one said, 'we'll give you a giseng party.' They invited someone from the bank, from the foreign ministry. Each of the men had a girl assigned to them, to rub their necks, serve them liquor or tea, fill their plates, even feed them. The girls were agog with the presence of this very pregnant Western woman. They were clearly nervous." She had no one assigned to her, but periodically one of the nearby gisengs would disdainfully plop some food onto her plate. "I felt like a little dog. Afterward, I said to my contact that I felt as if I'd just been through fraternity hazing. 'Yes, I hope you've learned your lesson,' he said."

In contrast, China posed fewer problems based strictly on sex. "Because of the nature of an authoritarian regime, my problems there were the same as any other journalist's. I even had some advantages. I seemed less threatening to many of the Chinese. I was often accompanied by a child, and the Chinese love children. . . . Chinese women, who were often wary of foreign males, were still curious enough to talk to me. For example, I could talk to them about sex. There were male journalists who would swear to you that there is little premarital sex [in China]. I can tell you that if you talk to women there, you find out that's not true."

Once Linda and Jay took an outing to an area of Beijing where wall posters had appeared for the first time. Jay, whose Chinese was better, went off to read the posters. Linda was trying to watch her son and take notes at the same time. A Chinese woman came over to her and, in perfect English, volunteered to watch the baby while she took notes. The heck with wall posters, Linda decided, and sat talking to the woman, learning how her family had been affected when her husband had lost his job and been jailed during the Cultural Revolution.

Women simply may speak more freely to other women wherever they are. Joanne Omang was helping cover the 1982 election in El Salvador and went with a carload of correspondents to an area where a body had just been found. "I always found it easier to go up to the women and start talking. Sometimes a woman would break into this long and heart-rending story, and the men I was with couldn't understand it. They'd say, 'I talked to her already and she didn't say that to me.' " There might also be a class element involved, Omang says, in that impoverished women, peasants, and workers, as dazed victims may be reluctant to talk to foreign journalists who are male and whom they link with authority.

"I never felt on the part of the authorities any discrimination" in Moscow, Charlotte Saikowski recalls about her years as *Christian Science Monitor* correspondent there from 1968 to 1972; nor was any ever involved at the *Monitor*, she says. "You have to remember that the *Monitor* is a small newspaper and was founded by a woman as one of the last things she did in her life." A woman was also an early Washington bureau chief at the *Monitor*.

"Still, in some ways, it might have been easier as a correspondent in Moscow being a male. You could meet a Soviet citizen in a bar. . . . Russian men would tend to be more assertive and strike up a conversation with a man. But I would talk to women. Russians can be very talkative. They open up in five minutes. Women might do that even more. They tell you their problems, their love life." Saikowski found that as a reporter in the Soviet Union, "you were always working around the margins to determine what's on the minds of the leadership, but you could always write about the people. What you could do best was give the flavor of life for your readers."

To do that, Saikowski, who spoke Russian and had taught English in Poland immediately after World War II, traveled frequently. She talked to a generation of Russian women in their late 30s and early 40s who had never married because so many men had died in the war. "To a Russian, this is a very deep tragedy." Without quoting the woman directly, she told one survivor's story of "the stigma of not being married." She didn't have this kind of rapport in Japan, however, because there Westerners, especially women, are always outsiders.

Listening for the story takes a certain knack. Many men have it. But "women are better listeners than men," says Karen Elliott House, foreign editor for *The Wall Street Journal* who won the Pulitzer Prize for listening to Jordan's King Hussein.

"Women don't envision themselves having the jobs men have. If you're a woman, you listen as opposed to telling them what *you* would do. In the Middle East that is particularly true, where they ask you what you would do first, to find out where you're coming from and second, to waste your time." Her prize-winning articles grew out of a series of conversations she had with Hussein in Jordan and later in India at a meeting of leaders of nonaligned nations. She went to dinner with Hussein five nights "because he had nothing else to do." His mind wasn't on the summit but rather on what he was going to do about President Reagan's proposed peace plan. She listened, and he talked more and more, and finally she produced a masterful look at how his position evolved.

"There are almost no women foreign correspondents who are bombastic," says Barbara Crossette of *The New York Times*. That makes it easier for them to deal in cultures that are more subtle than America's. Crossette, who did some Central American reporting before being assigned as Bangkok correspondent, found that women have other advantages overseas. Going to a refugee camp, for example, a woman can not only find out the official line that the men in charge want her to find out, but she has more access to women in the camps as well. "The women who talk to you are just women, not officials; they tell you what's going on."

Further, Crossette says that women may bring to foreign reporting a broader background. Not only do they need to know the politics and history of a region, but they know that "things like fashion say a lot about a society." If Islamic yuppies are trying to find fashionable clothes that still allow them to obey religious laws, that tells you something. You can read a house-and-garden magazine in Indonesia or visit a shopping center anywhere in the Third World and find out much about the culture.

"There's no reason to keep women out of foreign assign-

213

ments," Crossette adds. There's no heavy equipment. And the guerrillas never discriminate—just so you can keep up."

"On balance," said Judith Miller, who was Cairo bureau chief for *The New York Times*, "being a Western woman in the Arab Middle East has been an advantage professionally. Because I am a Westerner, the official and informal rules that restrict the freedom of Arab women have seldom applied to me. As a woman, however, I have been keenly aware of these rules. At times profiting from the virtual invisibility of women in some Arab countries, I was able to gain access to places, such as Saudi prisons, from which my male colleagues would almost certainly have been barred. In a few countries I have been granted interviews simply as something of a curiosity. In countries that denied me visas or refused to let me return, however, my nationality and what I wrote on my first visit were greater barriers than my sex."[10]

Similarly, Joanne Omang was able to get into a Chilean prison when other Western reporters—men—were being stopped. She showed her passport, was waved on through, and got all the interviews she needed. The guards simply didn't imagine that a woman would be a reporter. "Being a woman was sometimes a protective coloration. They'd start to clear a room of press before a meeting, and I'd just stand back in the wallpaper. I'm almost six feet tall and don't look Latin, but I'd get to stay and hear because women weren't considered people, so they may not have taken me seriously. I got an interview once with Chilean President Pinochet because they assumed I wasn't going to be very political."

In Nicaragua, President Anastasio Somoza gave more interviews to Karen de Young of *The Washington Post* than to many other reporters. "He hated my guts, but he was such a chauvinist figure, so sure of his charms."

A woman in the pool of foreign correspondents is still sufficiently rare that she stands out. In Vietnam, Tracy Wood found it was easier for the briefing officers to remember the women, to put a name and face together. Maggie Kilgore found that Defense Secretary Melvin Laird singled her out at press conferences, and he slipped her information on his trips to Vietnam.

Being a woman helped in a curious cultural way in Vietnam. Asians have softer speaking voices; so do women. "Sometimes it was easier for me to talk to the Vietnamese than it was for the men," Tracy Wood recalls. "I could sometimes see the Vietnamese flinch when the American men, especially the military or reporters, with their hard, loud voices, would bellow their commands or questions. My colleagues would almost flatten them against the wall with their voices." In Latin America, photographer Susan Meiselas noticed that most men stood while interviewing the shorter Latins; Joanne Omang often sat down.[11]

Being women helped Edie Lederer and Tad Bartimus in Phnom Penh in a way they'd just as soon not duplicate. They and French photographer Christine Spengler were in the old Hotel Royale during a shelling attack. "For a blink of time," Bartimus told a Vietnam correspondents' reunion in New York in 1986, "the AP's Cambodian coverage was handled entirely by women. Granted, we were huddled under a sagging iron bed. And we didn't know much about the size of artillery shells, or how to plot coordinates, or Clausewitz's principles of military tactics. But we got the story, and we got it out. We were ahead of the competition. And we lived to tell about it." What Bartimus delicately didn't tell that group was that in their scramble to find something to use to try to plot the coordinates of the shells as they fell, all the women had was a Tampax. It worked fine.

Women go abroad for the same reasons men do. Tracy Wood, for example, says that at the time when she was in line to go to Vietnam, working out of UPI's bureau in Sacramento, she had covered all the antiwar demonstrations in Berkeley. "I was 26 or 27 and my peers, a lot of the people I knew, were caught up in the war in one way or another. I knew the antiwar side. I wanted to see the war side myself." Women go to learn, as Judith Miller did, that there is no one definable Arab world. They go to write about the Indian people, not politics; about street vendors in Lima and the farmers in the Paraguayan outback, or they simply go because of the kind of irresistible pull that Georgie Anne Geyer felt for Latin America.

Men and women abroad face many of the same problems. Anyone working in countries during a revolution or under authoritarian rule has to be prepared for harassment or violence. Anyone trying to work and travel in the Third World, where airline connections may not exist until next Thursday, if then, has to be flexible, tireless, patient—and tough. But until society more completely reverses its attitudes, women must be tougher. To get the assignment. To adjust to cultures that put even less stock in their independent existence than they do in the United States. They must even be tougher to ward off unwanted sexual advances in societies that do not regard such advances as untoward, advances that may seem laughable in retrospect but frustrating when they occur.

The joy of the story often overcomes whatever frustrations occur. After getting an especially significant interview in Guatemala, Georgie Anne Geyer remembered, "At moments like this the sacrifices one makes to be a foreign correspondent—husband, children, the house with a view of the lake, the comforts of normalcy, and the reassurances of conformity—seemed, quite simply, irrelevant. The joy is a matter of personal transcendence and at the same time of a deep penetration of the world; of an odd sense of movement both ways."[12]

Everyday Indignities

The day Fannie Foxe jumped into the Tidal Basin in Washington after Rep. Wilbur Mills was stopped for drunk driving in her questionable company, *The New York Times* prepared a profile of the congressman. Eileen Shanahan, who had covered Mills as chairman of the House tax-writing committee, was in the office the entire day—not sitting behind a post—but she did not get the nod. She helped the man who did, and as he was finishing, he wondered aloud to her why she hadn't drawn the assignment. She wondered the same thing to the man who made the assignment.

"You weren't here. I didn't see you."

CHAPTER

13

Forbidden Turf

In sports, players hold out for better contracts. In the newspaper business, sports departments and photography departments have held out against women entirely or given them only marginal assignments. Long after the doors to the newsroom opened to women, both these sections were still considered no place for a lady.

Male or female, sportswriters and photographers have more in common than not. They need to land the job and get the good assignment, and they need to know how to write briskly on deadline or how to get close to a disaster scene and take the most graphic shot. They must work odd hours and travel frequently.

But there have been differences. Mary Garber of *The Winston-Salem Journal-Sentinel* couldn't sit in the press box at sports events. Sara Krulwich was denied a pass to the sidelines to photograph University of Michigan football games while she worked for her college paper.

Melissa Ludtke of *Sports Illustrated* sued to win access to the Yankee locker room for vital postgame interviews after she was excluded during the 1977 World Series. Lesley Visser of *The Boston Globe* was physically ejected from the locker room at the 1980 Cotton Bowl. Jane Gross of *The New York Times* asked Cleveland manager Dave Garcia an innocuous question after one game in 1981. He replied, "Young lady, you obviously have not seen many baseball games." Minutes later, a male reporter asked him the same question. This time, he responded quite civilly.[1]

Lisa Nehus Saxon of *The Los Angeles Daily News* told a *Los*

Angeles Times reporter that Reggie Jackson used to strut by her in the locker room and ask her questions about his nude body. In response, Jackson called her a liar,[2] but Alison Gordon, who covered the American League for five years for *The Toronto Star*, said later that Jackson "would always make sure he got naked the fastest and stayed naked the longest" when female reporters were in the locker room.[3]

And Susan Fornoff of *The Sacramento Bee* received a live rat in a pink box from Dave Kingman of the Oakland A's.

Until recently, women have not been able to get jobs as sportswriters or photographers in any numbers, to win assignments to the best stories, or to have equal access with men to all aspects of the stories. The discrimination that women in other sections of the newspaper dealt with years ago, women who are sportswriters and photographers still cope with today.

Sports are the American ritual, far more so than politics. The long exclusion of women from covering all aspects of that ritual denied them not only their legitimate interest in sports but also their opportunity to report on a key aspect of American iife equally with male reporters. Photographs tell the story more eloquently than words at times. And the long exclusion of women in any numbers from newspaper photography departments denied those papers not only more varied perspectives but additional talent, which equals better photographs.

Histories of sportswriting and photography contain few women's names. Adela Rogers St. Johns, best remembered for covering Hollywood for Hearst newspapers, was one of the first women sportswriters.[4] Maureen Orcutt, a championship golfer, was a secretary at *The New York Times* and covered women's golf. Some women covered sports during World War II. Precious few women—Jessie Tarbox Beals, Consuelo Kanaga, and Marion Post Wolcott among them—were staff photographers for newspapers in the years between 1900 and World War II.[5]

The dean of female sportswriters is Mary Garber, who retired from *The Winston-Salem Journal-Sentinel* in 1986 to work part-time after covering athletic events for forty years. She started knocking on the paper's door in 1938, almost from the day she graduated from Hollins College. "That was the Depression and there weren't any jobs," she says. Garber was hired in 1940 as society editor.

She became sports editor on the "all-girl staff" during World War II. When the men returned from military service, Garber returned to the news staff and covered sports only part-time. In 1946, she started covering sports full-time. "I was mainly covering high school sports. They were glad to get anybody. You could have sent a two-headed monkey." In time, she covered college football and minor league baseball.

"I made no effort to go into the locker room. Women just didn't do that. It wasn't that big a thing anyway. The biggest battle in the 1940s was to get into the press box. Women weren't allowed." But Leon Dure, the paper's executive editor, wrote to the athletic director of four Southern Conference (now Atlantic Coast Conference) schools in 1948 saying it was up to the newspaper alone to decide whom it sent to the games. When you reject her, he told the officials, you are not just dealing with an individual, you are rejecting the newspaper.

"All the years I worked, there was absolutely nothing until the civil rights acts passed that made this company keep me, but they did and they backed me on everything," Garber says.

Postgame interviews weren't much of a problem when Garber worked for an afternoon paper. She'd wait while the players showered and dressed, and "I just got home an hour late. But when I switched to a morning paper with a game over at 10:30 or 11:00 and a deadline a half an hour later, I couldn't afford to wait. I got a lot of cooperation and help. Assistant coaches fished people out of the locker room for interviews." Bones McKinney, Wake Forest's basketball coach, moved his postgame talk with reporters outside the dressing room.

"When I started, I knew I couldn't go in. I knew I had to plan ahead." When locker rooms did open to women, Garber went on in with the rest of the writers. She admitted feeling funny about it because many of the athletes were young enough to be her grandchildren. "Now you have women trainers, women as team doctors. There are coed dorms and people living together before they're married. I'm 70 and this is hard to get used to, but the young men and young women don't seem bothered at all."

The locker room. In every article about women as sportswriters, the question inevitably comes up. For the conservative, the locker-room question is one of morality—turning women loose among those clean-cut young men. For the athletes, it's either no big deal or it's an intrusion on their turf by an outsider that they don't like. Male sportswriters react in various ways: with resentment at competition from a new source or at the realization that they, too, are outsiders in the locker room and not one of the team; with annoyance if postgame policies are changed; or with indignation that colleagues who happen to be women aren't treated fairly.

But for the women involved it is a question of having the same opportunity that male reporters have to do the interviews that tell what was going through a player's mind or what a coach's strategy was behind a certain play.

Television made newspaper sportswriters more dependent on extra insights gained after the game than they were before. Washington Redskins fans, for example, will have either gone to the game or watched it on TV. If the morning paper has only the game story, says Christine Brennan of her coverage of the Redskins for *The Washington Post*, "then they aren't going to continue to read the paper. Of the 5 W's and H"—the journalistic guideline that all stories tell who, what, when, where, why, and how—"you have to have why and you have to get that after the game—in the locker room."

The old tactic of pulling players out of the locker room after a game for women reporters won't sell anymore. Women (a) know the tactic really doesn't work and (b) won't put up with second-class status anymore. When Tony Dorsett of the Dallas Cowboys is surrounded by press at his locker, for example, it would take a brave public relations man to pull him away. Without the interview in the locker room, the reporter misses the player in the background, taping an injured ankle, and can't feel tensions that may be dividing a team in a slump.

"If you have to wait until a player has showered and is on his way to the team bus, you get him the eleventh time the question has been asked and all the originality, all the spontaneity, the emotion, is gone," Brennan says. "You almost hope that the team that wins has an open locker room. It's not an overriding concern, but just enough to bother you." Access to the locker room, then, is to today's women who are journalists what access to the National Press Club and the dignitaries who spoke there was for the women of the Washington press corps in the 1960s.

Access to locker rooms is only one part of the job of the

221

sportswriter, but it has to be dealt with. The first women who faced the access issue in any numbers appeared on the scene in the 1970s as newspapers hired more and more women. Among them were Betty Cuniberti, Lesley Visser, Stephanie Salter, and Lawrie Mifflin, along with Melissa Ludtke of *Sports Illustrated*; B. J. Phillips of *Time* magazine; Robin Herman, formerly of *The New York Times*; Diane Shah, former sports editor of *The Los Angeles Herald Examiner*; and Jane Gross, now a metropolitan staff reporter for *The New York Times*.[6]

Betty Cuniberti remembers the locker-room question as a no-win situation. She had started covering sports for *The San Bernardino Sun* after graduating from the University of Southern California in 1973 and then moved to the *San Francisco Chronicle*, following the Oakland Raiders. "I was the first woman to cover a National Football League team from training to Super Bowl, but I couldn't go in the locker room. Getting in would be a mixed blessing," she says. "If you got in, you had an opportunity to do the story. But you also looked like someone who would stoop to anything to get that story."

Once while Cuniberti was covering the San Francisco 49ers, the team pulled off an upset victory. Coaches promised her that they'd bring some of the players outside the closed locker room. "But they were so busy celebrating, they didn't come. Not one. I was going angrily down the tunnel and I saw Welles Twombley [another sportswriter], and he said, 'Betty, what's the matter?' When he found out, he said, 'I'll give you everything I've got.' He was showing a kindness, but it was so insulting that I'd have to do that that I muttered an obscenity and said I didn't want his quotes. Welles understood. The players said the next day that no one asked them to come out. They'd have come."

Lesley Visser of *The Boston Globe* used to feel like Blanche duBois—dependent on the kindness of strangers—because she couldn't get into locker rooms—or was pushed out. Visser thought all that was behind her on a beautiful New Year's Day covering the 1980 Cotton Bowl. In the third quarter a press-box official handed out armbands for locker-room access. "I thought, 'This is wonderful. It's a new day.' For the first time I could think of questions instead of whether I'd have a scene at the door. I felt terrific. Well, the game was between Houston and Nebraska and was won on a twenty-yard pass with twelve seconds left. There were a hundred reporters—one woman—and we sailed into the locker room and were interviewing the quarterback.

"I thought, 'This must be how it goes for them all the time.' Then from ten feet away came this booming voice of Bill Yeoman. 'I don't give a damn about the Equal Rights Amendment. I'm not having her in my locker room.' They bodily threw me out. The cameras were turned on me, and I'm trying not to cry on the five o'clock news. I'm thinking: I love sports and I love putting words together, but what is this all about?"

It is not only men who keep women out of locker rooms. At the 1986 U.S. Open, Hana Mandlikova, the defending champion, had just lost to Wendy Turnbull. Tennis players usually do interviews immediately after the games in a special room or tent, but this time the locker rooms were open for the first time. An official announced that Mandlikova wouldn't come to the interview room, so Visser and an ABC radio person went to the locker room. Visser went in and found Mandlikova crying with her coach Betty Stove. "She started yelling that I had no right to be there. I said I did. I knew I would get no interview, so I said I was leaving but I hoped Hana would reconsider." She did.

"You absorb X amount of the blows because you can't complain all the time," Visser says. For example, at an Auburn-Georgia football game a few years ago she was in the locker room, and they told her they were sorry but she'd have to leave. "They put it so nicely, I said I'm just gonna leave."

Some teams opened their locker rooms as a matter of course when women were first assigned to cover them in the mid-1970s. Hockey and basketball teams acted individually before any access rules were handed down, but baseball and football were slower off the mark. In 1977 Dodger manager Tommy Lasorda agreed to let Melissa Ludtke into the locker room for a game at Yankee Stadium. Baseball commissioner Bowie Kuhn overruled him, and Ludtke sued. The court ruled in Ludtke's favor the following year, but it was not official major league baseball policy to have open locker rooms until 1985, when the next commissioner, Peter Ueberroth, ordered equal access.

First women couldn't get in to locker rooms; then when they got in, they got hassled. When Helene Elliott was covering the

Mets and trying to do clubhouse interviews, outfielder Dave King-man kept yelling abuse in the background. Finally, manager Frank Howard called a closed clubhouse meeting. Elliott knew that Howard was himself uncomfortable having women in the locker room, but he told his players that she was the authorized representative of her paper and that they were to behave accordingly. Before the game the next day, outfielder Darryl Strawberry came up to her and said of Kingman, "You don't worry about him. You're okay with us."

For every bad guy, there are also good guys. Elliott remembers a television broadcast on which Dale Murphy of the Atlanta Braves was spouting off about women in locker rooms. Elliott and Claire Smith of *The Hartford Courant* asked for equal time. NBC said it would provide it only if they found another player to say what they wanted said. They asked Don Baylor of the Boston Red Sox, who simply said, "Where do you want me to be?"

"If a person is a professional athlete, if he can handle professional sports, he can handle this," Elliott says. "I'm not demanding to talk to players in the nude. I'm just demanding the chance to talk to them. Anytime you have naked people involved, there's going to be an element of titillation." The wife of a player on the New York Rangers hockey team once asked her, in effect, did she look at those naked men standing in front of her?

"I told her that, believe me, I know the eye color of everybody on the team."

Not long afterward, one of the players she was interviewing closed his eyes, put his hands in front of the eyes of players standing on either side, and said, "Prove it."

Could she?

"Didn't I have to?" Elliott replies.

Among the public "there is a great misconception of the locker room. It's the least sensual environment I've ever been in," says Lesley Visser. "I remember after a Celtics game. It's un-air-conditioned, people were pushing up against each other to talk to Larry Bird, and Diane Shah turns to me and says, 'Lesley, we fought to get in here.' "

"People perceive the locker room as a singles' bar with unclad men," says Sarajane Freligh of *The Philadelphia Inquirer*. She believes that support for keeping women out of locker rooms comes from the Sunday fan who wants to be doing himself what the women are doing. "You have this guy having his Velveeta on rye. He's living vicariously through sports, and he's jealous. He sees a woman doing this job when she should be in the kitchen fixing his grits."

Other sportswriters can be part of the problem. Freligh complained when she was covering Penn State football that she couldn't get the players she wanted to interview brought out of the locker room. Penn State set up an interview room so all reporters could have access, but reaching it involved riding a bus. "The university thought it could avoid being considered the heavy, and it did. I was blamed. I was called bitch, cunt, whore. I finally bought a Walkman and wore it in the press box so I wouldn't hear what they said."

Dealing with athletes in locker rooms has made it more difficult for women to cover baseball on a regular basis, Freligh contends. In other sports the locker room is the place where the athletes change clothes and go home. In baseball it's used as a clubhouse the whole season. "That's where they live. It's a real male world. . . . It's much larger, much more comfortable, they spend so much more time there." So it's a more difficult atmosphere in which to work.

Officially, the locker-room question is now behind women in areas where it has been raised. But in smaller cities where no women have yet covered sports, they'll still be tested, says Michelle Himmelberg of *The Orange County Register*. Resistance to women in locker rooms is already lower in the sports with more college graduates—basketball, football, and hockey as opposed to baseball —even though many college locker rooms remain closed. "If the athletes dropped in on a few classes, which we hope they did," says Christine Brennan, "they dealt with women more there. Just being on a campus teaches you there are different cultures, different worlds." Black athletes, too, generally get high marks for behavior toward women who are sportswriters. They're cooler, says one reporter; they also know what it's like to be outsiders.

According to the Association for Women in Sports Media, a support group that issued its first newsletter in March 1987, pro football, baseball, basketball, hockey, and soccer now all have equal access policies. The Detroit and Dallas football teams opted for a separate interview room rather than opening their locker rooms after games. In college sports the policy is uneven because individual schools and in some cases conferences govern the rules. The National Collegiate Athletic Association controls only post-season play and requires equal access.[7]

"I don't know where we go next," Sarajane Freligh says, "but we'll know we've gotten there when people don't ask us about locker rooms and when there are no interviews just because we're women sportswriters."

Once in the locker room, "you never know how to act," says Betty Cuniberti. "Once I was seen laughing during an interview, and that became the subject of so much speculation about me and that player. Yet a man I knew had an open relationship with a woman tennis player and no one minded. You don't know. Should you be friendly or aloof? I was friendly, and I was called flirtatious. Then I was distant and was called a snob. Finally I decided just to be myself."

Being a sportswriter can be hazardous to your social life. "For me," Cuniberti says, "writing the stories was the easiest part. The hardest part was just keeping your sanity and having some semblance of personal life. Women in sportswriting are the absolute test case. You are the subject of so many double standards that it absolutely wipes you out. Sportswriters travel so much that the group of sportswriters becomes your whole life. You have no opportunity for a home life."

Cuniberti left sportswriting when *The Washington Star* folded and now reports for the *Los Angeles Times*. She got out of sportswriting, she says, because of the travel, the locker-room situation, and the repetitive, boring nature of the subject matter. "Those people don't have much to say about the world. I mean, they're nice guys, but they're 20 or 30 years old and they have never done anything but sports."

The pressures on women to know their subjects and do their jobs better than men is intense. In her first year covering the New England Patriots for *The Boston Globe*, Lesley Visser says, she felt she was carrying the responsibility for all women. "That made me much more serious than I had to be. Everyone would go to dinner, and I'd go to my room and read the press guide. I had this fear someone would ask me about someone traded after the 1968 season."

226

Visser found that getting married helped her relationships with the men she covered. "Often as a single woman, my intentions were misinterpreted," she says. Now many of the athletes know her husband, sportscaster Dick Stockton. "That gives me an added credential, although we often go out after I've covered a game and the men will ask him about a play in the third quarter."

Newspaper readers hear more about these sexy issues—locker-room access and relationships with athletes—than they do about athletes who go about their business, do interviews graciously, and deal in a businesslike manner with all reporters, male or female. Jane Gross of *The New York Times* found a camaraderie and acceptance when she tried mentally to put herself in the shoes of the players, tried to absorb everything she could "of this alien all-male culture."[8]

She got spoiled, she wrote in an article for *The New York Times Magazine*, because, although the travel is debilitating, "it is also effortless and mindless." Impeccable arrangements are made for the comfort of the players; she became totally unused to carrying a suitcase, booking a flight, or battling for airport taxis. The travel also "creates an intimacy among the players and between the players and those of us who travel with them," Gross, now a metropolitan staff reporter for the *Times*, wrote. "When I think about the traveling, the first-person-plural pronoun—the 'we' that reporters must avoid because it suggests a closeness that defeats our purpose—comes naturally. While I never feel like a member of the Yankees in New York—where I sleep and wake in my own apartment, shop and cook, visit friends—on the road, I do, and I am not wholly sorry."

Gross talked of the exuberant camaraderie the teammates shared among themselves—and with her. It must be, she wrote, "what men seek in bars and at card games. I now see that this exclusion of women is not as malicious as it seems."[9]

The focus on the locker room also obscures the hard work of day-to-day coverage done by women who are sportswriters so that they can get and keep their jobs. Women have gotten these jobs because of the pioneers who preceded them and/or because a sports editor was open-minded. As Christine Brennan of *The Washington Post* says, "Behind every woman who is a sportswriter, there is a decent man." Women have also gotten their sportswriting jobs because other women demanded equality on the job.

"If there hadn't been a women's movement or a suit [against *The New York Times*], no one would have dreamed of putting a woman in the job of sports editor at the *Times*," said Le Anne Schreiber shortly after she moved into that job, which she has since left.[10]

Some of the women were sports fans as kids; in other families, sports was only part of the routine. "I cannot describe how fanatical I was," Brennan says of her childhood in Toledo, rooting for the Mud Hens baseball team and collecting baseball cards. The year she was 13, her father took her to Florida to see the Tangerine Bowl because the University of Toledo was playing the University of Richmond. Although she was named girl athlete of the year in high school, she was fascinated with politics as well as sports and found them parallel. "There are clear winners and losers, there's a lot of posturing, and it's famous people you're covering."

While attending Northwestern University, Brennan had internships at *The Toledo Blade* and *The Miami Herald*. She went to work at the *Herald*, where Paul Anger, the sports editor, was very supportive. "I was very lucky to go right to a place where I was given a fair deal. I was also put on the Miami University football beat right away. That's a testament to Paul Anger that he was going to treat me as a sportwriter, not as a woman sportswriter. I was 22 and had the third- or fourth-biggest beat."

Brennan says she never had to beat it out in the bush leagues and had comparatively few problems. "I tell Lesley [Visser] that you were beating on doors that I've walked through."

Helene Elliott, who had preceded Brennan as an intern at *The Miami Herald*, grew up in Brooklyn. Her parents were big sports fans. Elliott had a memory for numbers, and that fueled her interest in sports statistics. But when she told her high school adviser that she wanted to be a sportswriter, the woman laughed. She said, "Women can't be sportswriters. Be realistic. Pick something you can do." Elliott was sports editor of her paper in high school and worked on the college paper. Then she got a full-time job with *The Chicago Sun-Times*, landing a good beat—college football and basketball. She joined *Newsday* in 1979.

Despite their different backgrounds, women agree that there are times when they cover sports stories differently than men do. "Sometimes players will talk more openly to a woman," says Sarajane Freligh. "You ask questions that are different—it's not what everyone else gets. Players may tolerate an odd question, and they even sometimes say that no one ever asked them that before. Sometimes other sportswriters grimace when I ask something. But I notice when the guy's giving a good answer, they're all writing it down. If newspapers are indeed in their death throes because of TV, they need to be different. Women have that approach, and they ought to be encouraged."

Annette John-Hall, who has covered sports for *The Oakland Tribune* and *The Rocky Mountain News*, recalls suggesting a story to a colleague about a rookie who wasn't playing well. He started it with three paragraphs of statistics. "I would have written about the guy's knee surgery and his frustration at sitting on the bench. I'm not the kind who can rattle off statistics at the drop of a hat. What I do bring to the craft is a more human perspective. I think the reader wants to know what the guy is thinking when he hits a three-pointer at the buzzer, not how often he's done it before.

"When I was in the Bay Area there were a lot of women sportswriters. I'd read all their stories, and I realized that the main link that we all shared was that we looked at writing from that point of view."

One of those Bay Area writers was Stephanie Salter of the *San Francisco Examiner*, now an op-ed page columnist. She found that black basketball players would talk more openly to her than they did to men, and she developed a real bond with some of the players. One had a deformed child who had died, and he obviously wanted to talk to someone about it. It yielded a story that was both illuminating and sad.

Women who are photographers may operate along somewhat the same lines. They listen. They try to put subjects at ease. "Of course, there are the times when you know someone is not taking you seriously. But normally I've found it an advantage to be a woman," says Iris Schneider, staff photographer for the *Los Angeles Times*. "In getting a job, managers may be held up by the fact that you're a woman, but once you have the job and are on the assignment, I find people are less threatened by your presence. You can get into some places that men couldn't get into.

"Men are less sensitive to some delicate situations, such as when someone in a family has been murdered. I've found that the case in taking pictures of AIDS patients at San Francisco General Hospital. Obviously, there are men who are quite good in these cases, but as a rule people seem more relaxed with a woman photographer."

Janet Knott, the senior woman on the photo staff at *The Boston Globe*, says, "I have always believed that being a woman is an advantage. If you're unassuming, disarming, it's much easier to make people feel they're having a good time while you're taking a picture." Knott has found that "proving yourself takes longer if you are a woman in photography." Newspaper photography "is a physical medium, and the concept of a woman carrying all that camera equipment makes men uneasy."

Resourcefulness helps. Knott was covering the launch of the space shuttle *Challenger* when it blew up. "The story changed in a matter of seventy-two seconds," Knott says. "Some of my male colleagues stopped shooting. A male friend was much more emotional than I. I never allowed myself to feel the emotion of the moment. That's very important in a spot-news situation. I knew the reactions would be the story. I just kept clicking away. . . . When I went over to the AP trailers, there were hysterical people there, people running around. I've learned that though I'm with a big paper, when you're covering something like this you won't get the attention that the AP and *New York Times* get. So I drove to the Space Center airport to try to get my film on a plane. The Eastern strike had cancelled the closest connection, so I called *The Orlando Sentinel*." Photographers at the Space Center had had difficulty getting shots transmitted because of all the excitement, but Knott sent thirteen pictures.

Generally speaking, Sara Krulwich, a veteran of nearly a decade at *The New York Times*, agrees that being a woman ultimately helped her in her career timing along the way. But it was not always so. In college, she wasn't allowed to cover football because the credentials said no women were allowed on the field. "There may have been a women's movement in 1969 but not in Michigan.

"Somewhere I got the energy and had the moral sense that I was correct, so I just went down on the field because I had the credential. People said, couldn't I read? And it said right there I couldn't be there, but I forced the issue. I had to work just to get the privilege to be on the sideline. But it's funny: football was so dull for the people who had to be there that when I met the university president, he knew every single hat I had on at every game that season."

In 1973, when she was job-hunting, Krulwich says, "there were picture editors who specifically said they didn't hire me because they'd feel bad having me as the bottom person on the ladder—having me as the cleanup person at night. They'd feel guilt at putting girls on the street. At *The Hartford Courant* the guy told me, 'We'd be hiring half a photographer.' " By contrast, at *The New York Times* she had two weeks of orientation and then was sent to the South Bronx at night.

News photography opened to more women in the 1970s because of the affirmative-action requirements that many newspapers imposed upon themselves under pressure from the women on the staffs or because lawsuits at other papers prompted defensive maneuvers. "If you were fresh out of college and had the proper credentials in 1975, it seemed fairly simple to get hired at one of the large metropolitan dailies," said Jennifer Werner, staff photographer at *The Seattle Post-Intelligencer*.[11]

But a decade later, most of the papers had fulfilled their affirmative-action goals and saw little need to round out their staffs any further, Werner added. "It is still common to find that on a newspaper photo staff of fifteen there are only one or two female shooters"—although she said several papers have "a long history of hiring women photographers and hiring them in numbers" such as *The Philadelphia Inquirer*, *The Miami Herald*, *The* [Louisville] *Courier-Journal*, and *The* [Nashville] *Tennessean*.

Women are getting good training, so there are plenty of women who can do the jobs, she said, but with women underrepresented in news management, other women don't get hired, and they still aren't taken seriously. In preparing a report for the National Press Photographers Association (NPPA), Werner found that women still feel that "they have to go the extra mile, be willing to work longer hours, develop picture stories on their own time, and be able to handle any assignment that may be thrown their way." Werner reported that the women also felt that their assignment editors "sometimes assign sex roles to their photographers

231

at the same time they assign stories or photo 'beats' to cover." Men get sports, and women get children and old people.

In the early days of women's push into photography, women who got jobs found they were working in photo departments that were like locker rooms, not like newsrooms, says Mimi Fuller Foster, who worked as a photographer for thirteen years at *The Cincinnati Post* before joining *The Atlanta Constitution*, where she became a picture editor. There were no women in any role.

When she started at the *Post*, there were *Playboy* foldouts on the newsroom wall and cartoons. "They had to take them down. They didn't like that. . . . The chief photographer would not let me work at night. It was not that I especially wanted to, but it meant that I was not in the regular rotation. That made the men mad. I felt it was important that I do the same things that everybody else did. It took a couple of years before I was in the regular rotation.

"The chief photographer was never willing to go to bat for me." Foster covered the Cincinnati Reds but was denied clubhouse access. "I was competing with the *Enquirer*, and that meant I couldn't attend celebrations after a big victory. I couldn't compete equally. He would never fight that. If there was a really big game, they would send somebody else with me." Not until a younger group of men came in was she treated more equitably, Foster said.

Many women have worked their way into full-time newspaper jobs through freelancing, and indeed many of the best-known women photographers still are freelancers, such as Susan Meiselas, who has especially turned her lenses on the fighting in Central America; Mary Ellen Mark, whose photographs appear in *The New York Times Magazine*; and Ulrike Welsch, who worked for *The Boston Herald Traveler* five and a half years and for *The Boston Globe* nine before quitting to work for herself in 1981.[12]

Iris Schneider was teaching on New York's Lower East Side and pursuing photography as a hobby when a friend suggested she try to get some assignments. She did some work for the Girl Scouts and the American Heart Association. She was back at her school after classes one day when she took a photograph of an elderly black woman teaching chess to black and Hispanic kids. She sold *The New York Times* on the idea of doing a story on the woman, and the paper sent a reporter. "I'll never forget the first

232

time I walked into the newsroom of *The New York Times*—for someone who had never thought of photography as a career, that was very heady." Eventually, she became a full-time staff photographer for the *Los Angeles Times*.

Schneider became one of about ten women on the *Times* photography staff. Generally speaking, however, "women are still very much alone in this profession," Jennifer Werner says. To try to overcome the isolation, the National Press Photographers Association has established a women's committee. It has focused on problems women photographers face by holding regional meetings and conducting seminars with veteran women photographers. The committee has also established a job bank and has studied the chemicals used extensively in color photography that could be hazardous to women who are pregnant or are planning to be.

Werner feels that the newspapers should be helping in these studies so that their female employees can have equal health protection. But, as with other issues, she adds, "If you want equality, you've got to do something about it."

"Women's needs are different from those of fifteen years ago when women struggled just to get a foot in the door," Werner said in the NPPA report. "Now the major issues are ones dealing with parental leave and child care. Many women who have been in the business for a number of years are now facing an either-or decision: whether to raise a family or pursue a career. The profession is still very inflexible regarding these issues, for they are typically thought of as being just women's problems. The women's committee would like to see true equality in our profession, not by denying that there are real differences between men and women but by recognizing and affirming those differences. The profession will change and become more responsive to women only when all the standards and values are no longer exclusively defined by men."[13]

Rules against the same newspaper or competing papers hiring married couples hurt journalists in all departments, but they may especially hurt photographers because photo staffs are small. As April Saul of *The Philadelphia Inquirer* and her husband, Steven Zerby, also a photographer, were building their careers, they found that "in the cities that still had two newspapers, the papers were

233

often nervous about putting two spouses in competition, and Steven and I wondered which of us would be happy working for the lesser paper, knowing that no matter how successful he or she became, the other—the better—paper would be forever out of reach."[14]

The doors to darkrooms and sports departments opened late for women. Women who are photographers don't see the replenishment of their ranks that they'd like to see; projections are mixed on the sportswriters' side. Lesley Visser worries that young women may not be hearing about the good things about sports reporting —the good competition, the entertainment, the variety of people one meets. "It's a problem. You don't always want to be doubted. You don't want it thought that genetically you can't recognize a safety blitz." But Michelle Himmelberg counts 250 women now active as print sportswriters. Christine Brennan predicts there will be more as more women participate in sports.

"No one has ever given me one good reason why women shouldn't cover sports," says Betty Cuniberti. "The only one that comes up over and over is that darned locker room question. But if you go to a game, look around the stadium. There are lots of women. They aren't dragged there. Women who hate sports don't go to games. Sports is a world for men and women, as spectators as well as participants."

Everyday Indignities

Vivian Vahlberg, who covered Washington for *The Oklahoma City Times, The Daily Oklahoman*, and *The Colorado Springs Sun*, reported on the vote that admitted women to the National Press Club in 1971 from the balcony, "where we were allowed to sit."

She later served eight years on the Press Club board. She'd make points, she recalled, "and they would be ignored or forgotten. Then a man would make the same point, and it would be discussed."[3]

CHAPTER

14

Diapers on the Front Page

In 1962 Lois Wille, who was reporting on welfare-related issues for *The Chicago Daily News*, discovered that the area's public health establishment refused to give out birth-control information. That meant that poor women had no way to get contraceptives. Clinic workers told her that they would be fired if they even referred women to Planned Parenthood.

Wille's city editor was a man of good social conscience, but he was a Catholic in a very Catholic city and was reluctant to run the stories after she spent months on them. He even ran them by a friend—a local monsignor—who had no vehement objections, but still the series sat. Wille fidgeted. "I finally had to help it along. The only way it finally got in was when I said *The Chicago American* was writing the same series. It finally went in because they were afraid they'd be scooped."

As a result of Wille's articles, the public aid department of Cook County and the city health clinics started providing birth-control information and services. *The Chicago Daily News* won the Pulitzer Prize for Wille's articles. The Pulitzer committee especially commended the *Daily News*'s courage in tackling a sensitive subject and providing a public service.

A man might have heard about the birth-control issue the same way Wille did, while working her beat. But would he have viewed it as a story in 1962? And would he have pushed as hard to get the story? The fact is that it was a woman who did the story where men had not. Wille brought to her job a different experience, a different sense of what was important in the basic daily lives of readers, especially readers who were women. Her presence in the newsroom gave that experience an outlet and gave her newspaper a story—and a distinction—that it might not otherwise have had.

Wille, who became associate editor and then editor of the editorial page of the *Chicago Tribune* after the *Daily News* folded, had not only worked on the women's pages but had also covered urban problems in the days when Mayor Richard J. Daley ran Chicago. Wille was in the vanguard of women who not only covered the traditional stuff of newspapers but also started to change the definition of news by writing stories on subjects that had rarely been written about. As one woman—now a managing editor—said, "Women don't cover fires any differently. Women don't cover prison breaks any differently. But I do think having more women in the newsroom adds a perspective that we need." Some editors wanted to call it the "women's angle," and they might have had something if they hadn't put the stories into a ghetto, hadn't considered them lesser views on lesser news.

"Women often became experts in fields where they were not vying against men," says Patricia O'Brien, who reported on social issues—as well as politics and tax legislation—for Knight-Ridder in Washington. In Chicago, for example, Lois Wille found that if she wanted to do a series on how badly the Cook County juvenile court was operated, she could because "nobody was writing about that. . . . It was not so much things I dug out, but once I did a story, I was inundated with people coming to me. All you had to do was show you were interested. People would see a female by-line, and they thought I'd be receptive."

Carol Richards of *Newsday* had the same experience. "After the 1976 election, I started covering more social issues" such as health and aging, says Richards, who then worked for Gannett News Service. "It was like shooting ducks in a barrel. It was the greatest beat in the world. Nobody was covering it that way. Papers were putting my stories on the front page. My bosses were surprised I had thought of it. I was surprised that nobody else had thought of it. Perhaps that was a woman-y thing: to look at the way people live rather than at government institutions."

Lest this sound like an argument for segregating women into welfare and equal-rights stories, be assured that it is not. It *is* an argument for considering that stories about life at home deserve just as much attention as stories about life in the House and the Senate and the White House—and for recognizing that in many instances it was women who first made sure those stories got attention.

Susan B. Anthony had it right as far back as 1893, when she said, "As long as newspapers and magazines are controlled by men, every woman upon them must write articles which are reflections of men's ideas. As long as that continues, women's ideas will never get before the public."[1] For that very reason—because female journalists had to survive in a man's world—women long resisted writing anything other than what the big boys wrote. Since then, they have proved they can be political writers, foreign correspondents, sportswriters. They have found their voices in that arena and are now willing to take on issues that they recognize as news in traditionally uncovered arenas.

Twenty years ago women had fewer options. Many felt that they would be shunted aside if they wrote only about women. Women still don't have full equality of subject matter, although women have now covered defense and Capitol Hill for *The Washington Post*, the United Nations for *The New York Times*, AT&T for *The Wall Street Journal*, and the White House for the *Los Angeles Times*. Now, too, there is a better chance that they share in the definition of news. That's the difference.

Many men always write stories that detail the human condition, and some women never do. But one of the ways American newspapers today differ from American newspapers of two decades ago is the presence of more women who assign, report, and edit the news. The greater the variety of people who gather the news in the community and the world, the greater the variety of news that will be gathered.

It is impossible to distinguish absolutely between the influence of women in the newsroom and that of women entering the work force. Who really causes coverage to change—newsmaker or newsperson? Women outside the newsroom made news by entering politics in greater numbers, demanding an end to job bias in fact as well as in law, having children later, and insisting on better day care. Women inside the newsroom saw the stories outside the newsroom. As the years passed, they gathered more confidence that going after these uncovered stories of social change wouldn't relegate them to the status of lesser beings.

It is, however, a relatively straightforward task to ask women who are journalists whether they do their jobs at all differently from the way men do them. Their answers, layered one on top of the next, show the added element women have brought to American newspapers.

Education was long considered an acceptable subject for the lone woman in the newsroom. Women were teachers; women could write about the schools. As schools became battlegrounds of ideologies and as education reform became a hot issue, the second-class status of education writers changed. Like Latin American coverage, education proved to be an area where women went when there were few other straight news areas they could cover and where events caught up with their expertise.

With Mom in the newsroom today, coverage of children may be the biggest area of change. It cannot be an accident that newspapers started paying more attention to the problem of child abuse at a time when there were more women on the staffs to pay attention.

Elizabeth Rhodes of *The Seattle Times* always read the little fillers that occupy the bottom of columns throughout newspapers —especially the ones about crime. "Not because I like crimes, but because I am fascinated by human psychology and why people do what they do." Skimming the paper, she once came upon a three-inch story about a man charged with second-degree murder in the fatal scalding of a toddler. The man, the mother's boyfriend, "claimed he was only trying to clean up the kid's mess, but he held him under hot water so long, the child's skin literally fell off."

She'd read other stories about children killed by adults, and every time the charge brought was second-degree murder—or less. Adults killing adults got nailed for first-degree murder. There seemed to Rhodes to be a double standard of justice. "As a mother I was angered. But as a reporter I was curious."

Rhodes was working as a general assignment reporter for the "Scene" feature section of the *Times*. She had none of the traditional background that would have gone into covering the story. Although she had worked for both *The Miami Herald* and

The Charlotte Observer for a total of ten years before going to the *Times*, she had never covered courts, cops, or city hall. "I had to learn all the stuff—all the legalese, all the way to research records and find records that weren't there." She systematically examined every child-abuse death that had occurred in three counties in the Seattle area over five years and then compared the outcomes in those cases with others in which adults killed adults.

"I discovered that judges didn't see it as murder" when children were killed. "They'd say, 'He didn't mean it.'" Rhodes's articles—"Getting Away With Murder"—began with the example of little Tina Ford, who when she died two days after her fourth birthday, was so dehydrated and undernourished that she only weighed what a two-year-old would weigh. The aunt with whom she lived had pleaded guilty to manslaughter and served only twenty-four weeks in jail.

Tina's case was not isolated, Rhodes wrote: "More than 20 local children have died of abuse or neglect since 1980. Those who killed them often got sentences that amounted to a slap on the wrist: a year or less in jail. By comparison, in 22 local cases where adults beat adults to death, the most frequent sentence was life in prison."[2]

"Since then," Rhodes says, "they've really applied the law. Many things had been legal as long as you could demonstrate lack of intent. The corporal punishment laws have been changed. There is now a list of things you can't do—no burning, cutting, suffocating." Rhodes won the Penney-Missouri first place award for her series on child murders.

Washington State's laws may have become more humane, but California's moved in the opposite direction in the fall of 1987—but not without the outraged observance of a *Los Angeles Times* editorial. Editorial-page intern Bonnie Heald, a parent and a recent graduate of the University of Southern California, spotted a bill in the legislature that would narrow the definition of child sex abuse, under the guise of clarifying the procedures under which children could be removed from abusive parents. The bill—backed by a fundamentalist group called Victims of Child Abuse Laws or VOCAL, which felt its children were its business—so narrowly defined child abuse that youngsters would have had to suffer permanent injury or disfigurement to be removed from their homes or, in the case of sex abuse, deep bleeding or bruising. Heald doggedly reported on the real harm inherent in the bill, which passed the California legislature in a last-minute log-drive. But her reports were to no avail; Gov. George Deukmejian signed it, despite protests from concerned legislators and social workers alike. The public was informed, even if the governor was unmovable.

What happens to children when they are taken from neglectful or abusive parents? Are they any better off, or are they warehoused and forgotten? Lois Timnick of the *Los Angeles Times* has written extensively about overcrowded conditions and lack of counseling for children in crisis at MacLaren Children's Center, run by Los Angeles County. Timnick also found that some children were being returned to abusive homes. And she has reported extensively on the critical shortage of foster-care homes in the Los Angeles area, the inadequate screening of prospective foster parents, and the lack of county support for foster parents who are coping with difficult children.

Bad care for children and the need for good care have both become much more frequent subjects for news stories. In the fall of 1986, the *Los Angeles Times*'s column-one spot on the front page—the space reserved to showcase special stories—carried a story about Texas firms that used day care as a perk to try to recruit or hold female employees. Significant as the story was in raising the sophistication of day-care coverage, it may have been as significant that the byline on the story was a man's. The author, J. Michael Kennedy, and his wife, Rebecca Trounson of *The Houston Chronicle*, had just become parents.

Missing children have drawn intense press and political attention as well. Their plight captured the imagination—and the milk cartons—of America for a time. Yet in the middle of that heightened interest, one woman reporter was suspicious of the rising statistics and the public belief that children were being randomly abducted. Diana Griego of *The Denver Post* had been assigned by then–city editor Vikki Porter to write a story about dentists who implanted coded microdots into the teeth of children whose parents feared they might turn up missing. Griego tried to get accurate statistics about how many children were indeed missing. And she kept asking herself why parents might fear abduction. "Something wasn't right," she said.[3]

"I had just graduated from the California State University

at Fullerton the year before, so I remembered something I learned in an investigative reporting class: 'If something doesn't sound right, check it out,' the instructor told us. 'There's probably a story there.' " Griego had been told by experts that 1.5 million children disappeared each year, 50,000 of them abducted by strangers, but an FBI agent told her those numbers were impossible. "In fact, the FBI had investigated only sixty-seven cases of children kidnapped by strangers the year before, he said." The director of one missing-children organization admitted that those statistics may have been pulled out of a hat.

Griego told her city editor what she'd found, and Porter told her to keep digging. With veteran reporter Louis Kilzer, Griego kept working, finding that most of the missing kids were runaways and children kidnapped by a parent who did not have custody. *The Denver Post* won the 1986 Pulitzer Prize gold medal for public service for their articles.

Children's health has drawn new attention as well. In the fall of 1986, four Rochester, New York, hospitals and one in Buffalo decided not to use a new brand of diapers because they suspected that the products caused a severe skin infection in some infants. The Rochester *Democrat and Chronicle* ran the story on its front page to alert those parents in Rochester who might be using the same kind of diapers.[4] "It's a myth that only women are interested in these issues, and that they only read the feature pages," says Barbara Henry, editor of the *Democrat and Chronicle*.

"The spate of stories on children may be because there are more mothers in the newsroom," says Mindy Cameron, city editor of *The Seattle Times*. There are stories of children as victims and about their everyday lives. "We are treating children as people. Women have a recognition that things are really happening here and we should take a look at it."

Elizabeth Rhodes drew an even more personal connection. "I had a child in 1983. Before June 1983 I did almost no kid stories. I resisted them, in fact. Then every night I'd go home to this sweet, defenseless little girl. I could see both sides of it. How much they need protection, but how sometimes they make you so mad. . . . Having her and being responsible for her made a big difference doing that story. . . .

"I don't think newspapers have a lot of respect for mothers.

This newspaper is better than others because a lot of us are mothers and they'd be hard put to put us down."

With more women as foreign correspondents, children figure more in international coverage as well. After the disaster at the Chernobyl nuclear plant, Felicity Barringer of *The New York Times* spotted an item in the Soviet press about children from nearby Pripyat being taken to one of the prime Young Pioneer summer camps near Yalta. "Nobody had talked to anybody from Chernobyl, and I figured that the kids had undergone a really traumatic experience and might talk about it."

Barringer's colleagues, Serge Schemann and her husband Philip Taubman, were dubious. They thought everyone had read all they ever wanted to read about Chernobyl. But Barringer persisted and at the last possible moment got Soviet authorities' permission to go. The children did talk to her, and the *Times* played her story, "The Children of Chernobyl," on the front page.[5] "I don't know whether I'd have done it if I hadn't been a mother," Barringer says.

Just as serious coverage of children has increased with more women in the newsrooms, so has coverage of women as women. Virtually every woman interviewed for this book could point to at least one story—usually more—that she did that she felt a man might not have done or would have approached differently.

Abortion is the most obvious women's health issue that has drawn unrelenting front-page coverage. That coverage would have occurred even if women had never set foot in newsrooms because abortion exploded into a major political issue. But abortion would not have become the issue that it is today if no women had stepped into newsrooms and boardrooms and squadrooms—and stepped out of the control of men because they could control whether they got pregnant.

Men and women alike have covered the abortion story. But Betty Anne Williams, assistant managing editor at the Rochester *Democrat and Chronicle*, found herself pursuing the issue into terrain previously uncovered when she was with the Associated Press in Washington. "I was the first person to write about how the federal government subsidizes abortions for military personnel, whether that's good or bad. I had to go over military records. They weren't used to that kind of question."

243

There remains much room for other, new kinds of questions in abortion coverage. Men still direct much of the coverage, and so even though abortion is a major political issue, it is still often covered like any other campaign or legislative drive instead of like the fundamental threat to established power of men over women that it is. For example, some of the male religious and political leaders who oppose abortion clearly fear that women who can control their bodies will escape their control in other ways. This is an element of the debate that rarely appears in many news stories or even in editorial comments. Many older male editors—who wouldn't be caught dead reading feminist literature—simply cannot see that element of the story. Yet that fear may form part of the basis of the objection to abortion by those who connect freedom of choice for women—whether for careers or contraception—with what they perceive as diminishing returns for men. The rigid do in fact lose when they hold that notion; the flexible see that freedom of choice for women unleashes enormous energies for the good of all. The resistance of the rigid—and the true motivation for it—is an area of coverage that deserves exploration because it is fundamental to public policy.

Abortion. Rape. Toxic shock syndrome. Battered women. Joann Byrd, executive editor of *The Herald* in Everett, Washington, remembers interviewing rape victims who she is not sure would have talked as freely, if at all, to a man. She also did a story about a transsexual—a difficult story for the conservative community of Spokane, where she was then working. "I think that at least the macho men might have been uncomfortable. I spent days with the man preparing for that surgery." She was able to do those stories, Byrd feels, because "people were relatively comfortable with me. I was young and short. I didn't ask hostile questions, but I got the same information. People were not frightened by me."

In her study of women in the media, Jean Gaddy Wilson of the University of Missouri quoted a male columnist about the effect of having more women making news decisions. "We had a story about a legislator who was brought up on a statutory rape charge," the columnist had said. "There were two women on the desk that night. Two guys on the desk may have nudged each other and said, 'See what ol'——— has been up to,' and buried it in the paper. But not these two women. They put it on the front page. They didn't overlook it. I think the feeling at the paper is that men and women will treat the news differently."[6]

From paper to paper, big and small, women frequently have improved newspapers' rape-law reform coverage. *The New York Times*, for example, regularly runs wrap-up stories suggested by a national correspondent and fed by memos from other reporters around the country. Grace Lichtenstein did a national roundup on changing rape laws more than a decade ago. "The reason I had the idea was because Susan Brownmiller was my friend, and she was writing the book [*Against Our Will: Men, Women and Rape*], and I was interested. It ran on page one."

Ever irreverent, Lichtenstein also managed one of her fondest dreams at *The New York Times*: she got rock and roll on the front page for the first time—a story on a relief concert for Bangladesh.

Women have also often had to be groundbreakers in covering stories about gays. "The idea that there could be a gay synagogue, for example, I thought was a good story," Lichtenstein says. "Homosexuality was a more touchy subject for men. As a heterosexual woman, I could write that story for *The New York Times*. Gays had been invisible. Judy Klemesrud had done stories on gays for the 'Living' section, but this was for the news section."

Marlene Cimons of the *Los Angeles Times*, one of the first reporters to spot the dimensions of the Acquired Immune Deficiency Syndrome story, initially found difficulty in getting good play for the AIDS stories that are now routinely on the front pages. Because it was a disease that initially seemed to affect only gay men, the story made male editors uncomfortable until they fully recognized the broad public-health implications and until it became clear the disease affected a broader segment of the population. This hypersensitivity let the origins of a major plague go uncovered and may have fed the initial apathy that retarded financial aid for research on the disease.

Their handling of stories on toxic shock syndrome revealed more male squeamishness and "the blindness of sexism," as Molly Ivins of the *Dallas Times-Herald* calls it. "If it was an aftershave that was killing them, I don't think it would take any time at all to get on page one." But menstruation was an old taboo, and who wanted to run stories about tampons anyway? Yet toxic shock was killing people, primarily women who used tampons.

Toxic shock frightened many women. After one development in the story, *Los Angeles Times* editors decided at their page-one meeting (at which no women were regular participants) not to put the story on the front page. John Lawrence, who was then in charge of economic coverage, asked several of the women who worked for him if they thought it should have been on page one. They said yes, emphatically. So Lawrence and Paul Steiger, then the *Times*'s business editor, put together a team to examine the business aspects for a big Sunday feature. "He had the sense to ask," says one of the women, Pamela Moreland. And he had a substantial number of women in his business section that he could ask.

Not all the toxic-shock coverage was done by women, to be sure. James Worsham, now of *The Kansas City Star*, was then a business reporter for the *Chicago Tribune* and won both an in-house award for best domestic reporting and a national consumer journalism award for a six-part series that he, Charles Madigan, and Ann Marie Lipinski did in May 1981 on the controversy over Rely tampons and their removal from the market. Harry Nelson covered the story extensively for the *Los Angeles Times*. As already mentioned, Nan Robertson won the Pultizer Prize for her article interspersing her own trauma with the search for answers to the toxic-shock mystery by scientists, physicians, and businesses.

Coverage of women's health questions, then, seems to have been a beneficiary of the presence of more women in the newsroom. Reporters are exploring another aspect of the physical well-being of women as well—wife-beating. Few newspapers had touched the topic. It's hard to know why, because it seems like an obvious crime story, but here's one possible explanation. Men who run newspapers, like men who run police departments, are used to their ability to take charge, to get out of bad situations. Although perhaps sympathetic to the victim in individual wife-beating cases, they still tend to blame the victims because they can't understand why a woman wouldn't leave an abusive man. Never having been dependent (or so they think—I remember vividly my father's wounded vulnerability whenever he had a cold and took to his bed), they didn't recognize the difficulties a dependent woman has in deciding to leave, then in getting the financial and physical ability to do it. So few newspapers noticed the stories, either. But Eileen McNamara at *The Boston Globe* did.

McNamara had heard about two state judges in Somerville, Massachusetts, outside Boston, who were giving battered women a hard time for seeking restraining orders against their husbands. After the body of Pamela Dunn, who was pregnant, was found in the nearby Lexington dump, McNamara got a tip to listen to the tapes of the hearing at which Dunn had asked for a restraining order.

"On the recordings of the March hearings," she reported in the *Globe*, "[Judge Paul P.] Heffernan can be heard scolding the 22-year-old Arlington woman for wasting the court's time 'on a situation which in my opinion clearly is a little bit out of control.' . . . He berated her for securing a police escort when she returned to the couple's apartment to retrieve her clothes, telling the officer who accompanied her, 'I think you've been duped in this case.' At the couple's final appearance, Heffernan told Paul Dunn, 'you want to gnaw on her and she on you, fine, but let's not do it at taxpayers' expense.' "[7]

The woman's husband was arrested in Florida and convicted of murder. The judges stepped aside from the bench until the investigations were completed, and two other judges have been stripped of their authority to hear such cases. A special investigator concluded that Heffernan was guilty of gross misconduct; formal charges were lodged against him by the judicial performance commission.

Reflecting on the subjects on which women writers write, Pat Fisher of *The Seattle Times* sums up what several women say. "One of my subjects is children, whether it's education, safe toys, abortion, abuse, delinquency: I'm interested in it all. Ninety percent of the editorials that are done on those subjects are done because I'm here." In her office there is an award from the Alliance for Children, Youth and Families naming Pat Fisher journalist of the year. "I'm proud of that."

Abortion, child care, and rape-law reform are issues of the women's movement, and it took women in the newsroom to see them as stories. "I always felt a responsibility to cover those stories," says Sharon Dickman, now an assistant metropolitan editor for *The Baltimore Evening Sun.* "A lot of things were going on in 1972 and 1973 and 1974 that weren't being covered."

Dickman remembers doing a series on working mothers in the mid-1970s. "It wasn't as if I was going through it and believed in it as a cause and said because of that I'd get working mothers on the metro pages. It was new. It was out there. It wasn't like we were making it up. Now when you look back, if there hadn't been some of us who felt responsible, when would those stories have gotten into our papers?"

Margie Freivogel of *The St. Louis Post-Dispatch* feels the same way. "If I could dispel what I feel I ought to write and write what my instincts tell me, I might write what people really want to read. I decided I had to trust my instincts." Coverage of routine Washington legislation is just that—routine. Coverage of women in politics, says Freivogel—"that's a real movement of historical significance, and this other stuff nobody's going to remember next week."

The women at the *Maine Times*, a weekly published in Topsham near Bath and Brunswick and best known for its environmental coverage, have consistently followed the women's movement. Back in the early 1970s, virtually all the staff was female, and the paper put out an issue devoted almost entirely to women. "We put out a sequel in the mid-1970s, and we would not have put the energy into that if we weren't women," says staff writer Phyllis Austin. Even today, "if we don't have a woman on the staff who is committed to social issues, they don't get written about."

Why, Austin was asked, do women write these stories? "They see a story immediately, they know it affects their lives, their relationships. It's really where the heart is. When we covered those things, we were vitally interested in them, and they touched our lives, and we knew they touched others' lives. We knew their importance. They're not at arm's length, as it so often is with men who do these stories."

The major change shaping women's lives in the last two decades has been their unprecedented entry into the work force. Coverage of working women has grown far more sophisticated than just "first-woman" stories, although such stories still exist. It is rare that physical or marital descriptions accompany such stories, and there's far less of the "petite mother of two" phraseology tucked away in the story about a firefighter or a city council member.

Especially important in the modern coverage of working women has been *The Wall Street Journal*. It has moved not only from declining to interview women for jobs in years past to having women in prominent reporting and editing jobs, but it also now gives prominent attention to questions about marriage, day care, promotions, clothing conformity, and sexual harrassment. Once in the 1960s a senior *Wall Street Journal* editor told a female applicant that it wasn't true that his paper didn't hire women, it just hadn't hired any since 1944. Today its stories about hiring and working with women reach the audience that most needs to read them: America's corporate leaders.

"I think it's important to write about the role of women for the readers of *The Wall Street Journal*," says Karen Elliott House. "Not only are these important stories, they deal with the issues people talk about. More time is spent over the dinner table and in the bars in talking about people's roles—what it's like to work for a woman, how do you deal with a woman who works with you, the frustration of people whose female boss goes off to play with her kid. Everybody's looking for clues on how to deal with that. These stories are enormously well read."

The change of attitude toward women in the work force and of women toward working, as well as the shift in the number of working women with young children, is one of the key trends in twentieth-century social history. *The Wall Street Journal* has recognized that trend, as have the business sections at some major newspapers; the *Los Angeles Times*'s business section has, for example, repeatedly focused news and opinion columns on questions of day care and pay equity.

Covering women in the work force can mean hard work—physically hard work. In 1950 Marvel Cooke wrote a memorable series for *The Compass* in New York about the way white women took advantage of their domestic help, the "slave market." Each morning, at a number of pickup points, women employers came to choose among the domestic workers who congregated along the sidewalk. For several mornings in a row, Cooke's husband drove her from their home in Harlem to a spot near one of the pickup points in the Bronx. No matter what she wore, Cooke, a well-educated woman, didn't have the care-worn appearance of the rest of the women on the corner, and the other workers distrusted her. And employers wouldn't hire her. "The women would come down and look at me; I didn't look as if I knew anything. There was a bet on at the paper that I would not get the job."

She went back for several days and was passed over. "I had just given up, saying, 'I'm going to the ten-cent store here and have a bowl of soup because I'm hungry.'" Just then a woman came along late and gave Cooke a job.

"The girls on the corner had begun to believe I was authentic because I turned up two or three days and they told me, 'You're new. One of the things you have to watch is to set your time because they have a way of turning the clocks back.' Well, I went through the paces. I did everything that woman asked me to do, including iron. And I don't iron well. The very last thing I'll do is put a wrinkle in it. But I ironed curtains with these ruffles all around, and I did a beautiful job. . . . Then she gave me something else to do. She ate and didn't offer me anything to eat. She gave me something else to do. I said, 'I really can't do it.' I looked at my watch and it said three o'clock. 'My children are coming home'—I don't have any children—'my children are coming home,' I said. . . .

"She had turned her clock back to 1:30. I said, 'But it's 3.' I was paid all of seventy-five cents an hour. I said, 'I know I set my watch by your clock when I came in and my watch says 3, so I expect to be paid for five hours.' She paid me. But she said, 'You will come back next week?' Of course, she never saw me again. . . . I called the office to say that I had had a job and I was going home and rest up and I'd be in the next day.

"That turned out to be one of the best series they ever had. . . . *The Compass* had a truck with a great big sign on it. It said, 'READ: I WAS A SLAVE BY MARVEL COOKE.'"

In this series Cooke evoked her most powerful images in the article of January 11, 1950. She wrote that the corner in front of Woolworth's at 170th Street was beginning to feel like home.[8] "It seemed natural to be standing there with my sister slaves, all of us with paper bags, containing our work clothes, under our arms.

"I recognized many of the people who pass. I no longer felt 'new.' But I was not at peace. Hundreds of years of history weighed

250

upon me. I was the slave traded for two truck horses on a Memphis
street corner in 1849. I was the slave trading my brawn for a
pittance on a Bronx streetcorner in 1949. As I stood there waiting
to be bought, I lived through a century of indignity."

From that day to this, women reporters have had a special
eye out for working women. Pam Moreland, then on the business
section at the *Los Angeles Times*, covered an event at which a group
of working women gave its "Scrooge of the Year" award to a local
bank. She saw the possibilities for a bigger piece on 9 to 5, the
union organizing among secretaries. Her article appeared in the
coveted column-one spot on the front page.

In the entertainment industry as well as in other aspects of
American business, women have been organizing to try to get
more directing, producing, and writing jobs for women in television and films. Connie Koenenn, editor of the *Los Angeles Times*
daily "Calendar" entertainment section, has tried to have her section reflect that development, just as it covers other elements of
the industry such as emerging technologies, changing trends in
movie and TV story lines, acting awards, and rising stars.

"There's a fear of making something seem legitimate that
isn't, and I understand that," Koenenn says. But she also insists
that reporters talk to women as well as men at the film and TV
conferences they cover to find out their concerns. "It's not as if I
said go and cover something that wasn't there. It was something
to cover. There is a woman. Go cover her. Or there are no women.
Cover that, too. Men do not even see the lack of women. Women
always do."

By 1984, a consensus emerged among some women at the
Los Angeles Times that the paper needed to take a more systematic
look at women in the workplace. Directed by Linda Mathews, who
was then on the national desk, a team of women outlined a possible
series, won the paper's commitment to the project, and worked
on the project off and on for six months. Starting the Sunday
after Labor Day, the twenty articles and one editorial focused on
the movement of women into the work force, family concerns like
child care and marital stress, women as executives, bias against
women in politics, and the uncertain employment future for
women.[9]

In the course of preparing the series, women encountered

251

all the problems faced by the women about whom they were writing. One who worked on the series quit before it ran to spend more time with her child. Another quit to write books and be her own boss. One was called home when her mother had a cancer operation. And one was pregnant and had barely finished her work on the series before giving birth to a daughter.

As important as the information the articles imparted was the fact that they appeared for ten days in a row on the front page of the *Los Angeles Times*. Three of the articles ran in column one. That play said to the public that one of the best papers in the country felt the subject of women in the workplace was worthy of serious, consistent news coverage. It was true for those ten days at least.

Everyday Indignities

I cannot report others' Everyday Indignities about being ignored without some of my own. I understand Vivian Vahlberg's feelings about ideas she mentioned that fell on deaf ears of male colleagues, only to be mentioned later by one of the men and then thoroughly discussed. It's happened more than once at *Los Angeles Times* editorial pages conferences, although not recently. Once, at least, my boss, Anthony Day, called one of my colleagues on his supposedly bright new idea, saying tartly, "Kay just said that."

But in other times past, as he asked those of us seated around the table for our ideas for the next day's editorials, he forgot to call on me. I worried that being ignored meant the subjects I wrote about sometimes would not see the light of day. I thought that perhaps I was oversensitive, until I saw it happening time and time again to my then new colleague, Gayle Pollard. One does not enjoy being the female equivalent of Ralph Ellison's *Invisible Man*. I never said anything. She finally did. With vigor. It doesn't happen anymore.

CHAPTER

15

The Newsroom Evolution

At 5 P.M. each afternoon the senior editors at *The New York Times* meet to decide what stories will go on the front page the next morning. Two women regularly attend that meeting: Soma Golden, the national editor, and Carolyn Lee, the photo editor. Sometimes there is a third, Nancy Newhouse, who edits the lifestyle sections. "I've never really felt as if I'm *the* woman at the 5 P.M. meeting," insists Golden. "I certainly don't represent all women. . . . But I am female. I do have some strong feelings" that may differ from those of the men in the room, she adds.

She does indeed have strong feelings, and she has used them to argue onto the front page a story about fears among heterosexuals that bisexuals might be spreading Acquired Immune Deficiency Syndrome. A man who knew of their concerns might have argued just as passionately, she says firmly. She adds that executive editor Max Frankel has proved committed to beefing up lifestyle coverage in general because it's important and it's what people read. If asked, Golden would probably also point out that that kind of story is hardly the only kind that she pushes for page one.

The point is, though, that a woman—Soma Golden—was the national editor of *The New York Times*, and she was the one who was positioned at that meeting to get that story onto the front page of that paper, the most widely respected in the country. That may be one among many reasons—talent, experience, chutzpah —why Max Frankel put her there. She had heard the anguish among women who had had relationships with gay men and who feared they might get AIDS, and of gay men who feared they might have the disease or have unwittingly transmitted it.[1] And she wasn't afraid to say that it was an important story.

Soma Golden started out as an economics reporter at *Business Week* and then at *The New York Times*; then she became an editorial writer, then the Sunday business section editor before becoming national editor in January 1987. The point is that not only do women make a difference in covering stories that, for want of a better term, are "women's issues," they also make a difference in covering medical stories, business issues, politics, foreign affairs, nuclear disarmament, and, as we have seen, even baseball.

Golden is willing to acknowledge a difference: in that page-one meeting she is a person with two children and a husband who also works full-time. "I may represent someone living life on the edge," someone trying to do it all who feels it is terribly important to live her life at home so that there is still a family to come home to when the job is done. In other words, she feels she is not so much representing women as representing families. Men have families, too, and increasingly take them into account, but balancing these concerns still puts more strain on women than men.

"That's where I'll affect coverage—and that's where I have to affect the *Times*." Not only must she make the staff changes to improve news coverage, but she knows that the paper's attitude must change toward news coverers who are increasingly two-career family people as well.

And finally, Soma Golden's management philosophy—"I'm not afraid somebody is going to look better than me"—also shows a different outlook that women bring to that traditional male stronghold, although again she draws back from making the sweeping assessment that only women have that attitude. The men who are going to be successful in the coming years have it, too. But women may well have a head start because they aren't as used to being number one. Says Golden, "I have a fantastic assistant in Dan Lewis. I am delighted with that. I don't want all the credit. There's enough to go around."

Let's take news coverage first. Golden, who studied economics at Radcliffe, got a master's degree in journalism at Columbia University and went to work for *Business Week* in the fall of 1962. So she's watched economics reporting for the better part of two decades. "Surely somebody's told you that in those days business sections of newspapers typically were the places that if you were a boozer or something else," that's where you were stashed. "It was clear to women that that was an area of newspapers where the men were weak."

So a few women started covering economics, and they could do well because for a long time nobody in the newspaper hierarchy paid any attention to them. It was a good entry-level job for the women who figured that out—again, rather like Latin America was for women who wanted to be foreign correspondents. Still, there were precious few—Eileen Shanahan, columnist Sylvia Porter, and a few others. Then came recessions and inflation, and economics became a big story—and there were the women like Soma Golden and Lisa Myers, now with NBC but then a reporter for *The Washington Star*, to analyze it.

Obviously, men still edit business sections, or many of them, and they deserve credit where credit is due for the sections' emerging readability. But women were instrumental as well, proving that they could not only read balance sheets—quite contrary to the "scatterbrain" stereotype of the woman who can't balance her check book—but also that they could ask questions consumers wanted asked. Women still like to shop, and even many of those who don't at least know what questions to ask corporate executives if they can't find the product or service they want at the department store, the grocery chain, or the hardware store.

Life on the business pages at many newspapers, however, is not like life in businesses shown in television commercials, the ones where the woman executive rushes in with the solution to a client's computer system problem with one brilliant insight. What if as many women covered corporate finance or banking as cover retailing? What if more women covered the oil industry than covered the entertainment industry? Would they ask questions about employment practices, about flexible working hours, about better serving consumer needs? You betcha, as Ellen Goodman would say.

In covering all aspects of business and labor—not just women in the work force—women do still face some barriers. Just as some labor unions have not welcomed women as members, they have not looked favorably on women reporters. Huntly Collins, covering labor for *The Philadelphia Inquirer*, says that one of her goals was to "open some channels of communications with the building trades unions, whose leaders hadn't talked to reporters—even men—for years." She interviewed the head of the plumbers' union. "He's about six foot six and 250 pounds. We developed some rapport, and at the end of the interview he thanked me and shook hands. Then he said, 'I never shook the hand of a lady before.' "

Sara Fritz stood out in the crowd of men when she covered the AFL-CIO first for United Press International and then for *U.S. News & World Report* in the 1970s. "It was really a shock to them when I showed up." She overcame the normal raunchy comments and developed a sparring relationship with AFL-CIO President George Meany at his news conferences "because he remembered me. He knew how to work an audience, and he picked me as a foil. I always asked him when he was going to retire. 'Don't call me, I'll call you,' he'd say. And I'd say, 'You do that.' He was ill the day he decided to retire, but he did have someone call me."

Breaking into business or labor reporting is much like starting out as a sportswriter. As Lawrie Mifflin, deputy sports editor of *The New York Times,* says, the hurdle now is convincing people in the world of sports—and she could have said business or labor—"the athletes and the general managers, that you are serious and knowledgeable. As soon as you've done that, you've solved that problem. But it is still a problem because there is still an inclination that a woman isn't going to know as much or isn't going to work as hard."

There is still that inclination because women are outsiders, just like blacks and Latinos and Asians, and now even white men who grew up on farms are outsiders. But outsiders often are excellent reporters, male or female. They see different stories, ask different questions—or use different sources.

Fran Dauth got some of her best stories in the San Francisco Bay area in the early 1970s from secretaries in the government offices. "There was a room where they had coffee at about ten o'clock every morning, and I went most every day. I liked them. I also didn't think it would hurt to know them."

They helped. When she was working on a story surveying Oakland's commissions to see how many women and minorities had been appointed—"a natural now, but a story that hadn't been done then"—she got the commission list but found she didn't know many of the people. One of the mayor's secretaries did. After her stories revealed that the commissions were made up overwhelmingly of older white males, the pressure was on when a key vacancy occurred. The city fathers wanted to keep the opening quiet so that they wouldn't have to appoint a minority in this last gasp of the white Republican administration of Oakland, Dauth recalls. Only city council members knew. But Dauth got the information anyway, and no one in authority could figure how. They simply weren't asking the right people when they tried to plug the leaks.

Women also ask different questions. When Anne Roark of the *Los Angeles Times* was with *The Chronicle of Higher Education*, she found herself assigned to interview a theoretical mathematician who had just won a $150,000 grant for promising young scientists. "We had nothing in common," Roark recalled. "We couldn't relate to each other." So Roark asked him, " 'What's your day like?' He looked at me like I was crazy. No one had ever asked him a question like that. He said, 'I sit . . . and think.' It was probably the best piece I'd ever done," Roark said.[2]

Some questions open new areas to explore; others open only areas of aggravation. One of the most persistent questioners who occasionally throws strikes in from left field and other times strikes out has been Sarah McClendon, who has run her own news service in Washington since 1944. McClendon has annoyed Presidents and other journalists alike. Saying that it is her goal "to be a bridge between big government and little people," she has regularly risen at presidential press conferences to ask questions about which no one else was thinking. Criticized even by some of her allies as too much of an advocate, McClendon has nonetheless forced some presidential answers on questions about the homeless, veterans' benefits, and sex discrimination.

She's been the target of two editorials in *The New York Times*. One was for a question she asked about Defense Department management. The *Times* felt she "assured herself of the television spotlight, as usual" through wild, unsubstantiated charges "in as McCarthyesque a performance as we have seen in some time, even from Miss McClendon."[3] And in 1973 the *Times* accused McClendon of "boorish behavior" when she questioned Nixon about the Veterans Administration, adding that "her excess of volume and verbosity and her tendency toward rude interruptions of Presidential replies would be offensive even in a less exalted setting."[4]

That editorial was an "excess of volume" for *The New York Times* itself. Although newspapers rarely publish letters from their own reporters, in this case the *Times* published one from Eileen Shanahan, then in its Washington bureau, who wrote that McClendon deserved "appreciation, not condemnation, for the questions she has asked Presidents over the years." Shanahan pointed out that McClendon questioned President Eisenhower's decision to send troops to Lebanon without congressional authorization and had raised many questions about waste in the Pentagon, "often with specific examples that were corrected because she brought them to public attention. She has repeatedly exposed with her questions instances of invasion of privacy by the Government.

"Mrs. McClendon is reviled, I fear, largely because so many people find tough-mindedness in a woman an unattractive trait. A man who had asked the same questions as Mrs. McClendon would not be criticized by the *Times*," Shanahan said in closing.[5]

Willingness to ask the obvious question or a hostile question is an asset for investigative reporters. Mention investigative reporters, and some people think of Carl Bernstein as played by Dustin Hoffman—mooching cigarettes, scribbling notes on rumpled paper, and camping in unsuspecting people's doorways. But more and more the investigative reporter is a Carla, not a Carl. Miriam Ottenberg of *The Washington Star* was one of the best—she won the Pulitzer Prize in 1960 for a series of articles on baby selling. *The Washington Journalism Review* called Mary Hargrove, special projects editor for *The Tulsa Tribune* in Oklahoma, the "best in the West" for her work investigating the Penn Square Bank failure and the finances of Oral Roberts's ministry.[6]

Claire Spiegel, who started investigative reporting while still at the Columbia School of Journalism, was thoroughly hooked on it at the New York *Daily News*, probably because of "something about the New York press environment and the premium put on scoops and stories that shook people up." Spiegel later joined the *Los Angeles Times* and has broken major stories about bidding on city housing contracts, stress pensions for police, and misused antipoverty funds.

"You have to be someone who doesn't like the in-crowd, is

knocking the in-crowd." Women have an advantage, Spiegel says, in that they are "viewed as nonthreatening." If you're camped out at a source's house, you aren't as ominous. "Or if I knock on somebody's door after 7 P.M. and they hear a woman's voice, they may think I'm in trouble and let me in."

Traditional beats can yield nontraditional stories if you want them to. I covered federal regulatory agencies for the Newhouse News Service in the 1970s. Flat decision-making stories—"WASHINGTON—The Federal Communications Commission today announced . . ."—were common then. I tried instead to show how the Commission affected (or didn't affect) programs for children on television or what Federal Trade Commission rules about hearing-aid sales meant to the hard of hearing. I explored issues that the agencies were asked to decide but wouldn't; these issues were often far more relevant to the public than those they did act upon. The approach is fairly common now, but it was not then.

Science and medical writing are evolving as well. Again, not because women can explain nuclear physics or brain surgery any better or even as well as some men, and certainly not because women have been groomed for years and years as scientists or doctors or science writers or medical writers. But take the example of Jane Brody, whose "Personal Health" column has run in *The New York Times* since 1976. She tried to foster coverage of more human concerns about medical questions in her very first job interview with Clifton Daniel, then managing editor, before she joined the *Times* in 1965.

"He asked what I thought of the science writing at *The New York Times*. I said it was fine as far as it went, but it didn't go far enough. What did I mean? It covers innovations, discoveries, technology, but it doesn't do much for helping people live better lives, I said. He asked me for an example. I picked epilepsy. While there had been no breakthroughs, there still had been advancements to help people function better, but epileptics still faced discrimination. That should be written about. It just so happened that Clifton Daniel's brother-in-law is epileptic."

So Brody started covering the human side of medicine. "That's what I became known for—writing not what people think they should read but what they want to read."

Science writing and business writing, okay; let women do it.

But the holiest of holies is national security. War, weapons: perhaps even more sacred to men than covering politics or the power-I football formation is covering the ultimate power, nuclear weapons. Women can't possibly understand that. If we let them do this, we'll have no secrets left. The sanctity of the treehouse will be totally destroyed.

Geneva Overholser writes foreign-policy and national-security editorials for *The New York Times*. She has often found herself the only woman in some rarefied discussions. "At some point if you are going to be any good at all, you have to set aside the appearances of knowing it all." That creates a new problem in turn, she says, because among national-security professionals "there's great emphasis on appearing to know all there is to know.

"So you have to go ahead and ask the basic questions. I think women are more willing to ask basic, very broad questions. That's probably true of anybody who isn't part of the priesthood—and of course more women [than men] haven't become part of that priesthood." Insiders seem to distrust the public, feeling it doesn't understand national-security questions, but Overholser contends it is journalists' job "to give the public the information and it makes the decisions." In that way the press—the outsiders—can help demystify arms control.

Sometimes an elementary question yields the day's most revealing answer, as Overholser found during a session between Sen. Albert Gore, Jr., of Tennesee and the *Times*'s editorial writers. "It was a typical conversation about the Allies' fears over the zero-zero solution, the probability of difficulties over verification in the INF agreement, et cetera. Then I said that one thing that concerns me particularly is the huge gap between the public, with its fears and yearnings on this issue, and leaders and experts, whose thoughts tend to be locked into very small terrain. 'Can you help with that problem as part of a campaign?' I wondered.

"Gore came alive. He sat forward and said, 'That's really what I want to do. It's what I do best. If I have a good twenty minutes with people so that I can explain things—I find they really want to hear it.' " Gore's response was evidence to Overholser that "so often the broader, more human question that occurs to us (and seems a bit unorthodox or out-of-tune) is very useful and quite welcome."

When former White House Chief of Staff Donald Regan made his now infamous comment that women weren't interested in arms control because they didn't understand throw-weights, he was hooted at soundly by men and women alike. By one in particular. Meg Greenfield, editorial page editor of *The Washington Post*, who has described herself as a latecomer to feminism, says, "I knew instantly the absurdity of Regan's remark. . . . I was writing all that stuff when he was still on Wall Street. It was so ridiculous because he doesn't know which end of the missile you light."

Having women as these top editors and as editorial writers has reshaped the dialogue as well as the coverage of the other precious commodity—politics—as well. Every election year, politicians make the rounds seeking newspapers' endorsements for their candidacies. Sometimes all the top editors and the publisher of a newspaper participate in questioning a presidential or mayoral candidate; sometimes only a handful of editorial writers do the work. In obscure races in which candidates lack clear public identities, the kind of information elicited to aid voters depends directly on the kind of questions editorial writers ask.

Thus, it is important for women to be present at endorsement interviews to raise issues that only women seem vitally concerned about, says Nancy Grape, editorial writer at *The Portland Press-Herald*. Grape once wrote a column that criticized Maine's governor for thinking he had fully addressed women's issues if he discussed the number of women he had appointed to jobs. "What about day care?" she asked. Women on editorial pages may be especially important in smaller cities, Grape adds, where institutional discrimination may be stronger. Those local newspapers must be particularly vigilant, she says, and be sure they keep after politicians and organizations that buttress the idea that it's still okay for men to have a special position.

And woe be to the politicians these days who aren't prepared to deal with these questions. They are finding more and more women on editorial pages—although still few as editorial-page editors at major papers. And more and more, the women do speak up.

"I know some women might like to think we are the same" as men, says Barbara Henry, editor of both the morning and the afternoon Rochester papers. "We are different. We make different decisions." She describes her papers as "top heavy" with women in management; as a result, the papers pay more attention to social issues such as child care and pay equity. "We deal with these issues more on our opinion pages. Those questions tend to be asked more of politicians running in this area. They know they're going to get asked those questions when they come in here." Rochester elected a woman to Congress—its second in history—less than a month after Henry made that comment.

Even the newspaper columnists are different with women among them. Yes, there is still George Will and his quota of quotations, but foreign affairs now shares the spotlight with family affairs. Writers like Judy Mann and Dorothy Gilliam, Ellen Goodman and Anna Quindlen find their subjects in private as well as public life.

Even as they themselves represent an evolution in the world of newspaper columns, the individual women columnists themselves continue to evolve. For example, syndicated columnist Joyce Maynard, a former *New York Times* reporter, spoke with pride about writing about the "very important things [that] were happening under our roof" in rural New Hampshire.[7] But as her world changed and was threatened, Maynard's column changed as well. When the federal government talked about putting a nuclear waste dump literally right where her family lived, Maynard started writing about the issues as well as working against the dump.

Ellen Goodman and Anna Quindlen are probably the best-known of these columnists nationwide, Goodman because of her long syndication by *The Washington Post* Writers Group and Quindlen because of her Wednesday forum in *The New York Times*. The two women tackle many of the same questions about relationships, but each has her own style. Goodman moves from the reality—say, Gary Hart's withdrawal from the Presidential race—into the realm of personal reactions and human ties. Quindlen often moves in the other direction—from the personal to the universal. Quindlen is a more open book—no less perceptive, but her own persona shows more in her pieces than that of the private person who is Ellen Goodman.

"I didn't want to write just light stuff or just politics" in starting to write a column, Goodman says. "I felt it was important to do both. I wanted to try to break through this false dichotomy because people don't live all one way or the other. I didn't want to draw lines between private lives and public lives but rather to connect these lives.

"Voice is something you find inside and let out. You just develop it. I mean, look, what are the big stories? Aside from the blip of Irangate, they are social change, AIDS—that's what people talk about. . . .

"Because of the time I began the column [the early 1970s], I was more able to write as who I am without excising the woman part of it. Earlier than that, a lot of women had to follow the male model—or they followed the woman's model and they were writing advice to the lovelorn. Coming when I did, I didn't have to adopt a falsetto baritone. At that point, editorial writers had pretty much written off female readers. If they had any reader in mind at all, it was the white male decision maker."

"My column," says Anna Quindlen of "Life in the 30s" in *The New York Times*, "is my telephone conversation voice. It's what I talk about on the phone. Newspapers don't cover that ground. If they do, they cover it as sociology but not as human emotion. Emoting is what I do best."

Just as she has said in print, she really does write the column upstairs while her two sons watch television downstairs or go to school or tell the neighbors Mommy doesn't work. Quindlen's style cannot be mistaken for Goodman's; it is often more confessional, the realizations of a woman in her 30s who now understands, for example, what her mother was saying or thinking when she, Anna, was an uncomprehending youngster. Goodman writes more straight political commentary than does Quindlen, but both focus more than other columnists on what people take into the political world and away from it rather than on the events of the political world itself.

Many women who are reporters and editors, then, can readily identify what makes their work different from that of men. But it has proved to be far harder to measure these differences or to capture in statistics how well or ill newspapers cover women. The evidence almost has to be anecdotal, which simply won't please the people who don't believe women have made a difference.

But several studies have been done. One, by Pam Reich, who was at the time a graduate student at the University of Missouri, found that *The Los Angeles Herald Examiner* ran only a few more stories about women under the editorship of Mary Anne Dolan than it had under that of her predecessor James Bellows, who had brought Dolan to the paper.[8] However, more stories about women appeared on the front page when Dolan was editor, and the stories were more issue-oriented than tied to specific events.

"That would appear to be a major difference, since one of the main reasons cited for women's news not receiving coverage is that it is often not event-oriented—newspapers have to be willing to seek the news out," Reich concluded. Remember: that's the same reason—newspapers are event-oriented—that David Broder gave for the (male) press missing the beginnings of the women's movement.

Quantifiable or not, newspaper coverage has clearly changed since the years when editors first laughed at "women's lib," ran "leg art" prominently, and thought women were interested only in recipes. Newspapers now carry more stories from unconventional sources, some of whose voices were first heard by women reporters on their staffs.

Hearing different things—or hearing the same things differently, as Elizabeth Rhodes of *The Seattle Times* puts it—is a trait that carries over to the way some women manage employees, given that chance. And the way they manage affects the product they help manage. Management, then—like the business coverage, editorials, and column writing that have been traditionally men's domain—is another area that is getting a transfusion of new blood and new approaches, new people with new ideas—but not enough and not in enough places.

Without Sandy Banks, a black woman, on the *Los Angeles Times*'s metropolitan desk, for example, Marita Hernandez would not have found as sympathetic an ear when she became aware of developing opposition to a new state prison in East Los Angeles, a heavily Latino area. Some of the male editors had pooh-poohed the story; they told Hernandez that although state Assemblywoman Gloria Molina, who represented the area, was upset with the planned construction, Molina, a Latina, was on the outs with the Democratic establishment in Sacramento and was sure to lose.

Hernandez knew from talking with community people that the resentment ran deeper than the surface politics. She went to Banks, who knew from her own dealings with the black community that neighborhood energy could sometimes overcome political reality. She told Hernandez to keep checking. The community did block the prison project for a time; the legislature eventually tried to resolve the issue by deciding to build two prisons, one in Democratic East Los Angeles and another in a rural Republican area. No matter what the resolution was, the point is that these two women and the awareness they had of community dynamics helped the *Times* handle a major political story that it might otherwise have missed, at least initially.

Women on the desk sometimes simply ask reporters different questions. "I want to make sure we just don't go to men to see what Riverside or San Diego is thinking," says Marcia McQuern, who has been city editor in both cities.

"I think women may be probably a little more sensitive to discrimination issues, too," McQuern adds. "We've been there. We know what it feels like. So we may be more aware of questions about hiring and promoting people. . . . We can be saved from some embarrassing insensitivities, the unconscious demeaning things, by having a variety of people in our newsrooms—and the paper is better for it. Fewer of them are happening now that women are there raising the questions."

Had a woman been in a position of real responsibility on the *Los Angeles Times* desk in 1979, when Jane Byrne was elected mayor of Chicago, would this story have run?

CHICAGO—It has been more than a century since Mrs. O'Leary's cow kicked over a lantern and started the famous fire that destroyed the heart of Chicago.

Now, 198 years later, another blaze is scorching the foundations of this city. Chicago has been Byrned.

The modern-day arsonist is not a careless housewife or an establishment-hating radical. She is a diminutive, 44-year-old mother with ash blonde hair, green eyes and a posh northside apartment.

The day after torching one of the most powerful

political organizations in the nation, her most threatening act was to have her fingernails manicured at a fashionable beauty salon.

Jane Byrne, the woman whose 15,000 vote victory over incumbent Michael A. Bilandic in Tuesday's Democratic mayoral primary shocked the Chicago machine and the nation, is a study in contradictions.[9]

Byrne was the first woman mayor of a major U.S. city and had tossed out the machine. She was finally named in the fifth paragraph by, you guessed it, a male reporter. It is a measure of the changing times that the senior editors had the grace to grimace the next morning when asked about the story, and one almost felt safe in predicting that its like would not appear in papers at the close of this decade.

Almost safe, that is, until a Sunday in November 1987 when the *Los Angeles Times* carried a feature story by Jerry Gillam about the rising number of highly paid female lobbyists in the state capital. A valid story, it nonetheless focused on whether these women used their bodies to get votes. The fifth paragraph read: "The women insist that they lobby exactly the same way men do, get the same sore feet from running around the Capitol buttonholing lawmakers—and resent speculation that their sex appeal helps them round up votes from male legislators."[10]

Whose speculation? It's never identified. Sacramento is a notoriously sexist environment, to be sure, but no editor sufficiently challenged the story to alter its focus. It should also be noted that the *Times* had no women in its Sacramento bureau at the time this story was written nor any on the government desk that handled the story.

More women work at American newspapers now than did even in 1979, when the Byrne story appeared. But this sexist coverage still appears because women remain a minority among decision makers. The male mentality still fawns over Fawn Hall, a bit player in the Iran-contra hearings but pictured profusely because of her "God-given beauty." The press appeared in droves the day she testified. As Nikki Finke of the *Los Angeles Times* pointed out, Hall, the secretary to Lt. Col. Oliver North, was treated like a figure in a sex scandal, a person lacking dignity.[11]

Newspapers also can still be accused of the "bimbo factor." Donna Rice, a single woman, was identified, pursued, and treated as a notorious type; she was described more regularly as a blonde than as the Phi Beta Kappa college graduate that she is, while Gary Hart—and it was he, not the woman, who withdrew from the presidential race because his credibility and judgment had been tarnished—was never described as a lanky strawberry brunet.[12]

For these reasons, women still need to be vigilant on newspaper desks and in editorial-page meetings as "thought police," says Anna Quindlen. "If you work at *The New York Times*, you never have to worry about 'shapely blonde' showing up as a description. But the term 'womanizer' is one you can argue about. Is it sexist? Then there was the whole issue of using Ms. on second reference to women.[13] The *Times* resisted its use for years, but women kept the heat on and finally convinced the *Times* to change "because [using] Mrs. leads to inaccuracies."

Women editors may be as likely to run stories as sensational as men are, but Linda Cunningham, executive editor of *The Trenton Times*, believes women may think twice about the ways a story might hurt its subject. "We will still run it, but our approach raises enough red flags that we can cover the holes in the story."

Some draw a harder line. Scott McGehee, former managing editor of the *Detroit Free Press* and now an executive with Knight-Ridder, says, for example, that she would never have run a photograph of the Pennsylvania state official who killed himself by sticking a gun in his mouth. Many male editors, of course, also choose not to run the most graphic photos. "I'm certainly not here to say women have a lock on sensitivity, but I think they are willing to ask some questions and raise some different points."

Women are not universal paragons of virtue, wit, and wisdom, of course. Sometimes they're just plain not very smart. The late Jerry Belcher of the *Los Angeles Times* remembered a woman with whom he had worked years ago in northern California who had so little confidence that when she filled in for her boss during his vacation, she looked at the page makeup for the same month the year before and laid out the pages exactly the same way, day by day, no matter what the news was.

Mary Anne Dolan, former editor of *The Los Angeles Herald Examiner*, sees great timidity among female managers. Once they get into positions of responsibility, not enough women continue to demonstrate the energy and initiative that they had to show in order to get there in the first place, she says. "Many who get to certain positions don't want to rock the boat in fear they might lose this tenuous opportunity—so then they don't use the opportunity."

Some women also have a real need for male approval, she says. They keep looking around for the man who's really in charge. "They don't stand up for any ideas of their own." Others are of mixed minds when they get a top job; they can't remember why they wanted it. "That fights against risk taking." After decades in the back row of reporters, standing outside male semicircles around male political candidates, a few women have earned positions of authority. And says Dolan, "Big surprise—we don't know how to handle power."

One writer I interviewed said she sometimes sees women managers "striving to be too hard," out-machoing the men. "You don't have to crucify someone to make a point." Another woman who has been a top editor comments that "the opportunity to be with the men was bringing out the worst" in some women.

Generally speaking, though, female manager after female manager says that she thinks women are more collegial and less wed to the "feudal lord-serf arrangement," as Beverly Kees of *The Gary Post-Tribune* puts it. "I'll talk it through with someone, not bark out an order and expect it followed. At some point, though, I have to say, 'I hear you, but we still have a paper to put out.' " Or, as Rosalie Wright of the *San Francisco Chronicle* puts it, "I do not believe in creative tension."

Empathy in the editor's office brings all kinds of twists. Linda Cunningham found that her approach of caring about people and their problems can yield more openness in the newsroom. "The staff tends to view you as a mother-confessor. Now that has a downside, too. Everybody puts their monkey on your back, and they may not take you too seriously. They'll go to the woman with their problems, and they'll go to the man for a decision."

The male newsroom model inevitably produces a militarylike chain of command, accompanied by an insistence that work is all and that outside concerns should fall before the needs of the workplace. That model necessarily means that the person at the top must behave like a general in charge of obedient troops. In newsrooms this mentality has produced the hard-hitting investigative reporter who chases his prey down the halls and who, when he gets to be an editor, chews nails before he talks to reporters. The modern male editor, to be sure, communicates far better than his predecessors did, but he can still be oblivious to the concerns of the people who work for him.

This top-down pattern of leadership is changing throughout industry. But it still has sufficient hold in business in general and in the newspaper business specifically that women often take the path of least resistance and do what the men do. When women succeed, they may be accused of being too tough or too work-oriented—traits admired in men operating within that model.

Where there are more women in management, where individual women have the confidence to do things differently if they see the need, there may be less confrontation and more consultation. Women may do better in this environment. It isn't like the rough-and-tumble good old days of the front page and slam-bang journalism; it may go farther toward providing the better-balanced product that is vital if newspapers are to survive in an increasing competitive communications world.

Many journalists never want to be managers; they were initially attracted to the business as reporters and writers, and reporters and writers they intend to remain. But some women are starting to speak a different piece. "I enjoy management," Karen West, associate city editor at *The Seattle Times*, says. "I'm good at it. I was born at the right time. The doors have been opened by the pressures from women going before, and what I want to do is to bring other women along behind."

Where West has succeeded in managerial jobs from Washington State to *The Washington Post*, it has partly been through her ability to communicate—to tell people why she is doing what she is doing. Good male managers do that, too, but generally speaking women communicate more. For a long time, private relationships were women's main link to the world; they may simply be translating that need to work out relationships into the professional sphere. As social critic Elizabeth Janeway puts it, "we've had to figure out how to get along without simply giving orders that will be obeyed."[14]

Managerially, "my style is much more participative than the men who preceded me," says Kay Fanning at *The Christian Science Monitor*. "But you know, I learned nurturing, mothering a staff, from a man who happened to be my husband, Larry Fanning." Women, she says, "find themselves a little better able to listen to readers than to dictate what they should think. Being sensitive doesn't have to be soft. But you don't have to have the macho image of newspapers—the one that says 'listen to us because we have all the answers.' "

The bottom line for newspapers is to have the diversity to survive in an increasingly diverse society. I have said that often; I cannot say it too often. "Only if you have those different points of view in your newsroom will you see different stories," says Nancy Woodhull, who heads the Gannett News Service and helped start *USA Today*. "I have a very different attitude from most people who go into journalism. I didn't see people in politics as an important event. It may be what people talk about because the media puts it on the front page and then people talk about it. But generally it's the things people do" in their daily lives that interest readers.

"I'd be crazy to run a newspaper and not put the World Series on the front page just because I'm not interested in it," Woodhull says. "Men do that kind of thing all the time on stories in which they are not interested."

Women may be more open to a variety of stories because they are tugged in more directions. "A man who wants to go into banking simply learns bankspeak. His family is subservient. He rules," Woodhull adds. "A woman has to understand bankspeak. She has to understand soccerspeak. She has to understand ballet-lessonspeak. She has to deal with the in-laws. She has to get along with all kinds of people. Women in the home have always been the facilitators."

A newsroom evolution is occurring: in the traditional beats, in the new beats that are being created to reflect the changing society, and among managers as well as the managed. Stories may now get into print without the foot-dragging a Lois Wille encountered because now a Lois Wille and a Soma Golden and a Nancy Woodhull are helping make the decisions. Individuals do make a difference, if still individually.

271

In too many places, at too many times, the new approaches are not institutionalized and the new beats are not firmly part of the definition of news. All too often, if the woman who has covered these issues is away on a fellowship or if the woman who has shepherded the stories onto the front page is on vacation, the digging into new areas slows down. These issues won't be firmly part of the evolving definition of news until more women are in positions not only to report them as news but to see that they get in the paper.

Everyday Indignities

Mary Anne Dolan had just been named managing editor of *The Los Angeles Herald Examiner*. Only a few women had ever held such a high job in the newspaper industry. One of the men she would supervise came over and effusively, almost unctuously, congratulated her. She was understandably pleased. Then he said he'd been out to all the card shops to get a card for her, but the only ones they had were congratulations for having a baby.

CHAPTER

16

The Glass Ceiling

Conversation buzzed softly at the reception for women editors at the annual convention of the American Society of Newspaper Editors (ASNE) on San Francisco's Nob Hill in April 1987. The women drank a toast to Katherine Fanning of *The Christian Science Monitor*, who was taking over as ASNE president. She would be the first woman to be president in the sixty-year history of the organization, which often serves as a collective voice for newspapers on questions of freedom of the press, access to information, and professional standards.

The women gathered in the Fairmont Hotel's Fountain Room had another cause for celebration. With them was the new editor of the half-million-circulation *Miami Herald*, Janet Chusmir, whose new job at one of the nation's biggest papers put her squarely in the forefront of women in the newspaper business.

The reception could fit into one of the Fairmont's smaller meeting rooms because few women are top editors. Questioned on this, Susan Miller of Scripps-Howard, an ASNE board member, said there were still only seventy-eight women who belonged to the vast organization which has about six hundred currently active editors among its members.

Fanning, who comes from a cultured, moneyed background and carries herself accordingly, is not given to feminist rhetoric. Nonetheless, she smiled and said she hoped ASNE "wouldn't have one token and then wait another sixty years." In both her off-the-cuff reception remarks and her acceptance when she formally took the ASNE gavel, Fanning said that she was taking on the presidency "in the name of all those women who have been laboring in the newsrooms all these many years and years."

The newsrooms that ASNE members oversee may be dotted with women now; but the offices of the newspaper brass that ring those newsrooms are still for the most part filled with older white men. Not only does that mean that individual women are not advancing in proportion to their overall numbers in the news business, which is unfair; it also means that newspapers are being denied their experience in planning their coverage, experience that might be relevant to some of the very readers the newspapers seek to attract and hold—which is shortsighted.

The dearth of women in top jobs is an industrywide condition. It is especially damaging at the nation's biggest papers, the ones that could provide leadership because they are on virtually everyone's list of the tops in the business.

When I started to work on the *Los Angeles Times* in 1978, there was one woman's name on the masthead: Jean Sharley Taylor. Her responsibility as associate editor was for the "View" lifestyle section, the arts coverage, the book review, real estate, food, and travel. No woman headed coverage of metropolitan, foreign, national, Washington, or business news or editorials. Two women had been foreign correspondents.

Nearly ten years later, there was still one woman's name on the masthead: Jean Sharley Taylor. One other woman, Narda Zacchino, was editor of the Orange County edition. Still no woman headed coverage of metropolitan, foreign, national, Washington, or business news or editorials. In the intervening years, the metropolitan editor's job had changed hands, as had the jobs of national editor, foreign editor, business editor, book editor, Sunday Opinion section editor, op-ed page editor (twice), and "View" editor (three times). All were filled by men with the exception of the op-ed job, which was handled by a woman who had since left for another section of the paper. And one more woman had become a foreign correspondent.

The Washington Post is probably best of the top three papers in the country in the visibility it accords women in top jobs, but not without having faced an equal employment complaint in the 1970s. At the *Post*, Meg Greenfield has headed the editorial page staff for ten years. Karen de Young was foreign editor before going to the London bureau. Margot Hornblower headed the New York bureau before leaving to work at *Time* magazine. Elsie Carper has been assistant managing editor since 1972. Mary Hadar edits the "Style" section. The *Post* has women as foreign correspondents based, among other places, in London, Tokyo, Moscow, and Central America. And although board chairman Kay Graham may not be a blazing feminist, she is a highly visible woman, a corporate leader, and the woman in the newspaper business best known to the public at large. Even so, no women's names were fed into the rumor mills of speculation as to who would succeed *Post* Executive Editor Benjamin Bradlee.

The New York Times had only one woman—Charlotte Curtis, its op-ed page editor—in the power loop, the uppermost circle from which top editors regularly come, until late 1986. Shortly after naming his new team, executive editor Max Frankel argued that some women had already been on their way up—that the woman he named national editor and one who turned him down for another key job, among others, had been in that power loop. The fact remains that despite a lawsuit concluded in 1978, no women were in the running for the very top jobs eight years later when Abe Rosenthal retired. Frankel did promote Soma Golden to national editor; Karen Arenson succeeded her as Sunday business editor, and Judith Miller was named Washington news editor.

At that same time, *The New York Times* had columnist Flora Lewis based in Paris, Sheila Rule in Africa, Barbara Crossette in Bangkok, Marlise Simons in Rio de Janeiro, and Shirley Christian in Buenos Aires. Other women who had reported from abroad included Anne O'Hare McCormick, Nan Robertson, Judith Miller, Jo Thomas, and Gloria Emerson.

Kay Fanning and Janet Chusmir are the only two women who edit major papers in the United States. The first ever to head a big-city paper that she didn't also own was Mary Anne Dolan at Hearst's wobbly *Los Angeles Herald Examiner*.

The Associated Press had no women bureau chiefs until 1975, when it named Tad Bartimus to head its outpost in Anchorage, Alaska, and Edie Lederer for Lima, Peru. By mid-1987, there were three women as chiefs of domestic bureaus out of forty, and three more overseas out of thirty-six. United Press International named Helen Thomas to head its White House coverage in 1975.

By mid-1987, UPI had twenty-six women among its ninety-eight bureau chiefs within the United States. Seven of UPI's top thirty jobs, from editor to regional editor, were held by women.[1]

Overall, by 1986 women made up only 12.4 percent of the nation's most senior newspaper editors—the editors, associate editors, managing editors, and editorial-page editors. These are the people who have the ultimate authority over what stories appear in the paper, who is hired to write and edit them, where the stories will run, and what the paper's position will be on key issues. That was an increase from 5.2 percent in 1977. At that rate, it will take until nearly halfway through the twenty-first century before women achieve parity in top management ranks, according to the projections of Dorothy Jurney. Her survey showed that about three-fourths of the nation's daily newspapers have no women among the senior editors. Half of the biggest newspapers had at least one woman in a top job, obviously meaning that half didn't.[2]

The smallest newspapers—those under 25,000 circulation—had the most women in top jobs, 15.2 percent in 1986. That should not be surprising; women are 55 percent of all employees, business and editorial, at the smallest papers but only 28 percent at papers over 100,000 circulation. And at the very biggest papers—those over 250,000 circulation—women made up only 10.3 percent of top editors in 1986. In 1977, 3,025 men and 165 women held directing editors' jobs. By 1986 those figures were 2,987 men and 421 women.

To David Shaw, a *Los Angeles Times* reporter who covers press issues, those numbers mean that when he interviews people for his articles, he talks to "far too few" women because women simply aren't in the responsible jobs. Shaw, who has covered the press for the *Times* since 1974, has written on about eighty topics in that time. He has done stories on almost all areas of the paper, from editorial pages to obituaries to White House coverage to book reviews and food sections, and he has found the highest percentage of women as food editors, restaurant critics, and religion editors.

"I was very conscious that I had interviewed few women. I went out of my way to talk to more women because if you're writing about what it's like to be a foreign correspondent, it may be different to be a woman. Generally speaking," Shaw adds, "I talk to the top editors. The vast majority of them are male." By late 1987, at least, Shaw himself had never done an article for the *Times* on the role of women in the newspaper business although he had just finished a look at wine writers.

In summary, there seems so far to be little room at the top for women in American newspapers despite their movement in increasing numbers into the newsroom since the mid-1960s. Male managers deny that there is a glass ceiling barring women's advancement, but women are definitely bumping their heads against something up there. It is not lack of experience, and it is not lack of ability, and it is not lack of sheer numbers.

Kay Graham recognized the problem—"the invisible barrier separating middle-management women from the power positions"—and told a Washington audience that she had realized that dismantling that barrier would be more complex than just waiting for women to serve long enough to advance. "As overt sexual discrimination has waned, subtle sexual prejudice has come to the fore as a barrier to women's progress," Graham added.[3]

"It's stupid in our business to have leadership not reflect its readership," says Allen H. Neuharth of Gannett newspapers, who founded *USA Today*. "And what's the readership? The readership is half or more women, and it does not seem to make good business sense or professional journalistic sense to me to have the leadership of newspapers not reflect the readership of the audience they're after. I'm not saying the formula has to be exactly what the audience is in a given community, but if your readership is 55 percent women and 45 percent men or vice versa and your newspaper leadership is ninety to ten, then something's wrong."

The picture is better at the middle-management and reporting levels. In a massive 1985 survey of the newspaper work force, Jean Gaddy Wilson of the University of Missouri found that women were 21 percent of newspapers' city editors, 66 percent of the feature editors, 90 percent of the lifestyle editors, and 35 percent of its copyeditors. They were 36 percent of the nation's general news reporters and 57 percent of its feature writers. Women were still only 9 percent of editorial-page editors, 8 percent of photography directors, 2 percent of sports editors, and 5 percent of sportswriters.[4] "In general," Wilson found, "as newspaper circulation decreases, the percentage of women employed increases."

Fully one-third of the journalism work force is female. That figure is likely to increase because journalism school enrollment is now over half female; Wilson reported that 46 percent of the newest hires are women.

Why does it matter whether women are managers? "As long as you send human beings into the field to witness things and come back and write up their own version, you will have a very subjective business in which you will see only glacial change in the actual news coverage," says Solveig Torvik of *The Seattle Post-Intelligencer*, who has been an assistant city editor as well as reporter. "You'll see it faster with women as assignment editors, executive editors, managing editors, publishers."

Torvik shares the belief of many journalists—mainly reporters—that "the single most appalling part of the newspaper business is management." Men aren't particularly trained for it before they take over; women couldn't do worse. "I think it helps enormously to have at least one woman in a newsroom in a decision-making capacity because it adds a better balance to the newspaper. Most males who go into the newspaper business are congenitally untrained to be managers. More attention is paid to an individual performance through more humane methods by women—not all women necessarily. But they do show some concern for egos, and everyone in journalism has an ego," Torvik adds. "You become the mother hen to a bunch of seventh graders."

In addition to women's movement—or lack of it—into management, there are other measures of professional status that help tell the story. How well are women paid? Where do their stories appear? Do they win assignments to Washington? Do they win the Pulitzer Prize? Do they receive the major fellowships?

Pay. "Women's salaries lag behind men's in almost every newspaper job in almost every circulation category," Wilson concluded after assessing responses to a detailed questionnaire returned by 648 publishers. "Even when women and men with the same length of service are compared, women's salaries in a majority of cases lag behind those of their male counterparts in the same job at newspapers of a similar size." Female publishers earn on the average eighty-three cents for every male publisher's dollar. Women who are photography directors or sports editors make only 60

279

percent of what men earn in those jobs—usually because they hold the positions at smaller papers where salaries are lower. "It is generally the case that, at the largest newspapers, women are paid three-fourths or more what men make."

Wilson found that younger women, newer to management, face less pay discrepancy compared with male employees than women with longer service records. The dollar figures: women in the lowest managerial category earn salaries that average $11,000 less than men's in that category. Women with twenty-six to thirty years' service earn $22,000 less on average than men in that category. Women are now almost half of journalists with one to five years' experience, and the average salary difference between men and women in that category is $3,500. Among professionals with thirty-five years' experience, women are only 10 percent of the total, and they earn $7,000 less than men with comparable experience.

The pay inequity was so glaring on the copy desk at *The Houston Chronicle* in the 1970s that Karen Carter staged a novel protest. She draped a bra over the copy-desk sign and labeled it "Equal Work—Equal Pay." The boss, described by Carter as a bit of a martinet, came in. Complete silence. He saw the bra, strode toward his office, turned briskly on his heel, pointed to the offending object, and announced, "Boys, we're going to fill those cups with gold." The women got a raise.

Bylines. Few people sit around and count bylines, so little hard evidence exists. I asked a journalism class at the University of Southern California in 1985 to critique one edition of the *Los Angeles Times* each week regarding its coverage of and by women. My students found that usually one woman's byline appeared on the front page, that women's bylines generally were clustered in the business and "View" sections—rarely in sports—and that women's bylines might appear on a range of subjects but that men's bylines rarely appeared on a story focused mainly on women.

That same year, the Women's Media Project of the National Organization for Women's Legal Defense and Education Fund tallied women's bylines and found *USA Today* was best and *The New York Times* was worst. Reviewing newspapers around the country over two two-week periods (one during the presidential election, one soon afterward), NOW-LDEF ranked *The Boston Globe* second, followed by *The Atlanta Journal, The Washington Post,* the *Detroit Free Press, The Cleveland Plain Dealer,* the *Chicago Tribune, The Wall Street Journal, The Philadelphia Inquirer,* the *Los Angeles Times,* and *The New York Times. USA Today* had 41.5 percent of its page-one articles by women, while only 10 percent of the front-page articles in *The New York Times* were written by women. Overall, 23.7 percent of the papers' articles were written by women.[5]

Columnist Ellen Goodman was one of the few newspaper people who wrote about the survey, commenting that it was "one front-page story that ended up in the back of the paper." Goodman noted that "the researchers had to go to page one to find these inequities. Newspapers have changed enough so that women are filling in behind the front lines. . . . But the bad news is these women are not getting equal prime space. After all, the front page is still the front page. This is where the big story, the news that editors label 'important,' gets placed. . . .

"The media not only reports what's happening in the larger society, it reflects what's happening. This study reflects the big plateau that now ranges all across the professions. The entry-level jobs are much more open; women are now getting stuck at a higher level." Goodman added that it's not so much getting on page one that is important; it's being one of the people who decide who gets on page one. "There are more women in the Reagan Cabinet meetings than in most editorial meetings."

And she concluded: "There are a lot of theories about the current plateau in journalism. They'll sound familiar to women in other professions. There is less room near the peak of a pyramid and less mobility. Women have just amassed enough numbers to begin an inexorable push upward. In time"—remember that word, time—"they will inevitably percolate to the top. But before you buy that theory, remember one law of physics: Nothing percolates unless you apply a whole lot of heat."[6]

Washington assignments. Washington, the seat of national power, is also a seat of press power. It is also an avenue for advancement. The 1985–86 congressional directory listed as accredited personnel six women from *The New York Times* out of fifty staff members, six for the *Los Angeles Times* out of thirty-five, two for *The Boston*

Globe out of ten, five at Knight-Ridder out of thirty-three, thirteen for Gannett out of forty, five for *Newsday* out of eleven, two for *The* [Baltimore] *Sun* out of fifteen, three for *The Christian Science Monitor* out of ten, ten for *The Wall Street Journal* out of fifty-two, and five for Scripps-Howard out of thirty-three.[7] Although visible on Capitol Hill and at the White House, few women have yet to cover defense and national security issues. Five women were Washington bureau chiefs by 1987: Charlotte Saikowski of *The Christian Science Monitor*, Cheryl Arvidson of the *Dallas Times-Herald*, Mary Leonard of *The Detroit News*, Kathy Lewis of *The Houston Post*, and Beth Frerking of *The Denver Post*.[8]

Pulitzers. Journalism is accused of praising itself not faintly but too well. The Pulitzer Prize, newspapers' top award, began in 1917. In 1937 Anne O'Hare McCormick of *The New York Times* became the first woman to receive a Pulitzer. By 1987, thirty-three of the prize winners out of 315 in writing categories had been women; no women were among sixty-one cartoonists who had won prizes, and only two women, one of them an amateur, were among sixty-three photo prize winners. Only two women have won Pulitzers for editorial writing. The lack of women in these categories reflects less the capacity and more the rarity of women cartoonists, photographers, and editorial writers. Women are best represented in the investigative category, followed by commentary and criticism. In 1987 twelve of the sixty-five judges helping to select prize winners were women. The number of female judges has risen slowly since 1972, the first year women served on juries; that year there were five.[9]

Fellowships. In recent decades, several programs have been set up at major universities to bring journalists onto campus for sabbaticals. They take courses, hold seminars with leading thinkers and doers, and talk shop with other journalists from around the country and around the world. Each year eighty to one hundred people apply to the leading programs at Harvard, Stanford, and Michigan; twelve are chosen for each campus.

Nieman Fellowships began at Harvard in 1938. The first women holding Niemans were Mary Ellen Leary of Scripps-Howard, based in San Francisco, and Charlotte L. FitzHenry of the Associated Press in Chicago, during the 1945–46 school year. Women won fellowships then off and on until a dry spell between 1959 and 1967, when they were totally shut out, at least among American participants. Overall, there have been seventy-three women out of a total of 598 Niemans, or 12.2 percent. In 1984 there were more women than men in the program for the first time, and in 1985 and 1986 half the classes selected were female.

The Stanford Professional Journalism Fellowship originated in 1966. Seventy of the 321 American journalists selected have been women, or 22 percent. The highest number of women in the program, now known as the Knight Journalism Fellowships, in any given year has been six in 1984, 1985, and 1988.

Michigan started its program in 1973 and has had forty-four women out of 174, or 25.2 percent. Six women were in one class of ten fellows in 1985.[10]

Among Alicia Patterson Fellows given grants to travel and do research, the first woman was selected in 1969, three years after the program for journalists began. Since then, women have held about 30 percent of the hundred fellowships granted.

These are the overall yardsticks. Who are the people behind them, and what difference do they make?

In 1987 two women reached the pinnacle of the profession. Both Katherine Fanning and Janet Chusmir had always intended to write but didn't start their careers until they had had children and had established themselves in other roles. Fanning came from a family wealthy enough to start its own private school after finding the local public school in Joliet, Illinois, inadequate. Chusmir's father was a Boston businessman—he sold leather and shoemaking materials to shoe companies—and her family was so business-oriented that she had to threaten not to go to college at all if she weren't allowed to major in journalism. Katherine Fanning virtually started at the top, while Janet Chusmir worked her way up from reporter. Fanning took over as head of a newspaper founded by a woman whose Christian Science beliefs she shared; Chusmir moved upward in a chain of newspapers dominated by men.

Fanning's route to newspaper editing was "as circuitous as the twisting Alaska Highway" that took her and her three children

283

in a bulging Buick station wagon to Anchorage and *The Anchorage Daily News*. She "had had it easy growing up as an only child" of a bank president and his wife, Fanning acknowledged, but she realized that many people weren't as fortunate as she was. She attended Smith College, taking every writing course offered. But she deferred her dream of a New York magazine career because her mother wanted her to come back to Chicago, "join the Junior League, and behave like a Chicago society woman."[11]

She married Marshall Field, who ultimately took over as publisher of his father's *Chicago Sun-Times* and later bought The *Chicago Daily News*. In 1963 her marriage fell apart, in part because of Field's emotional problems. Divorced, she moved to the Old Town section of Chicago with her children, became politically active, and joined both the Urban League and the Church of Christ Scientist.

Two years later she set out for Alaska because she had friends there and because she "wanted adventure, the outdoors, the sheer beauty of the place. I liked the general feeling of energy, the feeling that it was the frontier, the sense that it didn't make any difference that you came from a family with a big name." She took a job as librarian at *The Anchorage Daily News*. "Certainly I hadn't become a trained reporter by this time," she later recalled. "But in the Alaska of the Sixties, you could break into the newspaper business—or any business—with the appropriate mixture of curiosity, enthusiasm, and gall. I never would have dared to try it in Chicago."

Back in Chicago on a visit, she again met Larry Fanning, who had been hired by Field as editor of *The Chicago Daily News*. They married that fall. The Fannings returned to Alaska, bought *The Anchorage Daily News*, and hired a team of young reporters. He became editor; she did some reporting and worked on the business side. The paper, which hadn't been a moneymaker, continued to show a loss, but it made itself a presence. The *Daily News* editorially advocated gun control in a state where almost everybody owned a gun, and it supported the Alaska native claims movement. It published a thirty-two-part series on the dangers of laying the oil pipeline across Alaska, and advertisers pulled away. Then Larry Fanning died of a heart attack in February 1971.

Kay Fanning became editor. "It often surprised me when

others treated my opinions deferentially because I was the boss. My style was to look for consensus to develop, but if that failed, I found I could make the tough decisions." The paper continued its investigative reporting on the pipeline and the opportunities for corruption surrounding it. For its reporting on the Teamsters and their political and financial impact in Alaska, the *Daily News* won the public service Pulitzer Prize. Four months later the paper nearly closed because of its financial problems. The McClatchy Newspapers bought the *Daily News*. Fanning stayed on at the *Daily News* for four years, then was asked to take over at *The Christian Science Monitor* in June 1983.

At the *Monitor*, Fanning says, she has influenced both the content of the paper and the style in which it is managed. She helped develop a series of articles on women in the developing world, reported by Kristin Helmore. "It used to be assumed that only women were interested in child care. Now both [sexes] are." The *Monitor* runs more stories reflecting that shift as well, stories written and edited by both young men and young women. Fanning initiated three new departments in the paper, "Home and Family", "Arts and Leisure," and "Ideas." For several years the *Monitor* has consistently provided the best coverage of ideas and how their application—or lack of application—affects society.

Women in top newspaper-management jobs are important, Fanning says, because "an all-male-dominated press does not reflect society any more than an all-female-dominated press would be reflective." But there has been movement toward a better balance. "When Carol Sutton was named managing editor in Louisville, she was one of the women featured on the *Time* magazine cover. That was a real novelty then. Many women are managing editors now. A good many groups have seen that it is good for their newspapers to have women in the leadership roles. This is not to say there is not a long way to go."

Her election as ASNE president was more "an effect rather than a cause" of shifting momentum. "I sensed they really wanted to find a woman president," Fanning says. At the women's reception at the ASNE meeting, Fanning commented that the organization needed to look at why more women were not in top editing jobs and what ASNE should or could do about it. Stressing the importance of women in top management, she added, "There is no doubt in my mind that women have a very special quality to bring to management decisions in newsrooms."

Standing off to the side as Fanning made her comments was Janet Chusmir. Like Fanning, Chusmir started later in the game than most. At 16 she had gone off to Boston University, fallen in love, accelerated her studies, graduated, and got married at 19. She and her husband, at first a real estate developer and now a college professor, moved to south Florida. Chusmir raised two children and became active in her community. At 33, she started work as a freelancer. She was to be paid ten cents an inch, but when she turned in longish stories, her editors set a top fee of $2.50 a story. In 1963 she started writing for *The Miami Beach Daily Sun*, which was owned by Knight organization executives. When it folded, she went to *The Miami Herald*.

Chusmir was on a team of reporters that went to political conventions and Apollo space missions. She covered bills in the legislature that recognized trends in the broader society. "I got a reputation of getting the story nobody else could get," Chusmir says, explaining that she got into a funeral that was supposed to be closed to the press simply by putting on her black dress and walking in. She got on board Hubert Humphrey's boat cruising off Miami simply by showing up and saying to the crewman, "Didn't so-and-so say I was coming?" They evidently thought she was so-and-so's mistress, she says. It worked.

Eventually Chusmir moved into management; she worked briefly as assistant city editor supervising the specialized reporters, then became "Living Today" editor. Two and a half years later she became assistant managing editor for features.

In 1982 she went to Boulder as publisher of the small Knight-Ridder paper, *The Daily Camera*. In 1987 she returned to Miami as executive editor, one of the first editors of a major paper with primarily a features background. Chusmir arrived at a critical time for the *Herald*. Not only had it just stirred controversy by reporting presidential candidate Gary Hart's dalliance with a Miami woman, but it was also grappling with how best to serve its changing community, an uneasy mix of white and black, Cuban, Salvadoran, and Nicaraguan cultures.[12]

Until Fanning and Chusmir were named to their jobs, Mary Anne Dolan had been the sole female editor of a major American daily newspaper in recent times. At *The Los Angeles Herald Examiner*, a paper that never rebounded after a crippling strike in the 1960s, Dolan had the unenviable task of competing with the massive *Los Angeles Times*. But under Dolan's direction and that of her predecessor James Bellows, the *Herald Examiner* often heard the day-to-day concerns of readers, which enabled it to outperform the *Times* on occasion. Dolan, who had worked on *The Washington Star* before going to Los Angeles, was a smart, stylish editor. She knew the *Herald Examiner* had to be different or it would not survive in a sea dominated by what the paper's gossipy "Page 2" feature irritatingly called "the Gray Whale, Mother *Times*."

"There are two kinds of newspapers" in Dolan's analysis: "the traditional, older, historically established, important dull newspapers" and the "newer, MBA school of newspapering." The former has the "we-the-boys-run-the-show-here mentality," respectful of tradition and deferential to its legendary figures, who are all men. Young men buy into that legend and do the same things that have always been done to get to be part of the newspapering elite. The latter type of newspaper is high-tech, computer-oriented, stylish, slick, and usually associated with chain ownership. "There is no sense of the joy of editing" there, says Dolan, who nevertheless acknowledges that it is these organizations—Gannett is among them—that offer opportunities for women.

Dolan didn't want her paper fitting either the dull or the joyless category. She had twin goals: to provide better entertainment coverage, especially about what people watch on television, and to focus on women. To survive, she argued to the Hearst higher-ups, "we have to make the *Herald* important to women." Women, she knew, held a variety of jobs and had risen to management levels all over Los Angeles. "I didn't want to make it into a paper of women's news but to sort through subject matter with the idea of what women readers might be interested in."

Dolan knew that "the risk was returning to overly simpleminded laudatory stories about women in order to have stories about women. So we tried to choose stories demonstrably important to all of us—to avoid at all costs the woman-talking-dog story." Once, for example, Dolan moved a story on pre-Olympic predictions on Los Angeles traffic snarls inside, out of its planned page-one spot, to make room for a long wire-service report on discrimination against women in pension plans. Toni Carabillo, former president of the Los Angeles chapter of NOW, praised Dolan, who left the *Herald* in 1985, for having her paper carry "issues that no other newspaper would have on its front page."[13] In contrast, Carabillo added, women often found news that was important to them in the back pages of the "View" section of the *Los Angeles Times*.

For women in the newspaper business, the first real breakthrough since newsroom doors opened wider in the 1960s had been Carol Sutton's appointment in 1974 as managing editor of *The Courier-Journal* in Louisville. Sutton, who had attended the University of Missouri Journalism School, was originally offered a secretarial job at *The Courier-Journal* and took it. Within a year, she was working on the city desk and in 1963 was named women's editor, one of the pioneering group that changed the women's pages.

Sutton not only took the women's section in new directions, she also nurtured the careers of many young men and women, especially women and minorities. They were "Carol's chickadees," as one woman called them. "Most of our training came from her," says Maureen McNerny, who worked for Sutton and later became features editor and then arts and entertainment editor at *The Courier-Journal*. "She had an uncanny ability for bringing out the best in people, and she expected the best."

But rank did not always have its privileges. Sutton used to tell a story about getting a call from her children's school when one of them was sick. Sutton had been out of the office, and the person on the line sounded very relieved when she was finally reached. Sutton asked why the school hadn't called her husband, who was an educational consultant—he could have left his job to pick up the child. That had never occurred to them. After Sutton was named managing editor, publisher Barry Bingham told *Newsweek* that he had asked her whether her new reponsibilities as well as caring for two preteenage daughters would be too much strain. "I don't think I would have asked that if she had been a man," Bingham conceded.[14]

Sutton directed the paper during its coverage of court-ordered busing to achieve school desegregation and became the paper's senior editor in 1979. She died of cancer in 1985.

Sutton's paper was sold to the organization that is clearly the best in terms of recruiting and promoting women into top management jobs: Gannett. Its commitment is a story unto itself (Chapter 17).

Second to Gannett in its reputation for hiring and advancing women is the Knight-Ridder chain. It hasn't as many papers, and it has more of an insider's point of view, so it hasn't been as brisk and brash as Gannett. But women who advance in an establishment chain with such name papers as *The Philadelphia Inquirer*, the *Detroit Free Press, The Miami Herald*, and *The San Jose Mercury News* have advanced in a world of the old-boy network. They have also advanced in a world of generally higher quality papers than all but the biggest and newest of Gannett papers.

In addition to Janet Chusmir as executive editor in Miami, Knight-Ridder has, among others, Scott McGehee—former managing editor at the *Detroit Free Press*—as an assistant to the senior vice president overseeing newsside operations at three of the organization's newspapers; Deborah Howell, senior vice president and editor at *The St. Paul Pioneer Press*; Beverly Kees, editor of *The Gary Post-Tribune* in Indiana; and Jennie Buckner, managing editor for the afternoon operations of *The San Jose Mercury News*.

Knight-Ridder strikes an outsider as a cautious organization, one that "won't promote a token," as one of its editors said, one that has acted to move women and minorities up the ladder—but not precipitously. Some good women have gotten away, including Nancy Woodhull to head Gannett News Service. She once worked at the *Detroit Free Press*.

Knight-Ridder has been focusing on the question for some years. In 1981 Knight-Ridder asked several of its top women to appear together on a panel at its editors' meeting in Detroit on "What It's Like to Be a Woman Editor." The panelists were Jennie Buckner, Janet Chusmir, Deborah Howell, Beverly Kees, and Scott McGehee. They spoke quite candidly by all accounts, and their candor hasn't affected their careers. Says Buckner, who had moved from assistant city editor at the *Detroit Free Press* to various management jobs at *The San Jose Mercury News*, "Then we were seen as exotics. Now we are seen as working colleagues. Then that really was a question for them." Now it isn't.

Smaller papers, and even big ones outside the East Coast

corridor, have often done well by women, too. "People talk about Texas as if it was Bombay," says Rena Pederson, editorial-page editor at *The Dallas Morning News*. "You would find people more progressive in Dallas than at *The New York Times*." Pederson, a graduate of the Columbia School of Journalism, worked for UPI and the AP in Dallas and for *The Houston Chronicle* in Washington. She traveled to the Far East on a Jefferson Fellowship and has worked thirteen years at the *Morning News*. Interviewed in 1986, she said, "We have a woman associate editor, a woman who is editorial-page editor, a woman as foreign editor, a woman as business editor. Can you find something like that at *The New York Times*? Can you find something like that at the *Los Angeles Times*?"

Joann Byrd became executive editor of *The Everett Herald* in Washington in 1981, when she was 38. She had the same adjustment problems faced by many women, especially by women who are relatively young when they reach the top. "Men my age and younger tend to treat me as a professional," Byrd says at 43. "It's older ones who have difficulty. They apologize if they swear, they don't know whether to open doors, they aren't quite comfortable."

At the *Herald*, a paper with fifty-six thousand circulation, the page-one meeting has regularly been attended by the same number of women as men, sometimes more. That alters the dynamic in a way no one who has never been profoundly in a minority can ever understand. It gives the women freedom to speak up and out; it gives men a sense of equal participation with women that they may never have had before.

It also changes the results of some meetings. Karen West, who was city editor at the *Herald* before working for *The Washington Post* and now *The Seattle Times*, remembers an incident when a man was being interviewed for a top management job. In a meeting with some of the top staff, he was asked some managerial question, and "he said you have to treat women differently." When pressed, West reports, "he said what he meant was that at certain times of the month women are more emotional, more sensitive.

"There was a slight pause. There were four women managers in the room. The first voice was male, who said he thought that was ridiculous. The men were better feminists, and the women never had to say anything. At that moment he lost any hope of getting that job. If he had been sitting in the room with all men, he might not have had that reaction. But the men at the *Herald* knew different because they worked with women. A remark like that today is known as a dumb thing to do. It draws groans."

Small can be beautiful for women. Big may be glamorous, but it's rarely as open to change. The possibility for power, impact, and influence is unrivaled at *The New York Times*, the nation's most prestigious newspaper. But the reality of seeing women obtain that power, impact, and influence is another matter entirely.

The New York Times is not the biggest newspaper in the country. It is not always the best. But it is always the paper of record, the paper to beat. It is the paper that opinion makers read, the paper that people around the country read for the thorough view of the world that their local newspaper cannot provide. It is also an insular paper in that it draws its executives from its own ranks, ranks that until the last decade held few women and encouraged few to aspire to management levels.

The sex discrimination lawsuit against the *Times* that was settled out of court in 1978 put pressure on the paper to open its doors more widely to women. Judging by what they say publicly even years later, the suit did not convince *Times* managers that they had been unfair. But the lack of women in top jobs, the differences in pay, and the comparative scarcity of women's by-lines during the era immediately before the lawsuit are sure signs that the *Times* did not look for talent in women as it did in men. The fact that even today Max Frankel can quickly name only a short list of women who might be ready for higher managerial jobs is a direct result of inequities that persisted even after the suit was settled. Eight years was sufficient time to start righting old wrongs, and publisher Arthur O. Sulzberger, and his executive editor Abe Rosenthal made few changes.

If attitudes at the *Times* are changing—and that remains debatable among the leaders and the followers there—it is because the sheer number of women available as trained, energetic young journalists has started to alter the ratios. The process has been furthered by the appointment of Max Frankel as executive editor. Frankel is neither as mercurial as Rosenthal nor as oblivious to the contributions women can make.

Women's perceptions affect the urgency with which the paper deals editorially with some issues, Frankel indicates. "A man

291

might be just as outraged to see abortion clinics bombed as a woman is. But while I saw abortion as desirable social policy, a woman sees it as part of her right—or at least certain women do. When that is a right, an undeniable part of your being, the issue plays differently in your mind. That's why it's important to have women. It's the same reason you wouldn't want the staff all Catholic, all Jewish, all white."

To try to compare the outlook of the new editor with that of the former editor, I interviewed Abe Rosenthal, newly named associate editor, the day after I interviewed Frankel. I asked him where the stimulus had come from when the *Times* was changing its coverage of the women's movement in the 1970s. Rosenthal did not name Judy Klemesrud, although her name had come up in another context; he did not mention Eileen Shanahan's reporting out of Washington, nor Grace Lichtenstein's stories on issues related to changing roles for women. In short, he did not mention any reporters' names. "In the beginning," he said, "the stimulus came from outside. From Betty [Friedan] and Gloria [Steinem]; there were others, but those are the ones I knew. There weren't enough women on the staff" to have altered the coverage, he added.

If the attitude at the top has changed, has that attitude percolated down to other editors? "It's very clear to them, but I think I was pushing on an open door," Frankel says, adding that his assistants seemed pleased to have female candidates on their lists for promotion. Frankel says he's now dealing with managers and job candidates in their 40s, so "their peers, their boss, the whole environment in which they function supports this now." He adds that he thinks male managers "want to go home and say they have a woman deputy." The next question is do they want to go home and say they have a woman boss?

What *The New York Times* is to the nation, the *Los Angeles Times* is to the West Coast in general and California in particular. On some stories, on some days, it is better than *The New York Times*. Its sports coverage is broader. It covers entertainment as a business and as a social force. It covers the press in a systematic, analytical way and has done so longer than the *New York Times*. Its foreign correspondents capture the flavor of the country they cover. But while the paper has stylish writers, few capture the offbeat nature that makes Southern California Southern California or the diversity of the city as well as its writers capture Paris and Cairo.

The *Los Angeles Times* tends to unleash its resources on block-buster projects about social issues, but it doesn't maintain ongoing daily coverage of them the way it does for politics or foreign affairs. Some of its middle-level editors make conscientious efforts to organize regular social-issue coverage, but there are too few different voices contributing ideas to the process.

Although it is by no means automatic that the presence of a woman in a newspaper's hierarchy changes that paper's focus, it often does. But the woman with most managerial responsibility at the *Los Angeles Times* is not taken as seriously as she could be. Part of that is due to the culture in which she works. Until she left the "View" editorship at the *Times*, Jean Sharley Taylor had marched a clean line upward for herself and for women. A good writer, a thoughtful student of social change, she had been an outstanding feature writer on the *Detroit Free Press* and a ground-breaking editor as women's sections made the transition to stylish looks at contemporary life.

Named associate editor in 1976, she joined what had been an all-male-forever masthead. Trying to be heard in the upper echelons in which she has had to work cannot be easy. It's lonely there. The leadership simply does not take women seriously, especially women who come from a feature-side background. It can say it does, but its record says otherwise. It is a leadership that sincerely believes it has been fair to women but that creates jobs for white male after white male.

Even in that context, Taylor has had the opportunity to place women in jobs that would make a difference at the *Los Angeles Times*. Asked how she thought she had done in this regard, Taylor cited the women brought in as assistants on the "View" section, in arts coverage, and as assistant book editor. Assistant, assistant, assistant. On Taylor's turf, three new "View" editors have been named in my time at the *Times*. All men. A new book editor. Male. An executive arts editor. Male. A deputy associate editor. Male. His assistant. Male. A magazine editor. Male. Taylor did put women in the line jobs where they do much of the work of putting out daily and weekly sections. One woman was named fashion editor;

another, Connie Koenenn, was hired as an assistant arts editor and moved up only after a separate daily arts section was created.

The problem is not uniquely Taylor's nor uniquely that of the *Los Angeles Times.* Journalists at paper after paper have affirmed this judgment: that women operating alone in a male hierarchy often lack the independence that would enable them to function with the talents that brought them there. Operating alone at the top is never easy; it is difficult to retain the courage of your convictions. The problem may fade as generations change and as more women enter management from the general news route rather than from the feature pages. We are not there yet, and we ask a great deal—not only that the pioneers pioneer in getting to the top, but that they continue to do so when they get there. Men who are still making the appointment decisions must pick enough women of strength that the women can operate comfortably in the upper realms. We do not have the luxury yet of asking for less. (And we still must *ask.*)

On back-to-back days in October 1985, I visited the *New York Times* and *Washington Post* newsrooms. There, wandering around, talking to reporters and editors, were Abe Rosenthal, the *Times* executive editor, and Ben Bradlee, the *Post* executive editor. At the *Los Angeles Times*, editor Bill Thomas is rarely in the newsroom. His office is on the second floor; the newsroom is one floor above. The *Times* management style is hands-off. Pick the people, and let them do their job. Those managers receive direction from the top about financial goals. They certainly received direction about the importance the paper placed on outstanding coverage of the 1984 Olympics. In the past, however, they have not received similar direction—or have not been made to believe it if they did get it—about hiring and promoting women and minorities.

The perception of many women at the *Los Angeles Times* is that they are ignored when promotion opportunities roll around. This perceived indifference has not only left most desks at the *Times* manned—and I use the word literally—by males; it has also cost the paper in talent and morale. Although stories of personnel machinations are essentially boring to anybody not affected, some examples here will illustrate the *Times* women's perception of where they stand.

Sharon Rosenhause came to the *Los Angeles Times* as an editorial writer in 1974, then went to India for eighteen months as the *Times*'s first female foreign correspondent. When she came home, she covered city hall, including the thorny issue of local cable-television franchising. She served as assistant metropolitan editor handling government copy, then was named by Narda Zacchino to be city editor in Orange County as the paper sought to improve its daily news coverage in that potentially huge circulation area south of Los Angeles. She made all the stops. Finally she wanted to come back to Los Angeles to an editing job. Nothing could be found for her. So she went to the New York *Daily News*, the nation's biggest daily metropolitan paper, as assistant managing editor.

Linda Mathews joined the *Los Angeles Times* as a metropolitan reporter in 1967. She went to Harvard Law School and covered the United States Supreme Court out of the Washington bureau. When her husband, Jay, was assigned by *The Washington Post* to cover China from Hong Kong, Linda sought unsuccessfully to get a *Times* assignment. She went to work, as already described, for the Asian *Wall Street Journal* and ultimately was rehired by the *Times* to cover Beijing. She returned to California as op-ed page editor, then assistant national editor. She would have been a logical candidate for advancement had the *Times* been seeking to advance women. The *Times* wanted to hire Norman C. Miller, Washington bureau chief of *The Wall Street Journal*; Miller got the job of national editor, and Mathews soon shifted to deputy foreign editor.

In recent years, the Washington bureau has lost Ellen Hume to *The Wall Street Journal*, Eleanor Randolph to *The Washington Post*, and Eleanor Clift to *Newsweek* after a year of covering the White House. All three were front-page regulars.

You could say that Grace Lichtenstein, a writer and a skier, can write a feature as gracefully as a skier carves perfect tracks in new snow. Available to the *Los Angeles Times* after a few years as a freelancer, Lichtenstein was told by the "View" section, which was just starting new health and fitness coverage, that there were no suitable openings. Jackie Tasch was leaving the metro desk after serving as weekend editor and being told that she wasn't tough enough on her writers; no other job was found for her at the paper. Job freezes occur at the *Times* as they do everywhere else, but openings were created for Miller; for Richard Eder to leave *The New York Times* and review books out of Boston; for Shelby Coffey when the *Los Angeles Times*'s parent, Times Mirror, sold the *Dallas Times-Herald*; for John Lindsay when he was about to go from *The Los Angeles Herald Examiner* to San Diego. All are men of experience, but in this pattern of creating jobs for men and not for women, there seems to be a double standard, and it has irked women at the *Times*.

"I think the perception is a genuine perception," publisher Tom Johnson acknowledged in an interview. "I've had a number of people on the staff who've expressed themselves to me. I do believe that each of those situations that you've described has almost been sort of a specific step at the time, but when you look at it in total, there is a reason to come to that conclusion. To that, I can only say that I'm aware of it. And I am redoubling our efforts as far as future choices. . . . I think it's a valid perception, something that is troubling to me and others here and something that we must address."

Johnson issued a new affirmative-action plan in 1987 because he didn't think the *Times* was making progress as rapidly as it should. The plan "establishes goals in each of the departments and it ties the annual bonuses" to success in meeting those goals. Johnson says. Previous efforts had been "very successful as far as statistics—general statistics—among the entire work force—minorities, women. But the lack of progress in the middle-management and executive . . . groups is evident by analysis of the composition of those groups."

The message that women and minorities must be considered and promoted, although it is "continually being emphasized in some of our meetings and retreats, is perhaps not coming down when decisions are made." For example, the *Times* has surveyed its management and drawn up a list of potential successors to those who now edit the paper. Looking through the list of names, Johnson says that, "it is very clear that there are more men in the system than women when you look at—these are management jobs throughout—in the system, probably three to one or more of numbers. . . . I think we're going to have to give extra emphasis to selection of women, provided other professional experiences and qualifications are reasonably evident."

Why hasn't such a policy been more forcefully enunciated and administered in the past?

Bill Thomas took over as editor in 1971, and the paper has changed dramatically for the better since then. His first priority, he says, was to organize responsibility that "was diffused to such a point that I didn't know who the hell was supposed to do what, so I couldn't call on them to do it." Once he got key people in key positions, he focused on writing areas, changing the range of stories that the paper runs.

"Now women fit as well into that as men. I don't even think of women [separately]. So in the process—I'd like to be able to say in 1971 or 1972, I vowed by God, I'd move women into top positions. I just didn't do that. I thought frankly it was going to take care of itself, and I used to say so because . . . totally truthfully the quality of the women coming along was so good at that point that I just figured why worry about that when I still have a lot to worry about in [getting] blacks and Latinos. The problem now is not having enough women, not having enough professionals, . . . the problem is at the top. Now maybe that's taking care of itself, but it's taking a lot longer than I thought it would."

Less than three months after these interviews with Johnson and Thomas, the *Times* made its first major editorial personnel change under the new plan. It named a white male as the new "View" editor. The job had not been posted; none of the three female "View" assistant editors was interviewed for the position; and no other women at the paper were sounded out about the job. The women were bothered less by this one appointment to one job than by the ongoing pattern of overlooking women as well as the "clandestine" fashion in which the job had been filled, as they put it in a protest letter to the publisher.

Newspapers like *The New York Times* and the *Los Angeles Times* may be too big and too corporate to change easily. Newspaper management style has changed; groups meet and plan projects and budgets and new bureaus where once an iron-willed or over-worked editor did it all. Corporateness has bred collectiveness. And groups tend to be more cautious. They don't take risks. And if the group is still mostly or entirely white males, it won't be as likely to take a chance on a woman, a black, a Hispanic, or an Asian-American.

For hope of change, "I think you really have to look at the next generation rather than this one," says David Laventhol, president of Times Mirror. "This one is men who are 50 and running newspapers. When they were 30 and coming up, they came up in mostly male organizations." They weren't, he implies, used to dealing with women as equals.

The *Los Angeles Times* is one of the best papers in the country; it can also be better. It can make better use of its resources. It is wasting and losing talented women. This is especially short-sighted given the preponderance of women in journalism schools, the snazzy women winning fellowships, the smart women already on its payroll. With all of Times Mirror's resources in general and the *Times*'s in particular, Gannett should not have the best reputation for hiring and promoting women; the *Los Angeles Times* should and could.

To survive, newspapers need to provide a broader range of news—not just about Iran and the contras and how the American government handles those questions, fundamental as those issues are—than television can provide. They need to focus those same staff resources, the same relentless daily coverage, the same open inside pages, on the ramifications for society of everything from the lack of adequate child care to the search by environmentalists and other groups for harmony between humans and the land. Newspapers need to examine day after day the national scandal that suicide is the second-leading cause of death among teenagers in the United States.

Newspapers must examine why Americans today want happy-talk news and happy-talk Presidents so that even serious journalistic attempts to examine contemporary problems make readers turn the page to the funnies. It cannot provide that range with the same old interchangeable faces running America's newsrooms.

Everyday Indignities

Ellen Hume, now a political reporter for *The Wall Street Journal*, was covering a shareholders' meeting of an aluminum storm door manufacturer in her early days of writing business features for the *Detroit Free Press*. The chairman of the company leaned over and said, "Honey, wouldn't you rather be covering fashions?"

"I kept my mouth shut because I had a job to do, but afterward on the elevator, I said to the PR man—with all the other men there—'You had better train your boss. Someday the law may make him hire some women. Surely he wouldn't ask a black reporter if he wouldn't rather shine shoes.' "

CHAPTER
17

Breaking Through: Commitment at the Top

No matter how critical the portrait of Allen H. Neuharth, no matter how derisive of *USA Today*—the McPaper, fast news in a fast-food world—and of the Gannettoids the organization spawns, virtually every profile of the man and his organization gives grudging affirmation to Al Neuharth's affirmative actions.[1] Gannett recruits women and minorities. Gannett promotes them. Gannett bases others' promotions in part on their affirmative-action performance. Others talk about rating people for the job by looking beyond race and gender; Gannett looks squarely at race and gender and does something.

Life is hardly perfect for women at Gannett, just as it is hardly perfect for anybody. But Gannett is unarguably the industry leader in finding talented women and absorbing their ideas. In this book on women in the newspaper business, Gannett deserves separate consideration as an object lesson in what can be done. If other news organizations had Neuharth's commitment, the glass ceiling would long ago have been shattered.

Gannett has ninety-one newspapers, including *USA Today*, with a combined circulation of more than six million. Twenty-three women are publishers of Gannett papers, including Cathy Black at *USA Today*. The two Rochester papers have a woman editor, Barbara Henry. Eighteen others have women in the most senior editing positions, such as managing editor. Of 5,737 total news employees, 2,256—or 39 percent—are women.

Speaking of Al Neuharth and his efforts, *Los Angeles Times* publisher Tom Johnson says, "He deserves major credit for doing the best job in the business so far, and I think it's also been very good for the others because those who say that progress can't be made . . . just look at that organization."

Gannett, although a big organization, has the advantage that most of its newspapers are small. "It's easier to make change at smaller papers. You can have more impact," says Christy Bulkeley, the first woman Neuharth named to publish a daily newspaper. Al Neuharth himself is another factor. His presence is *the* presence in the organization, his style is its style, for better or for worse. Gannett did not have a reputation as a recruiter of minorities and women when Neuharth arrived; if its reputation lives beyond his regime, it will be because he selected people around him who believe as he does that it's right for business as well as just plain right.

What Al Neuharth and Gannett do in regard to women and minorities is important; why they do it is revealing. Neuharth's motivations show that unless a top executive has a personal reason for doing something, it simply will not command his or her deepest commitment.

Neuharth is a flashy journalistic outsider, a man who makes the gossip columns with his personal life and the business pages with his corporate life, a man who dresses in gray and white to match his hair, even as he colors American newspapers red, yellow, and green. His penthouse office is not that of a gray corporate man—not with its polished brass desk and onyx top, its gold-plated manual typewriter, its TV screens in a bank along the ceiling. Articles criticizing the Gannett corporate culture and "the clones that ate American journalism" have appeared in publications as diverse as *Savvy* and *The New Republic*. Neuharth is regarded as a messenger bearing bad news from the corporate future more often than a messiah of American journalism.

When Neuharth was two years old, his father died of injuries from a farm accident. Neuharth was brought up by his mother, Christina, and an older brother, Walter. That fact alone has given Neuharth what he describes as "a personal strong philosophical reason for not only preaching but practicing equal opportunity for males and females and minorities." Speaking of his widowed mother, who worked as a waitress, a seamstress, and a house-keeper to support her family, Neuharth adds, "I saw in that little

301

town in South Dakota where I lived that she had to work twice as hard for half as much income. I didn't think that was fair. And I don't forget that. That's the personal side of it."

That he attended public schools and then the public university in South Dakota meant that Neuharth mixed with people from all walks of life. "I had a high school graduating class of twelve boys and twelve girls. It was pretty small, but nonetheless it was a microcosm of America if you multiplied it many times over, because there were sons and daughters of bankers, lawyers, merchants, farmers. The only thing lacking in my small town was the racial balance. But the religious balance was there. . . . And then by design I went to the public university. . . . That was after World War II, and then we had some representation from blacks and Orientals—not as heavy as you would get in an eastern school— and again young men and women whose backgrounds covered every walk of life. So I think it is fair to say that I am comfortable with people of nearly every economic level—*every* economic level—men or women, blacks or white," Neuharth says.

Neuharth got another push toward affirmative action from his former wife, Lori Wilson. Once a Florida state senator, Wilson actively backed the Equal Rights Amendment. Those who knew the couple say she reinforced Neuharth's basic concern for fairness toward women that his mother had established.

In college, Neuharth worked summers on small newspapers in South Dakota with 18,000 to 20,000 circulation, then went to the much larger *Miami Herald.* Not growing up on a single major newspaper made it easier, he says, to become critical of generally accepted editing approaches. He put thought into action when he founded *USA Today* in 1982.

Critics say *USA Today* trivializes the news, capsulizes it, jazzes it up so that serious analysis suffers. Its staffers wonder if a new Pulitzer Prize category shouldn't be created for "best investigative paragraph." There is a tendency toward unrelenting cheerfulness and old-fashioned American boosterism in a world that is not always a happy place.

But there is also no question that *USA Today* consistently runs on its front page stories that attract readers and affect people. The day I interviewed Neuharth, *USA Today* was playing across the top of the paper a report issued by the National Cancer

Institute bringing together the various changes in lifestyle and diet that people could undertake to try to reduce the risk of cancer. Every person in America has some concern, some brush with that disease. I read the story as I waited to interview Neuharth, then searched for it in *The New York Times*. I finally found it—a wire-service account on page A20.

My first question to Neuharth concerned this treatment of the news. I'm told "you're trying to cover the news more the way people perceive it rather than the way the press says they should perceive. . . . When did you come up with the idea that the big news organizations were veering away from how people viewed what was important?"

"I didn't come up with the idea that they were veering away from it," he responded. "I don't think they were ever on target with it.

"And I concluded quite a number of years ago—maybe because I'm fairly called a bit of a rebel editor—that too many male decision makers in newsrooms were editing newspapers for themselves or their male associates and the readers be damned. I spent . . . some early years working with male editors suggesting that the traditional approach to selection of subject matter, handling of content, maybe wasn't quite as perfect as most editors thought it was in the views of the reader. . . .

"In my judgment, back then a segment of our reading audience or potential audience that wasn't being adequately considered in our treatment of the news was the majority segment—females. It seemed to me that it made professional sense to have more females make those decisions and see if their orientation would be different."

Which came first, I asked Neuharth—the idea of expanding the direction of the news coverage or the insistence on having a broader range of people doing the coverage?

"I think I was compelled to move in that direction more by a feeling that the treatment of the news was not on target with the readers than I was in feeling that the newsroom had too damned many males in it. I think it happened that way, but they came together rather quickly."

Unlike many women, blacks, Hispanics, and Asian-Americans —and some white males—who share Neuharth's views, he was in

303

a position to put his ideas into play. Neuharth rose quickly at *The Miami Herald*, from reporter to Washington reporter to assistant city editor, executive city editor, and assistant managing editor. "For the first time, I was in a position to say that maybe when you are looking for subeditors, you have a row of reporters over here and three of them are female and ten of them are male, [and] you've got to look at them all."

He also brought into the news meetings people who still were considered society editors. Dorothy Jurney "was clearly, to me, a broad-gauged editor of women's pages" who helped "the guys in their part of the newsroom understand what the hell folks wanted to read." After Neuharth left the Knight organization and joined Gannett, he could expand his impact. "I was not just involved in the hiring and decision making, but I was able to and expected to set overall policies for a lot of other people."

By the middle 1960s, Gannett was sending recruiting teams "not just in our little area of New York or to Columbia or Penn State but out to Missouri and Minnesota and Nebraska and North Carolina. And their assignment was to try to entice the best talent, men or women, white, black, or yellow to come to work for us. And because we had smaller newspapers than, say, *The New York Times* and the *Los Angeles Times*, it was easier for us to say this person may not become a Pulitzer Prize–winner in ten years, but he or she may be able to do a hell of a good job in Ithaca, New York, or Binghamton, or Rochester. And it was easier for us because we had a kind of minor league farm system and a lot of papers rather than a major league newspaper or two."

Indeed, Pamela Moreland of the *Los Angeles Times* remembers one ubiquitous Gannett recruiter. At a National Association of Black Journalists awards luncheon, people were asked to raise their hands if they had ever encountered Jerry Sass of Gannett as he traveled from campus to campus. "It may not have been half, but if not that, then at least one-third of the people in the room raised their hands," Moreland says.

Once women and minorities were recruited, Neuharth says, "we seriously set about trying to help make them become pro-motable and then promoted them. . . . Again, if we'd had only the *Los Angeles Times* and a few years later *The Hartford Courant* [as Times Mirror does], we probably wouldn't have been able to have done that. But when you've got these 15,000- to 20,000-circulation newspapers, it isn't as risky, and you're able to give them more help and let them learn on the job." Neuharth named Christy Bulkeley as publisher in Saratoga Springs, New York.[2] "That worked. She's good."

Even then, "there were some people at Gannett at high levels who felt that now that our token woman publisher had been named, that was enough. When I named the second one, I was told that. Buzz off! I said this was not a token thing, and we were going to continue trying it in hopes that it would work. Well, anyway, what I knew very well was that it was both the women who were promoted into key management roles and I who were on trial. But I was on trial in promoting men, too. It was just when they screwed up, it wasn't as highly visible."

By the time Neuharth named his seventh woman publisher— Sue Clark Jackson of the *Reno Gazette-Journal*, daily circulation, nearly 60,000—she had been an editor in Binghamton, New York, a 65,000-daily-circulation paper, and editor and publisher in Niagara Falls, daily circulation, 27,000. "I remember telling her then that my comfort level had just increased tremendously. I felt that I had to get beyond a half-dozen before I could say now I have demonstrated that we really do mean that the opportunities are available. Now I can demonstrate that they will be treated the same, and if they don't perform, we'll fire them." And it has happened. In at least one case, says the Gannett senior vice president for personnel, Madelyn P. Jennings, "we overpromoted, spent extensive time counseling and training, which didn't work," so the person was removed from the publishing job.

By now, altruism needn't be the only motivation for Neuharth's affirmative action. "It pays off financially, both in the general acceptance of your newspaper by the audience, and what does that do? It helps you in circulation, and it helps you in advertising. In general acceptance. I initially was pleasantly surprised—but surprised—at the general acceptance of some of the new approaches that women in decision-making roles were getting in certain communities." Ithaca, a college town, was no surprise; Neuharth figured that "if there are progressive thinkers anywhere—at Cornell University and Ithaca College—we ought to be able to get away with a woman publisher here. And that's the way we'd express it—can we get away with a woman publisher?" Pam McAllister Johnson is publisher of *The Ithaca Journal*, one of the few black publishers in the country.

But, says Neuharth, "I was surprised in Chambersburg, Pennsylvania." It is more of an agricultural and small industrial area. "I was somewhat surprised that the first woman publisher in there and the first woman editor had the level of acceptance in that community of what they were doing."

What about the cynics who say that the only reason Gannett can promote women is because it has so many small papers? That it isn't as likely to pursue affirmative action at the larger, better papers it has bought in recent years—*The Des Moines Register, The* [Louisville] *Courier-Journal,* and *The Detroit News*?

"I think we've demonstrated two things," Neuharth replies. "That we did in fact introduce women into the publisher ranks at our smaller newspapers, but we introduced most of our men into the publisher ranks at our small papers, too. . . . And the record shows that quite a number of those women did move up through the farm system. Again, another example of how far they've moved is that Sue Clark Jackson is one of four regional presidents. That's the second highest position we have."

Not only must people want management jobs and be qualified for them, Neuharth says, but the organization also must have the opening. "Our problem is in finding enough qualified people who are interested in more responsibility rather than saying, what are we going to do with this person who is sitting around looking for a bigger job and we don't have an opening."

When Neuharth says there's a lot of movement at Gannett, he literally means packing the pots and pans and linens and books and the cat and dog and moving. From Boise to Chambersburg and to Muskogee, Oklahoma—Marj Paxson's route; or from Rochester to Saratoga Springs to Danville, Illinois, and back to Rochester—Christy Bulkeley's route; or from Bridgewater, New Jersey, to Utica, New York, to Sioux Falls, South Dakota, to Burlington, Vermont—Donna Donovan's route. Critics have said that Gannett people barely have time to learn one community before they go on to the next, that people have to move or lose their place on the train to the top.

John Curley, Neuharth's successor as Gannett chief executive, told *Los Angeles Times* reporter Thomas Rosenstiel, "I think that criticism was more valid five or six years ago." Although some people like to move, he added, Gannett is now trying harder to place people in areas of the country where they grew up.[3]

Are women any more reluctant to move than men? "In the last fifteen years," Neuharth says, "I don't believe we have had any more women say, 'No, thank you,' to an opportunity for advancement that involved a move than we had men say the same thing. There are some of those cases where [people say], 'I love Honolulu' or 'I love Niagara Falls and I won't move,' but that's true of both men and women.' "

Neuharth is quick to insist that he not be portrayed as beating his breast and claiming all credit or responsibility. Gannett developed its reputation not only because of the commitment of Al Neuharth and his senior executives such as John Curley and *USA Today* Editor John Quinn, but also because Neuharth put people into the personnel jobs who demonstrated that he meant business.

"I spent quite a few years preaching this approach, and a hell of a lot of my decision makers in Danville, Illinois, or Fremont, Nebraska, or Reno, Nevada, weren't practicing it. The tough thing was to get the decision makers out there to believe that you meant it." Neuharth preached his gospel for about seven years with some success but felt he nearly always had to be personally involved in selections to get his message across.

Neuharth says he got tired of preaching to people who smiled and listened and continued doing what they were doing. "I named a woman as the senior personnel person in this company, and that was concrete evidence that I meant it." He encouraged that woman—Madelyn Jennings—to bring in Jimmy Jones, a black former New York Jets football player, to work with her. "And when you trot Madelyn Jennings and Jimmy Jones out at meetings of publishers and editors around in the Gannett group, it's pretty damned hard for the most stubborn traditionalist or simple-minded folks not to get it."

Jennings explains that affirmative action at Gannett has teeth in it because executives' bonuses are based in part not only on how many women and minorities they hire but also on how promotable those people are. "When you have money involved, the amazing thing about the American people is that they pay attention," she remarks. Every executive at Gannett, from department head on up, has as part of his or her management-by-objective rating a set of equal employment opportunity goals, putting people alongside profit and product in judging performance. A positive rating in all categories determines the percentage of money the person gets; a negative rating gets attention from the regional vice president.

Each Gannett executive also rates his or her staff members' potential to move to higher responsibility during the next year. "That surfaces a bank of names to the key vice presidents. . . . They specifically ask who's minority and who's female. It helps assess how weak or strong they are in those categories." Gannett also sends several hundred people to seminars at the American Press Institute and to internal seminars on a range of editing and management topics. "I look," Jennings says, "to make sure that among the people going there's a mix." Finally, says Jennings, "We never have a companywide meeting without equal employment being a topic."

Again, what about the question that Gannett can do it because it is a bunch of small papers?

"I don't consider *USA Today* small," Jennings replies. At Gannett, Jennings adds, "the assistant treasurer of the company is a woman. That doesn't have anything to do with small newspapers. We don't just have a few women publishers. We have them at all levels." Gannett is helped in this regard by its recruiting record. "If a company gets a reputation that it's not your name that matters or your race or your sex, people will want to come to work for you. It's reinforcing."

"If I were a woman working at a secondary level in a newspaper organization that did not have that commitment at the top and I saw no prospect of it being there in the foreseeable future," Neuharth said, "I'd get the hell out of there. There are enough companies—not just Gannett—there are quite a number of media companies where the commitment is there at the top. . . .

"I think it's going to take women individually or collectively either leaving that kind of employer, threatening that kind of employer, or suing that kind of employer. For the latter, there's no better example than the great Associated Press. It took a hell of a lawsuit to convince those damned male chauvinists on that board and in their management that they could no longer do it. In the last three or four years, you have seen some surprising progress made by some women in the Associated Press that without that lawsuit wouldn't have happened."

But all the named plaintiffs have left the AP.

"All of them?" says Neuharth in surprise. "Is that a fact? Well, it serves AP right."

Everyday Indignities

Narda Zacchino had just taken over as editor of the Orange County edition of the *Los Angeles Times*. Sharon Rosenhause was working with her as city editor.

One of the older photographers came in and announced that he'd just dropped by to meet "the girls."

Zacchino wasn't sure how she'd handle this guy, but the story had a happy ending. Coincidentally, she took one look at the bad working conditions in the darkroom and got a crumbling wall and faulty plumbing repaired. A few months later, the same photographer announced that it was clear that it had taken having a woman in charge to get the place fixed up.

CHAPTER

18

Is the Prize Worth the Price?

You can't wear a grubby Ohio State T-shirt to the hardware store because you're the town's newspaper editor, and you might meet a city council member. You're signed up to play in a local golf tournament, and some guy doesn't want women in his foursome—even though you're the town's newspaper publisher. You work twice as hard on your reporting beat because you don't want to appear to have let up since you had your baby. Your marriage breaks up, and you're not sure whether it was because you traveled and worked late or whether it would have happened anyway. You're on an assignment in a war zone and you're scared and you're not sure you can get the story, but you dare not show it, or you won't get a tough assignment again.

In the old days, you wouldn't have had these problems because you were female, and because you were female, you probably wouldn't have had the job of editor or publisher or foreign correspondent or even reporter. You had no worries about what you wore or whether somebody wouldn't play golf with you or whether you got overseas. You had to quit if you had a baby, and if your marriage broke up, you wondered if it was because you were frustrated by staying at home or if it would have happened anyway.

Women face decisions involving marriage, child care, mobility, office romances, personal courage, and personal stability as their roles in the newspaper business change. Personal life rarely figures in accounts of the professional life of male journalists; that is not to say it shouldn't. But one cannot write a book about women in the newspaper business at the close of the twentieth century without discussing these issues. Their resolution can still determine whether women will get all the jobs they are capable of doing and how well they will do them if they get them.

Too many employers have not yet realized that individual women make individual decisions on questions facing them, and that the reaction of one woman will not be another's, any more than one man's reaction is the same as the next man's. Women can only make these individual choices freely if their bosses and colleagues allow them the flexibility to do so—or if their bosses get uterine transplants and start having the children themselves, because it is balancing family and job that causes the most tensions.

The arrangements and adaptations are infinite. Margie and Bill Freivogel of *The St. Louis Post-Dispatch*, who have four children, split a job. Others have arranged live-in child care. Anna Quindlen quit *The New York Times* to stay home with her two sons, but she writes the popular "Life in the 30s" column for the paper. Karen Elliott House and Peter Kann of *The Wall Street Journal* brought their adopted baby Petra to the office for three weeks before they could find someone to handle child care. Peggy Andersen's son Joshua had a "day-care corner" at the Anchorage AP bureau when Tad Bartimus ran it a decade ago.

Older women exercised just as many options when their children were young. Janet Chusmir, editor of *The Miami Herald*, stayed home with her two children until they were near teenage, then started her journalism career at 33. Eileen Shanahan's husband prodded her to go back to work not long after their first child was born; she started at *The New York Times* while her two daughters were still growing up. Kay Fanning divorced her first husband and piled the kids into the car to move to Alaska, where she went to work for *The Anchorage Daily News*.

Job-splitting requires adaptability. The Freivogels, for example, told the Washington bureau where they work that it could have one of them anytime, no matter when a story broke, but it could never have both at once. So when President Reagan was shot, Margie staked out the hospital on her shift while Bill got the kids ready for bed. Time for the switch. Bill bundles the kids in their pajamas into a cab, heads for George Washington Hospital, meets Margie, takes her notes, and heads into the night while Margie gets into the cab and takes the kids back home to bed.

The Freivogels' arrangement came after a career of adjustments. Margie Freivogel, who was editor of *The Stanford Daily* at the height of campus protests, married after graduation and took a summer internship at *The Washington Post*. The couple moved to Boston when Bill went to Harvard Law School, but she was turned down at the *Globe* because the man interviewing her said, "Why should we hire you? You'll just get pregnant." Bill quit law school, and both Freivogels were hired by the *Post-Dispatch*, but Margie had to start on the women's page. Eventually, she became an education and environment reporter. After her first child was born, she became an assistant city editor. Both parents worked full-time but on different shifts to minimize the time away from home. On Saturday nights, Margie was the editor and Bill was one of two reporters she supervised. "We always found we got good ideas by talking over stories," so there was no problem in that regard, Margie says.

The Freivogels had always wanted to cover Washington, but it was hard to get two openings at one time in a comparatively small bureau. A job was offered to Bill at a time when Margie was pregnant. She said she wouldn't go if only he had a job. She didn't want to go to Washington without job security, so the pair made a counterproposal to share the job. Bureau chief Richard Dudman was receptive but had reservations, largely because he didn't know the Freivogels as well as their bosses in St. Louis had.

Enter Betty Friedan. Dudman attends a publishing party for *The Second Stage*, in which Friedan stressed the need to move away from the male model of work. Dudman and Friedan talk, he says he has a situation in his own office like one Friedan describes, and she says, sure, you should do it. So Margie and Bill Freivogel become a two-for-one package for *The St. Louis Post-Dispatch*. At first, they split the days they worked; when the paper shifted to morning publication, they worked different days because they often had to report and write in the same day.

"We're doing this," Margie says, "because back in 1971 I decided, 'I'm not going to be a second-class citizen for some indefinite period of time.' I didn't think at the time that I was doing anything particularly advanced. I just always thought I could do anything. I thought we women were farther along than I realized later we really were."

Job-sharing involves the children in their parents' work. The

Freivogel kids went to the 1984 Democratic Convention, where Bill was dubbed the "pool" reporter because he had the kids at the pool while Margie pursued the story of women's role. The children also traveled with Mom and Dad to the 1985 convention of the National Women's Political Caucus in Atlanta.

That same summer Dale Mezzacappa went off to New Orleans and the NOW convention with Matthew, who was still in diapers. A single parent, she was going on vacation after the convention, and it was easiest to take Matthew along rather than return to Philadelphia for him. Easiest, because NOW conscientiously provides child care at its conventions. All was fine until Sunday, the final day of the meeting, when the *Inquirer* decided it wanted a profile of NOW President Eleanor Smeal, who was originally from Pittsburgh.

The story was the least of Mezzacappa's worries; she was a veteran of six years at the *Inquirer* by then. The main problem was that with the convention over, so was the child care. So she interviewed Smeal while the collective hierarchy of NOW baby-sat with Matthew. She arranged with the woman who provided day care during the conference to take care of Matthew on Monday morning while she finished her piece. She packed the bags and finished the story but didn't have time to file it before heading off for the airport to make her connection to Atlanta. En route to Atlanta, she realized she packed the diapers in the suitcase that was checked through to Florida. "You can buy everything in the Atlanta airport but Pampers," she says. So there was Matthew, oozing slime, wandering off repeatedly, while his mother was trying to convince an indifferent clerk at the *Inquirer* to be patient while she transmitted her story from her computer through a pay phone. Each time she corralled Matthew, she hoped no thief would disconnect her computer in midsentence. All ends well that ends.

There are as many opinions on the effects of working mothers on children (and not nearly the concern with working fathers, of course) as there are working mothers. "I don't feel my job is the least bit shortchanged," said Anne Roark of the *Los Angeles Times* after her first child was born, "and I don't feel my child is the least bit shortchanged. I think there can be too much mothering." Roark has always done much of her writing at home and still does. "They just thought I was eccentric before. Now they're thinking I'm working at home because I'm a mother. I go into the office more now—totally for appearances. My problem may be unique, but appearances for women are very important."

After the birth of her first child, *Oakland Tribune* reporter Carol Brydolf worked part-time. "The work was much more intense. I wanted to show that I could be productive." She found she'd get "a really good story that was continuing and then spend a lot of time prepping somebody else. It's not a great deal" for the paper. But it can be good for the kids if you're working. "Your identity is not based wholly on them" or theirs on you, she says.

Mothers and fathers like Carol Brydolf and her husband, John Jacobs of the *San Francisco Examiner*, have realized that it's no sin to lighten up on their intense concentration on work a little while their children are growing up. More parents need to do that, and their newspapers need to see that it's not a devastating career setback. Jane Brody of *The New York Times* says that when her twin sons were little, she decided not to accept as many out-of-town assignments. "You've got a whole lifetime out there. I've been in the newspaper business for twenty-four years. What's three years that I stay close to home because I have toddlers?"

Cynthia Gorney, who writes for *The Washington Post* from the San Francisco Bay Area, took son Aaron with her to one conference—Women in Law—where there was "intense child care," but otherwise she didn't travel as much after she had children. She had been the kind of reporter who "loved getting in rental cars and driving around places I'd never been before." Once her husband Bill told her she'd been home only half the days that month—"and you can imagine the mood in which he told me this. When Mount St. Helens blew up, we were having breakfast and the desk called and said, 'Please be in Washington State in three hours.' I loved it."

Anna Quindlen stayed with her job as deputy metropolitan editor at *The New York Times* after her first child was born but quit when her second son was due. Reactions among men, she says, are changing, as more are married to women with careers, but she adds that newspaper executives still have "got to be more laissez-faire" in their attitudes. They let men take leaves for books and that's okay—"I would really love it if they'd do it for children." Quindlen's column lets her stay in the business if not in the office. "There are few people with kids any more visible than I am."

In one of her columns, Quindlen directly addressed her own

surprise when her elder son told his friends his mommy didn't work. Her decision to work part-time, she says, would have been unthinkable to her when she was younger. "At 25, I should have worn a big red A on my chest; it would have stood for ambition, an ambition so brazen and burning that it would have reduced Hester Prynne's transgression to a pale pink.[1]

"Now it seems as if there are so many years ahead to pick up where I left off, or backtrack if I need to, or change direction entirely. If I get the forty additional years statisticians say are likely coming to me, I could fit in at least one, maybe two new lifetimes. Sad that only one of those lifetimes can include being the mother of young children."

Women make adjustments of all kinds. Sandy Banks, who became an assistant metropolitan editor on the *Los Angeles Times* not long after the birth of her child, did so in part because desk work has a degree of predictability and accessibility, even though she found it not as creative as reporting. "The decision to go on the desk was made in large part for benefit to my own life," she says of her editing job. She later took over as head of Times Mirror's Metpro program, which trains young minority journalists. While still a reporter, she carried her baby with her on interviews for a story on the anniversary of the Watts riot and brought her into the office when she wrote. She did the story in the first place even though she was still recovering from childbirth because she didn't want it to seem as though she didn't think the story or the job was important.

Women who are older or in more powerful positions face the same questions but can sometimes afford different answers. Karen Elliott House, *Wall Street Journal* foreign editor, and her husband, Peter Kann, the paper's associate editor, adopted a daughter in February 1986 and had their period of adjustment. So did House's staff. News that they could indeed adopt Petra had come via phone call "right in the middle of Gerry Seib's release" from captivity in Iran while House was on another line with Seib's wife, correspondent Barbara Rosewicz. After Petra arrived, House's work patterns changed. Formerly, she had arrived at work at 6:30 in the morning to deal with correspondents in Europe and she'd stay late; with Petra in her life, House says she became more of a 9-to-5 person. She knows her staff was frustrated in her first days with Petra because she wasn't as accessible as she'd been.

Having children changes attitudes. "It may be that when you have a child, though, your job gets put into perspective," Sandy Banks says. "It used to be that I lived for my job. I went home and thought about it. I didn't watch the clock. I think I have a healthier attitude—but it's not necessarily the attitude that goes down well."

"Before I had a kid, I was the run-over-your-own-mother-for-a-good-story type of reporter," says Cynthia Gorney. "I'd go weep with the mother and go away. I was not unsympathetic, but I'd think, 'Boy, is this great copy.' Having a kid made me think what was important to me and not just what I was going to get as a writer."

For the thirtieth anniversary of Disneyland, Gorney decided to stretch the feature-writing form and just sat down and wrote an essay. "There was a confidence in me that had never existed before Aaron was born. I found out, 'I can say it.'" In some ways, she became her own authority and was astonished by the power of the feeling. "The sense of self that informs the voice was a lot stronger than it had been. I had always been an outsider. Being pregnant and having a kid made me feel it was the first time I did something that made me part of the world."

"There's a flip side," Gorney cautions. She says she has grown more impatient and sometimes gets quotes wrong. "Now I've been doing it long enough that I can see that such a mistake doesn't get into print. But I have a short attention span now. I am less jazzed by story qua story."

To marry or not to marry, to unmarry or not—each woman resolves that question in her own way as well. A book about men in the newspaper business would be highly unlikely to discuss men's marriages, except in a case of a Philip Graham marrying a Kay Meyer and becoming the favored son-in-law and publisher of *The Washington Post.* Many women in top jobs are divorced, and some never married; some agonize over that status, while others revel in it. But more and more are married or have married again. All seek a balance in their public and private lives.

Freelance correspondent Dickey Chappelle, married to a photographer for fifteen years and divorced in 1956, asked herself in her autobiography whether a woman could be both a foreign correspondent and a wife. "My answer is—never at the same time. . . .

"Good correspondents are created out of the simple compulsion to go see for themselves what is happening. There's competition for their assignments, and the odds are heavily in favor of the man or woman who yields to the fewest distractions in obeying the compulsion," Chappelle wrote in the book, published only three years before she died when she stepped on a land mine in Vietnam. "It's a 24-hour-a-day task till a story's done and you cannot know as you start covering an event where it may lead you. Till it's done, people you love always receive less evidence of love than the correspondent wants to give them. . . . Some marriages survive this deprivation indefinitely but mine (and most of them) did not."[2]

Even today, two and a half decades later, "it's a hard row to hoe to be a woman in a position of power," says Catherine Shen, publisher of the *Honolulu Star-Bulletin*. It's hard to be alone in a job like that, to be alone at the endless out-of-town meetings. You almost need to have a spouse, Shen says, "and I don't know too many men who are willing to be a spouse" in the anonymous context of appendage that the word implies. "It's hard to have two career people. It doesn't make for a personal life. The culture doesn't give much support."

Marrying a woman of status—a competitor, if you will—does not appeal to some men. The stories about the difficulties professional women encounter in finding mates have been blown out of proportion—they almost seem like scare stories played up to keep women in their place. But there is no question that if you want to get married, you may have a problem in a world in which commitment is difficult and youth is valued.

Moving somewhere to take a new job or to be with someone else who is taking a new job brings identity questions to the surface. Who am I? What am I asking someone else to do for me, or what am I being asked to do for him? What support systems am I leaving behind?

Alice Bonner moved to Africa with her then-husband Leon Dash of *The Washington Post*, giving up a carefully nurtured career and plunging herself into deep soul searching. Bonner, who now does college recruiting for Gannett, had decided in the tenth grade that she liked to write. Nonetheless, she says she was an unlikely newsperson. "I grew up in an extremely rural area of Virginia, in Southside, which is in Dinwiddie County near Petersburg. It is a part of the world that stood still for many years.

"In 1966, under a freedom of choice integration plan, I went to a white high school. I'd go to the library and read the few books on the news business. I didn't find any women. I didn't find any blacks. It looked like a challenge to me." Bonner went to Howard University. "I had felt the sting of integration and I wanted the comfort of a black school. I wanted to be in D.C. because Washington was the place to be for news."

Going to work for *The Washington Post*, Bonner covered the human resources agency of the District of Columbia, a "monstrously sized local HEW-type agency." The beat produced stories that helped her get a Nieman Fellowship at Harvard in 1977. But despite all the advantages at Harvard, Bonner found sexism hadn't disappeared. There were only two women Niemans that year— Molly Sinclair, now of *The Washington Post*, was the other. "Whenever there was a guest speaker, it was assumed that we women couldn't be other than spouses." Toward the end of the year when it had happened once too often, poet Archibald MacLeish spoke, and Bonner asked a question. " 'Whose wife are you?' he asked. And I burst into tears. That year a lot of things came together. I had always seen race as the important thing. That year made both of us realize the important things were shared because we were women."

When she returned to the *Post* from Harvard, she wanted to cover the Department of Health, Education, and Welfare but ended up covering congressional hearings on general assignment. "It wasn't such a big deal," she thought, to give it up when she married Dash and went to Abidjan in the Ivory Coast. She did some reporting there but mainly handled logistics. She also had a baby.

"I felt I was in the shadow of a man. I had had no way of anticipating the psychological impact of leaving my identity behind. I didn't know what it meant until I didn't have it anymore. A lot of things contribute to break up a marriage, but part of it was feeling that I had given up my identity."

Bonner left Africa, went back to the *Post*, and overcompen-

319

sated, she says, working harder than she needed to, even though the people at the *Post* were very supportive of her as a single parent. "If there are ways to have it all at once, I haven't met anybody who's done it," Bonner says. "I like the culture of our business. But there are some who don't. They work hard on relationships or family. Those are the people who have successful marriages. They don't hang out in the newsroom that extra time if there's a reporter who needs help on a story. You have to plan your life in phases—a career for a while, or a family. God, I don't know anybody who has both."

Bonner decided to move into personnel work because of her own experiences and because she had enjoyed working with young freelancers while she edited the *Post*'s "D.C. Weekly" section after her return from Africa. "I don't think I'd do anything different, but I do feel the need to have my lessons passed on. . . . I need to preach a little to people about that. The few women who do break through have to help some others get through. I don't think the male hierarchy is going to give up anything willingly. I believe in education, that once men see women aren't going to change everything, that women are not going to put a kitchen in the middle of the newsroom, things will get better."

Unlike Bonner, Felicity Barringer wrestled ahead of time about the impact on her own life of going abroad with a journalist husband. Barringer edited *The Stanford Daily*, married Philip Taubman after graduation, and went to work in 1973 for *The Record* in Hackensack, New Jersey. In 1976 she was hired by *The Washington Post*, first covering suburban Montgomery County, Maryland, then the state legislature. In 1985 her husband, who by then was working for *The New York Times*, was offered a plum: its Moscow bureau. But the *Times* adamantly opposed Barringer's writing for the *Post* from Moscow.

Taubman had turned down an assignment for *Esquire* in Vietnam so that Barringer could stay at the *Record*, so it wasn't as if the trade-offs had all been one-sided, Barringer says. "All of a sudden we realized we were in a rut. We needed a change, and we needed it pretty badly." They could stay in Washington and be comfortable or go to Moscow and grow during an invaluable spell of time for themselves and their two children. That she would not be able to keep her job at the *Post* was "a burr under the saddle," an uncomfortable consequence, but less relevant than the chance for a change. Barringer ended up working part-time for the *Times* in Moscow and got her own front-page stories.

Some elect to turn down foreign assignments or new jobs at home because of personal considerations. Laurie Becklund had majored in English and Spanish at Immaculate Heart College in Los Angeles, studied briefly at the Autonomous University of Mexico, and taught English in Mexico City. She had a master's degree in journalism from Columbia University and had worked on newspapers in Newport Beach and San Diego. While covering a Mexican presidential election, she became aware of potential stories along the U.S.-Mexican border. One series looked at the exploitation of Mexican women who crossed the border daily to find domestic work.

After she joined the *Los Angeles Times*, she was offered the job of Mexico City bureau chief. But she was considering marrying another reporter—Henry Weinstein, who writes about labor issues for the *Times*—and turned down the job. Weinstein offered to quit and go with her, but Becklund was uncertain that he could get another reporting job because Mexico City was not then the object of interest that it has since become.

By all accounts—although no one will confirm it on the record—Anna Quindlen was in line to become the first woman ever to hold the job of metropolitan editor—or any other key line news job—at *The New York Times*, but she turned it down to stay home with her children.

Some don't take the jobs. Some do. Donna Donovan was editor of the Gannett-owned *Daily Press* and *Observer-Dispatch* in Utica and had been married for two years to a legislative aide for the New York State Senate when she was named publisher of the Gannett paper in Sioux Falls, South Dakota, *The Argus Leader*.

Soon after she moved from Utica to Sioux Falls, she discovered she was pregnant with her first child. Her husband was wrapping up his work in New York and realized that he was giving up a career he had nurtured for many years. "It was a strain on our marriage. . . . And no one in Sioux Falls could understand the concept of a husband who would move for his wife, nor a husband who was unemployed for nine months. . . . It was a very, very tough time." From that experience, Donovan says she learned that

321

her family is her number-one priority. "My family does come before my job."

Professionally, Donovan loved the *Argus Leader* and found South Dakota receptive to leading roles for women. "If an organization didn't admit women, they changed the rules to welcome me." But then came another move, one for which "the time was not good." Her husband had just become established in a job he liked, and the couple had found many things they liked about living in South Dakota. He in effect said, "You've got to be joking," when she told him about her chance to become publisher of *The Burlington Free Press* in Vermont and a regional vice president. "But that move went completely differently. We were only separated two months. I traveled back and forth because of my new regional responsibilities, we found a house, and he had a job lined up. Things fell in place more smoothly."

Even though "it's not all twinkles, as in the Donovans' case," *Miami Herald* editor Janet Chusmir maintains that more and more women are willing to move. Decision makers will "forfeit some of the best talent in the industry" if they don't change their attitudes and keep an open mind about women's mobility. Employers treat men's decisions as individual decisions, not linked to gender; they should do the same for women, she added.[3]

Many single women face moving as well. You carefully construct a support system, but you have to build it again if there's a better opportunity. Leaving Washington, D.C., my own hometown, was wrenching, but leaving the Newhouse Washington bureau for the *Los Angeles Times* was a professional step ahead. I knew only two people in all of Los Angeles. Being single doesn't necessarily mean you're the only person you need to consider in making your decision—there are family and friends—but it does ease the complications, just as it does on a day-to-day basis. Nonetheless, establishing my role in a new surrounding—not to mention finding a new dentist, a new doctor, a new haircutter, a new place to live, a new kennel for Seamus the cat, and most of all, a new place to play tennis and new tennis partners—were a royal pain. At least I wasn't coming in as a boss, which adds definite limits on friendships.

Barbara Henry graduated from the University of Nevada at Reno and went to work as a reporter for the *Reno Gazette-Journal*, where she became wire editor, then city editor. She worked on *USA Today* for a year and a half and returned to the *Gazette-Journal* as executive editor. She had worked in Reno for a decade and a half but uprooted herself in her early 30s to become editor of the Rochester *Democrat and Chronicle* and Rochester *Times-Union*.

She's not very sympathetic with women who complain about newspapers but opt out of management. "You can't change it by not getting into it. Most people go from reporting to editing because they want to do things their way. You change it if you get into it. If you're persuasive, and you're willing to work on it, they'll listen."

To manage or not to manage—or even to aspire to manage; to report or to edit—these are critical points for women as they are for men. More women are pressing to go into management, but it's not to everyone's taste. "Management is sort of like taking out the garbage," says reporter Nina McCain of *The Boston Globe*. Somebody's got to do it, but she suggests it should be rotated so that no one is stuck for more than two years, and so no one takes a power trip or contributes to an us-versus-them attitude. Some don't like it; some do. Knight-Ridder executive Scott McGehee was pressed into service with thirty minutes' notice when *The Savannah Morning News* and *Evening Press* needed someone on the desk. She decided she was more suited to be an editor than a reporter and never looked back, eventually becoming managing editor of *The Detroit Free Press*.

Men and women alike go into the newspaper business either because they like to write or because they like to snoop. Some change their minds and decide they want to shape the news and direct the troops; others never veer from their original interests. They don't want to lose touch with the streets by being cooped up in an office. "There's a freedom and flexibility [to reporting] that you don't have when you're tied to somebody else's copy," says Kay Longcope, a veteran of more than sixteen years at the *Boston Globe*.

"With salaries what they are now, you can make a decent living as a reporter, and it's so much more exciting," says Hilda Bryant, a longtime reporter with *The Seattle Post-Intelligencer* who's now a television reporter. "The adventure is in reporting, not management." Management could be an adventure as well, Bryant

323

says, if there were more women publishers to help create a better overall climate for women in the newspaper business.

A number of women interviewed for this book said they had found that management as now constructed involved too much hassle for too little reward. Entry into management in the first place was too uncertain of reward, no matter how well you played the game. Why beat your head against a closed door? So they built a life separate from work, focusing on musical interests, sports, children, nature, educational programs, their communities —with the idea in mind that when they reached the end of their working days, they would not feel they had given only at the office. Who is to say they are wrong?

Women face scores of other questions, big and small. Even though women are now sprinkled throughout management ranks, "we're still asked if we can stand the pressure of being on the fast track, still asked if our husbands will mind not having dinner on the table at six o'clock. We're still asked if we'll cry when things don't go our way," Linda Cunningham, executive editor of *The Trenton Times*, told the New Jersey Press Association.

Controlling the emotions is supposedly the mark of a man —or of a woman in a man's world. But many a woman has sat through an outburst from a man that is written off to pressures or creativity. A woman who made such an outburst, however, would have been ostracized for letting her "raging hormones" get the better of her. No matter that there are sexist jokes; no matter that she receives indifferent treatment from her colleagues; no matter the groundless arguments advanced to dismiss her idea of reality that she hears—a woman can't walk out of a meeting in disgust. She'd be accused of having no sense of humor or of being emotional. Said Cunningham, "We cry in boardrooms no more often than our male counterparts throw temper tantrums in the hallways. We are here to stay."[4]

Domestic tasks that were standard for women for generations now go by the board. "I cooked my last meal six years ago," says Joann Byrd, executive editor of the *Herald* in Everett, Washington. "I am not responsible for anything at home. If I have a particularly bad spell, my husband even fills my car with gas. But he hasn't done my laundry yet. I realized that I cannot do it all. I cannot be a perfect mother, perfect wife, perfect daughter, perfect editor. I don't care if I'm a perfect housewife. You have to decide what's important. We are going to need to change our view of how much we can do and what." Or as Rena Pederson, editorial-page editor for *The Dallas Morning News*, says, "When I'm 50, I'll do my nails and clean my closet."

Private as the choices of managing a family, maintaining friendships, and making career moves are, several other questions that cannot be ignored are even more private. Sex. Fear. Loneliness. These feelings are as much a part of reporters' lives both at home and abroad as are their professional competence and their persistence in getting assignments. But they remain largely ignored in much of the reporting on reporters. However, they influence judgment on what stories get pursued, and they may give rise to conflicts of interest. So they belong in the picture if it is to be a full portrait, not just connected dots. As one foreign correspondent said to me, not only must you discuss professional questions, "you have to talk about sex. You have to handle the question of risks and of charges that a woman got a job or a story on her back."

These questions reflect people's perceptions of how women do their jobs. Sometimes these questions even cost women their jobs. Laura Foreman was fired from *The New York Times* because "she slept with a politician but kept right on doing the job she was hired to do," Eleanor Randolph noted in an *Esquire* rundown on sexual conflicts of interest.[5] Maggie Higgins was also dogged with questions about how she got stories.

Foreman's affair involved Henry J. "Buddy" Cianfrani, a free-wheeling South Philadelphia politician whom Foreman met on her beat as a political reporter for *The Philadelphia Inquirer* in 1975. Foreman wrote seven stories about Cianfrani after "he had changed from her source to her lover," Randolph wrote. Foreman left the *Inquirer* for a job at *The New York Times* before the relationship became an open issue and didn't tell her new editors about it. Once it did become known, the *Times* fired her; its editors felt they couldn't send her to cover any story. At that point, the *Inquirer* assigned two Pulitzer Prize–winning reporters to investigate the Foreman incident the way they would investigate any conflict-of-interest case about a government agency, so there were few secrets about the episode. Their findings were contained in a 17,000-word article.

"The Laura Foreman-Buddy Cianfrani affair put a lot of

people on notice that sex had become an official conflict of interest," Randolph wrote. Foreman taught reporters "that besides avoiding junkets and freebies and fat envelopes that come under the table, we also have to screen our bedmates. Failing that, we may have to change our jobs."

A comment by Abe Rosenthal of *The New York Times* would have landed him into any journalistic equivalent of Bartlett's *Familiar Quotations*. Said Rosenthal in a conversation to Gene Roberts of the *Inquirer*: "It's okay to fuck elephants—just don't cover the circus."

Love in the newsroom is still another matter. It happens all the time now, as there are more women in newsrooms. Reporter marries reporter. Questions intensify when boss woos employee; will one treat the other with preference? That was the question raised when Sally Quinn, who cut stiletto-sharp profiles for the "Style" section of *The Washington Post*, wed her boss, *Post* Executive Editor Ben Bradlee. Until she left the paper, the romance made some staff members complain that her copy got special treatment. But, Randolph commented in her article, "conflicts within the newsroom are far preferable to conflicts of interest that set newsroom loyalties against loyalties to news subjects."

What is curious is that women often seem to be the ones punished, questioned, and derailed for transgressions, while the men are considered regular fellows, or sexy devils. The female journalist who got the worst rap was Marguerite Higgins, who shared a Pulitzer Prize for coverage of the Korean War.

Higgins was an attractive, driven woman who seemingly did what she needed to do to succeed. "Am I getting a reputation for sleeping around?" she once asked her friend Judy Barden. "I'm afraid so," her friend replied. "Is that really so terrible?" Higgins asked. Barden later told Higgins's biographer Antoinette May, "I've never understood why people got so annoyed about it. God knows there were enough disadvantages to being a woman in a so-called man's world. The generals who were the main news sources certainly didn't want you—oh, well, they wanted you on their terms, in bed when it was convenient for them—but they couldn't be bothered other times. They didn't want you 'interfering with the men.' People accused Marguerite of taking advantage of men, but I could never understand that. Her relationships, sexual or otherwise, were mutually pleasurable associations. Whose was the advantage?"[6]

Marguerite Higgins was competitive and talented, and her colleagues sometimes looked bad in comparison. "Male journalists were always criticizing each other," *Life* magazine's Carl Mydans told May. "They'd say a man was dishonest in his reporting or lazy or possibly an alcoholic, but they never damned a correspondent by accusing him of sleeping around. This charge was constantly leveled against Maggie. It wasn't important enough to even consider in discussing a man and the worst thing they could think of in describing a woman. The men regarded reporting as their privileged territory. That a woman would invade the war area—their most sacred domain—and then turn out to be equally talented and sometimes more courageous was something that couldn't be accepted gracefully. . . . The competitive spirit and determination that would have been admired in a man were the very qualities that caused men to resent Maggie."[7]

Higgins continues to provide sexy copy. In *The Paper*, his 1986 book on *The New York Herald-Tribune*, Richard Kluger spent more time discussing Higgins's sexual activities than he spent on the news-reporting skills of many *Herald-Trib* staff members. Describing Higgins as "a five-foot-eight windblown blonde," Kluger added that she "had a voluptuously curved, unmistakably adult body that, by all accounts, proved useful in the advancement of her career. She did not flaunt its attributes but neither was she coy about her sexual appetite."[8]

Men can be counted on to think women have all the advantages owing to sex, Georgie Anne Geyer wrote in her autobiography, *Buying the Night Flight*. "What they supposedly meant was that because I was young and blond and female, I could get things from men. Frankly, I never quite understood the principle at work here. I just couldn't picture waking up at three in the morning with some stranger lying next to me and saying, 'Eh, Ché, *mi amor*, tell me where your missiles are?' Men apparently think this is the way it's done."[9]

Geyer has hiked through Guatemala to see the guerrilla activities and turned her brief imprisonment in Angola into a chance to interview her captors. She told of an encounter in Russia on a 1971 trip to finish research for a book on Soviet young people.

She had spent a pleasant day with her guide and a television journalist named Ivan in the countryside outside Tbilisi in Soviet Georgia. Ivan walked her to her hotel door. Half an hour later, he was back, pushed his way in, grabbed her wrist tightly, ripped her nightgown down the front, slapped her hard across the face, and announced that he knew she wanted him. She didn't. Finally she convinced him to leave. The reaction of the Russians and Americans in Moscow who learned about the fracas made her feel like the guilty party, which troubled her as much as the incident itself.[10]

In Islamic countries women have found themselves especially vulnerable, for in that world there is no room for women in the public sphere. "You are considered a fallen woman," Sharon Rosenhause says. "It simply was not safe to travel alone, and sometimes not even with colleagues. I was much more adventurous in India, but even there I always tried to travel with male colleagues," says Rosenhause, who was then with the *Los Angeles Times*. "I got used to being stared at by the Pakistani businessmen and tribal chiefs. Once I was in an elevator with a lone man, and the guy grabbed me. If you have to worry about protecting yourself physically, then it's damned hard to worry about doing your job."

Sometimes Rosenhause turned these attitudes to her advantage. Covering the coup in Afghanistan that precipitated the Russian invasion, Rosenhause realized that "the whole world was waiting to hear what happened. But there were all these correspondents, and one Telex in Kabul" for sending stories. Censorship had also been imposed. "Islamic society is so chauvinistic, it is hard to understand. The Telex operator would see all these guys around and me—and I wasn't first in line—but he sent mine first. I beat Reuters that day. I figured that since I had suffered indignities because of traveling in an Islamic country, I deserved it."

Judith Miller of *The New York Times* invented a husband named George to handle the eternal question, "Where is your husband?" that she encountered throughout the Middle East. The preoccupation with family life there demanded that she have a husband, or she'd never get past that question with Arabs.[11]

Sheila Rule came up against her own feelings in a way she never anticipated when she went to South Africa on assignment for *The New York Times*. "NOTHING PREPARES YOU FOR APARTHEID" read the headline on *The New York Times Magazine* article she wrote about her trip.[12] "Growing up black in America in the 1950s, I was familiar with the ignorance, fears, and furies of racism," but the "denials and slights I felt and saw in my country in no way reflect the oppression and jagged-edged existence experienced by black South Africans."

Looked on by many everyday South Africans as their "sister from America," Rule could pretend to be a resident of a black township when stopped at a roadblock. And she was somewhat prepared for white reaction to a black reporter. But "I was in no way ready for the treatment I received from many black South African men on the city streets." As she took walks around Johannesburg to shake off the tensions, she was repeatedly confronted by men "who made lewd, persistent comments. Some of the remarks were made in African languages, as I was often mistaken as South African until I opened my mouth, but the message was brought home by tones and gestures. On several occasions, my breasts and buttocks were fondled.

"Certainly, black women in America have long been accustomed to black men's calls of, 'Hey, baby,' and, 'Mama, can I go with you?' But the approach of these men was, to me, flirtation gone mad. I was aware of the low status of women on the African continent, but in the black-ruled countries I had visited, I had never seen it emphasized with such bold, public aggression."

Rule was at first shocked; then she cursed the men who accosted her. One incident occurred on a street crowded with whites, and she did not want them to see two black people at odds. Finally, she asked black South African women about the problem. Some said it was accepted practice; others said it was just like the way Italian men behaved; others said the men were worthless.

"It was only after traveling to a desolate patch of oppression in the so-called homeland of Gazankulu that I began to understand some of the aggression. With candlelight illuminating her face as day gave way to darkness, a woman there told me that she had seen her husband for a total of about twenty months in twenty years because of the system of influx control, which often requires black men to travel to faraway places to work and live in bleak single-sex hostels, leaving their families behind. It is a system that tears apart families and leads to desperation."

329

Sex is an issue, then. So is fear. Fear is fear; it knows no sexual barriers. Marlise Simons, a stringer for *The Washington Post* at the time, was kidnapped by Mexican government troops, blindfolded, and tied up for several days soon after she arrived in the country in 1971. Later she was arrested in Chile during the 1973 coup, when the military was executing prisoners. Those experiences took her to the "outer limits of fear" and has made coverage of events since then seem far less threatening.[13] Maggie Kilgore says that nothing in her background prepared her for the midnight rocket attack that rattled her windows in South Vietnam or for her first near-hit in a helicopter skirmish.

In an article that Judith Miller of *The New York Times* wrote while based in the Middle East, she commented, "Other women may be cut out to cover wars, but Lebanon taught me that I am probably not among them." Still, fear may have driven her to dodge bullets to get the Beirut story. "Maybe my being a woman had made a difference after all. I had been so frightened most of the time in Lebanon that I was determined to prove I could be as fearless, as macho, as many of my peers. I had to demonstrate to them, to my editors, to myself, that women—and this woman, in particular—could be sent anywhere."[14]

A few years after she returned from the Middle East, Miller said in an interview that she found men still felt more need to prove their bravery than women did. Some even take silly risks to do so. "If ever there was a time I thought my life would be in danger, I didn't go. I don't believe in taking unnecessary risks. My job was to be alive to report the story."

Not long after the bombing of the Marine barracks in Beirut, however, Miller went with two companions to check small villages to see how the Shia Muslims were taking over the country. "I didn't know how dangerous that was. We could have just disappeared. Shortly thereafter I started agitating within my paper to close the *Times* bureau. I said, 'We're there to cover the story. Let's not be part of it.'"

Fear is an equalizer. Gloria Emerson found life perfectly equal for women in Vietnam—perfectly equal "to cover firefights, and be attacked by rocket-propelled grenades, and see things that will give them nightmares for years."[15]

There is fear of failure as well as fear for safety. Fear of failure can stretch one's limits—or push the limits of truth. Janet Cooke of *The Washington Post* was viewed as a stylish newcomer in a fast league. For whatever reasons, she made up a stunning story about a child who was a drug addict. She had made up part of her résumé as well. When her Pulitzer Prize was announced, the résumé hoax was discovered, then the story hoax as well. The *Post* returned the Pulitzer.

Sex. Fear. And loneliness. Traps for any reporter. Men who go abroad on reporting assignments give up friends, a culture they understand, the ability to establish roots in the best of cases, safety, and all personal ties in the worst of assignments. They, like the women who draw such assignments, get in return a life on the edge of the news and knowledge of how a different system works and that they can work within it. They may escape from boredom at home and work as well, or from personal situations that no longer work.

There was excitement and too much drinking in a schizophrenic situation like Vietnam, where primitive jungle fighting was often only minutes by helicopter from city nightlife. Edie Lederer of the Associated Press remembers that "Saigon was a place where people worked hard and played hard. Playing hard was important to relieve the tension. There was a lot of the live-for-today syndrome because you didn't know what tomorrow might bring. People didn't sleep a lot. There was a tremendous amount of partying, dining out. Some of that had a purpose. The more people you met, the better you knew what was going on."

More often, though, women working abroad, or as sportswriters or political writers constantly on the road, complain about the loneliness of hotel rooms, the tedium of travel. So do men. But there is a difference for women. "On Saturday night you find yourself in a strange city. You don't go for a walk or look at the strip joints," says Joanne Omang of *The Washington Post*. "When I would find myself with an evening in a new city where I didn't know anyone, I usually had a good dinner and went back to the hotel and read a good book. Whether that's worse or better than what men do, I don't know. I do know it saves you from cirrhosis.

"In the end, I didn't like that part. The loneliness, the endless hassle of living in the Third World and trying to travel, the struggle to make arrangements for a place to eat and sleep and go to the bathroom. I have·mixed feelings. After you're back, you realize you've had a rare opportunity to stretch yourself completely, to see how much work you can do, how well you can organize your time, how much patience you have. You test your reportorial skills, your physical stamina, your language ability. There are no limits to what needs to be done."

Ideally, there should be no limits to what can be done by women as foreign correspondents, or political writers, or copy-editors. There are, because they still work in a man's world, a world of toughness in which you don't show fear or loneliness or have personal problems. According to one school of thought, if women want to work in this male world, they should adapt to its rules and its schedules.

But increasingly women and like-minded men say they want to work in a human, humane world. It is time for an accommodation from more than one side, a joint understanding of the needs, hopes—and fears—of women and men in the newspaper business. That will enable women as well as men to participate fully in their profession—participation that already has demonstrably enlarged newspapers' view of the world.

Everyday Indignities

Molly Ivins of the *Dallas Times-Herald* figured that if a woman reporter presented herself seriously, she'd get taken seriously. With her added advantage of size—"I'm not just tall, I'm big"—she figured big people really would get taken seriously. "If I put on high heels, I really am intimidating—about six-four."

"But still, I'd go to see a Texas legislator and ask a question, and he'd say, 'Why worry your pretty little head about that? Why don't you come sit on my lap?' "

CHAPTER

19

Now What, and So What?

Sen. Edward M. Kennedy of Massachusetts visited the *Los Angeles Times*'s senior editors and political writers early in 1987. The paper's editor, William F. Thomas, described the session: "I sit in a roomful of people—when we had Ted Kennedy. And when I look around the room, we could have had a couple of women there, but we didn't have any. We didn't have any blacks, either. We didn't have any browns, either. We were just ten Anglo guys is what we were."

Women have brought to American newsrooms new perspectives on the news and different styles of reporting and managing. Entry into those newsrooms is no longer denied; advancement to senior editorships and plum assignments—advancement that would have put some women in that meeting with Ted Kennedy —remains limited. Women and minorities offer the promise of more thorough coverage of ever-changing communities and, through that improved coverage, improved circulation and advertising prospects in a world in which many other media compete for the newspaper reader's time and money.

Woman after woman interviewed for this book said that the biggest single factor blocking the fulfillment of this promise is the tendency of men to hire and especially to promote people just like themselves—that is, other white males from the same economic and cultural background. Not just occasionally, either, but over and over and over again, even in an era of supposed awareness of the need for affirmative-action plans for women and minorities.

In times past the replicated reporter was the fast-talking,

hard-driving guy who covered the cop shop; now it tends to be the young Ivy Leaguer in blue blazer, chinos, and loafers. "You can see them coming in the door, and they're marked for advancement almost from that moment on," says a *Washington Post* veteran, a woman. In contrast, women of talent have rarely been identified in the same way because there are rarely women of talent in management jobs to see themselves in that person coming in the door, green but potentially a star. "I never faced clear-cut discrimination," one *Boston Globe* reporter says, "but I never was channeled, either."

"The rooms at the top are filled with people who sacrificed family by working long hours," says columnist Ellen Goodman. "When they are looking for replacements, they look for people like themselves. Breaking a mirror is difficult. Why not have more like yourself because you did such a good job?"

In many professions, it may not matter that one generation of managers duplicates itself through its hires. But in journalism, Goodman says, it's different because "you're making decisions about what's news, about what's important. That affects how a community sees itself. If some people aren't there, then you're saying their news isn't important. The only way to have a chance to make better decisions is to have a more representative group making decisions. I'm not saying women will necessarily do it right, but that's the only way you have a shot at it at all."

No one shares power willingly. Newspapers haven't fully realized the truth in the line that "power is like yeast—spread it out and it grows." It doesn't diminish an organization to have many people in power; it simply taps more resources. But newspapering has been a male society until very recently, says Times Mirror President David Laventhol, and "male societies still like to keep it that way, emotionally if not intellectually."

Only when there is a top-down commitment not just to consider but also to hire and promote women and minorities for the top editing jobs—and then listen to them once they are there—only then will newspapers have the staff to help reach their fullest potential audience. That commitment from the top is the single most important factor in changing the status of women and minorities in the profession today. It must be matched with money for recruitment, training, salaries, and bonuses for executives who do well—and discipline for executives who don't.

Allen Neuharth of the Gannett newspapers said it should happen, and it happened. In contrast, three press leaders were targets of legal actions by female employees—*The New York Times* and the Associated Press were sued, and *The Washington Post* was the target of an Equal Employment Opportunity Commission complaint. As recently as the summer of 1987, nearly fifty women at the *Los Angeles Times* felt compelled to write their publisher outlining their concern over neglect of their aspirations, and seventeen black women at *The Washington Post* started meetings with management once they found they were clustered at the bottom of the pay scale. It should be a matter of concern to these organizations that a man they regard as a renegade—Neuharth —has a better reputation than they do for advancing women and minorities.

When the commitment is there, newspapers work to hire women and work to hold on to them. That commitment is entrenched as corporate theology at Gannett. Gannett finds people like Pam M. Johnson, the black woman who is publisher in Ithaca; Alice Bonner, the former Nieman Fellow eager to help recruit women and minorities at the college level; and Tonnie Katz, who was managing editor for *The Baltimore News American* when it folded. She considered working at the *Los Angeles Times*, but there was no job offering solid chances of advancement. Katz became managing editor of Gannett's *San Bernardino Sun* after Gannett officials said, in effect, "What can we do to make this woman happy?"

Gannett finds these people because it has a personnel department charged with looking for them. To their credit, many other papers also do have minority recruiters, but few have seen the same need to build a network of women to hire and promote as Gannett has.

Women hold positions in newspaper management today that I never dreamed of in 1960, when I was a dictationist for United Press International. But the scales are hardly balanced yet, especially at the nation's most prominent newspapers. These papers authenticate change when it shows up in stories on their front pages, through bylines of women and blacks as well as well as white males around the world. Women in prominent jobs at *The Christian Science Monitor* and *The Miami Herald* and the Gannett organization are all well and good, says a former *New York Times* reporter, "but it's too bad they don't count." There is a certain arrogance of power and provincialism in that statement, because of course they count. But there is also hard truth, because it is *The New York Times* and the *Los Angeles Times* that help set the agendas for people who can bring change to society. They should be the leaders, and they are not.

Advancing women in greater numbers into corporate newspaper hierarchies will not, of course, solve all the press's problems. Nor will it bring down the kingdom. It's a bit like what the anarchist Emma Goldman said about the effects of women's suffrage. The suffragists had argued that women would clean up politics and rid the world of war, disease, and vice. But Goldman observed that to assume a woman "would succeed in purifying something which is not susceptible of purification is to credit her with supernatural powers."[1]

How will women advance? Part of the answer lies with women themselves. They must prepare themselves better to tackle management jobs. But, one female publisher says, "the men who are in positions of power need to think that it's a wise business decision to get women and minorities in top positions. Otherwise, they're going to fail."

Elsie Carper, assistant managing editor of *The Washington Post*, puts it this way: "Women are heads of sections, women are assistant managing editors. But when are they actually going to run the papers? When are they going to be the managing editors? There are not many of them around the country."

Letting time pass unmolested is not the answer to Elsie Carper's question, although it is the answer executive after executive gives to the question of what will bring about change for women in the newspaper business. Time, says David Laventhol, president of Times Mirror. Time, says Max Frankel, executive editor of *The New York Times*. Time, says Meg Greenfield, editorial-page editor of *The Washington Post*.

And I'll be using a walker at the Old Feminists' Home before real change occurs if time alone is left to heal the problem of discrimination in the upper ranks of American newspapers. Bill Thomas, *Los Angeles Times* editor, said he had thought the question would take care of itself but obviously it hasn't. Recalling the Kennedy session, Thomas added that the pattern of men-only in top jobs and top meetings should be broken. "It's the time to do it. The raw material is there. It's time to skip some people over some other people." It is also time to do it, not just to talk about it.

Change in newspaper promotion policies won't occur until more editors and publishers change their attitudes about how women will react to a given assignment, a proposed move, or a change in working hours. Some have already changed their attitudes, but the attempt to abandon stereotypes needs acceleration. One woman's approach to covering a story, accepting an out-of-town assignment, or managing an office does not represent all women, any more than one man's attitude reflects the attitudes of all men. Just as women demand that they not be stereotyped, they must be more flexible themselves and not automatically discard a suggestion about a story or a change of scene just because they haven't done something that way before.

They must be willing to take some risks. Patricia O'Brien was a *Chicago Sun-Times* reporter who had attended college after her four children were born, often falling asleep over her typewriter at the kitchen table as she wrote her papers. She was no stranger to risk. Still, when approached about moving to the Knight-Ridder bureau in Washington, she said she didn't want to leave Chicago. She was just divorced and back from a Nieman Fellowship at Harvard. She left work one Friday, and on her way out she noticed that some coffee had been spilled on one of the desks. When she came in Monday, she saw the same coffee spill, the "same row of people hunched over typewriters, the same guy who I knew kept a fifth in his desk. I said to myself there are times that you make a change or you never will." She took the new job.

Stereotypes will change as more men work entire careers side by side with women, something most senior editors today have not done. Max Frankel, executive editor of *The New York Times* since November 1986, clearly differs from his predecessor, A.M. Rosenthal. Although Rosenthal said, "There is nothing on this paper that women cannot do," it was Frankel who finally let more women do more of those things. Frankel says that he is going to look beyond stereotypes of women in making promotion decisions. "Women are sometimes described as temperamentally too hot," Frankel says. "The quality we find admirably aggressive in men is called temperamental in women. If that's the only thing somebody can tell me as a reason a woman shouldn't be an editor, I am consciously discounting that."

"Women, never having been part of the white male establishment, look at it differently," says Joann Byrd, executive editor of the *Herald* in Everett, Washington. Because of that outsider status, women on the average may simply be more used to "ignoring who are men and women and looking at their skills"—and that's what it's going to take to bring change. From her earliest days on the city desk, Byrd says, "It didn't bother me that women were assigned to things they hadn't covered in the past. Nor was I worried about sending a man to do a lightweight puff piece if that's what we had to do."

Forget altruism. Forget even the theme advanced throughout this book that only after women entered the newspaper business in greater numbers did the portrayal of women more accurately reflect the reality of their lives. That is true, but newspapers could go on quite nicely with today's status quo, never putting women in top positions, and they would still offer a fairer presentation of women than they did twenty-five years ago. There has to be something in it for the person in power to bring in the powerless. Newspapers are first and foremost businesses, not public servants; over time, it simply should be good business for newspapers to have a range of people making news decisions if they want to retain readers and therefore retain advertisers. Corporations never forget the bottom line. Selling a better product by appealing to a wider variety of readers should be a bottom line issue.

Even as they finally move to advance women, editors still make some mistakes. Sometimes they groom a woman only to have her turn them down when she decides her family comes first or she doesn't want to move across the country. *The New York Times* learned that it needed to have more women in the pipeline, says editor Frankel, because "some are going to do that to you." Of course, Frankel goes on, "you also have men who are not as portable these days. They don't want to go overseas because their wives have jobs." The point is, adds Abe Rosenthal, that this time when a woman was offered a senior job and turned it down, there were four men available to choose from. "Next time, we will have four other women."

And some editors still discriminate. They have to be discriminating; if they didn't the 50 percent of the country's major papers that have no woman editor, associate editor, managing editor, or editorial-page editor would have women in some of those jobs.

Some papers are still combating the legacy of past discrimination. In the past, "some of our editors were real pigs—but that's the way they grew up," says Katharine Graham, board chairman and former publisher of *The Washington Post.* "There is probably discrimination in the upper half [of newspaper management ranks] because it's still run by people in their late 50s or 60s, and they're still in the old world."

Bill Thomas says he has tried to determine what still blocks women's progress. "Whether or not there's some hidden agenda still at work, I have a hell of a time making out myself. No one will confess it. No one admits to it. But I don't think I've talked to a single woman who wouldn't say that they feel there is still some feeling about their charging ahead," some negative feeling. "I'm not sure that everybody has dealt completely honestly about their feelings when this has come up. I do see, though, that there has to be a hell of a lot less of it just in the last five years simply because of what's happening to the women here."

Changing executive attitudes has often been left to time— or to the women, who must prove they can make decisions, produce the work, and be comfortable to work with instead of being made comfortable themselves. Social critic Elizabeth Janeway put it most succinctly: "Even companies that proclaim themselves 'Equal Opportunity Employers' seldom feel it is their duty to try to change the inside of executive heads. Reducing male sexism is taken to be a female task; which is like saying that racism is solely the problem of blacks or other minority members."[2]

When outsiders come inside, the insiders go right about their business as they always have, if there is no leadership to the contrary. A woman makes a suggestion; no one hears. A man makes the same suggestion five minutes later; everyone thinks it's a great idea. "I've said, 'You don't listen to me,'" says Muriel Cohen, a reporter who led *The Boston Globe*'s Pulitzer Prize–winning coverage of school desegregation. "'You hear a woman's voice and you turn it off the same way you do your mother or your wife.'"

Women's ideas may not be taken as seriously as men's even by the very men who consider themselves liberal. You can't know anything about foreign policy because you're female. And you can't get listened to if you talk about anything "womanly" because that's not vital to the men—or so they think. Where does that leave you?

Or you're invisible, ignored in a discussion. Or physically there isn't even a place for you. Fresh from her Nieman Fellowship, Patricia O'Brien found that *The Chicago Sun-Times* wanted to showcase her presence, and it announced proudly that she would join the paper's editorial board. But then when she wanted to go to the board's meeting, her boss looked flustered and said, well, he was sorry, but you see they'd neglected to get a chair for her.

The problem is, as Byrd and others acknowledge, that not all women respect their own skills. The chance to slug it out with the boys brings out the worst in some women. They forget other women as they enjoy their own success. They take on the coloration, the attitudes of the male society in order to succeed, and so it makes no difference that they as women are there. For real change to begin to occur, one female editor says, one woman has to get in among the main news editors who will be a real thorn in their side. She simply has to call them on every mistake they make, whether of omission or commission, in dealing with women in news stories and personnel decisions. For even more real change to occur, it will take getting several women—a critical mass, if you will—into key jobs at each newspaper so that women aren't afraid to advance their own ideas.

The man's world that is newspaper management today has given management a bad name with many reporters. They went into the business to write and report, and nothing they see in management ranks lures them to change their original vocation. So it may not be enough to put women in management; management styles themselves probably must change to attract now-disdainful reporters.

"Good management is invisible," says Christy Bulkeley, former publisher at Gannett papers in Saratoga Springs, New York, and Danville, Illinois. "Most of what they see is the poor management, and they don't want to be part of that system."

A big part of management is knowing how to think ahead, Bulkeley adds, remembering her days in Danville; there, post-election coverage had simply never been planned ahead of time. "You learn what decisions can be made outside deadline time. This doesn't have anything directly to do with home—however, it has come about from the push to accommodate women's needs," to make the most effective use of office time for women who couldn't

341

live at work. Women, especially mothers, "are natural translators and connectors, which is what newspapers are supposed to be," and those skills may help match the needs of the staff with the requirements of covering the news thoroughly and efficiently.

Corporations also must reexamine the notion that a person must go into management to advance his or her career or to move to get ahead. "You have to have the same standards, too," Bulkeley adds. "Men opt out of management, and they aren't put down for it. They don't say that about men who are still reporters— David Broder, Haynes Johnson. You've got to have your best people on the streets.

"Some women don't want to move. Male spouses aren't moving as freely as female spouses. Moving is an antidote for going stale, but if you find a place that you match, you should be able to grow without going stale and without having to move. There are plenty of men who have refused to move, and women as a class should be judged no differently."

Women have especially found management positions to be drains on home life. Narda Zacchino spoke of twelve-hour days that she loved when she took over as editor of the *Los Angeles Times* Orange County edition, but she found that several nights a week her husband and her young children were coming in to eat dinner with her in the *Times* cafeteria. "I could not be one hundred percent career woman, one hundred percent wife, one hundred percent as a mother. The day I came to that realization, my life changed. When I was just a reporter and a wife, I was okay, but then I felt as if I was failing about my children. I learned to do the best I could in all those areas. When I would leave at 7 P.M., there was a lot of work still to be done. But when I'd go home at 9 P.M., there was still a lot of work to be done."

Feminist author Betty Friedan has found that many women are holding themselves to impossible standards, standards men never met. They are trying to be perfect in the corporate world and perfect homemakers. Or as Friedan put it: "Must—can—women now meet a standard of perfection in the workplace set in the past by and for men who had wives to take care of all the details of living and—at the same time—meet a standard of performance at home and as mothers that was set in the past by women whose whole sense of worth, power and mastery had to come from being perfect, all-controlling housewives and mothers?"[3]

The answer is obvious. Both corporate attitudes and women's attitudes need to change, to meet somewhere in the middle of today's unrealistic expectations—for women and men alike. People should not have to live that way, working eighteen hours a day, said Christy Bulkeley during a lengthy conversation analyzing management questions. "This may be the contribution that women can make, giving more options to more people. Who lives seven years longer? Any change I'm part of has to make it possible for men to get that seven years back. The press is part of the problem here in our definition of who's successful. We have to change the way we report about successful people in their jobs. Moving on in two years to a bigger job is not the only way to be successful."

The concerns of women who do not want to go into management are "not excuses," Bulkeley said. "They are legitimate concerns that have to be talked through." Newspapers need to examine practices that turn off the out groups. They need to ask their female employees the old question, "What *do* women want?" They think they know; they do not.

They also need to have management training for everyone —not just women or minorities—because there is no great sign that men know what they are doing in handling personnel any more than women who have not had the opportunity. Women who don't do well in management sometimes would have failed no matter what. Others could learn how not to fail or be uptight if someone cared to teach them. The same traits that make good reporters do not invariably make good managers. Newspapers notoriously resist management training, contending it doesn't fit their needs. But it can be tailored to them.

About a year after Sharon Dickman became the first woman on the *Evening Sun* desk in 1979, she found she lacked some managerial skills. "People didn't talk things through. It was the kind of job they said you only learn by doing." She felt she benefited from more formal training—which the Sunpapers provided at her urging; by learning how to get the best work out of people; and by dealing with those with problems.

One of those problems is finding someone or some place to assure safe care for children, especially for children of journalists who travel or work odd hours. But as Katharine Graham of *The Washington Post* says, "The communications industry—and business in general—has yet to face up to what I believe will be the

343

most important issue in enabling women to combine careers and families. I'm talking about day care. In order for women to be able to remain on the job long enough to gain the seniority they need to win the top spots, the conflicts of career and child care must be resolved. I believe a new and vastly expanded approach to day care has to be a major part of the solution. Reliable day care at reasonable cost must become a reality in American life— as common as medical insurance and pensions, which were once thought to be revolutionary, too," Graham told an international women's media conference in Washington in November 1986. "We in the media have an essential responsibility to keep the public informed and aware of this issue. We must all work on it together, starting now."

As the journalistic work force becomes increasingly female, editors and publishers will have to face that fact and provide more part-time work, offer flexible hours, and assist in some way with day care, whether through referral services, tax-shelter financial arrangements, or contributions to community child-care programs if on-site centers aren't appealing to management. All too slowly newspaper unions are starting to place such questions in their negotiating packages as young women—and their husbands —insist that they be there. The best hope for a breakthrough lies with the inevitable day when editors and publishers find that their young hot-shots, the reporters they want to keep, are women, and attention must be paid.

Child care remains a back-burner issue at many newspapers —among managers if not among the women on the staff. Some women have also found that editors view pregnancy as less important than a professional absence—writing a book or going to Stanford or Harvard—or than other health-related absences. To a woman, pregnancy may be just as formative an experience— probably more so—as writing a book. Maternity-leave policies are generous at some papers, stingy or inconsistent at others. On other issues related to children, progress is being made. Martha Hamilton of *The Washington Post* expresses special pride in a provision won by the Newspaper Guild that employees may use their sick leave to stay home with sick children.

Like male managers, women, too, have learned that advancement is not automatic. It's not like when they were growing up and their parents gave them approval when they did something well. In the business world it is not sufficient to do a job well and sit back and expect some reward. Women have to tell folks they're there and tell them what it is they want and why they ought to get it. It is not the way many women were brought up because it sounds like bragging—something a lady never did.

To find out what women can do for themselves—and are doing today—I asked a handful of women who are or have been newspaper executives for their suggestions. In the first place, replied Beverly Kees, editor of *The Gary* [Indiana] *Post-Tribune*, women can plan careers now. It never occurred to her when she was starting out that she could become an editor; the words "career path" were never used in her childhood. "That's a whopping change."

Karen de Young of *The Washington Post* has been a firm advocate of foreign reporting as a way of bypassing career roadblocks. "It skips a lot of steps . . . but not everybody likes that kind of life." When she was foreign editor at the *Post*, de Young offered overseas jobs to some young women who turned her down. "These were women with a proven track record, but they took into consideration things I hadn't. They saw themselves living in hotel rooms in South America for three years with no personal life. They were less willing to make sacrifices. It wasn't the danger and the discrimination. It was the desire not to live that way. Most of the women felt their fortune and some level of visibility were better attained in Washington. I find myself hoping women will get a bit more adventurous."

Speaking about career drives in general, Karen Elliott House of *The Wall Street Journal* echoed de Young. "I think women may have become conservative with success. When you have nothing to lose, you're willing to risk more. When you have something to lose, you feel like risking less, you try to fit in. I don't think women got as far as they have by being quiet. My own great fear is that women have peaked. They don't want to keep pushing forever. If you want it, you should ask for it. The worst thing that someone can do is say no."

Feminist fatigue may very well have set in even though women remain short of their goals. It has been hard to continually rev up when society in general is slouching toward conservatism, when the President of the United States was indecisive at best and hostile at worst to pleas that his administration was weakening the government's commitment to fair hiring practices, when the attorney general actively sought to weaken that commitment, and when the head of the U.S. Commission on Civil Rights made fun of women's attempts to achieve pay equity.

Women who are already in the executive ranks must not be reluctant to promote other women. Some women who are managers are more conscious of affirmative-action considerations and more likely than others to tell a subordinate whose final list of candidates for a job contains no women or no minorities to go back and try again. Others bend over backwards to appear fair, to fit into the men's club, and they end up appointing the same old faces to the same old jobs—men as the bosses, women as assistants. That is not being fair; it is being faithful to old standards.

"I never want to be labeled as someone who is only seeking women for key jobs," says Catherine Shen, *Honolulu Star-Bulletin* publisher, "but women have so far to go yet that I'm not worried about that."

"I named the managing editor, a woman," says Barbara Henry, executive editor at Gannett's two Rochester newspapers. "I didn't even think about it. She'd been in the newsroom eight years. She was the obvious choice. I felt that women were discriminated against for many years and there should be some atoning for past sins. . . . I still don't think women are anywhere near where they should be in any business."

Having women in the executive ranks can help—and should help—women with children. "Women in management jobs will make the accommodations to women to help schedule so they can work out their lives with kids," Henry adds. "It's not that men wouldn't have done it, but they didn't have anybody at their level saying they should do this. Now they have women who are counterparts."

"Women who get into positions of responsibility have to remember the young women behind them. There is a responsibility to the next generation. You have to spot people who may need a Dutch aunt talk," says Marcia McQuern, managing editor of *The Riverside* [California] *Press-Enterprise*. "You also have to be sure women don't use discrimination as an excuse. If you don't get a job or an assignment, you simply might not be good enough. You need to learn the things that will help you the next time."

Willingness to buck the male model in hiring and operating

346

style requires confidence that may only come with experience. "You have to have the strength to be yourself and trust your instincts," says Janet Chusmir, editor of *The Miami Herald*. "A lot of what I am was shaped by being home with children. You learn. You have to trust who you are and don't try to imitate the men." Or as Judith Clabes of *The Kentucky Post* in Covington told a TV interviewer, anyone who can handle the "terrible twos" of children should have enough confidence to run a newsroom.

"The ones who are there now have to be good," says Deborah Howell, editor of *The St. Paul* [Minnesota] *Pioneer Press*. "We're the ones who have to prove it. If you're not good—I'm scared that if we're not good it will rub off on other women. I got the job as executive editor because I was standing in line. There have to be enough women out there who cannot be denied. When I got the job as city editor, I didn't know another woman city editor. Now there are women city editors all over the place. There is nothing more plodding than a woman getting to be an editor. No women are considered hot shots. Women have had to fight it up from the trenches."

"Women have to believe that they are good," says Linda Cunnigham, editor of *The Trenton* [New Jersey] *Times*. "Until those women believe they are good, that they are talented, that they are entitled to be in the field, we can kiss good-bye any progress. You probably increase upward mobility by moving downsize in circulation. You've got to be in a position to relocate. And mainly you've got to accept the fact that it's okay to be calculating, to plan a career. Right now, women still tend to be reactive."

Pure demographics may change the pace. More women than men are enrolling in college now, and more women than men are graduating from journalism schools. Will time tell? Will the profession change appreciably as the products of journalism schools enter the journalism world? And, some ask, will that change be good or bad?

Today over 60 percent of mass-communication graduates are women. Not all these women go into newspapers. Some go into careers totally unrelated to journalism. Some go into public relations. Some go into advertising, and some into television. But 46 percent of the newest hires in newspapers are women. What will happen as those women move through the pipeline? What will happen if women become the majority in the profession?

347

In 1985 the University of Maryland School of Journalism issued a report called "The New Majority: A Look at What the Preponderance of Women in Journalism Education Means to the Schools and to the Professions." Directed by Maurine H. Beasley, associate professor of journalism, the report started a hot debate. It traced discrimination that women faced in the news business and in journalism education, outlined the challenges for journalism educators, and proposed some solutions.[4]

Some newspaper women found the report insulting in its implication that women's entrance into the field in greater numbers was somehow devaluing the jobs in pay and prestige. But what the report did was to call attention to the differences in women's and men's pay, found in study after study, and to call upon journalism educators to raise female students' consciousness of that fact so that they would insist on fair pay. The report's author, Maurine Beasley, did not condone women's lower pay; she warned that if pay didn't go up, especially at community newspapers where many young people begin their careers, journalism would lose the benefit of the brightest young men and women.

The thrust of the Maryland report was indeed to combat and not condone discrimination. Nonetheless, it contained loaded words: "With the tilt in journalism school enrollments to almost two-thirds female, educators and professionals in the field have compelling reasons to act upon these disturbing prospects:—Journalism and related communications fields may become 'pink-collar ghettos' in which salaries and status are lower in relation to other major professions. Female-dominated fields such as teaching, social work, nursing and librarianship traditionally have been lower-income professions. Although salaries in journalism-related fields (some of which already are noted for low pay) may not decline, there should be concern that they will not rise as they might if these fields remained predominantly male."

In the past, women became teachers, social workers, and librarians because other professions—especially law and medicine —were closed to them; they could not even gain admission to the schools that they would have to attend to obtain professional credentials. Women went where they could get jobs, in fields that often paralleled what had been their roles in the home, nurturing, and educating. Thus, pay was low because women had nowhere else to go and employers knew it.

348

Journalism was low-paid before women ever got through the door. If the pay remains low in some parts of the business, it's not women's fault. Women have more job options now—law, medicine, and journalism among them—so it's less likely that particular fields will become feminized and thus lower paid because they are women's only options. The newspaper world is in no immediate risk of a complete female takeover, at least not as long as top management remains more than 80 percent male. Newspapers are vital to the functioning of the country—to disseminating information about everything from football to the federal government—and thus men are not likely to flee in droves even as women enter the business. Newspaper work remains work of influence and status.

What is happening more than feminization at the grassroots reporting level is equalization. The march from the women's page to the front page is hardly complete, and the move upward in newspaper hierarchies is still restricted by people who don't yet see the advantages to sharing power, but these shifts are under way. People aren't used to that dynamic. A story conference changes when half the participants are female. A personnel meeting or a seminar at Harvard, Stanford, or Michigan changes when half the participants are female. There is indeed security in numbers. Women become more willing to speak up in page-one meetings about a story they know concerns many readers, to assert their own ideas on who might make a good sports reporter or foreign correspondent, or to raise a question that elicits a new line of thought. The shift is under way but hardly complete.

What if it happened? What if more women were in charge? "Assume for a moment," asks *Detroit Free Press* publisher David Lawrence,[5] "that women do not instinctively see the world in terms of conflict and controversy. Might we then stop covering politics as though it were a football game? Might we see less emphasis on who is up and who is down and who beat up on whom? Might our coverage emphasize the substance of the candidates, their philosophies, the issues and the choices facing us?

"I can hardly wait."

I have seen enormous changes. I have not seen enough change. I, too, can hardly wait.

Notes

The material in this book is based on interviews, most lengthy, some only fleeting, with the following journalists, who generously shared their time and their thoughts. I used the present tense when quoting from these interviews; material from other sources is footnoted and referred to in the past tense. Those journalists are Cheryl Arvidson, Edith Evans Asbury, Phyllis Austin, Sandy Banks, Karlyn Barker, Felicity Barringer, Tad Bartimus, Betty Bayé, Mary Lou Beatty, Laurie Becklund, Marylin Bender, Chris Black, Alice Bonner, Diane Borden, Betsy Wade Boylan, Benjamin Bradlee, Christine Brennan, Jane Brody, Hilda Bryant, Carol Brydolf, Jennie Buckner, Christy Bulkeley, Mary Lou Butcher, Joann Byrd, Mindy Cameron, Elsie Carper, Karen Carter, Leyla Cattan, Lisa Chung, Janet Chusmir, Shelby Coffey, Muriel Cohen, Jane Conant, Maureen Connolly, Marvel Cooke, Barbara Crossette, Betty Cuniberti, Linda Cunningham, Grace Darin, Fran Dauth, Linda Deutsch, Karen de Young, Sharon Dickman, Mary Ann Dolan, Angela Dodson, Donna Donovan.

Jerelyn Eddings, Helene Elliott, Katherine Fanning, Carmen Fields, Pat Fisher, Mimi Foster, Max Frankel, Margie Freivogel, Sarajane Freligh, Sara Fritz, Dorothy Gilliam, Soma Golden, Ellen Goodman, Cynthia Gorney, Katharine Graham, Nancy Grape, Meg Greenfield, Mildred Hamilton, Kay Pinkham Harris, Barbara Henry, Diana Henry, Marita Hernandez, Michelle Himmelberg, Sue Hobart, Ann Holmes, Karen House, Toni House, Deborah Howell, Karen Howze, Evelyn Hsu, Ellen Hume, Molly Ivins, John Jacobs, Madelyn Jennings, Susan Jetton, Annette John-Hall, Pam M. Johnson, Tom Johnson, Laurie Johnston, Dorothy Jurney, Tonnie Katz, Beverly Kees, Maggie Kilgore, Connie Koenenn, Janet Knott, Sara Krulwich, David Laventhol, Mary Ellen Leary, Edie Lederer, Claudia Levy, Fran Lewine, Flora Lewis, Grace Lichtenstein, Frances Lide, Kay Longcope, Nina McCain, Scott McGehee, Mary

McGrory, Eileen McNamara, Margaret Dempsey McManus, Otile McManus, Maureen McNerny, Marcia McQuern, Judith Martin, Linda Mathews, Nancy Hicks Maynard, Dale Mezzacappa, Judith Michaelson, Lawrie Mifflin, Judith Miller, Pamela Moreland, Patt Morrison.

Ruth Cowan Nash, Allen H. Neuharth, Patricia O'Brien, Joanne Omang, Carol Ostrom, Geneva Overholser, Marj Paxson, Rena Pederson, Ginny Pitt, Gayle Pollard, Anna Quindlen, Eleanor Randolph, Elizabeth Rhodes, Carol Richards, Maggie Rivas, Caryl Rivers, Anne Roark, Nan Robertson, Lori Rodriguez, Sharon Rosenhause, A. M. Rosenthal, Charlotte Saikowski, Stephanie Salter, Janet Sanford, Iris Schneider, Eileen Shanahan, Gerry Shanahan, David Shaw, Isabelle Shelton, Catherine Shen, Beth Campbell Short, Peg Simpson, Bill Sing, Claire Spiegel, Ann Sullivan, Mary Swanton, Jackie Tasch, Jean Sharley Taylor, Bill Thomas, Helen Thomas, Jackie Thomas, Lois Timnick, Solveig Torvik, Kelly Tunney, Virginia Tyson, Gerry van der Heuvel, Lesley Visser, Jennifer Werner, Karen West, Lois Wille, Betty Anne Williams, Theo Wilson, Tracy Wood, Nancy Woodhull, Rosalie Muller Wright, Anne Wyman, and Narda Zacchino.

1 Out of the Picture

1. *Webster's New Collegiate Dictionary* (Springfield, Mass.: G. & C. Merriam, 1959), p. 565.
2. Gay Talese, *The Kingdom and The Power* (New York: World Publishing, 1969).
3. Richard Kluger, *The Paper* (New York: Alfred A. Knopf, 1986), p. 402.
4. Not wanting to pull a Joe Biden, I readily acknowledge that Lee Dembart, an editorial writer at the *Los Angeles Times*, was the first person I heard using the expression that most news is "olds."
5. David Broder, *Behind the Front Page* (New York: Simon and Schuster, 1987), p. 128. Discussion of press coverage of Betty Friedan and the women's movement begins on p. 125.

2 Publishers and Pundits

Few comprehensive histories of women in the newspaper business exist. The best remains Ishbel Ross's *Ladies of the Press* (New York: Harper, 1936), but it is obviously dated. An excellent source of biographical material on the best-known historical figures in the field is *Great Women of the Press* by Madelon Golden Schlipp and Sharon M. Murphy (Carbondale, Ill.: Southern Illinois Press, 1983). Other good sources include

Marion Marzolf, *Up From the Footnote* (New York: Hastings House, 1977); and Barbara Belford, *Brilliant Bylines* (New York: Columbia University Press, 1987).

1. Schlipp and Murphy, *Great Women*, pp. 1–11.
2. Susan Henry, "Journalistic Comrade: Eliza Otis and the Beginnings of a Newspaper Dynasty" (Paper prepared for the Association for Education in Journalism and Mass Communication, August 1986).
3. Kluger, *The Paper*, p. 286. See also Alden Whitman's article on Helen Reid in *Notable American Women: The Modern Period* (Cambridge, Mass: The Belknap Press of Harvard University Press, 1980), pp. 574–75.
4. Ralph Martin, *Cissy* (New York: Simon and Schuster, 1979), p. 272.
5. Ibid., p. 338.
6. "Alicia Patterson Is Dead at 56," *The New York Times*, July 3, 1963, p. 27; "Alicia Patterson," *The New York Times* editorial, July 6, 1963; "This Is The Life I Love," by Alicia Patterson as told to Hal Burton, *The Saturday Evening Post*, February 21, 1959, p. 19; *Editor and Publisher*, July 13, 1963, p. 11; *Current Biography*, 1955, pp. 474–76; and James Boylan's entry on Alicia Patterson in *Notable American Women*, pp. 529–31.
7. *Current Biography*, 1965, pp. 364–66; Deirdre Carmody, "Dorothy Schiff Agrees to Sell Post to Murdoch, Australian Publisher," *The New York Times*, Nov. 20, 1976, p. 1; Wolfgang Saxon, "The New York Post Has a Long History," *The New York Times*, Nov. 20, 1976, p. 29.
8. *Time*, Nov. 3, 1980, p. 103; Richard West, "Grace McClatchy Dies; Headed Papers," *Los Angeles Times*, Oct. 18, 1980, p. 24 (McClatchy's full name was Grace Eleanor McClatchy).
9. Gail Sheehy, "Cinderella West: California's Unknown New Queen of the Press," *New West*, May 24, 1976, pp. 50–69. See also Alexander Auerbach, "Helen Copley: Novice Takes Firm Control," *Los Angeles Times*, Jul. 19, 1975, p. 1; and Terry Christensen and Larry Gerston, "The Rise of the McClatchys and Other California Newspaper Dynasties," *The Californians*, Sept.–Oct. 1983, pp. 8–24.
10. David Halberstam wrote at length about Kay and Philip Graham in *The Powers That Be* (New York: Alfred A. Knopf, 1979). See also Jane Howard's "The Power That Didn't Corrupt," *Ms.*, Oct. 1974, p. 47.
11. Schlipp and Murphy, *Great Women*, p. 49, quoting from William Harlan Hale's 1950 biography, *Horace Greeley: Voice of the People*.
12. Letter from Margaret Fuller to Samuel Ward, March 3, 1845, cited

in Bell Gale Chevigny, *The Woman and the Myth* (Old Westbury, N.Y.: The Feminist Press, 1976), p. 295.

13. Ibid., p. 465.
14. Schlipp and Murphy, *Great Women*, p. 88.
15. Ibid., p. 93.
16. Ibid., p. 135.
17. Ibid., p. 138.
18. Ibid., p. 147. Ross's *Ladies of the Press* also discusses Nellie Bly at length.
19. Schlipp and Murphy, *Great Women*, p. 149.
20. Ibid., p. 150.
21. Ross, *Ladies*, p. 63.
22. Ibid., p. 65–66.
23. Schlipp and Murphy, *Great Women*, pp. 112–20. See also Margaret Culley's article on Dorothy Dix in *Notable American Women*, pp. 275–77.
24. Schlipp and Murphy, *Great Women*, pp. 121–32.
25. Elinor Langer, *Josephine Herbst* (Boston: Atlantic–Little Brown, 1983), as well as Langer's article on Herbst in *Notable American Women*, pp. 333–35.
26. Schlipp and Murphy, *Great Women*, pp. 21–36.
27. Paula Fass on Parsons in *Notable American Women*, pp. 527–529. See also Dorothy Townsend, "Louella Parsons, 1st Hollywood Gossip Queen, Dies at 91," *Los Angeles Times*, Dec. 10, 1972, p. 1; Murray Illson, "Louella Parsons, Gossip Columnist, Dies," *The New York Times*, Dec. 10, 1972; *Current Biography*, 1942, pp. 631–32.
28. George Eells's entry on Hedda Hopper in *Notable American Women*, pp. 350–51. See also *Current Biography*, 1942, pp. 391–92; "Hedda Hopper, Columnist, Dies; Chronicled Gossip of Hollywood," *The New York Times*, Feb. 2, 1966, p. 32.
29. Jack O'Brien, "She Does What She Always Wanted to Do," Associated Press, Oct. 20, 1943; Associated Press, "Sigrid Arne Has Covered Seven World Conferences," Apr. 21, 1945; *Current Biography*, 1945, pp. 15–16.
30. Linda Steiner and Susanne Gray, "Genevieve Forbes Herrick: A Front Page Reporter 'Pleased to Write About Women,' " *Journalism History* 12 (Spring 1985), pp. 8–16. See also Ross, *Ladies*, pp. 539–42.
31. William Shirer, *The Nightmare Years 1930–1940*. (Boston: Little, Brown, 1984), p. 118.
32. Ibid., p. 118.
33. Marion K. Sanders, *Dorothy Thompson: A Legend in Her Times* (New York: Avon Books, 1973), p. 330. Sources on Dorothy Thompson

include Vincent Sheean, *Dorothy and Red* (Boston: Houghton Mifflin, 1963); Ross, *Ladies,* pp. 360–66; Schlipp and Murphy, *Great Women*; Kluger, *The Paper*; Jo R. Mengedoht, in *Dictionary of Literary Biography,* Vol. 29, *American Newspaper Journalists, 1926–1950.* Edited by Perry J. Ashley. (Detroit: Bruccoli Clark, 1984), pp. 343–50; and Paul Boyer's entry on Thompson in *Notable American Women,* pp. 683–86.

3 The Roosevelt Rule

1. Maurine Beasley, *Eleanor Roosevelt and the Media* (Urbana and Chicago: University of Illinois Press, 1987), pp. 25–36. See also material on Lorena Hickok by Jean Christie in *Notable American Women,* pp. 338–40; Joseph Lasch, *Love, Eleanor* (New York: Doubleday, 1982); and Ross, *Ladies,* pp. 203–09. Ross discusses Eleanor Roosevelt's press conferences on pp. 309–22.
2. Marie Manning, *Ladies Now and Then* (New York: E.P. Dutton, 1944), pp. 207–8.
3. Bess Furman, *Washington Byline* (New York: Alfred A. Knopf, 1949), p. 36. See also "Bess Furman Dies; Capital Reporter," *The New York Times,* May 13, 1969, p. 47; Ross, *Ladies,* pp. 345–47; and Susan Ware's article in *Notable American Women,* pp. 256–57.
4. Furman, pp. 58–59.

5 Bridging the Gap

1. Helen Thomas, *Dateline: White House* (New York: Macmillan, 1975), p. 3.
2. "Aggie Underwood," *Air California Magazine,* Oct. 1979, p. 42.
3. Bruce Henstell, "Newspaperwoman Tells All About It," *The Reader,* July 31, 1981, p. 1.
4. Ibid., p.5.
5. Jack Smith, "No-Nos for News," *Los Angeles Times,* Aug. 3, 1980, p. vi.
6. Henstell, "Newspaperwoman," p. 6.
7. Stan Leppard, "Exclusive! Aggie's Torrid Era at Helm of Paper Bared," *Long Beach Press-Telegram,* Aug. 24, 1980, p. L/S 2.
8. Ibid., p. L/S 2.
9. Charles Nazarian, "That's Agness With a Double 'S,' " *Valley News,* Dec. 7, 1980, pp. 4–7. See also Joelle Cohen, "Aggie Underwood, an L.A. legend, dies at 81," *The Los Angeles Herald Examiner,* July 4, 1984, p. 10; Jerry Belcher, "Aggie Underwood, First Woman City Editor of Major Paper, Dies," *Los Angeles Times,* July 4, 1984, p. 1.

10. Leppard, "Exclusive!" p. L/S 2.
11. Nan Robertson, "Toxic Shock," *The New York Times Magazine*, Sept. 19, 1982, p. 30.

6 Through the Door

1. Antoinette May, *Witness to War* (New York: Beaufort Books, 1983), pp. 49–52.
2. Murray Illson, "May Craig, Feisty Capital Writer, Dies," *The New York Times*, July 16, 1975, p. 40.
3. Calvin Trillin, "Covering the Cops," *The New Yorker*, Feb. 17, 1986, p. 39.

7 The Girls in the Balcony

1. Fran Lewine, "Women's National Press Club/Washington Press Club History," Oct. 1985, pp. 1–2.
2. Don Larrabee, "A Chronology on the Admission of Women Journalists to Membership in the National Press Club," 1985, p. 1.
3. Lewine, *Women's*, pp. 2–3.
4. Memo from Bill Lawrence to the National Press Club Board of Governors, Nov. 27, 1959.
5. Letter from Doris Fleeson to Secretary of State Christian A. Herter, Mar. 11, 1960.
6. Letter from Doris Fleeson to Helen Thomas, Mar. 11, 1960.
7. Thomas, *Dateline*, p. xvii. See also Eleanor Clift, "Helen Thomas: Dauntless Dean of the White House Press," *The Washington Journalism Review* (Nov. 1986), pp. 26–31.
8. Letters from Helen Thomas to Edward Lahey and others, May 20, 1960, and responses from Walter T. Ridder, Jun. 10, 1960; John L. Steele, May 23, 1960; Walter Trohan, Jun. 8, 1960; Drew Pearson, May 23, 1960; K. G. Crawford, Jun. 19, 1960; and James Reston, June 14, 1960. These letters are part of the Washington Press Club files at the National Press Club Library.
9. Merriman Smith, "In crisis times even ridiculum is grave," *Nation's Business*, Jan. 1962, p. 23.
10. Art Buchwald, "A Lady in the Balcony," *The Washington Post*, Aug. 29, 1963.
11. Letter from Bryson Rash to I. William Hill, Nov. 20, 1963.
12. Letter from Bryson Rash to I. William Hill, Dec. 9, 1963.
13. Notes by Jessie Stearns Buscher, Nov. 27, 1962, in Washington Press Club file.

14. Vera Glaser, "Rocky's Kickoff Viewed As Snub," *The Washington Star*, Dec. 29, 1963, p. E-3.
15. Lewine, *Women's*, p. 5.
16. Letter from Pauli Murray to A. Philip Randolph, Aug. 21, 1963.
17. Lewine, *Women's*, p. 6.
18. Women's National Press Club presentation before President's Commission on the Status of Women, Apr. 15, 1963.
19. Report by Frances Lewine to Women's National Press Club, Nov. 21, 1963.
20. Letter from Windsor P. Booth to James Symington, May 19, 1966.
21. Larrabee, *Chronology*, p. 3.
22. Letter from William D. Hickman to National Press Club board, Jun. 4, 1970.
23. Larrabee, *Chronology*, p. 4.
24. All comments are from the tape of the National Press Club meeting, Jan. 15, 1971.
25. Robert Ames Alden, "Women and the National Press Club—pro," an open letter to National Press Club members, Jan. 1971.
26. Harrison Salisbury, *Without Fear or Favor* (New York: Times Books, 1980), pp. 94–95.
27. Ibid., pp. 94–95.
28. Bella Stumbo, "Counter-Gridiron: Birth of a Tradition," *Los Angeles Times*, Apr. 8, 1974, sec. IV, p. 1. See also "The Counter Press," *The San Francisco Examiner*, Apr. 7, 1974, p. A12; Judy Flander, "Ladies Night at the Gridiron," *The Washington Star*, Mar. 23, 1975, p. A3; and Don Shirley, "Counter-Gridion: Bingo!" *The Washington Post*, Mar. 24, 1975, p. B1.
29. Katharine Graham speech at the National Press Club Tribute to Newswomen, Washington, D.C., October 22, 1985.
30. Thomas, *Dateline*, p. xviii.

8 Stylizing the News

1. Ross, *Ladies*, p. 425.
2. Ibid., p. 441.
3. Ibid., p. 442–43.
4. Ibid., p. 457.
5. Manning, *Ladies*, p. 126.
6. Ross, *Ladies*, p. 425.
7. David Laventhol, *Los Angeles Times* management conference speech, Jan. 28, 1987.

8. Marylin Bender, *The Beautiful People* (New York: Coward McCann, 1967), pp. 76–78.
9. Kluger, *The Paper*, pp. 623–25.
10. Bender, pp. 104–105. See also Robert D. McFadden, "Charlotte Curtis, a Columnist for the Times, Is Dead at 58," *The New York Times*, Apr. 17, 1987, p. B6; "Charlotte Curtis; Pioneer Women's Editor of the New York Times," *Los Angeles Times*, Apr. 17, 1987.
11. Georgia Dullea, "Judy Klemesrud, 46, Is Dead; Reporter for Times 19 Years," *The New York Times*, Oct. 13, 1985, p. 52.
12. Memo, "Re: Women at the Washington Post," from women at *The Washington Post* to Katharine Graham, Benjamin Bradlee, Philip Geyelin, and Howard Simons, Apr. 12, 1972, p. 3.
13. Marj Paxson, in Judith Clabes, ed., *New Guardians of the Press* (Indianapolis: R.J. Berg, pp. 121–29.

9 Political Crossroads

1. Peg Simpson, "Covering the Women's Movement," *Nieman Reports: Special Issue on Women and Journalism* (Summer 1979), p. 20.
2. Ibid., p. 21.
3. Ibid., p. 23.
4. Geraldine Ferraro and Linda Bird Francke, *Ferraro: My Story* (New York: Bantam Books, 1985), p. 73.
5. Kay Mills, "Democratic Women Are Ready to Run," *Los Angeles Times*, May 9, 1984, sec. II, p. 7.
6. Ferraro and Francke, *Ferraro*, pp. 71–72.
7. Eleanor Randolph, "Women Take to the Ferraro Trail: Composition of Press Corps Engenders Questions of Fairness," *The Washington Post*, Jul. 30, 1984, p. A4.
8. Peter Boyer, "The Three Phases of Ferraro's Press," *The Washington Journalism Review* (Nov. 1984), p. 25. See also David Shaw, "Press and Ferraro: A Case Study," *Los Angeles Times*, Dec. 5, 1984, p. 1, and "Ferraro's Silence on Her Finances Led to Scrutiny," *Los Angeles Times*, Dec. 6, 1984, p. 1; Alex S. Jones, "Ferraro Campaign Delivers Coup de Grace to Boys on the Bus Era," *The New York Times*, Nov. 3, 1984, p. 9; and Jean Gaddy Wilson, "Campaign Coverage," *Ms.*, Dec. 1984, pp. 124–25.
9. Ferraro and Francke, *Ferraro*, p. 322.
10. Sara Fritz, "A Change in Style," *Nieman Reports: Special Issue on Women and Journalism* (Summer 1979), pp. 24–25.
11. Ferraro and Francke, *Ferraro*, p. 321.

12. Terry Hynes, "Doris Fleeson," in Ashley, ed., *Dictionary of Literary Biography*, Vol. 27, pp. 104–6.
13. Sara Sanborn, "Byline Mary McGrory: Choice Words for Bullies, Fatheads and Self-righteous Rogues," *Ms.*, May 1975, p. 59.
14. Jane Mayer, "The Girls on the Bus Move Past Tokenism on the Primary Trail," *The Wall Street Journal*, Jun. 6, 1984, p. 1.
15. Mary McGrory, "Women: Ferraro's Magic," *The Washington Post*, Jul. 29, 1984, p. C1.
16. Simpson, "Covering," p. 21.

10 If The Suit Fits . . .

1. "Grace Glueck Tribute to Attorney Harriett Rabb Recalls Beginning of Suit at Times," *Media Report to Women*, Washington, D.C., Dec. 31, 1978, p. 2.
2. Joan Cook and Betsy Wade, "Our Shot at History." Tape of talk at the Schlesinger Library, Radcliffe College, May 1, 1986.
3. Ibid.
4. Judith Coburn, "Women Take the New York Times to Court," *New Times*, Oct. 2, 1978, p. 20.
5. Cook and Wade, "Our Shot."
6. Ibid.
7. "N. Y. Times Pays Males $3,735 More Per Year Attributable to Sex Discrimination Alone—Experts Report Study to Federal Court," *Media Report to Women*, Washington, D.C., Apr. 1, 1978.
8. Coburn, "Women," p. 26.
9. Ibid.
10. Salisbury, *Without Fear*, p. 399.
11. Cook and Wade, "Our Shot."
12. Charges are detailed in the class-action complaint filed in U.S. District Court in New York for Sylvia Carter, Marilyn Goldstein, Marian Leifsen, and Jane McNamara "and all others similarly situated" in 1975, and the settlement is outlined in the consent decree, 75 Civ. 52 (JRB), signed Feb. 26, 1982.
13. Sharon Dickman, complaint filed Aug. 23, 1974, Maryland Commission on Human Relations, Baltimore, Md.
14. Memo from women at *The Washington Post* to *Post* executives, 1970.
15. Memo, "Re: Women at the Washington Post," Apr. 12, 1972.
16. Robbie Grant, "Hello, Handsome, Get Me Rewrite," *Working Woman*, Jun. 1979, p. 34.

See also Joan J. Cirillo, "Suit Suite," *Quill* (December 1984), pp. 14–18; Thomas B. Morgan, "The Times Are They A Changin'?" *New York Woman*,

Notes

Mar./Apr. 1987, p. 134; Marion Knox, "Women and The Times," *The Nation*, Dec. 9, 1978, p. 635.

11 Women of Color

1. *Report of the National Advisory Commission on Civil Disorders* (New York: Bantam Books, Mar. 1968), p. 385.
2. American Society of Newspaper Editors news release, Apr. 9, 1987. See also *ASNE Chronicle*, Apr. 10, 1987, p. 4, published by the *San Francisco Chronicle* for the 1987 ASNE Convention.
3. Ellis Cose, "The Quiet Crisis: Minority Journalists and Newsroom Opportunity," Institute for Journalism Education, University of California, Berkeley, July 31, 1985.
4. Jane Arnold, "The Columnists," *Savvy*, Oct. 1985, pp. 38–39.
5. Jerelyn Eddings, "More Voices for the Choir," *The Baltimore Sun*, Nov. 19, 1986.
6. In 1984 three other female journalists committed suicide. The deaths were unrelated, but especially since all were women of talent, the suicides and any connection they might have had to the pressures of newspaper work gave pause to the living.
7. Leanita McClain, *A Foot in Each World*, Clarence Page, ed. (Chicago: Northwestern University Press, 1986).
8. Ibid., p. 13.
9. Round-table discussion of Asian-American journalists held for Associated Press Managing Editors at *USA Today*, Mar. 8, 1987.

See also S. Lee Hilliard, "Pressing for Power," *Black Enterprise*, Apr. 1985, pp. 42–50; Jill Nelson, "Integration When? A Tale of Three Cities," *The Columbia Journalism Review*, Jan.–Feb. 1987, pp. 41–51, and "Gilliam's Progress," pp. 52–53; Jill Krementz, "Karen Howze: Organizing the Daily life of a Newspaper—and a Family," *Savvy*, Mar. 1986, pp. 59–62; and Bebe Moore Campbell, "To Be Black, Gifted, and Alone," *Savvy*, Dec. 1984, p. 67.

12 Trenchcoats Come in Women's Sizes, Too

1. Margaret Fuller, from *At Home and Abroad*, quoted in Chevigny, *The Woman*, pp. 464–65.
2. May, *Witness*, p. 127.
3. Kluger, *The Paper*, p. 448.
4. Ibid., p. 447.
5. Gloria Emerson, quoted by Tad Bartimus of the Associated Press in a speech to the Overseas Press Club's Vietnam Correspondents Reunion in New York, Nov. 21, 1986.

6. Georgie Anne Geyer, *Buying the Night Flight* (New York: 1983) Delacorte Press, pp. 47–48.
7. Hilda Bryant, "Tea in an Ammo Dump with the Afghan Rebels," *The Seattle Post-Intelligencer*, Aug. 1, 1980, p. A14.
8. Eleanor Randolph, "The Sharing of Stories," *The Washington Post*, Nov. 15, 1986, p. C1.
9. Anthony Astrachan, *How Men Feel* (Garden City, N.Y.: Anchor Press, 1986), pp. 4–8.
10. Judith Miller, "Mideast Odyssey," *The New York Times Magazine*, Aug. 12, 1984, p. 36.
11. Ann Marie Cunningham, "The Outer Limits of Fear," *Savvy*, Aug. 1982, p. 54.
12. Geyer, *Buying*, p. 9.

See also Pamela Constable, "Witness: The Truth About Covering Latin America," *The Boston Globe Magazine*, Sept. 20, 1987, p. 12; Leslie Bennetts, "Women at War," *Vogue*, Nov. 1983, p. 438; Thomas Morgan, "Reporters of the Lost War," *Esquire*, Jul. 1984, p. 49; Sue Chastain, "Dodging the Same Gunfire as Their Male Colleagues," *ASNE Bulletin*, Dec.-Jan. 1984, p. 10; Joanne Omang, "How the Fourth Estate Invaded the Third World," *The Washington Journalism Review*, Jun. 1982, p. 45; Joanne Omang, "Reporting 'Under Fire,' " *The Washington Post*, Oct. 23, 1983, p. L1; Grace Lichtenstein, "Have Pen, Will Travel," *The Washington Post*, Jan. 11, 1983, p. C2.

13 Forbidden Turf

1. Jane Gross, "A Woman Reporter in Yankee Country," *The New York Times Magazine*, Oct. 25, 1981, p. 113.
2. Tom Friend, "Reggie," *Los Angeles Times*, Oct. 5, 1986, p. iii-3.
3. Virginia Watson-Rouslin, "The Men's Room," *Quill*, Jan. 1987, pp. 20–24.
4. Jean C. Chance, "Adela Rogers St. Johns," in Ashley, ed., *Dictionary of Literary Biography*, Vol. 27, pp. 310–12.
5. C. Zoe Smith, "Great Women in Photojournalism," in *Women in Photojournalism* (Durham, N.C.: National Press Photographers Association, 1986), pp. 7–12.
6. Roger Angell, "The Sporting Scene: Sharing the Beat," *The New Yorker*, Apr. 9, 1979, p. 46.
7. Susan Fornoff, "Who has an open-door policy? Writers' guide to major sports," Association for Women in Sports Media newsletter, Mar. 1987, pp. 4–5.
8. Gross, "Woman Reporter," p. 32.
9. Ibid, p. 36, 40.

10. Paula Dranov, "Girls in the Locker Room," *Cosmopolitan*, Feb. 1980, p. 232.
11. Jennifer Werner, "Being a Woman and a Photojournalist in 1986," in *Women in Photojournalism*, p. 17.
12. Smith, in *Women in Photojournalism*, p. 12, and Ulrike Welsch, "It Takes Guts to Quit Your Job," in *Women in Photojournalism*, pp. 62–63.
13. Werner, p. 22.
14. April Saul, "A Brick Wall Called Nepotism," in *Women in Photojournalism*, p. 39.

See also Julie Rovner, "No Guts, No Glory," *The Washington Woman*, Dec. 1986, pp. 18–22, 46; Sally Tippett Rains, "An End to the Open Locker Room Dilemma?" *The Sporting News*, Apr. 8, 1985, p. 44.

14 Diapers on the Front Page

1. Interview with *The Chicago Tribune*, May 1893.
2. Elizabeth Rhodes, "Getting Away with Murder," *The Seattle Times*, Jul. 28, 1985, p. 1.
3. Diana Griego, report on Denver Post Pulitzer Prize in *Times Mirror Today* (Summer 1986), p. 1.
4. Michelle Fountaine Williams, "Superdiapers in a bind at 5 hospitals," *Rochester Democrat and Chronicle*, Oct. 15, 1986, p. 1.
5. Felicity Barringer, "Children of Chernobyl," *The New York Times*, Jun. 5, 1986, p. A1.
6. Jean Gaddy Wilson, report on women in the newspaper business, International Women's Media Project meeting, Washington, D.C., Nov. 1986.
7. Eileen McNamara, "2 Judges Withdraw From Cases," *The Boston Globe*, Oct. 15, 1986, p. 1. See also "Court challenged in Massachusetts," *The New York Times*, Nov. 30, 1986, p. 61.
8. Marvel Cooke, " 'Mrs. Legree' Hires Only on the Street, Always 'Nice Girls,' " *The Compass*, January 11, 1950.
9. "Women in the Workplace," *Los Angeles Times*, Sept. 9–19, 1984. Series of articles by S. J. Diamond, Cathleen Decker, Nancy Yoshihara, Sara Fritz, Doris Byron Fuller, Karen Tumulty, Kathleen Hendrix, Joan Sweeney, Maria LaGanga, Bella Stumbo, and Kay Mills. Series edited by Linda Mathews.

15 The Newsroom Evolution

1. Jon Nordheimer, "AIDS Specter for Women: The Bisexual Man," *The New York Times*, Apr. 3, 1987, p. 1.

2. Paula Montez, profile on Anne Roark for University of Southern California Journalism 467, Apr. 16, 1985.

3. "Abuse of the Press Conference," *New York Times* editorial, Sept. 27, 1969, p. 32; "President Forgets About an Appointee He Named," *The New York Times*, Sept. 27, 1969, p. 16.

4. "Questionable Questions," *The New York Times*, Feb. 27, 1974, p. 38.

5. "In Praise of Mrs. McClendon," *The New York Times*, Mar. 26, 1974, p. 40. See also Francis X. Clines, " 'Maybe I Wasn't Lady-fied,' " *The New York Times*, Jul. 30, 1982, p. B4.

6. Alan Prendergast, "Best in the West: Tulsa Troubleshooter Mary Hargrove," *The Washington Journalism Review* (Jul.-Aug. 1987), pp. 21–25.

7. Heather Vogel Frederick, "Reports from the Homefront: Columnist Joyce Maynard's 'beat' is her own rural backyard," *The Christian Science Monitor*, Sept. 14, 1987, p. 23.

8. Pam Reich, "Pam Reich Compares News Coverage of Women's Issues Under Los Angeles Herald Examiner Editor Mary Anne Dolan With Coverage by her Male Predecessor," *Media Report to Women*, Mar.–Apr. 1983, p. 11.

9. Bob Secter, "Tiny Blonde Has the Clout in City of Big Shoulders," *Los Angeles Times*, Mar. 1, 1979, p. 1.

10. Jerry Gillam, "Lobbyists in State Capitol: These Women Take Up Issues, With All Things Being Equal," *Los Angeles Times*, Nov. 8, 1987, Part I, p. 3.

11. Nikki Finke, "The Fawning of American TV," *Los Angeles Times*, Jun. 11, 1987, p. V1.

12. "The Strawberry Brunet," *The New York Times*, May 17, 1987, p. 26. See also Susan Anthony, "Hart News Coverage and the 'Bimbo Factor,' " *The New York Times*, Jun. 23, 1987, p. A30.

13. *The New York Times*, June 20, 1986, p. B12. See also Betsy Wade, "A Triumph of Reason," *Ms.*, Sept. 1986, p. 96; Paula Kassell, "Miss, Mrs., Ms." *New Directions for Women*, Sept.–Oct. 1986, p. 1.

14. Elizabeth Janeway, *Improper Behavior* (New York: William Morrow, 1987), p. 225.

See also Bernice Buresh, "Critical Mass," *Quill*, Sept. 1984, pp. 14–20, 35. Buresh, a Boston University professor, was far ahead of her time with the insight in this article.

16 The Glass Ceiling

1. The AP designates fewer of its offices as bureaus than does UPI, hence the difference in the number of domestic bureaus.

2. Dorothy Jurney's reports appeared regularly in *ASNE Bulletin*. The one cited appeared in Oct. 1986.

3. Katharine Graham, "The 'Glass Ceiling': Women's Barrier to Top Management." Speech to the International Women's Media Project, Washington, D.C., Nov. 12, 1986.

4. Jean Gaddy Wilson, "Women in the Newspaper Business," *presstime*, Oct. 1986, pp. 30–37.

5. Survey by the Women's Media Project of the NOW Legal Defense and Education Fund, Apr. 8, 1985.

6. Ellen Goodman, "Few Women Behind the Headlines," The *Hagerstown* [Maryland] *Morning Herald*, Apr. 23, 1985.

7. Congressional Directory, 1985–86. (Washington, D.C.: U.S. Government Printing Office), pp. 918–32.

8. "Movers and Shakers," *The Washington Journalism Review* (Feb. 1986), p. 8. Also "Beth Frerking appointed chief of D.C. bureau," *The Denver Post*, Sept. 7, 1987.

9. "The Pulitzer Prizes, 1917–1983," Columbia University; listings from 1984–87; and correspondence from the office of the administrator of the Pulitzer Prizes.

10. Figures obtained from Harvard, Stanford, and Michigan.

11. "Katherine Woodruff Fanning," in Clabes, ed., *New Guardians*, pp. 59–72. See also Suzanne Wilding, "The Lady is a Newspaperman," *Town and Country*, Jan. 1986, pp. 114–16, 166–67; Alex Jones, "Woman Named to Head Newspaper Editors' Group," *The New York Times*, Apr. 11, 1987; "Monitor editor leads U.S. editors' group," *The Christian Science Monitor*, Apr. 10, 1987; Michael Harris, "Toward a More Genteel Fourth Estate," the *San Francisco Chronicle*, Apr. 6, 1987.

12. Thomas Rosenstiel, "Latinos and Papers Clash in Miami," *Los Angeles Times*, Jan. 9, 1987, pp. 1, 14. See also Rosenstiel, "Journalism History Made," *Los Angeles Times*, Jun. 12, 1987, p. iv-1.

13. Jay Mathews, "Sex Appeal in L.A.," *The Columbia Journalism Review*, (Jan.–Feb. 1983), pp. 7–8. See also Barbara Fryer, "Lou Grant Is . . . a Woman?" *Los Angeles*, Apr. 1982, p. 128.

14. "Ms. M.E.," *Newsweek*, Sept. 2, 1974, p. 50. See also "Carol Sutton, ex-managing editor of C-J, dies," *The* [Louisville] *Courier-Journal*, Feb. 20, 1985, p. E7.

See also Terri Schultz-Brooks, "Getting there: women in the newsroom," *The Columbia Journalism Review* (Mar.–Apr. 1984), pp. 25–31; Christine Doudna with Carla Rupp, "Up the Masthead: The Push for Power in the Press," *Savvy*, Sept. 1980, pp. 24–32; Carla Marie Rupp, "Improvements are sought in covering women's news," *Editor and Publisher*, Oct. 18, 1980, pp. 38–39; Fred Barnes, "The Post vs. The Times: Which Is Better?" *Washingtonian*, May 1987, pp. 132–43; and Beverly Kees, in Clabes, ed., *New Guardians*, pp. 95–102.

17 Breaking Through: Commitment at the Top

1. These articles include Phil Weiss, "Invasion of the Gannettoids," *The New Republic*, Feb. 2, 1987, pp. 18–22, and Louise Bernikow, "The Paper Tiger," *Savvy*, Mar. 1983, pp. 39–43, 84–85.
2. Bulkeley was the first female publisher of a Gannett daily, while Gloria Biggs was Gannett's first female publisher for a weekly, *The Melbourne Times*, in 1973.
3. Thomas Rosenstiel, "Gannett Chairman Expands Empire Advancing Into the Major Leagues," *Los Angeles Times*, July 6, 1986, p. IV-5.

See also Peter Prichard, *The Making of McPaper: The Inside Story of USA Today* (Kansas City: Andrews, McMeel and Parker, 1987); Alex S. Jones, "The USA Today Story; Neuharth's Obsession," *The New York Times*, Jul. 3, 1987, p. D1; Carl Sessions Stepp, "Gannett's Thunderbolt," *Quill*, Jul.–Aug. 1986, pp. 16–21; Eleanor Randolph, "Curley's Task," *The Washington Post*, May 25, 1986, p. F1; John Wilke, "Al Neuharth Steps Back, But He'll Keep Gannett on a Tear," *Business Week*, Jun. 2, 1986, p. 34; and Barbara Matusow, "Allen H. Neuharth Today," *The Washington Journalism Review* (Aug. 1986), pp. 18–24.

18 Is the Prize Worth the Price?

1. Anna Quindlen, "Comfortable as a Person, Not a Personage," *The New York Times*, Jan. 14, 1987, p. 15.
2. Dickey Chappelle, *What's A Woman Doing Here?* (New York: William Morrow, 1962), pp. 140–41.
3. Janet Chusmir, "Women will move—if the offer is too good to refuse," *ASNE Bulletin*, Jan. 1986, p. 21.
4. Linda Grist Cunningham, "We've come a long way, baby," *Editor and Publisher*, Nov. 24, 1984, p. 52.
5. Eleanor Randolph, "Conflict of Interest: A Growing Problem for Couples," *Esquire*, Feb. 1978, p. 55.
6. May, *Witness*, pp. 117–18.
7. Ibid., pp. 164–65.
8. Kluger, *The Paper*, p. 440.
9. Geyer, *Buying*, p. 58.

10. Ibid., p. 163–72.
11. Judith Miller, "A Mideast Odyssey," *The New York Times Magazine*, Aug. 12, 1984, p. 36.
12. Sheila Rule, "Nothing Prepares You for Apartheid," *The New York Times Magazine*, May 4, 1986, pp. 62, 72.
13. Ann Marie Cunningham, "The Outer Limits of Fear," *Savvy*, Aug. 1982, p. 50.
14. Miller, "Mideast," p. 36.
15. Quoted by Sue Chastain, " 'Dodging the same gunfire as their male colleagues,' " *ASNE Bulletin*, Dec.–Jan. 1984, p. 11.

19 Now What, and So What?

1. Nancy Woloch, *Women and the American Experience* (New York: Alfred A. Knopf, 1984), p. 346.
2. Elizabeth Janeway, *Cross Sections* (New York: William Morrow, 1982), p. 112.
3. Betty Friedan, *The Second Stage* (New York: Summit, 1981), p. 80.
4. Maurine H. Beasley, *The New Majority: A Look at What the Preponderance of Women in Journalism Education Means to the Schools and to the Professions* (College Park: University of Maryland, October 1985).
5. David Lawrence, "The Myth of the Pink Collar Ghetto," *The Washington Journalism Review* (Jan. 1986), pp. 21–23.

See also Susan Miller, "What women—and their bosses—should do to keep women climbing up the management ladder," *ASNE Bulletin*, Jan. 1986, pp. 13–20.

Everyday Indignities

1. Jane O'Reilly, "Click! The Housewife's Moment of Truth," *Ms.*, Spring 1972, p. 54.
2. Andree Brooks, "Women in the Clergy: Struggle to Succeed," *The New York Times*, Feb. 16, 1987, p. 15.
3. Deborah Churchman, "Vivian Vahlberg: The Struggle to Have It All," *The Christian Science Monitor*, May 25, 1982, p. 18.

Acknowledgments

Acknowledgments, read, mean little to all but a few readers; written, they mean everything to the writer. They can convey only partially the debt that is owed to the people who have provided advice, information, and singular patience.

First among these people is my mother, Mary S. Mills. A former English teacher, she has always expected clear expression; a quiet, gracious but determined woman, she has always made me knock on doors that I was not sure would open; a mother, she has always been there when the discouragement was deepest. I simply could not have done this book without her faith in me. Thank you, Mother.

Countless women and men spent hours with me in 150 interviews for this book; each person, each interview, helped inform my judgment. Their names are listed in the Notes section. Not all are quoted directly, but all informed my thinking as I wrote this book. Thank you, too.

The idea for this book germinated in a 1979 talk on press coverage of the women's movement for the Center for Research on Women, as it was known then, at Stanford University and took life after professional pep talks from my longtime friend Dean Mills. He and his wife Sue encouraged me when publishing prospects looked bleak and then read my drafts when publishing looked possible; they and their sons Jason and Jesse shared my thoughts through the entire process. In long after-tennis talks, Connie Koenenn helped shape many of the ideas that fill this book, any she cares to claim. My professional feminist consciousness was first pricked years ago by Eileen Shanahan, and without her help and advice, I would not be wherever it is I am today.

In Los Angeles, others who aided and abetted with their various talents were Mary Bryant, Betty Friedan, Susan Henry, Carol Nagy Jacklin, Ann and Bert Lane, Wendy Lazarus, Suzanne and Gerry Rosentswieg, and Iris Schneider. Herman Hong, my computer guru, kept me on line with special humor. I owe thanks to others across the country—Joan and Ken Kaplan, Jane Bernard-Powers, Jim and Sandi Risser, Martha and Harry Press, Marion and Harry Lewenstein, Nancy Hicks Maynard, Steve Ponder and Gaye Vandermyn, Solveig Torvik, Karen West, Pam Conklin, Nannerl Keohane, Phyllis Austin, Caryl Rivers and Al Lupo, Jane and Ned Cabot, Sharon Rosenhause, Frances Lear, Paula Parker, Huntly Collins, Richard and Susana O'Mara, Sharon Dickman, Ernie Imhoff, Carl Schoettler, Amanda Harris, Natalie Fobes, Bill G. Ferguson, Martha Hamilton, Claudia Levy, Rebecca Trounson, and Betsy Wade Boylan. The sisters at Redwoods Monastery provided a quiet, harmonic retreat for the final manuscript editing.

Jean Gaddy Wilson of the University of Missouri generously shared her thoughts with me based on the information from her massive study on women in the newspaper business, as did Dorothy Jurney, who for years was the only person keeping regular tabs on the number of women making it—and not making it—into top management. I first met both—and other valuable sources—at a Journalism and Women Symposium held on Labor Day 1986 at Estes Park, Colorado, through the instigation of Tad Bartimus, and I thank them all for getting me well started on my year's leave. These fifty or so women helped finish the year as well with reinforcement and support.

Three libraries have provided valuable material. I especially must thank Patti Brown of the *Los Angeles Times* library, who countless times unearthed obscure clippings or major magazine articles. The *Times* librarian, Cecily Surace, gave me this access to the library, and I greatly appreciate it. Barbara Vandegrift at the National Press Club Library helped me trace the entry of women into that club, and Tom Reilly, director, and Robert Marshall, archivist, at the Urban Archives Center at California State University, helped with papers left by Agness Underwood.

The *Los Angeles Times* did not usually provide leaves for writing books until the spring of 1986, and I was the first person able to take advantage of this enlightened policy. I am grateful to Bill Thomas, the executive editor, for establishing the policy, and to Tom Johnson, the publisher, for authorizing my leave and for urging me to write "a hard-hitting book." And I especially thank my boss, editorial-page editor Anthony Day, who granted the leave and worked out the terms. He sent me on my way with encouragement and welcomed me back in the same vein. His editing and that of his deputy, Jack Burby, served as the example that guided me as I edited my own manuscript. Gayle Pollard, my colleague on the editorial page, has long been a sounding board, a base in reality, and a sharp stick in the ribs when I need it. Gillian Stormont and JoD Jones, of the editorial-page staff, were mainstays in keeping me in contact with the office.

It is said of Diane Cleaver, my agent, that she never gives up. Thank goodness. She knew the project would work, even at times when I was about to chuck it, and she was right. It is also said that editors delight only in excising your words. Not true. Cynthia Vartan of Dodd, Mead exists to make other people look good. She left me alone when I needed to be left alone, and she told me I was wordy when I needed that, too. If book publishing had more people like Diane Cleaver and Cynthia Vartan, I would have started writing books long ago.

No foundation, no organization supported this book financially other than the publisher, Dodd, Mead. I did not apply to any press-related foundations for obvious reasons of conflict of interest. The lack of readily available support for writers who are not academics speaks poorly for the chances of independent authors to do independent work. That's a sour note, but at least it makes one less group to acknowledge.

The one remaining acknowledgement is to the hundreds of women, named or unnamed in this book, who have worked on newspapers in this century and the last. Women who are journalists today stand on their shoulders, and we must never forget what they did in order that we can do what we do today toward changing the outlook of the American press and even the definition of what it considers news.

Index

Index

Cook, Joan, and *The New York Times* suit, 158, 160, 163, 164
Cooke, Janet, 331
Cooke, Marvel, 66, 249–251; career of, 176–179
Copley, Helen, 20
Copley News Service, 139
Costanza, Midge, 133
courtesy titles, 138–139, 158, 268
Cowan, Ruth, 45, 152, 198; career of, 41–42
Craig, May, 87, 94, 104
Crawford, Kenneth, 98
Croly, Jane, 15, 23–24
Cronkite, Walter, 55–56
Crossette, Barbara, 165, 213–214, 276
Crouse, Timothy, 128
Cuniberti, Betty, 222, 226, 234
Cunningham, Linda, 268, 269, 324, 347
Curley, John, 306, 307
Curtis, Charlotte, 6, 119, 276; career of, 120–121; on *The New York Times* suit, 159

Daily Oklahoman, 40, 235
Dale, Ed, 58
Dallas Morning News, 195, 290, 325
Dallas Times-Herald, 62, 83, 114, 116, 145, 245, 282, 296, 333
Daniel, Clifton, 57, 120, 260
Darin, Grace, 51, 84
Dash, Leon, 318, 319
Dauth, Fran, 79, 85, 89, 257–258
Davis, Nancy, 160
Day, Anthony, 253
Demaris, Ovid, 70
Dempsey (McManus), Margaret, 5, 71–73
Denver Post, 241–242, 282
Des Moines Register, 306
De Toledano, Ralph, 104
Detroit Free Press, 74, 115, 185, 281, 289, 293, 299, 323, 349
Detroit News, 268, 282, 306; women's lawsuit, 149, 167
Deutsch, Linda, 88–89
Devroy, Ann, 145, 146
De Young, Karen, 209, 214, 275, 345
Dickman, Sharon, 167, 247–248, 343
Dillman, Grant, 201
displaced homemakers, 121
Dix, Dorothy, 26, 27
Dodson, Angela, 121, 186
Dolan, Mary Anne, 265, 268–269, 273, 276, 286
Dolan, Maura, 146
Donovan, Donna, 306, 321–322

Dowd, Maureen, 146
Downie, Len, 171
Dudman, Richard, 313
Dunnigan, Alice, 101
Dure, Leon, 220

Eddings, Jerelyn, 184–185
Eder, Richard, 295
editorial writers, 184–185, 247, 253, 262–263, 282
Eisenhower, Dwight, 64, 105, 141, 197, 259
El Paso Times, 200
Elliott, Helene, 173, 223, 228
Ellis, Virginia, 144
Emerson, Gloria, 75, 120, 201, 276, 330–331
Equal Employment Opportunity Commission, 151, 154, 167, 168–171, 202
Equal Rights Amendment, 11, 49, 58–59, 130, 134, 223
Everett Herald, 81, 244, 290–291, 324, 339

Fanning, Katherine, 271, 274–275, 276, 312; career of, 283–285
Fanning, Larry, 271, 284
Farenthold, Frances, 127
fear, as motivating force, 330–331
fellowships awarded to women, 282–283
Ferraro, Geraldine, 7, 12, 135, 136, 137, 139, 140, 142
Field, Marshall, 284
Fields, Carmen, 84, 187, 196
Finke, Nikki, 267
Fisher, Pat, 183–184, 247
FitzHenry, Charlotte L., 282
Fleeson, Doris, 87, 94, 96, 97, 128; career of, 140–141
Folliard, Eddie, 113
Ford, Gerald, 131
Foreign Affairs, 32
foreign correspondents, 197–216, 345
Foreman, Laura, 325–326
Fornoff, Susan, 219
Foster, Mimi Fuller, 232
Frankel, Max, 164, 165, 254, 276, 291, 337, 338, 339
Franklin, Barbara, 12–13
Franklin, Benjamin, 16
Freed, Ken, 152
Freivogel, Bill, 312, 313–314
Freivogel, Margie, 81, 248, 312–314
Freligh, Sarajane, 224–225, 226, 228–229
Frerking, Beth, 282
Fresno Bee, 20

371

Index

Index

376

377

Index